Macroeconomic Analysis in the Classical Tradition

T0312078

Macroeconomic Analysis in the Classical Tradition explains how the influence of Keynes's macroeconomics, including his changed definitions of some key macroeconomic concepts, has impeded many analysts' ability to readily resolve disputes in modern macroeconomics.

Expanding on his earlier work—*Macroeconomics without the Errors of Keynes* (2019)—the author delves into more aspects of macroeconomic theory and argues for a revision of Keynes's contribution to the field. Attention is given to theories and concepts such as Say's Law, the quantity theory of money, the liquidity trap, the permanent income hypothesis, 100% money, and the Phillips curve analysis. The chapters work to build a careful critique of Keynes's economics and make the case that the classical macroeconomics of Smith, Say, Ricardo, Mill, and others could help resolve present-day policy disagreements and redefine macroeconomic priorities.

This book provides essential reading for advanced students and scholars with interest in the foundations of Keynes's theories and current debates within macroeconomic policy.

James C. W. Ahiakpor is Emeritus Professor of Economics at California State University East Bay, Hayward, USA.

Routledge Studies in the History of Economics

The Economic Thought of Sir James Steuart
First Economist of the Scottish Enlightenment
Edited by José M. Menudo

A History of Feminist and Gender Economics
Giandomenica Becchio

The Theory of Transaction in Institutional Economics
A History
Massimiliano Vatiero

F.A. Hayek and the Epistemology of Politics
The Curious Task of Economics
Scott Scheall

Classical Liberalism and the Industrial Working Class
The Economic Thought of Thomas Hodgskin
Alberto Mingardi

English Economic Thought in the Seventeenth Century
Rejecting the Dutch Model
Seiichiro Ito

Poverty in the History of Economic Thought
From Mercantilism to Neoclassical Economics
Edited by Mats Lundahl, Daniel Rauhut, and Neelambar Hatti

Macroeconomic Analysis in the Classical Tradition
The Impediments of Keynes's Influence
James C.W. Ahiakpor

For more information about this series, please visit www.routledge.com/series
/SE0341

Macroeconomic Analysis in the Classical Tradition

The Impediments of Keynes's Influence

James C.W. Ahiakpor

Routledge
Taylor & Francis Group

LONDON AND NEW YORK

First published 2021
by Routledge
2 Park Square, Milton Park, Abingdon, Oxon OX14 4RN

and by Routledge
52 Vanderbilt Avenue, New York, NY 10017

Routledge is an imprint of the Taylor & Francis Group, an informa business

© 2021 James C.W. Ahiakpor

British Library Cataloguing-in-Publication Data
A catalogue record for this book is available from the British Library

Library of Congress Cataloging-in-Publication Data
A catalog record has been requested for this book

ISBN: 978-0-367-85987-9 (hbk)
ISBN: 978-0-367-72193-0 (pbk)
ISBN: 978-1-003-01624-3 (ebk)

Typeset in Bembo
by Deanta Global Publishing Services, Chennai, India

To my most influential professors at the University of Toronto: Jack L. Carr (Monetary Theory) and Samuel Hollander (History of Economic Thought)

Contents

Figures

Tables

Preface

John Maynard Keynes was undoubtedly the most influential economist of the 20th century, although his academic training was in mathematics, not economics. Keynes learned his economics "on the job," as Robert Skidelsky (1983: 166) has noted. Keynes continues to hold great attraction for some economists seeking resolution to current macroeconomic problems mainly because he was the "public economist" *par excellence*. Keynes was prominent in public debate on how to cure the persistent problems of high unemployment and economic stagnation in Great Britain during the inter-war years, particularly after Britain went back to the gold standard in 1925 at the pre-war parity. Keynes also was invited to participate in the June 23-July 2, 1931, Harris Foundation conference in Chicago to suggest policies to address the ongoing Great Depression (Davis 1971). Even after Keynes's economics got severely eclipsed by monetarism, new classical macroeconomics, real business cycle theory, and Austrian economics since the 1970s, Keynes's ideas on how to manage an economy in crisis still fascinate some who believe in their relevance.

Books such as *Capitalist Revolutionary: John Maynard Keynes* (2011), by Roger Backhouse and Bradley Bateman, and *The Elgar Companion to John Maynard Keynes* (2019), edited by Robert Dimand and Harald Hagemann, and the launching of a new journal, *Review of Keynesian Economics*, in 2012, attest to the continued fascination of some scholars seeking the relevance of Keynes's ideas to addressing current economic problems, especially since the financial crisis of 2007–8. Keynes's claim to have shown the irrelevance of classical economics to addressing an economy's problems outside of the full employment of labor in his *General Theory of Employment, Interest and Money* (1936) appears to be the basis of such belief, even as he himself by 1946 disowned some arguments being made by his ardent followers on the basis of that book. Clearly, there is a need to clarify and extend Keynes's own disavowal of his indictment of classical economics in his 1936 book and subsequent journal articles before 1946.

This book complements my arguments in *Macroeconomics without the Errors of Keynes* (2019), in which I explain how Keynes's errors in interpreting such important classical economic concepts as saving, capital, investment, and money led to his misrepresenting the classical theories of the level of prices—the Quantity Theory of money—interest rates, and an economy's adjustment process. I also there argue the alternatives to (a) the modern aggregate demand–aggregate supply explanation of the level of prices that derives from Keynes, (b) interpretation of the Great Depression by Milton Friedman and Anna Schwartz (1963) under Keynes's influence, and (c) David Hume's (1752) explanation of the adjustment of prices and wage rates to changes in the quantity of money by such Keynes-influenced scholars as Eugene Rotwein (1955), Morris Perlman (1987), and Carl Wennerlind (2005). I here extend my clarification of the impeding influence of Keynes's changed meaning of these classical concepts on modern analysts' ability to (a) interpret correctly Say's law of markets, (b) recognize Ricardo's contemporaneous equivalence of taxation and debt financing of government spending, (c) recognize the classical origins of antidepression policy recommendations during the Great Depression in the US, (d) recognize the detraction from Keynes's misrepresentation of saving by the modern focus on permanent income as the principal determinant of consumption spending, championed by Milton Friedman (1957), to the neglect of Adam Smith's (1776) explanation of the near contemporaneous "consumption" or using up of savings by borrowers, (e) recognize the Phillips curve analysis as merely a subset of the classical forced-saving doctrine, (f) recognize the considerable harm to an economy's growth prospects from adopting 100% reserves against demand deposits, as championed by Irving Fisher (1935), and (f) seek solutions to macroeconomic problems from classical macro-monetary analysis.

Modern macroeconomic analysis, mostly inspired by Keynes (1936), has advanced in technical sophistication, such as the Dynamic Stochastic General Equilibrium modeling, in almost complete oblivion to Keynes's own caution about the usefulness of the mathematical approach: "Too large a proportion of recent 'mathematical' economics are mere concoctions, as imprecise as the initial assumptions they rest on, which allow the author to lose sight of the complexities and interdependencies of the real world in a maze of pretentious and unhelpful symbols" (1936: 298). Such has been the fate of modern macro-monetary analysis that it does not first address the conceptual problems with Keynes's changed definitions of saving, capital, investment, and money. Jacob Viner (1936), Henry Simons (1936), and Frank Knight (1937), all of the University of Chicago, in their reviews of the *General Theory* note Keynes's distortions of the meaning of classical concepts, just as does A.C. Pigou's (1936) review. But Keynes's contemporaries failed to pursue that aspect of his "revolution" or misrepresentation of classical economics; Pigou, Alfred Marshall's successor at Cambridge, also was not much interested in the history of economics, which he regarded "the wrong opinions of dead men" (Robert Leeson 1998: 135 and Don Moggridge 1992: xvi). Few sought to correct Keynes's distortions of the meaning of these concepts with direct references to works by David Hume, Adam Smith, J.-B. Say, David Ricardo, or John Stuart Mill. Dennis Robertson's efforts tended to be limited to Marshall's *Principles*, which did not impress Keynes of his errors. Furthermore, J.R. Hicks's (1937) IS-LM model (originally IS-LL) served to distract the profession's attention from such pursuit.

Hicks's disavowal of the usefulness of the IS-LM model 40 years later was much too late. Without noting the language distortion aspect of Keynes's "revolution" in economic thought, Joseph Schumpeter, in his very influential *History of Economic Analysis*, declares Keynes "Ricardo's peer" ([1954] 1994: 1171) and regards Keynes's new macroeconomic analysis "a novel view that was attractive to some as it was repellent to others … an achievement, frank recognition of which is the *greatest* and *most deserved* of the compliments that may be paid justifiably to the memory of Lord Keynes" (ibid: 1180-1; italics added). Hardly has any subsequent Keynes biographer paid attention to Keynes's distortions of the meaning of economic concepts; not even David Laidler's *Fabricating the Keynesian Revolution* (1999) recognizes the significance of such distortions in Keynes's "revolution."

In a similar vein, Milton Friedman (1968b: 15), in effect, urges economists to accept Keynes's new "language and apparatus"; he declares: "Rereading the *General Theory* has … reminded me what a great economist Keynes was and how much more I sympathize with his approach and aims than many of his followers" (1970b: 134). Friedman also regards the *General Theory*, some of whose arguments Keynes later disowned, "a great book" (ibid: 133). This even as Friedman's undergraduate teacher at the University of Chicago, Henry Simons (1936), in his review of the *General Theory*, observed that Keynes's criticisms of classical economics in the book "will impress only the incompetent" (quoted in Roger Backhouse 1999: 68). Paul Samuelson also studied his undergraduate economics at the University of Chicago from 1932 to 1935 from the likes of Aaron Director, Lloyd Mints, and Henry Simons. But he gave all that up during his graduate studies at Harvard (1936–40) to have become one of the most effective propagators of Keynes's new economics, beginning in 1948 with the first edition of his popular textbook, *Economics*; see Samuelson (1985) and Ahiakpor (2019: 2).

My arguments in this book, as in the previous ones as well as in Ahiakpor (1998b), are aimed at explaining how modern macroeconomic analysis and policy formulation can benefit from discarding Keynes's changed meaning of economic terms, especially saving, capital, investment, and money, by returning to the language of classical macro-monetary analysis. The latter is also more consistent with the language of the marketplace where, for example, savings correctly are recognized as funds devoted by households to acquiring interest- and/or dividend-earning financial assets (including bank deposits, bonds, and stocks) and are distinguished from cash hoarding.

James C.W. Ahiakpor
September 2020

Acknowledgments

Writing the five articles that form the bases for Chapters 4, 6, 8, 9, and 10 benefited from comments I received at the various conferences at which I presented their original papers. As usual, I also benefited from comments from referees for the journals, including those that rejected my submissions. I also thank the journals that published the articles: *American Journal of Economics and Sociology* (2004), *Journal of the History of Economic Thought* (2009, 2013), *History of Political Economy* (2010), and *History of Economic Ideas* (2018). Several of my colleagues, particularly, Greg Christainsen, Shyam Kamath, and Steve Shmanske, have given supportive comments on my work. I also have benefited from discussions of these issues with Thomas Humphrey and Roger Sandilands. I am grateful to all of them without implicating them in any remaining errors of argument in the book. Those are mine.

I thank the College of Business and Economics at Cal State East Bay for funding my conference travels to present the papers upon which I base most of the chapters in the book. I have found the exposure to skeptical conference participants to be very stimulating indeed.

I also would like to thank Ms. Natalie Tomlinson and her colleagues for handling my manuscript proposal at Routledge and getting it to its ultimate approval. Finally, I cannot thank Ms. Elizabeth Graber enough for her enthusiastic encouragement that I pull together the deleted chapters from my 2019 book manuscript to constitute a new monograph and to have guided its approval for publication at Palgrave Macmillan. I regret that I ended up having wasted her time and effort on the project for not having kept in mind my contract obligation to Routledge regarding future monographs. I am in her eternal debt for having made this book possible, at least at this time.

1   Introduction

The pervasive impediment of Keynes's
influence in modern macroeconomic analysis

Ten years after the publication of his very influential *General Theory of Employment, Interest, and Money* (1936), Keynes (1946) disowned some of the arguments being made in his name by several of his ardent followers, especially Joan Robinson, Richard Kahn, and Nicholas Kaldor. Keynes lamented "how much modernist stuff, gone wrong and turned sour and silly, is circulating in our system" (1946: 186). In the article, Keynes also recalls his statement in the House of Lords that he was attempting "to use what we have learnt from modern experience and modern analysis, not to defeat, but to implement the wisdom of Adam Smith" (ibid). Keynes earlier declared, "I am not a Keynesian" (Hutchison 1981: 123). Also, after a 1944 dinner meeting in Washington, D.C., Keynes told his wife, Lydia Lopokova, and Austin Robinson at breakfast that "I was the only non-Keynesian there" (Hutchison 1977: 58). However, it appears Keynes did not connect the new language (definitions) he had introduced into modern macroeconomic analysis with the tenacity of his followership.

As previously discussed in Ahiakpor (1998b, 2003b, and 2019), Keynes's changed meaning of such important economic terms as saving, capital, investment, and money from their classical definitions (see Jacob Viner 1936, A.C. Pigou 1936, and Frank Knight 1937) was mostly responsible for his ardent followers' persistence in their views. This even as Keynes (1937b) acknowledges that "the clue to the peculiarity of my new doctrine is to be found in my definitions of Income, Saving, Investment and such other terms" (249–50). His followers did not, and many still do not, question the accuracy or appropriateness of his new definitions. For example, Michael Lawlor ignores practically everything written in criticism of Keynes's *General Theory* and claims, "My reading of Keynes manifestly does find him to be a variety of what I suppose is now called 'Post Keynesian'" (2006: 5). That is the variety of Keynesians who do not accept the market equilibrating process of supply and demand analysis. Thus, Lawlor describes his research project as, "How Keynes Came to Be a Post Keynesian" (ibid).[1]

Milton Friedman also failed to take into account his teachers', Jacob Viner (1936) and Frank Knight (1937), criticisms of Keynes for having changed the meaning of economic terms. Thus, employing Keynes's new meaning of concepts, Friedman declares, "Rereading the *General Theory* ... has ... reminded me what a great economist Keynes was and how much more I sympathize with his approach and aims than with those of many of his followers" (1970a: 134).[2] This after his observing that "The *General Theory* is a great book, at once more naïve and more profound than the 'Keynesian economics' that Leijonhufvud contrasts with the 'economics of Keynes'" (ibid: 133). These observations follow Friedman's (1968b: 15; italics added) earlier declaration that "in one sense, we are all Keynesians now; in another, no one is a Keynesian any longer. We all use the *Keynesian language* and apparatus; none of us any longer accepts the initial Keynesian conclusions." Friedman's dissent on "Keynesian conclusions" derives from his faulting Keynes's explanation of the Great Depression as having indicated the impotence of monetary policy to revive an economy from a depression (1970b, 1997).[3] Nevertheless, he notes, "Keynes's bequest to technical economics was strongly positive" (1997: 13).

Judge Richard Posner's 2009 declaration that he had become a Keynesian after reading the *General Theory* is another excellent example of how Keynes's changed meaning of economic terms has been greatly influential in gaining him followership.[4] Posner, for decades, had been hailed as a prominent member of the economic libertarian philosophy movement. He associated himself with the Chicago School of Economics (of which Milton Friedman was a leader) and ran a joint blog, "The Becker-Posner Blog," with the Nobel Economics laureate, Gary Becker, between December 2004 and May 2014. Posner's account of the novelties he found in reading the *General Theory* includes (a) Keynes's declaring "consumption is the sole aim and object of economic activity," but without Posner's acknowledging Adam Smith (*WN*, 2:179) earlier having made the same observation,[5] (b) Keynes's treatment of saving as nonspending but as cash hoarding and thus injurious to an economy's growth, (c) Keynes's treatment of consumption as the driver of an economy's growth, along the lines of the discredited expenditure multiplier process,[6] (d) Keynes's treatment of investment as only the purchase of physical goods, unrelated to the issuing and purchasing of financial assets, (e) Keynes's treatment of government expenditure as not depending upon the public's income through taxation and issuing debt (bonds), (f) Keynes's treatment of interest rates as being determined by the supply and demand for central bank money rather than by the supply and demand for credit, of which variations in central bank's money supply are a minor part, (g) Keynes's emphasizing the pervasiveness of uncertainty about the future, and (h) Keynes's inviting control over the economy by government bureaucrats; they necessarily must suffer the same ignorance about the future as private business operators.

It also has not helped the correct appreciation of classical macro-monetary analysis that Keynes attributed two incorrect assumptions to it, namely, (a) that there is always full employment of labor and (b) business people form expectations about the future with complete certainty or that they have perfect foresight. The full-employment assumption greatly has helped to distract attention from classical economic analysis since the occurrence of involuntary unemployment tends to be the norm in practically all market economies. However, A.C. Pigou's (1941) strong denials of the relevance of the full-employment assumption to classical macroeconomics analysis appear to be undermined by his *Lapses from Full Employment* (1945). The latter book appears to argue that, but for the lack of free competition among workers for jobs and fluctuations in the labor money demand function, there will always be full employment: "In stable conditions, apart from frictions, immobility [among wage-earners] and so on, thorough-going competition among wage-earners would ensure the establishment and maintenance of full employment except in circumstance which we are very unlikely to meet with in fact" (1945: 25). Pigou even entertained Keynes's (1936: 263–4) argument that, for a reduction in money wage rates in a period of high unemployment, nominal interest rates also must fall if the rate of unemployment is to decrease (Pigou 1945: 12–17).[7] A more helpful explanation would have been to show the irrelevance of the full-employment assumption to the classical theories that Keynes claimed needed it for their validity, including the theory of interest rates, determination of the level of prices—the Quantity Theory of Money—and inflation, the forced-saving doctrine, and Say's law of markets.[8]

The second assumption, the alleged certainty of expectations about the future, has tended to persuade many that Keynes's macroeconomics is more relevant to the world of uncertainty than classical analysis. Now it is common knowledge that some pay astrologers to foretell the future while many economic forecasters tend to be in demand as business consultants or by the news media to foretell the future of the economy. This even though classical analysis includes sellers' adjustment of their supplies to actual market conditions when reality conflicts with their expectations, e.g. Smith's (*WN*, 1, 63–70) description of producers' adjustment of their supplies to the "effectual demand." Smith also explains,

> The establishment of any new manufacture, of any new branch of commerce, or of any new practice in agriculture, is *always a speculation*, from which the projector promises himself extraordinary profits. These profits sometimes are very great, and sometimes, more frequently, perhaps, they are quiet otherwise.
>
> (*WN*, 1: 128; italics added)

Similar discussions of producers revising their production plans to suit market conditions in conflict with their expectations are discussed in the context of the law of markets by Jean-Baptiste Say, David Ricardo, James Mill, and John Stuart Mill, e.g. "the calculations of producers and traders being of *necessity imperfect*, there are always some commodities which are more or less in excess, as there are always some which are in deficiency" (J.S. Mill 1874: 67; italics added). Alfred Marshall (1920: 289) also declares that "we cannot foresee the future perfectly."

However, without Keynes's contemporaries having countered sufficiently his misrepresentations of classical macroeconomic analysis regarding the above two assumptions, it has been hard to stem his onslaught on the relevance of classical analysis at all times. Thus, one of the main reasons Richard Posner gave for his conversion to Keynesianism was economists' inability to predict the onset of the 2008 financial crisis—"The vast majority of them had been blinded by the housing bubble and the ensuing banking crisis; and misjudged the gravity of the economic downturn that resulted" (2009: 28).[9]

As discussed in Ahiakpor (2019, Chapter 1) the greatly favorable treatment of Keynes's macroeconomics in Joseph Schumpeter's highly influential *History of Economic Analysis* (1954) in contrast with that book's derisive treatment of classical macroeconomic-monetary analysis (Hume, Smith, Say, Ricardo, and J.S. Mill) also has helped to impede the correct understanding of classical analysis. Thus Schumpeter coins "The Ricardian Vice" derisively to mean "an excellent theory that can never be refuted and lacks nothing save sense" ([1954] 1994: 473; see also 541, 618, 653n, 668) to describe most of classical analysis. But with respect to Keynes, Schumpeter turns the "Ricardian Vice" into a praiseworthy characteristic—being attractive and convincing:

> Keynes was Ricardo's peer in the *highest sense* of the phrase. But he was Ricardo's peer also in that his work is a striking example of what we have called above the Ricardian Vice, namely, the habit of piling a heavy load of practical conclusions upon a tenuous groundwork, which was unequal to it yet seemed in its simplicity not only *attractive* but also *convincing.*
>
> ([1954] 1994: 1171; italics added)

Schumpeter also praised Keynes for having "freed [economists] from scruples [regarding 'functions of inequality of income concepts']. His analysis seemed to *restore intellectual respectability* to anti-saving views and he spelled out the implications of this in Chapter 24 of the *General Theory*" ([1954] 1994: 1171).

Now the classics taught that saving, which is the purchase of interest- and/or dividend-earning financial assets, and not cash hoarding, contributes to economic growth. Alfred Marshall (1923: 46; italics added) also explains that "in 'western' countries even peasants, if well to do, incline to invest the greater part of their savings in Government, or other familiar stock exchange securities, or to *commit them to the charge of a bank*." But in Keynes's definition, saving is merely non-consumption (1930, 1: 172; 1936: 61–5, 74, 210), and equivalent to cash hoarding (1936: 166–7). Investment, on the other hand, means only the purchase of capital goods (1936: 62). Thus, Keynes's definitions prevented him from recognizing the validity of the classical argument that saving promotes investment and economic growth. Keynes (1930, 1936) instead came up with his paradox of thrift, in which increased saving decreases an economy's growth; Ahiakpor (1995) elaborates.

Schumpeter failed to recognize the error of Keynes's definitions and argued instead that Smith and A.R.J. Turgot's linking savings with investment was "their most serious shortcoming" ([1954] 1994: 324, n. 2). Schumpeter also bemoans the classical argument that saving supplies "capital," arguing: "What a mass of confused, futile, and downright silly controversies it would have saved us, if economists had had the sense to stick to those monetary and accounting meanings of the term [capital] instead of trying to 'deepen' them" ([1954] 1994: 323). He could have benefited from John Stuart Mill's (*Works*, 2: 70–2) "third fundamental theorem regarding Capital," for example. Thus the Keynes–Schumpeter view of saving and investment has become a standard critique of classical analysis by most modern macroeconomists.[10]

Schumpeter also praised the impact of Keynes's macroeconomic analysis:

> Particularly in its bearing upon saving, interest, and underemployment, this message seemed to reveal a novel view of the capitalist process not only … to the public and "writers on the fringes" but also to many of the best minds in the sphere of professional analysis—a novel view that was as attractive to some as its was repellent to others … *an achievement*, frank recognition of which is the *greatest* and *most deserved* of the compliments that may be paid justifiably to the memory of Lord Keynes.
>
> ([1954] 1994: 1180–1)

Schumpeter indeed concludes his chapter on Keynes with: "In a history of economic thought Keynes's policy recommendations—time-bound as they were—and certain characteristically Keynes's doctrines—which are losing their hold already—may be much more important" (ibid: 1184).

It has been a long struggle to publicize Keynes's misrepresentations of classical macroeconomic analysis against such powerful influence as Schumpeter's. Thus, a referee for the proposed manuscript for this book reacted to my explaining Schumpeter's praise of Keynes's work to the detriment of the classics by declaring it as "completely false." Referring to Schumpeter's application of the "Ricardian Vice" to Keynes, but without the label, the referee argues,

> Schumpeter strongly objected to Keynes' theory (his review of the *General Theory* is worldwide famous for being a spiteful and harsh criticism) and his History of economic analysis states that the *General Theory* was "a striking example of […] piling a heavy load of practical conclusions upon a tenuous groundwork." The doubt arises about the author ever really read Schumpeter at all.[11]

Indeed, other than Keynes's money (cash) supply and demand theory of interest rates that Schumpeter (1936) praised for having followed his own, his review of Keynes's *General Theory* was mostly critical. However, Schumpeter's subsequent writings on Keynes, beginning with his 1946 memorial, was mostly positive; see also my discussion in Ahiakpor (2019: 6–7).

Subsequent authors of texts in the history of economic thought or analysis and macroeconomics have followed Schumpeter's praising Keynes's economic analysis to the detriment of the classical alternative. They include Don Patinkin's very influential *Money, Interest and Prices* (1965), Mark Blaug's *Economic Theory in Retrospect* (1996), and Robert Ekelund, Jr. and Robert Hébert's *A History of Economic Theory & Method* (2014). David Laidler's *Fabricating the Keynesian Revolution* (1999) hardly utters any criticisms of Keynes's misrepresentations of classical and early neoclassical macroeconomics.

The purpose of this book is to clarify the extent to which Keynes's changed meaning of saving, capital, investment, and money, along with his incorrectly attributing the assumptions of full employment and certainty of expectations about the future by entrepreneurs, have impeded modern macroeconomists' appreciation of classical macro-monetary analysis. The impediment has afflicted even some of those who have found faults with Keynes's analysis or are inclined to side with classical policy conclusions, including monetarists, new classicals, and Austrians. The arguments in this book complement those of my *Macroeconomics without the Errors of Keynes* (2019). Indeed, seven of the chapters were to have been included in that book. I had to delete them to meet the word count permitted in my contract.[12]

In Chapter 2 I explain how the failures of Gary Becker and William Baumol (1952), William Hutt (1974), William Baumol (1999, 2003), Samuel Hollander (2005a), Steven Kates (1998, 2003, 2015, 2018, 2019), and Alain Béraud and Guy Numa (2018a, 2019) to employ the classical definitions of saving, capital, investment, and money, rather than Keynes's versions have impeded their correct assessment of Jean-Baptiste Say's explanation of the law of markets. I illustrate in Chapter 3 how the same problem led Roy Grieve to argue that Keynes could successfully have criticized John Stuart Mill's restatement of Say's law of markets. The chapter elaborates my 2018 published critique of Grieve's 2016 article, "Keynes, Mill, and Say's Law: The *Legitimate* Case Keynes Didn't Make against J.S. Mill," in the *Journal of the History of Economic Thought.*

In Chapter 4 I explain how employing the classical meaning of saving as the purchase of interest- and/or dividend-earning assets could have saved Robert Barro (1974) from incorrectly claiming that increased saving would result from increased government deficit spending, which would prevent aggregate demand from rising. The correct interpretation of saving by James Buchanan (1976) also could have spared his claiming that Barro's argument already had been made by David Ricardo, thus giving modern macroeconomics the wrong version of Ricardo's equivalence theorem. The chapter draws upon my 2013 article, "The Modern Ricardian Equivalence Theorem: Drawing the Wrong Conclusions from David Ricardo's Analysis," in the *Journal of the History of Economic Thought.*

In Chapter 5, "Milton Friedman's permanent income hypothesis: A diversion from Keynes's misrepresentation of saving as non-spending," I explain how Friedman's (1957) failure to interpret saving in the classical tradition led to his elaborate arguments to reconcile an apparent conflict between household budget data showing a rising saving-income ratio as incomes increased and national income data failing to show the same in Simon Kuznets's (1952) study covering several decades in the US. With that work, Friedman has diverted economists' attention from recognizing the validity and significance of Adam Smith's declaration, "What is annually saved is as regularly consumed as what is annual spent, and nearly at the same time too; but it is consumed by a different set of people" (*WN*, 1: 359). Smith's argument forms the basis of subsequent classical macroeconomic analysis, especially J.-B. Say's statement of the law of markets. The chapter also explains the failure of temporary government remedies to increase "aggregate demand" to address economic recessions as not arising from the recipients of government relief basing their consumption expenditures on their permanent incomes but by the 100% crowding out of government expenditures. The chapter furthermore clarifies the extent to which Friedman's formulation of his permanent income hypothesis is but a subset of Keynes's own arguments in Chapters 8 and 9 of the *General Theory*; the same observation applies to Franco Modigliani's work on the consumption function too.

In Chapter 6, "The classical heritage of monetary theory and policy at Chicago and Harvard before the Keynesian conquest," I explain the error of David Laidler and Roger Sandilands's (2002a) claiming that it was Lauchlin Currie who informed John Williams, his doctoral thesis supervisor at Harvard, about the requisite monetary policies to cure the ongoing US depression. They further allege that Williams passed on Currie's policy prescriptions to the January 1932 Chicago conference. Laidler and Sandilands base their claims on the similarities between a 1932 memorandum to cure the depression prepared by three young Harvard Ph.Ds, Lauchlin Currie, Paul Ellsworth, and Harry White, and the Chicago Harris Foundation conference recommendations sent to President Herbert Hoover. However, it is foundational to classical monetary analysis that a falling level of prices results from the growth in the demand for money (currency) having exceeded the growth of money's supply. Also, a falling level of prices causes the opposite of the classical forced-saving mechanism, resulting in business losses and rising unemployment. The solution then is to find ways to increase the quantity of money and to restore the level of prices.

Most of the participants at the January 1932 Chicago conference, including Jacob Viner and several others from the University of Chicago, Gottfried Haberler, Lionel Edie, John Williams, and Irving Fisher, were well aware of the classical principle. Keynes, pre-1936, also adopted much of the classical monetary analysis. Currie also notes, "My theoretical approach had been influenced by Keynes since my London School of Economics days in 1922–25, and at Harvard throughout the Depression I had bootlegged [Keynes's] heretical views on fiscal policy … [and] considered myself a Keynesian from way back" (1972: 139, 141). Laidler and Sandilands might have argued otherwise had they not attributed too much novelty to Currie's thinking about monetary issues. They subsequently admit my point, noting that "monetary thought in both [the Universities of Chicago and Harvard] drew on a common quantity-theoretic heritage whose lineage can be traced back at least to David Hume (1752)" (2010: 573). The chapter is based upon my 2010 article, "On the Similarities between the 1932 Harvard Memorandum and the Chicago Antidepression Recommendations," published in the *History of Political Economy*.

In Chapter 7, "100% money: A harmful proposal appropriately ignored," I explain the danger posed to economic prosperity by some luminaries in modern macro-monetary analysis, including Irving Fisher, Frank Knight, Milton Friedman, James Tobin, and several other Nobel laureates, by their urging the adoption of 100% reserve banking in the US. Fisher led the call with his book, *100% Money* (1935), claiming that it would "keep checking banks 100% liquid; prevent inflation and deflation; cure or prevent depressions; and wipe out much of the National Debt." Underlying the claims is the erroneous belief that commercial banks create money (checkable deposits) out of "thin air" and destroy them when they recall loans. By so doing, it is alleged, the banks also cause inflation and economic booms sometimes and deflation and depressions at other times at their whim. Proponents of the 100% reserve system want to turn commercial banks into mere warehouses for the public's short-term savings rather than being intermediaries between savers and borrowers. They see little discouragement to the public from their being charged custodial and clerical fees by banks rather than the public being paid interest on their checkable deposits.

The chapter explains the fundamental flaws behind the 100% money proposal, including (a) the belief that banks create deposits out of nothing, (b) the belief that loan repayments contract bank deposits, (c) the belief that variations in the level of prices are caused by variations in demand deposits rather than the quantity of central bank money relative to its demand—the classical Quantity Theory of Money, (d) the belief that the proposal replicates the 1844 Bank Act of England that applied to Bank of England notes, not to bank deposits, and (e) the belief that the proposal would encourage more saving and investment for economic growth. The 100% reserve proposal also completely ignores Adam Smith's (*WN*, 1: 341) explanation of the "judicious operations" of fractional reserve banking creating a "wagon way into the air" to promote economic growth. The institution of deposit insurance in the US, beginning from January 1934, mostly has eliminated the danger that fractional reserve banking earlier posed.

Keynes's (1930, 1936) commingling of money (cash) with savings with banks and his insistence that banks do not depend upon the public's savings to lend have contributed to the view that adopting the 100% reserve rule would promote economic stability and growth. The chapter explains how attention to the classical literature on money and banking, particularly in David Hume and Adam Smith, would have helped proponents of the 100% money to recognize their error. Most students of money and banking as well as commercial bankers appear better to understand the danger to economic prosperity that the 100% reserve proposal poses than many other economists; see, e.g., Harry Brown (1940) and Douglas Diamond and Philip Dybvig (1986).

In Chapter 8, "Keynes's liquidity trap Is impossible: Classical monetary analysis helps to explain," I clarify how Keynes's (1930, 1936) sometimes commingling of money (cash) and savings in bank deposits to define money has served modern macro-monetary analysis poorly. That definition of money has allowed acceptance of Keynes's mistaken view that it is possible for money's demand curve to change shape to become perfectly horizontal at some unspecified, low level of (long-term) interest rates. But limiting the meaning of money to cash (specie in classical analysis or central bank notes in modern times) and recognizing that money's demand curve always takes the shape of a rectangular hyperbola, as the classics and early neoclassicals explained and Keynes (1933: 229, n. 2) earlier also recognized in John Stuart Mill's work, we can readily recognize the error of Keynes's (1936) liquidity trap argument. Variations in interest rates shift a downward sloping money demand curve rather than cause movements along it. Furthermore, people have other useful things to do with their incomes than to devote them all to hoarding cash when long-term interest rates have decreased to some low level. Income earners' utility maximization at three margins, namely, consumption, saving, and cash hoarding, assures that Keynes's liquidity trap would never occur. Don Patinkin, Milton Friedman, Paul Krugman, and David Laidler are among notable macro-monetary analysts who have not recognized the flaw in Keynes's argument. The chapter is based upon my 2018 article published in the *History of Economic Ideas*.

In Chapter 9, "The Quantity Theory of money, the forced-saving doctrine, and the Phillips curve analysis," I explain that the modern Phillips curve analysis is but an illustration of the classical forced-saving doctrine with respect to wage rates. A.W. Phillips (1958) matches rising prices with rising nominal wage rates and falling prices with falling nominal wage rates. But he does not link the rising prices to increasing quantities of central bank money relative to its demand and falling prices with the opposite, as explained in the classical Quantity Theory of Money. The behavior of nominal wages tends to lag behind unanticipated movements in the level of prices, while changes in the demand for labor tend to follow the behavior of prices. This is what explains the decrease in the rate of unemployment when prices are rising, before the rise of nominal wage rates, as explained in the classical forced-saving doctrine. The reverse occurrence follows the unanticipated falling level of prices that results from the growth of money's excess demand.

Phillips's 1958 analysis eschews the Quantity Theory analysis, following Keynes's (1936) relegation of that theory's relevance to only a state of full employment. This again is how Keynes's influence has impeded the application of classical macro-monetary analysis. The chapter is based upon my 2009 article, "The Phillips Curve Analysis: An Illustration of the Classical Forced-Saving Doctrine," published in the *Journal of the History of Economic Thought*.

In Chapter 10, "The future of Keynesian economics: Struggling to sustain a dimming light," I update my 2004 article with the same title published in the *American Journal of Economics and Sociology*. I explain that modern followers of Keynes's macroeconomics will have a hard time defending their belief when they come to recognize the errors of Keynes's defining saving, capital, investment, and money differently than the classical economists did. Correcting Keynes's definitions eliminates such standard Keynesian arguments as (a) government expenditures have a multiplier effect on an economy, (b) there are autonomous consumption, business, and government expenditures, rather than all expenditures depending upon income, (c) there is no necessary link between saving and investment, (d) interest rates are determined by the supply and demand for central bank money rather than by the supply and demand for credit, of which variations in central bank money form a minor part, and (e) a government's management of aggregated demand is necessary to assure economic stability and growth. The Keynes followers also will have the problem of sustaining their belief when they are confronted with textual evidence that the classical theories are not founded upon the assumptions of full employment and that entrepreneurs form expectations about the future with certainty.

Thus, I identity five analytical pillars upon which Keynesian macroeconomics is founded but none of which sustains serious scrutiny. They are (1) that savings are not spent; they do not provide the funds for investment spending as classical economics argues; (2) that consumption spending sustains and drives an economy's expansion through a multiplier process; (3) that the rate of interest is determined by the supply and demand for money (cash) or liquidity, not by the supply and demand for "capital" or savings; (4) that there are no equilibrating tendencies in a monetary economy to restore it to full employment once involuntary unemployment has occurred; and (5) that the classical theories of interest, the price level, inflation, and the law of markets (Say's Law) are all founded upon the premise that full employment of labor always exists.

In Chapter 11 I draw some policy conclusions that derive from interpreting classical macro-monetary analysis without the impediments of Keynes's influence. They include (a) no need for aggregate demand management or stabilization policies through cutting or raising taxes; production is the principal source of incomes for spending; (b) matching central bank money creation to variations in its demand by the public to sustain the level of prices—zero inflation targeting; variations in the public's savings included in modern M1 or M2 are not the source of inflation or deflation; (c) promoting increased saving through limited taxation to promote economic growth with low interest rates; (d) that imposing 100% reserve on checkable deposits mostly hurts an economy's prospects for growth; (e) leaving interest rates to their determination by the supply and demand for credit in various markets; and (f) not interfering in labor markets with minimum wage legislation. Thus, recent publications looking towards Keynes's *General Theory* for guidance to deal with economic problems are searching in the wrong place, I argue.

Notes

1 For a description of the seven major schools of modern macroeconomics, including the post-Keynesians, see Ahiakpor (2019, Chapter 1).
2 Robert Dimand and Harald Hagemann (2019: 1), strong Keynes adherents, cite Friedman's inclusion of this statement in his 1997 article to open the "Introduction" to their edited volume on Keynes without noting that Friedman was repeating an earlier

observation, a point Friedman himself makes in note 6. Friedman also points out that he wrote the article in 1988 (p. 3). Thus, Dimand and Hagemann's use of the statement as if it were a 1997 revelation to Friedman and their also not indicating that Friedman dismissed Keynes's indictment of classical economics as relevant to the "special case" [of full employment] to be "wrong" is quite misleading.

3 Ahiakpor (2019, Chapter 5) explains that Friedman's employing Keynes's broad definition of money (M1 or M2) to contradict Keynes's explanation of the impotence of monetary policy during the Great Depression is incorrect and misleading. The problem was mostly the shaken confidence of the public in banking institutions that led to a significant contraction of savings; see also Chapter 7.

4 Robert Dimand and Harald Hagemann (2019: 1) interpret Richard Posner's declaration as his having been "shocked to discover that he found the [*General Theory*] admirable, readable and helpful in understanding the world," and evidently applaud Posner's conversion to Keynesianism. This even though Posner writes of the *General Theory* as containing "heresies ... puzzles, opacities, loose ends, confusions, errors, exaggerations, and anachronisms galore" (2009: 32).

5 Smith (*WN*, 2: 179) argues, "Consumption is the sole aim and purpose of all production ... The maxim is so perfectly self-evident, that it would be absurd to attempt to prove it." Keynes (1936: 104) uses that observation to trash the benefits of saving, including in the form of sinking funds, because he did not recognize that savings are borrowed to be spent by issuers of IOUs.

6 See Ahiakpor (2001 or 2003b, Chapter 12).

7 Pigou there makes no effort to employ the classical (and Marshall's) supply and demand for savings or "capital" theory of interest rates; see Ahiakpor (1990 or 2003b, Chapter 5). It is also well known that Pigou was not much interested in the history of economics to have effectively countered Keynes's misrepresentations of the classics. He is noted to have declared his lack of interest in "the wrong opinions of dead men" and urged Dennis Robertson to get on "with constructive work of his own" rather than to be criticizing Keynes's work (see Robert Lesson 1998: 135).

8 See Ahiakpor (1997a or 2003b, Chapter 10) for such demonstration of Keynes's errors in the attribution of the full-employment assumption.

9 Posner evidently did not recognize the irony in his reasoning, namely, that three varieties of Keynesian economists—neoclassical Keynesians, new Keynesians, and post-Keynesians—also missed predicting the onset of the financial crisis!

10 The puzzle of how saving finances investment afflicts Posner's (2009: 30, 31) assessment of modern non-Keynesian macroeconomic analysis; he also embraces Keynes's "paradox of thrift" proposition.

11 In my response to the referee's comments, I gave a more complete account of Schumpeter's "Ricardian Vice" and his differential application of it to Keynes and the classics. It is remarkable that someone regarded to be highly knowledgeable as to be consulted by Routledge would turn out to be not so. My 2019 book contains similar reactions to my proposed manuscript as well as to journal submissions that were not published. Several of my journal publications correcting Keynes's misrepresentations of classical macroeconomics have taken from three to four years and several rejections before their acceptance.

12 Five of these chapters are based upon my published journal articles. They are chapters 4, 6, 8, 9, and 10.

2 Interpreting Say's law of markets or outlets correctly

The impediments of Keynes's influence

Introduction[1]

Several analysts correctly have noted the error of Keynes's (1936: 18, 25) interpreting Say's Law as "supply creates its own demand." They include William Hutt (1974), Steven Kates (1998, 2015), William Baumol (1999, 2003), Petur Jonsson (1997, 1999), James Ahiakpor (2003a, 2018b), Samuel Hollander (2005a, 2011), and Alain Béraud and Guy Numa (2018a, 2018b, 2019).[2] However, the influence of Keynes's definitions of saving, capital, investment, and money in modern macroeconomics in contrast with their meaning in classical economics, and his having attributed the assumption of always full employment of labor to Say's Law still appear to have impeded the law's correct interpretation among the Keynes's critics. Thus, some side with Keynes's view of the law's inapplicability in the short run, e.g. Baumol, Hollander (2005a), and Béraud and Numa (2018a and 2018b), while some others interpret the law differently than Say stated, e.g. Steven Kates (1998, 2003, 2015, 2018, 2019). Béraud and Numa (2019) also claim "a proximity of ideas between Keynes and Say" while finding Keynes's criticisms of Say's "system … to be ill founded" (229).

William Hutt (1974) aims to "rehabilitate" Say's Law but he does not focus on restating Say's own arguments. Rather, he tries to show "what Say really meant" or "what Say ought to have meant" (1974: v), albeit in his attempt to counter Keynes's criticisms of the law. Thus, instead of the production of a commodity creating a demand, an outlet, or a market for other produced goods and services, as Say argues, Hutt focuses on explaining the "market-clearing process" as the essence of Say's Law. He also agrees with Joseph Schumpeter's incorrect assessment "(a) that Say did not *fully* understand the 'law' to which his name has become attached; and (b) that in his defense of the 'law' against acute but economically illiterate critics, Say was sometimes very 'woolly,' slipping, at times, into serious fallacy" (1974: 4; italics original). Hutt also employs definitions of saving, investment, and money that are contrary to those Say adopted from Adam Smith. He defines saving as "The process of (a) replacing … the real value of that part of the stock of assets and the flow of services which is exterminated by consumption, or (b) adding to the stock of assets";

investment as "The entrepreneurial *process* of choosing the prospectively most profitable forms in which services are embodied into assets for replacement"; and money as "All assets the value of which arises, or is enhanced, because they are demanded and held *wholly or partially* for the monetary services they render" (1974: 16, 17; italics original). Hutt's arguments thus turn out not to be very helpful in explaining Say's law of markets or outlets.[3]

Say's law of markets deserves the prominence in macroeconomic analysis it lost, following its misrepresentation by Keynes (1936, 1937a, and 1939). Say proposed his law to counter the notion among "adventurers in the different channels of industry" that "When the demand for their commodities is slow, difficult, and productive of little advantage, they pronounce money to be scarce; the grand object of their desire is, a consumption brisk enough to quicken sales and keep up prices" (1821a: 132). The true explanation for slackened sales is the reduced production of other commodities for reasons other than insufficient demand since it is from productions that purchasers derive their incomes, money serving mainly as the medium of exchange. Say reaffirms the point in his second letter to Malthus: "Whatever be the cause which limits production, whether the want of capital [funds] or of population, of diligence or liberty, the effect is, in my opinion, the same; the productions which are offered on one-side are not sold, because sufficient commodities are not produced on the other" (1821b: 31–2). Say meant his proposition to assist in enlightening "the views of the agents of industry, and to give confidence to the measures of governments anxious to afford them encouragement" (Say 1821a: 132). Thus, Say argues: "the encouragement of mere consumption is no benefit to commerce; for the difficulty lies in supplying the means, not in stimulating the desire of consumption; and we have seen that production alone, furnishes these means" (1821a: 139). Also, "It is the aim of good government to stimulate production, of bad government to encourage consumption" (bid).

Understanding the impediments of Keynes's influence over the correct interpretation of Say's Law will help to promote a more consistent macroeconomic analysis and policy formulation for the efficient economic management, away from stimulating consumption or aggregate demand rather than removing what real obstacles there may be to production, as Say intended. Ahiakpor (2003a) clarifies Keynes's success with misrepresenting Say's Law; here we explain the impediments of Keynes's influence on some recent interpreters of Say's arguments who yet recognize Keynes's error of rendering the law as "supply creates its own demand." We start with recognizing more extensively than in the secondary literature Say's indebtedness mostly to Adam Smith's *Wealth of Nations* in formulating his law of markets or outlets.

J.-B. Say's indebtedness to Adam Smith for the law of markets or outlets

To appreciate the correct meaning of Say's law of markets or outlets, it helps to recognize that Jean-Baptiste Say was mostly restating Adam Smith's exposition of the working of markets for produced goods and services in the *Wealth of Nations* (1776).[4] That background is also helpful in interpreting Say's use of such concepts as saving, capital, investment, and money consistently with Smith's rather than the meanings introduced into modern macroeconomics by Keynes (1930, 1936) to the detriment of Say's Law's accurate interpretation. Say argues in his long introduction to the fourth edition of his *Treatise* that Smith's treatment of political economy was the best written in the 18th century: "Whenever the Inquiry into the Wealth of Nations is perused with the attention it so well merits, it will be perceived that until the epoch of its publication, the science of political economy did not exist" (Say 1821a: xxx-viii).[5] Say's very high regard for the usefulness of Smith's work to him includes his noting:

> Many principles strictly correct had often been advanced prior to the time of Dr. Smith; he, however, was the first author who established their truth … He has furnished us, also, with the true method of detecting errors; he has applied to political economy the new mode of scientific investigation, namely, of not looking for principles abstractedly, but by ascending from facts the most constantly observed, to the general laws which govern them.
>
> (1821a: xxxviii–xxxix)

However, Say also believed Smith's statements of the principles of political economy in the *Wealth of Nations* are significantly distracted with historical illustrations. Such details, Say believed, divert readers' attention from the core principles he considered very important both for those in government and the general public to understand the nature of a market economy in order to promote the adoption of efficient economic policies. Thus, rather than believing it is the lack of money or demand for commodities that causes a business slow-down and businesspeople calling upon governments to subsidize their productions or to increase the quantity of money, it is rather a reduction in some productions that causes a low demand for other productions (Say 1821a: 132; 1821b: 5). The point underlies the corrections to mercantilist ideas about the role of money and the benefits of business subsidies that Adam Smith criticizes in his *Wealth of Nations*; Smith himself followed David Hume's arguments in "Of Money" and "Of the Balance of Trade."

Furthermore, Say argues, "[Smith's] fundamental principles, too, are not established in the chapters assigned to their development. Many of them will be found scattered through the two excellent refutations of the *exclusive* or *mercantile system* and *the system of the economists*, but in no other part of the work" (1821a: xliii; italics original).[6] Thus, Say believed,

> We are … not yet in possession of an established text-book on the science of political economy, in which the fruits of an enlarged and accurate observation are referred to general principles, that can be admitted by every reflecting mind; a work in which these results are so completed and

well arranged as to afford to each other mutual support, and that may everywhere, and at all times, be studied with advantage.

(1821–: xlv)

Say's writing his *Treatise* was to remedy the absence of such a textbook.

However, rather than always citing Smith in his restatements of the principles, Say frequently paraphrased Smith's arguments, along with those of a few others, including David Hume's. He explains that he wrote the *Treatise* after first studying what had been written by others, forgetting them, and then restating what he had learned:

> To prepare myself for attempting so useful a task [of writing a textbook], I have thought it necessary attentively to peruse what had been previously written on the same subject, and afterwards to forget it; to study [relevant] authors, that I might profit by the experience of so many competent inquirers who have preceded me; to endeavor to obliterate their impressions, not to be misled by any system; and at all times be enabled freely to consult the nature and course of things, as actually existing in society.
>
> (1821a: xlv)

Say adds: "Having no particular hypothesis to support, I have been simply desirous of unfolding the manner in which wealth is produced, distributed, and consumed" (1821a: xlv). This may explain his subsequent elaborations or clarifications of his arguments in later editions of his *Treatise* to be more consistent with Hume's and Smith's monetary analysis or to address new economic episodes.[7]

Nevertheless, Say mostly cited Adam Smith as his guide to explaining the law of markets. He writes to Thomas Malthus,

> I revere *Adam Smith*—he is my master. When I took the first steps in political economy, and when still tottering I was pushed by the advocates of the balance of commerce on the one side, and the advocates of net produce on the other, I stumbled at every move—he [Smith] shewed me the true path. Supported by his *Wealth of Nations*, which shews at the same time his own intellectual wealth, I learned to go alone. Now I have ceased to belong to any school.
>
> (1821b: 21; italics original)

Indeed, Say was not always consistent with Smith's principles in some of his statements or defense of the law of markets, as some of his disputes with Ricardo illustrate; see Ricardo (*Works*, 1: 236–7). Thus, rather than citing such deviations as Say's having recanted or undermined his law of markets, it is best to note them as minor inconsistencies.[8] On the core principles of the law of markets or outlets, Say did not waver, as we encounter next.

The core of Say's law of markets or outlets

Keynes (1936: 18–19) drew upon John Stuart Mill and Alfred Marshall to state his understanding of Say's law of markets as "supply creates its own demand." Had he consulted Say's own *Treatise* or Say's *Letters to Mr. Malthus*, he would have found Say explaining the law as a two-part proposition: (a) that the production of a commodity immediately creates a demand, a market, or an outlet for other produced goods and services (not labor[9]) and (b) that productions can only be purchased with or by other productions.[10] Thus, a producer employs labor, equipment, machinery, and rents land or building, to produce a commodity so as to derive utility from the product's direct consumption or to acquire some other useful commodities (including money) or services in exchange. Extend that understanding to all other producers and we obtain the link between all markets for produced goods and services (but not for labor). The more each person (or firm) produces, the more demand or outlets they create for the productions of others; the less they produce, the less demand or outlets they create for the productions of others. Thus, Say argues, we "ought to be firmly convinced ... that the more producers, the more consumers there are" (1821b: 60).

In Chapter 15 of the fourth edition of his *Treatise*, Say well explains:

> A man who applies his labour to the investing of objects with value by the creation of utility of some sort, can not expect such a value to be appreciated and paid for, unless where other men have the means of purchasing it. Now, of what do these means consist? Of other values of other products, likewise the fruits of *industry*, *capital*, and *land*. Which leads us to a conclusion that may at first sight appear paradoxical, namely, that *it is production which opens a demand for products*.
>
> (1821a: 133; italics added)[11]

In his first letter to Thomas Malthus, Say also argues:

> Since the time of Adam Smith, political economists have agreed that we do not in reality buy the objects we consume, with the money or circulating coin which we pay for them. We must in the first place have bought this money itself by the sale of productions of our won.
>
> (1821b: 2)

That is, demand for commodities is founded upon productions or supply rather than the other way around as Keynes (1936) argues.

Also, the proposition does not amount to Say having claimed that "the *costs* of output are always covered in the aggregate by the sale-proceeds resulting from demand" (Keynes 1936: 20; italics original). Some goods may be sold at a loss while others are sold at profitable prices, Say (1821a: 135) explains: "It is observable ... that precisely at the same time that one commodity makes a loss, another commodity is making excessive profit."[12] Furthermore, Say explains,

"The trade of speculation ... is sometimes of use in withdrawing an article from circulation, when its price is so low as to discourage the producer, and restoring it to circulation, when that price is unnaturally raised upon the consumer" (1821a: 141n).

The creation of demand from production is also instantaneous, according to Say:

> It is worth while to remark, that a product is *no sooner* created than it, *from that instant*, affords a market for other products to the full extent of its own value [utility]. When the producer has put the finishing hand to his product, he is *most anxious* to sell it *immediately*, lest its value should diminish in his hands.
>
> (1821a: 134; italics added.)

A producer is even more eager to sell when prices are expected to fall, but may be less so when prices are expected to rise. Say also explains that money (cash or specie) serves merely as a convenient intermediary in the market exchange process: "almost all produce is in the first instance exchanged for money, before it is ultimately converted into other produce" (1821a: 133–4). This is the source of the characterization, "*C–M–C*," commodities exchanged for money to be exchanged for commodities, to represent Say's explanation.[13] Kates (1998: 30) thus misinterprets Say's argument with his criticism:

> Rather than arguing that the production of one good enables its producer to sell that good for money and then buy something else, Say looks at the process from the opposite direction. Say argued that the production of one good permits others to exchange what they have produced for money which can then be used to buy that first good.[14]

Thus, besides the amount of money one desires to hold in readiness against future purchases, one no sooner receives money in exchange for commodities than one seeks to exchange the money for some other commodities, including acquiring financial assets (saving). Say argues:

> Nor is [a seller] less anxious to dispose of the money he may get for it; for the value of money is also perishable. But the only way of getting rid of money is in the purchase of some product or other. Thus, the mere circumstance of the creation of one product *immediately* opens a vent for other products.
>
> (1821a: 134–5; italics added)

Now opening a vent does not mean the exchange is immediately completed or it is completed at cost-recovering prices. Such an extension of Say's argument just invites misinterpretations, as in Hutt's insistence on the determination of market-clearing prices as the essence of Say's Law: "Say's Law directs attention to actual *transactions*—the values (prices) of services and assets which are necessarily demanded when they are actually supplied" (1974: 27–8; italics original).[15] Say also notes, "to receive money in exchange is called, *selling*, and to give it, *buying*" (1821a: 220; italics original).[16] Similarly, Smith (*WN*, 1: 460) explains:

> The man [other than a retailer] who buys does not always mean to sell again, but frequently to use or to consume; whereas he who sells, always means to buy again ... It is not for its own sake that men desire money, but for the sake of what they can purchase with it.

Say also follows Smith[17] closely in recognizing the purchasing power conveyance function money (cash) performs in the market exchange process rather than money's acquisition being the substance of the exchange. In normal market conditions, the quantity of money in an economy sufficiently serves to facilitate the exchanges. If not, alternative means of exchange, including credit instruments, may be devised, Say (1821a: 134) argues. Say includes among money's substitutes, "bills at sight, or after date, bank–notes, running credits, and write–off" (1821a: 134n).[18] Smith's version of the same argument is,

> If money is wanted, barter will supply its place, though with a good deal of inconveniency. Buying and selling upon credit, and the different dealers compensating their credits with one another, once a month or once a year, will supply it with less inconveniency. A well regulated paper money will supply it, not only without any inconveniency, but, in some cases, with some advantages.
>
> (*WN*, 1: 458)

A greater abundance of goods relative to money (gold and silver coins) over a period of time leads to more money flowing into the economy after prices have fallen, along the lines of Hume's price-specie-flow mechanism that Smith (*WN*, 1: 378, 457, 460) also argues. Similarly, Say explains,

> As soon as there is a supply of money sufficient to circulate all the commodities there are to be circulated, no more money is imported; or, if a surplus flow in, it emigrates again in quest of a market, where its value is greater, or where its utility is more desired.
>
> (1821a: 273)[19]

Say understood such price-specie-flow mechanism as deriving from the fact that,

> It is seldom or never that any body *keeps in his purse or his coffers* more *specie* than enough to meet the current demands of his business or consumption. Every excess beyond these demands is rejected, as bearing neither utility

nor *interest*; and the community at large is fully supplied with specie, as soon as each individual is possessed of the portion suitable to his condition and relative station in society.

(1821a: 273; italics added)

Thus, Say recognized that money received in payment for one's sold production may be used to purchase other goods and services, and some held against future purchases,[20] and the rest lent or invested in financial assets (FA) to earn interest or dividends (savings). That is, income earners (households) spend their disposal incomes on consumption, saving, and cash holding: $Y(1 - t) = C + \Delta FA^d + \Delta H_h$. Importantly, "No political economist of the present day can by saving mean mere [cash] hoarding," Thomas Malthus (1836: 28) reminds us. When more money is demanded to be held than has been supplied, its value rises (commodity prices fall), while when more interest- and/or dividend-earning financial assets are demanded (increased supply of savings), their prices rise or interest rates or dividends fall. Both Hume's Quantity Theory and the theory of interest (interest rates being determined by the supply and demand for savings), adopted by Smith, are employed in Say's analyses.

Thus, interpretations of Say's Law as being relevant only to a barter economy, e.g. that of John Henry (2003: 196), are incorrect.[21] Henry also incorrectly contrasts Say's economy in which money is (allegedly) neutral with Keynes's in which "money cannot be neutral: money does affect output, and thus employment" (ibid.). Missing Say's analysis of financial intermediation by banks, Henry also yet follows Keynes to mischaracterize Say's economy as one in which commodities are sold for money to purchase a greater quantity of commodities: C–M–C' (2003: 194). But what Say describes is an economy in which people may exchange commodities for money in order to purchase other commodities: C–M–C. However, the production process is one in which capitals (savings) are borrowed to be invested in producing commodities intended to be sold at a profit.[22]

Say also discusses in his *Treatise* the factors that may cause disruptions to an economy's well-functioning, none of which pertains to the deficiency of consumption demand. They include "wars, embargoes, oppressive duties [and] dangers and difficulties of transportation" (1821a: 142). Other instances include (a) "times of alarm and uncertainty, when social order is threatened, and all undertakings are hazardous"; (b) "the general dread of arbitrary exactions, when every one tries to conceal the extent of his ability"; and (c) "times of jobbing and speculation, when the sudden fluctuations caused by gambling in produce, make people look for a profit from every variation of a rise, and money in prospect of a fall" (ibid.). In such conditions, Say observes, "capitals remain inactive and useless to production … there is no circulation, but of such products as cannot be kept without danger of deterioration; as fruits, vegetables, grain, and all articles that spoil in the keeping," the latter being sold at a loss (1821a: 142); see also (Say 1821b: 57–8).[23] Say envisions some dire consequences from these disruptive causes, including "families before in tolerable circumstances [becoming] more cramped and confined; and those before in difficulties [being] left altogether destitute. Depopulation, misery, and returning barbarism, [would] occupy the place of abundance and happiness" (1821a: 140). However, Say also believed that such "concomitants of declining production ... are only to be remedied by frugality [increased saving, not cash hoarding], intelligence, activity, and freedom [of enterprise]" (ibid.).

Item "c" in Say's list above reads like some the factors leading to the 1929 US stock market crash and subsequent business contraction during the Great Depression (1930–3) as well as the US housing market bubble's bursting in 2007–8, followed by the financial crisis, contracted production and increased unemployment. Clearly then, Say's explanations of the law of markets or outlets recognize the occurrence of economic recessions, reduced production, and the accompanying increased rate of unemployment of labor. He just did not make consumption deficiency their cause. Indeed, it is quite incongruous to claim that we can have the overproduction of all commodities (or demand deficiency) in a recession or a depression while there are also observed decreased production all around and increased unemployment.[24] Keynes's view that Say law presumes the economy is always operating at full capacity and there are no obstacles to full employment of labor is clearly a misrepresentation.[25]

In the absence of the above disturbances to an economy's well-functioning, Say also recognized that some goods may remain unsold if they do not meet the needs (preferences) of others in the marketplace or others have not produced enough to be able to purchase what has been brought to market: "the glut of *a particular commodity* arises from its having outrun the total demand for it in one or two ways; either because it has been produced in excessive abundance, or because the production of other commodities has fallen short" (1821a: 135; italics added). Some may interpret Say's explanation as his referring to "insufficient demand." Say rejects that explanation because no one produces but with the object to consume or sell. That is why it is the reduced production by others that results in the "excessive abundance" of what has been brought to market. Say's explanation directs attention to understanding the obstacles to production while the insufficient-demand explanation misdirects attention to demand stimulation, even as "Consumption is the sole aim and purpose of all production ... The maxim is so perfectly self-evident, that it would be absurd to attempt to prove it" (Smith *WN*, 2: 179).[26] Say also notes, "A bad harvest ... hurts the sale of commodities at large. And so it is also with the products of manufacture and commerce ... the stagnation of one channel of manufacture, or of commerce, is felt in all the rest" (ibid.). Say (1821a: 86–90; 1821b: 65–6) also discusses the emergence of unemployment owing to the displacement of workers by machinery even as the rate of production has increased.

Say's arguments above found elaborations by James Mill, David Ricardo, and John Stuart Mill, among others (see Becker and Baumol 1952, Jonsson 1997, Ahiakpor 2003a), and became absorbed into Alfred Marshall and Mary Marshall's *Economics of Industry* and Marshall's *Pure Theory of Domestic Values* and *Principles*, to which Keynes (1936: 19–21) refers. The subsequent elaborations have tended to focus on explaining the occurrence of some unsold goods as arising from the mismatching of production with the nature of demand rather than from the overproduction of all goods, including money, e.g. John Stuart Mill's summary: "Nothing is more true than that it is produce which constitutes the market for produce, and that every increase of production, *if distributed without miscalculation* among all kinds of produce in the proportion which private interest would dictate, creates, or rather constitutes its own demand" (1874: 73; italics added).

John Stuart Mill's summary may give the misleading impression that producers create demand for their own products. Hutt's (1974) rendition as productions create demand for competing products better states what Say has argued. Thus, although Mill concludes his essay by noting the "temporary excess ... of commodities generally, *not in consequence of over-production*, but of a want of commercial confidence" (1874: 74; italics added), the view still persists with some analysts that there could be an overproduction of all goods, including money, because of insufficient consumption demand. But Mill also argues:

> I know not of any economical facts ... which can have given occasion to the opinion that a general over-production of commodities [insufficient demand] ever presented itself in actual experience. I am convinced that there is no fact in commercial affairs, which, in order to its explanation, stands in need of that chimerical supposition.
>
> (*Works*, 3: 575)

Mill gives credit for "having placed this most important point in its true light ... principally, on the Continent, to the judicious J.B. Say, and in this country to Mr. [James] Mill" (3: 576). Mill (*Works*, 3: 574) also regards "the notion of general oversupply" an "irrational doctrine."

Keynes's difficulties with Say's law of markets or outlets

Although Keynes may not have read Say's *Treatise* or Say's *Letters to Mr. Malthus*, he could have understood Say's two-part proposition of the law of markets or outlets as (a) production immediately opens a vent, an outlet, or a market for other productions, and (b) productions can only be purchased by or with productions from the writings of John Stuart Mill and Alfred Marshall that he quotes in the *General Theory* (1936: 18–20). Both Mill (*Works*, 3: 574) and Marshall (1920: 590–2) also explain the disruption to production and employment from a commercial crisis, even if not as detailed as outlined in Say's *Treatise* noted above. There was thus little legitimacy for Keynes's claiming in the preface to the French edition of the *General Theory* that, in formulating his law of markets, Say implicitly assumed "the economic system was always operating at full capacity ... a theory so based is clearly incompetent to tackle the problems of unemployment and of the trade cycle" (1939: xxxv). He also concludes the preface with: "in the theory of production [the book] is a final break-away from the doctrines of J.-B. Say and that in the theory of interest it is a return to the doctrines of Montesquieu" (1939: xxxv).[27]

In the *General Theory*, Keynes argues that Say's Law implies "that there is no such thing as involuntary unemployment" (1936: 21) or "that there is no obstacle to full employment" (1936: 26). Keynes further assumes fixed labor-output coefficients in the production process in spite of Say's repeated emphasis on the plurality of the factors of production rather than focusing on labor alone in discussing the law of markets both in the *Treatise* and *Letters to Mr. Malthus*. Thus, Keynes defines "aggregate supply" of output as a function of labor employed, $Z = \phi(N)$ and "aggregate demand" also as a function of the amount of labor employed, $D = f(N)$. From such assumption, Keynes declares,

> The classical doctrine ... which used to be expressed categorically in the statement that "Supply created its own Demand" ... must mean that $f(N)$ and $\phi(N)$ are equal for *all* values of N, i.e. for all levels of output and employment; and that when there is an increase in $Z(= \phi(N))$ corresponding to an increase in N, $D(= f(N))$ necessarily increases by the same amount as Z.
>
> (1936: 25–6; italics original)

Most analysts' failure to separate the state of labor's employment in their interpretations of the law of markets thus appears to have inclined them to claim, along with Keynes, that the law may be valid only as a long-run proposition but not in the short run. Unemployment above the natural rate is a rather common phenomenon, especially in economic recessions. But, as Frank Knight also correctly points out in an October 1936 lecture, Keynes was incorrect to have included the state of the labor market in his interpreting Say's Law: "Say's law refers to *products* exchanged on the market—it does not refer necessarily to labor ... It says that a market tends to clear itself at a price. Keynes does not treat Say's Law as the classical economists did" (quoted in Cristiano and Fiorito 2016: 95; italics added).

Similarly, Schumpeter (1936: 704) criticizes Keynes's assumption that "variations in output are uniquely related to variations in employment," which "imposes the further assumption that all production functions remain invariant." Ricardo (*Works*, 1: 395n) approvingly quotes John Barton's (1817) arguing,

> The demand for labour depends on the increasing of circulating and not of fixed capital ... It is easy to conceive that, under certain circumstances, the whole of the annual savings of an industrious people might be added to fixed capital, in which case they would have no effect in increasing the demand for labour.

Ricardo, however, adds a correction to Barton's argument: "It is not easy, I think, to conceive that under any circumstances, an increase of capital should not be followed by an increased demand for labour; the most that can be said is, that the demand will be in a diminishing ratio" (ibid.). Say's own view is that the introduction of machinery frequently throws some workers out of employment (1821a: 86–90; 1821b: 65–6). However, the production of machines requires labor: "Machines cannot be constructed without considerable labour, which gives occupation to the hands they throw out of employ" (1821a: 67). But criticisms of Keynes's assumption of fixed labor-output coefficients in production virtually have disappeared from modern interpretations of Say's Law.

Also, according to Keynes (1930, 1: 172; 1936: 210), saving means only the non-consumption of one's income; savings are a withdrawal from the expenditure stream. Capital for Keynes (1936: 62) means only capital goods, the same meaning he attaches to investment—only the purchase of capital goods. However, with Keynes's changed meanings of saving, capital, and investment, it was difficult for him to see how saving would not impair an economy's production through a reduction on the demand for produced consumption goods. Thus, Keynes declares, "[the classics] are fallaciously supposing that there is a nexus which unites decisions to abstain from present consumption [saving] with decisions to provide for future consumption; whereas the motives which determine the latter are not linked in any simple way with the motives which determine the former" (1936: 21). But the nexus is the rate of interest determined in the credit or capital markets. Had Keynes understood Smith's (*WN*, 1: 358–9) defining saving as the acquisition of interest- and/or dividend-earning financial assets, and capital as first the savings of income earners and subsequently the funds employed in the sphere of production to acquire fixed capital and circulating capital—raw materials, produced goods yet to be sold, funds to pay wages before the receipt of revenues [wages fund], and cash-on-hand—Keynes could have recognized the credit or capital markets as the connecting medium.[28] Instead, Keynes (1936: 186–92) failed to recognize interest rates as being determined by the supply of capital (savings) relative to the demand for capital (investment-demand); see Ahiakpor (1990 or 2003b, Chapter 5).

Keynes also could not make meaning of Smith's declaring, "What is annually saved is as regularly consumed [used up] as what is annually spent, and nearly at the same time too; but it is consumed by a different set of people" (*WN*, 1: 359), and endorsed by J.-B. Say (1821b: 39). But Say (1821b: 39) followed Smith's explanation, "What is annually saved is as regularly consumed as what is annually spent; and nearly at the same time too" (*WN*, 1: 359). Thomas Malthus (1836: 38) repeats Smith's explanation and declares, "No political economist of the present day can by saving mean mere hoarding." John Stuart Mill (*Works*, 2: 70) too adopts Smith's explanation. Alfred Marshall (cited in Keynes 1936: 19) repeats the point. However, Keynes's commingling money (cash) and savings with depository institutions, both in his *Treatise* and the *General Theory*, impaired his treating the quantity of money supplied relative to the quantity demanded as determining the level of prices as Say did, following Smith and David Hume. Say's (1821a: 352–3) treating money as mostly the conveyer of savings to borrowers rather than its being the substance borrowed, again following Smith (*WN*, 1: 373–4), is missing in Keynes's analysis.

However, from his misunderstandings, Keynes (1936: 21) declares his objection to the classical view that "an act of individual saving inevitably lead to a parallel act of investment."[29] Also, Keynes objects to "the social advantages of private and national thrift [saving], the traditional attitude towards the rate of interest, the classical theory of unemployment, the quantity theory of money, the unqualified advantages of laissez-faire in respect of foreign trade and much else (ibid.)." These legacies of Keynes's misreading of the law of markets have impeded in varying degrees the correct interpretation of Say's Law by some of those who yet have faulted Keynes's defining the law as "supply creates its own demand." We discuss these below.

The impediments of Keynes's influence on some recent interpreters of Say's Law

a)   William Baumol

William Baumol has been an important contributor to the secondary literature on Say's Law. However, in spite of his having studied Say's own writings, which include Say's making no necessary link between production and the level of employment, Say's denying demand deficiency as a cause of economic contractions, and Say's arguing Smith's view of savings being spent reproduc- tively by borrowers,[30] he sides with Keynes's claim that Say's Law is inapplicable in the short run. Baumol argues, "As a loyal Keynesian, I conclude that where the Keynesian literature is *directly* at odds with the Smith-Say-Mill-Ricardo positions, I am driven to vote for the former ... I am convinced that the behavior of demand can be responsible for recessions and depressions" (2003: 34; italics original). And, although Baumol (1999) recognizes that the "main literature on the Law of Markets does, indeed, maintain that there cannot be a general failure of demand," he insists, "except perhaps in the very short run" (197). This after his having translated from the second edition of Say's *Treatise*, Say's own declaration, "I cannot conceive that the products of the labour of an entire nation can ever be overabundant since one good provides the means to purchase the other" (quoted in Forget 2003: 55–6).[31] Baumol also sides with Keynes's view that an increased rate of saving would impede an economy's growth, at least in the short run: "whether an upward (rightward) shift in the savings function will ever, indeed more than rarely, serve to impede growth or prevent it, at least in the short and intermediate run ... I am driven to vote for my fellow Keynesians" (2003: 35).

Baumol may have been inclined to side with Keynes because he misin- terprets Say as having disagreed with Smith's (*WN*, 1: 359) explaining that all savings are spent or consumed reproductively. Baumol (1999: 200) cites Say's reference to 1813 when capitals slept "at the bottom of the coffers of the capitalists" for want of demand as evidence of Say's disagreement with Smith's explanation. But Say agreed with Smith, restating the argument in his second letter to Malthus thus:

> You assume implicitly as fact, that a production saved is abstracted from every species of consumption; although in all these discussions, in all the writings you attack, in those of Adam Smith, of Mr. Ricardo, in mine, and even in your own [*Principles of Political Economy*, p. 31], it is laid down that a production saved is so much substracted [*sic*] from unproductive consumption to be added to capital, that is to say, to the value that is consumed reproductively.
>
> (1821b: 39)

Baumol also does not dispute Keynes's definitions of saving and investment that make it easy for interpreters of Say's Law to doubt the law's validity always. He argues, "There is an abundance of passages in the writings of Say and others advancing the claim … from Adam Smith, that income not devoted to consumption will always be spent on investment, and without delay" (1999: 201). But Say, like Smith, recognized disposable income being spent in two other ways besides on consumption, namely acquiring cash for its liquidity services and purchasing interest- and/or dividend-earning financial assets (saving). Thus, when saving is recognized as supplying the funds to be employed in the sphere of production, rather than being cash hoarding, the logic of Say's Law can be seen as sound; see also J.S. Mill's third fundamental theorem respecting capital (*Works*, 2: 70–2) and Marshall (1923: 46). Besides the unhelpfulness of Say's own statement that "many savings are not invested, when it is difficult to find employment for them" (1821b: 49n),[32] Baumol there appears to repeat Joseph Schumpeter's (1954) error in employing Keynes's definitions of saving and investment. Schumpeter argues, "every economist *should* have known that the Turgot-Smith-J.S. Mill theory of the saving and investment mechanism was inadequate and that, in particular, saving and investment decisions were linked together too closely" ([1954] 1994: 513; italics original), and that "the decision to save does not *necessarily* imply a decision to invest; we must also take account of the possibility that the latter does not follow or not follow promptly" (ibid.: 514; italics original). It is by treating investment as only the purchase of capital goods that the direct link between saving (ΔFA^d = demand for financial assets) and investment (ΔFA^s = supply of financial assets) through variations in the level of interest rates is lost on Baumol, Schumpeter, and Keynes.

   Baumol (1999: 198) furthermore misrepresents Say's (1821a: 87n) suggestion to a "benevolent administration" to relieve the short-term pain of technological unemployment: "provision for the employment of supplanted or inactive labor in the construction of works of public utility *at public expense*, as in construction of canals, roads, churches, or the like" (italics added). The suggestion is consistent with the law of markets since Say was not arguing that such expenditures would add to aggregate consumption spending. The funds would be taken from the public who otherwise would have spent them too; see also Say (1821b: 32–3). Keynes (1936), on the other hand, viewed such public works as stimulating aggregate demand to revive an economy from a recession or depression.[33]

b)   Samuel Hollander

Samuel Hollander has written extensively on the economics of Adam Smith, J.-B. Say, David Ricardo, Thomas Malthus, and John Stuart Mill. Yet in Chapter 5 of his 2005 book on Say, he argues the validity of Say's Law only as a long-run proposition, allowing overproduction in the short run, which is consistent with Keynes's view. Hollander could have treated Say's interpreting the French industrial depression of 1813 that resulted from a contraction in the agricultural sector, as being consistent with Say's Law even in the short run, namely, "production creates demand or outlet for other productions." As Say argues, "A bad harvest ... hurts the sale of commodities at large" (1821a: 135). Had agricultural production not declined, there would have been more demand for manufactured goods than occurred that year. Instead, Hollander argues, "in [Say's] later writings in particular, he recognized aggregate-demand contraction as one source of depression and general unemployment, going beyond Ricardo who allowed only that inadequate demand for goods characterized depression brought about by monetary or credit contraction" (2005a: 189). This even though Hollander (2005a: 205) also cites Say's own emphasis on production as the determinant of demand: "as the value we can buy is equal to the value we can produce, the more men can produce, the more they will purchase."

Furthermore, Say, like Smith, defined money (specie) as one of the commodities produced for exchange with other produced goods and services. Money is also demanded to be held because of its surety against future needs, besides its exchange facilitation function. Thus, exchanging commodities for money to hold does not violate Say's proposition that the production of a commodity immediately opens a vent for other commodities. But apparently to allow for the violation of Say's Law in the short run, in concert with Keynes's claims, Hollander changes the "immediate" opening of demand from a production to only a "potential" opening. He claims that all of Say's various formulations of his law, "*strictly speaking* imply only the potential to purchase" (2005a: 205; italics original). Hollander follows that statement with, "Say also cites a passage from his *Traité* asserting more strongly that the potential is fulfilled" (ibid.), but that does not substitute for Say's own statement of the "immediate" opening of a vent for other commodities by a production. However, Hollander (2011: 27) subsequently declares Keynes to have "misinterpreted his predecessors disgracefully," citing Ahiakpor (2003a) as illustration.

c)   Steven Kates

Steven Kates has been a strong defender of Say's Law against its criticism by Keynes since the mid-1990s. But several of his writings on Say's Law appear to have been impaired by Keynes's influence. First, he does not divorce the law from a close link with the labor market, just as Keynes did, following Malthus. Thus, Kates (2018: 279) considers incorrect Ahiakpor's (2018b: 267) statement, "Say's Law explains the coordination of markets for produced goods and services (not labor) by variations in relative prices, the value of money, and interest rates in a monetary economy." He argues, "Mill was very specific that 'demand for commodities is not demand for labour,' which is the very essence of Say's Law" (Kates 2018: 279). The irony is that the Mill declaration rather delinks the market (demand) for commodities from that of labor. Mill (*Works*, 2: 88) also explains, "The demand for commodities is a consideration of importance rather in the theory of exchange [markets], than in that of production"; whereas the consideration of labor's demand belongs in a theory of production. Moreover, labor is not one of the commodities exchanged in Say's Law; see also Say's (1821b: 15, 23–4) objections to Malthus's inclusion of labor in the discussion of his law of markets.

Second, Kates (2015, 2018) does not interpret saving as the purchase of interest- and/or dividend-earning financial assets as Say, Ricardo, and John Stuart Mill did, following Adam Smith; he appears to follow Hutt (1974: 16).[34] Rather, almost like Keynes, Kates treats savings as accumulated goods: "Saving is discussed [by Mill] in real terms. The source of resources with which to invest are made available only because some resources have been saved; that is, not used as current consumption" (2015, 48). Also, Kates claims, "A classical economist thought of 'saving' … in real [rather than financial] terms, as that part of the *stock* of the existing resource base devoted either to maintaining capital, or to producing additional capital aimed at increasing the future flow of output" (2018: 280; italics original). Furthermore, Kates insists, "In classical theory saving was the proportion of all existing land, labor, and capital used to add to the productive base of the economy" (ibid.).

Kates's above definitions of saving leave no room for interest rates to coordinate savings (supply of loanable funds) and investment-demand decisions in the credit market before the borrowed funds (capitals) are committed to acquiring fixed and circulating capital, the latter also including the wages fund. But Mill's (*Works*, 2: 70–2) third fundamental theorem respecting capital well explains that process; see also Mill (1874: 90–100). Say's own conception of saving, which he employs in his second letter to Malthus to counter Malthus's fears of too much saving, uses the financial or monetary (funds) concept:

> To the disciples of *Adam Smith*, who think that saving is beneficial, you [Malthus] oppose the inconveniences of an excessive saving; but here the excess carries its remedy along with it. Wherever capital becomes too abundant, the interest which capitalists derive from it becomes too small to

balance the privations which they impose upon themselves by their economy. It becomes more and more difficult to find good securities [IOUs]
for investing money, which is then placed in foreign securities. The simple
course of nature stops many accumulations.

(1821b: 40–1; italics original)

Interest is earned on loanable funds (savings), not on capital goods. Readers of
Kates's statements of Say's Law, aware that they do not directly acquire capital
goods when they save, thus could not be persuaded by Kates's arguments in
defense of the law.

Third, Kates appears to have been influenced by Keynes's (1936) adoption
of Eugene Böhm-Bawerk's interpretation of "capital" as only capital goods. He
thus agrees with Joseph Schumpeter's (1954) criticism of Say's exposition of his
law of markets. Schumpeter ([1954] 1994: 620) claims,

> The "practical" group of Say's pronouncements on the monetary ques-
> tions raised by his law may be rendered as follows: Unlike his interpreter J.
> S. Mill, he [Say] evidently did not think much of the practical importance
> of the phenomena that might be produced by widespread refusal to spend
> receipts promptly either on consumption or on "real" investment (that is,
> investment involving demand for goods and services).

But Say's analysis recognizes cash hoarding as a third form of "spending" one's
income, besides consumption and saving. However, accepting Schumpeter's
judgment on Say's exposition of the law of markets, Kates (1998: 34) argues:

> Unfortunately, Say's exposition was less than coherent than it ought to
> have been. Schumpeter ([1954] 1986: 625) was right when he wrote that
> Say "hardly understood his discovery himself and not only expressed it
> faultily but also misused it for the things that really mattered to him." Say's
> discussion had many gaps in logic, and has contributed to the misunder-
> standing of the law of markets.

Kates's and Schumpeter's failure to interpret saving or capital first in monetary
terms thus creates the confusion for them, not Say's having expressed his law
faultily.

Fourth, like Keynes (1936: 364), Kates (2015) also does not recognize the
wages fund derived from savings as constituting the demand for labor in Mill's
fourth fundamental theorem respecting capital. He claims: "the demonstration
that demand for commodities is not demand for labor requires no retreat into
classical presumptions such as the wages fund to explain why this may be the
case, or any reading into the text of some principle left unstated on the pages
of Mill's *Principles*" (2015: 45). But what John Stuart Mill sought to emphasize
in his fourth fundamental theorem is the role of savings or "capital" accumulation to hire productive labor services. Thus, Mill precedes that controversial

declaration with, "What supports and employs productive labour, is the capital [funds] expended in setting it to work, and not the demand of purchasers for the produce of the labour when completed" (*Works*, 2: 78). Mill then clarifies the source of labor's demand as "the amount of the capital, or other *funds* directly devoted to the *sustenance and remuneration* of labour" (ibid.; italics added). In Mill's chapter, "Of Wages," he also explains the demand for labor as being constituted by the "wages-fund of a country," that is, by the "circulating capital, and not even the whole of that, but the part which is expended in the direct purchase of labour. To this, however, must be added all *funds*, such as the wages of soldiers, domestic servants, and all other unproductive labourers" (*Works*, 2: 337; italics added).

Fifth, Keynes (1936: 116–7, 119) praises the usefulness of public works, "even of doubtful utility" (127), to increase aggregate demand and bring an economy out of a recession or depression. Nevertheless, Keynes also required to be fulfilled the condition that government's expenditure constitute "no reduction of investment in other directions" (117) for success. Furthermore, Keynes included the possibility of the multiplier effect of such spending to produce full employment (116–9). However, rather than pointing out the invalidity of Keynes's claims, Kates (2003: 77–9) argues that Keynes was saying nothing new that is not in Say's Law.

Kates bases the claim on several pre-1936 writers' having urged the use of public works. They include Fred Taylor ([1921] 1925: 203, cited in Kates 1998: 151), who believed such government spending in a depression would increase "total demand and so an increase in general prosperity." Thus, Kates (2003: 78) asks, "If both [Keynes] and his predecessors sought the same policy, where was the revolution? If both classical and Keynesian economics both indicated that there was a case for public spending, then where does the difference lie?" But Say's (1821a: 87n) suggested public works was a temporary relief for technological unemployment, not to relieve demand deficiency;[35] Keynes's multiplier argument is also a myth, being founded on the supposition that savings are not spent (Ahiakpor 2001).[36] Besides, Taylor (1925: 202–3) reached his erroneous conclusion by two arguments: first, missing the point that money is also a produced good in Say's analysis, and second, not specifying how "the public authorities" finance their expenditures.

In adopting Taylor's argument, Kates misses Mill's (*Works*, 2: 66) explaining the displacement of private spending by government taxes:

> [Government] may lay on taxes, and employ the amount productively … a great part of [the tax] would have been drawn from the fund for unproductive expenditure, since people do not wholly pay their taxes from what they would have saved, but partly, if not chiefly, from what they would have spent [consumed].

Mill (1874: 47–8) also ridicules the notion of large government expenditure promoting prosperity: "The utility of a large government expenditure, for the purpose of encouraging industry, is no longer maintained … It is no longer supposed that you benefit the producer by taking his money, provided you give it to him again in exchange for his goods." Say (1821b: 32–3) earlier argues the displacement of private spending by government spending, which contradicts Keynes's aggregate-demand increase argument.[37]

d) Alain Béraud and Guy Numa

Alain Béraud and Guy Numa (2018a) seek to clarify Say's statement of his law of markets or outlets beyond what Say explains in the fourth edition of the *Treatise*, the only edition translated into English, with their access to the fifth and sixth French editions. Their account, however, appears very much influenced by Keynes's work. They interpret some arguments differently than in the fourth edition of his *Treatise* but without the requisite textual evidence, which renders their contribution less than helpful.[38]

Thus, Keynes (1936: 20) accuses the classics of having introduced money "perfunctorily" into their analysis and that he was turning monetary theory into a theory of output as a whole rather than monetary theory explaining only the level of prices, that is, Keynes's arguing money's non-neutrality in the short run. Keynes (1936: 80–1, 328) also dismisses the meaningfulness of the classical forced-saving doctrine in which the lagging of factor costs, including wage rates, behind variations in the level of prices causes increased employment of labor when prices are rising and increased unemployment when prices are falling. But money's short-run non-neutrality is inherent in the classical forced-saving mechanism, which is a part of the Quantity Theory of money (Ahiakpor 2009). However, Béraud and Numa (2018a: 228–33; 2018b: 287) describe the same phenomenon—increased quantity of money initially stimulating increased production and employment until wage rates rise—without identifying it as such. Instead, they claim such explanation by Say as his having admitted a "contradiction between Say's Law and Say's actual monetary views" (2018a: 218); that "Say *conceded* … monetary expansion could promote increased expenditure and output" (2018a: 220; italics added); and Say "acknowledged [that] his monetary theory contradicted his initial framework in which commodities were purchased only with other commodities" (2018a: 231). But Say's own words they cite regarding the last claim are: "in spite of the principles that teach us that money plays only the role of a simple intermediary, and that products can *ultimately* be purchased only with products, more abundant money fosters all sales and the reproduction of new values" (ibid.; italics added).

Indeed, Say did not earlier argue that commodities (except money) exchanged directly with other commodities in a monetary economy but rather that money serves as a means of exchange—"the agent of the transfer of values" (Say 1821a: 135). Besides, whether money serves more than as a medium of exchange does not alter Say's fundamental proposition that "it is production which opens a demand for products" (ibid.). But failing to recognize the forced-saving analysis in Say's argument, Béraud and Numa draw the contrast, "Keynes stands out with his assumption of downward rigidity of money wages. This is not the focal point of Say's and Mill's analyses … Keynes's contribution is a macroeconomic model that formalizes markets interaction [*sic*] under a condition of money-wage stickiness" (2018b: 288). This in spite of their noting, "Say … admitted that some costs became sticky—particularly money wages" (2018b: 287).[39]

Also, producers of money, Say explained, immediately sought to exchange that commodity for other commodities for their own consumption or use, including lending at interest. It thus constitutes no contradiction of Say's explanation of the law of markets when he argues that the increased production of money "fosters all sales and the production of new values." But Béraud and Numa (2018a: 228) rather claim, "Say's endorsement of the quantity theory of money was far from strict. In *Cours* and in the fifth and sixth editions of *Traité*, Say detailed several monetary expansion scenarios that spurred prosperity."

Adopting Keynes's (1936: 210–1) view of savings as not being consumed or spent, Béraud and Numa's (2018a) also interpret Say's analysis as pertaining only to the long run. They argue, "All in all, for Say, the accumulation of capital generated higher output and thereby increased income, enabling increased consumption that *eventually* absorbed the surplus income" (2018a: 224; italics added).

Béraud and Numa (2018a: 231) furthermore claim that Say changed his mind regarding the law of markets because he acknowledged the short-term effect of an increased quantity of money on interest rates but interest rates rising subsequently, following the rise of commodity prices. However, that analysis also belongs in Hume's (1752) essay, "Of Interest," that Smith (*WN*, 1: 376) adopts. Hume argues that the level of interest rates is not ultimately determined by the abundance or scarcity of money (specie) but savings relative to their demand. Say (1821a: 353) also considers it "a great abuse of words, to talk of the interest of money; and probably this erroneous expression has led to the false inference, that the abundance or scarcity of money regulates the rate of interest." Indeed, Say (1821a: 353–4) observes, "The theory of interest was wrapped in utter obscurity, until Hume and Smith dispelled the vapour." Instead, Béraud and Numa (2018a: 229) follow Keynes's (1936, Ch. 13) liquidity (cash) preference theory of interest to claim that Say had "a conception of the interest rate defined as the reward for parting with cash"; they repeat the erroneous claim in (2019: 236).

Béraud and Numa's most serious undermining of a correct interpretation of Say's Law is their having adopted Clower and Leijonhufvud's (1973) so-called "Say's Principle" to contradict Say's own denial of a general glut of commodities in the *Treatise* (1821a: 135) and in his *Letters to Mr. Malthus* (Say 1821b: 24). They claim,

> Say … recognized that the failure to produce (or the failure of factor owners to sell their services) must have repercussions on the demand for output, because the demand for product was financed out of earned income.

Literally, this means that demand deficiency was possible and could lead to economic crisis. It could be that a glut could occur only in the short run, but it would still be a general glut.

(2018b: 287; italics original)

Béraud and Numa also draw on Hollander's (2005a: 214–9; 2005b: 384) altered version of Say's proposition, "a product is *no sooner created*, than it, from *that instant*, affords a market for other products to the full extent of its own value" (1821a: 134; italics added), to claim, "Say never meant that supply created its own demand, but simply meant that selling goods increased one's holding of money, thus *potentially*, but not necessarily, allowing the purchase of other goods with the proceeds of the sale" (2018a: 218; italics original); see also (2019: 231). They insist that Say's Law "was not that supply was necessarily equal to demand or that demand deficiency could not cause crises" (2018b: 287). But money was a produced commodity in Say's analysis. That is why there is no overproduction of all goods, including money, at the same time in his law of markets; see also John Stuart Mill (*Works*, 3: 572; 1874: 71). Besides, their argument confuses the intention of a producer from the realization of sales. Say's Law is about the opening of a market for other produced goods and services as a result of one's production.

Now the "Say's Principle" is an attempt to salvage Keynes's misrepresentation of Say's Law by alleging coordination failures between agents' plans regarding what to produce and what to purchase in return, based on their ability to sell factor services, including labor. Thus, Béraud and Numa employ a model in which there are "four types of commodities: factor services, products, financial assets, and money" (2018a: 239; italics added) rather than only produced goods and services; see also Béraud and Numa (2018b: 287; 2019: 234). But Say (1821b: 22–3) objects to Malthus's inclusion of labor among the "commodities" discussed in the law of markets. Besides, when some factor services are not sold, that must mean less output has been planned for production. We cannot then conclude that too much of everything, including money, will have been produced for there to arise a general glut of commodities.

Furthermore, the "Say's Principle" view is not the same as Say's explaining that "A buyer is effectively ready to buy as long as he has money to do so ... he can only obtain money with the products he created, or those created for him; hence the fact that it is production that generates outlets" (quoted in Béraud and Numa 2018a: 223; italics added). Money in Say's statement here refers to income, but Béraud and Numa interpret Say as arguing: "the buyer lacked money" (ibid.); they repeat the mistaken claim in (2019: 233). Keynes (1936: 20) similarly misinterprets a statement in Alfred and Mary Marshall (1879). But that is the very misunderstanding Say (1821a: 132) seeks to clarify about money in the market exchange process: it is not the scarcity of money that hampers purchases but the lack of adequate productions. Say (1821a: 133) further explains:

[Money's] whole utility [in the exchange process] has consisted in conveying to your hands the value of the commodities, which your customer has sold, for the purpose of buying again from you; and the very next purchase you make, it will again convey to a third person the value of the products you may have sold to others.

See also Smith (*WN*, 1: 306).

Also, note that Say in Béraud and Numa's (2018a: 223) quoted statement mentions "products," not factor services. Thus, Say (1821a: 86–7) could explain increased unemployment along with increased production, owing to the introduction of machinery, contrary to Keynes's firmly linking employment with the level of productions. Instead, Béraud and Numa (2018b: 286) claim, "the concept of 'unemployment' is not analyzed in Say's writing … It was used to designate work disruption during holidays. Say was perfectly aware that some individuals could not find employment, but he did not offer any theoretical explanation."

Conclusion

Say's law of markets makes perfectly good sense when read in the language of Adam Smith, where (a) saving means purchasing interest- and/or dividend-earning assets; (b) capital means the same thing as savings for income earners and then the funds employed by producers in the sphere of production; (c) investment means the acquisition of interest- and/or dividend-earning asset for income earners but the employment of borrowed funds by producers to acquire fixed and circulating capital, the latter including the wages fund and cash-on-hand; and (d) money means only cash (specie) or currency. The law applies only to produced goods and services, not labor services that have to be combined with other factors of production to create the products exchanged in the marketplace. Say also drew upon Smith's proposition of the purpose behind a producer's creation of a product, namely, either for their own consumption or for sale through the intermediary of money (cash). It is such intension behind production that underlies Say's proposition: "a product is no sooner created than it, from that instant, affords a market for other products to the full extent of its own value" (1821a: 134). Indeed, Say goes on to explain why some products are not sold while some are sold at profitable prices, as cited above.

Keynes's problems with Say's Law that made so much sense for the classical economists, particularly James Mill, David Ricardo, John Stuart Mill, on down to Alfred Marshall, arose mainly from his changed definitions of saving, capital, investment, and money. In Keynes's new language he could not understand how an economy is held together by market prices, including interest rates. To Keynes, savings are a withdrawal from the expenditure stream, capital means capital goods only, investment means the purchase of capital goods only, and money means variously cash or cash plus savings deposited with banking institutions, and sometimes even including treasury bills (Keynes 1936: 167, n.1). Keynes's incorrectly attributing the assumption of full employment of labor to Say's Law was another hindrance to his understanding. The lack of clarity or consensus over the meaning of Say's Law among analysts who have recognized the error of Keynes's describing it as "supply creates its own demand" easily can be traced to their having adopted Keynes's language rather than the language of Adam Smith in their interpretations.

Thus, the Great Depression that started from the United States and spread to the rest of the world can be understood as having arisen from the reckless credit inflation that preceded the US 1929 stock market crash, the 1930 Smoot-Hawley tariffs, the public's shaken confidence in several major banking institutions (Elmus Wicker 1996 and Milton Friedman and Anna Schwartz 1963, Ch. 7) that led to massive withdrawals of savings (deposits) from many other banks, and a great increase in the demand for money (cash) to hoard while the US Federal Reserve system, on the gold-exchange system, could not expand its currency to meet the demand. The latter resulted in price deflation, business losses, and increased unemployment, until the declaration of a banking holiday and the abandonment of the gold standard in March 1933 (see Ahiakpor 2019, Ch. 5). The experience well fits John Stuart Mill's explanation:

> From the sudden annihilation of a great mass of credit, every one dislikes to part with money, and many are anxious to procure it at any sacrifice. Almost everybody therefore is a seller, and there are scarcely any buyers; so that there may really be, though only while the crisis lasts, an extreme depression of general prices, from what may be indiscriminately called a glut of commodities or a dearth of money.
>
> (*Works*, 3: 564)

Keynes instead cited the Great Depression as proof of the inherent incapability of a free-enterprise economy to sustain itself without the intervention of government to restore aggregate demand from collapse and the inability of classical macro-monetary analysis to explain such phenomenon.

Say also outlined the remedies to an economy's malfunctioning in terms of addressing the hindrances to production, including "frugality [increased saving, not cash hoarding], intelligence, activity, and freedom [of enterprise]" (1821a: 140) but not the promotion of increased consumption.[40] None of Say's remedies is consistent with Keynes's preference for "a large extension of the traditional functions of government" (1936: 379) in order to override "capitalistic individualism" (1936: 381). Thus, Béraud and Numa's (2019: 240) latest claim that Keynes and Say "could readily have agreed ... on several issues, such as the possibility of aggregate-demand deficiency, the role of money in the economy, and government intervention through public works" can only be misleading.

Notes

1 This chapter draws upon my unpublished conference paper by the same title, discussed at the History of Economics Society Annual Meetings at Columbia University, New York City, June 20–23, 2019. I also restate some arguments in Ahiakpor (2003a). My drawing

upon Say's arguments in his *Treatise on Political Economy* (1821a) and noting his indebtedness to Adam Smith in developing his law of markets are new.

2 Gary Becker and William Baumol (1952) is more devoted to refuting the interpretation of Say's Law by Oscar Lange and Don Patinkin than critiquing Keynes's interpretation of the law as "supply creates its own demand." Thomas Sowell (1972: 4, 12, 19, 36, 119) unhelpfully repeats Keynes's rendition of Say's Law as "supply creates its own demand." Sowell (1972: 60–1) also depends upon arguments by J.C.L. Sismonde de Sismondi and Thomas Malthus to claim the possibility of a general glut of all commodities, including money, in contrast with Say's own denial of such and reiterated by David Ricardo and John Stuart Mill.

3 Hutt's (1974) treatment of Say's arguments appears to have influenced Steven Kates (1998), who also agrees with Schumpeter's assessment that Say did not fully understand his own law of markets. Kates (2015, 2018) rather incorrectly interprets John Stuart Mill's fourth proposition respecting capital as the true meaning of Say's Law. I elaborate below.

4 This very much explains the following his law of markets received in James Mill (1808) and David Ricardo's *Principles* (1817). It is with considerable justification that John Stuart Mill refers to Say as "the eminently clear thinker and skillful expositor" (3: 466). However, Mill's comment is in regard to Say's explanation of exchange values by market supply and demand.

5 Some claim that elements of Say's Law can be discerned from writers before Smith, including Josiah Tucker and A.R. J. Turgot, e.g. Hutt (1974: 6–7). However, Say (1821b: 24, 60, 82–3) in his letters to Malthus refers to his arguments as his "doctrine."

6 Say illustrates his charge with noting that "[Smith's] principles relating to the real and nominal prices of things, are introduced into a dissertation on the value of the precious metals during the course of the last four centuries; and the author's opinions on the subject of money are contained in the chapter on commercial treaties" (1821a: xliii). In fact, however, Smith's Volume 1, Book 2, Chapter 2 (302–50) of the *Wealth of Nations* is devoted to explaining money and banking, not to commercial treaties. See also Say's (1821a: 272) praising Smith's treatment of money and banking as "Smith's happiest efforts, yet it is not every body that comprehends his reasoning."

7 Because of such revisions, Béraud and Numa (2018a: 218) claim there is a "contradiction between Say's Law and Say's actual monetary views." But the monetary views in Say's later editions of the *Treatise* they cite are consistent with those of David Hume's (1752) *Political Discourses*, particularly, "Of Money," "Of Interest," and "Of the Balance of Trade," and which most classical writers, including David Ricardo and John Stuart Mill, endorsed without renouncing Say's Law or the Quantity Theory of money.

8 Noting that some of Say's arguments relate to "general excess, and not ... partial excess," Hollander observes, "Here is an invitation to misunderstanding" (2005a: 206, 207). But a general glut of all commodities, including money, resulting from too much production is impossible; I elaborate below.

9 Both in his *Treatise* and *Letters to Mr. Malthus*, Say emphasizes that labor alone does not create the products he discusses in the law of markets. Labor is in competition with other factors of production, particularly, machinery to be employed in production. Labor's wage rate relative to the rental rates of capital equipment thus very much determines how much of it is employed in production. Ricardo (*Works*, 1: 395) re-iterates the point: "Machinery and labour are in constant competition, and the former can frequently not be employed until labour rises."

10 Ricardo (*Works*, 1: 2912) affirms Say's second part: "Productions are always bought by production, or by services; money is only the medium by which the exchange is effected." After his brief quotations from Say's *Treatise*, Hutt (1974: 26) wonders "how Keynes could have continued with *The General Theory* if he had quoted passages like [those] for refutation instead of [the] unsatisfactory passage from J.S. Mill." However, the real problem with Keynes's use of Mill's work was his incomplete reading of it; see Ahiakpor (2003a).

11 Ricardo (*Works*, 1: 290) draws upon the second edition of Say's *Treatise* to argue that "No man produces, but with a view to consume or sell, and he never sells, but with an intention to purchase some other commodity, which may be immediately useful to him, or which may contribute to future production. By producing, then, he necessarily becomes either the consumer of his own goods, or the purchaser and consumer of the goods of some other person." Similarly, John Stuart Mill argues, "To produce, implies that the producer desires to consume [or to sell]; why else should he give himself useless labour?" (1874: 49).

12 Contrast with Becker and Baumol's (1952) misleading claim that Say's Law asserts "there will always be a market for all goods produced where we define a good to be something which can be sold at a price covering its costs" (372) and that "This argument is found in many places in Say's discussions of the Law" (372, n. 3).

13 However, it differs from Karl Marx's (adopted by Keynes) rendition, *CMC'*, where *C' > C*, allegedly to describe the capitalist mode of production (John Henry 2003).

14 See also Jonsson's (1999) noting some other lapses in Kates's (1998) treatment of Say's arguments, particularly his incorrect contrasting of Say and James Mill's accounts. Sowell (1972: 4) similarly gives an incorrect account of Say's Law, claiming, "An increased supply of output means an increase in the income necessary to create a demand for that output. Supply creates its own demand."

15 Hutt appears to have resorted to this extension of Say's argument to provide a justifiable explanation of the high rate of unemployment in Britain due partly to trade union resistance to wage reductions, but which Keynes (1936: 14, 16, 267) supported.

16 John Stuart Mill's equivalent statement Kates (1998: 73) cites approvingly is: "The sale of produce for money, and the subsequent expenditure of the money in buying other commodities, are a mere exchange of equivalent values for mutual accommodation."

17 Smith explains: "Money, by means of which the whole revenue of the society is regularly distributed among all its different members, makes itself no part of that revenue. ... The great wheel of circulation [money] is altogether different from the goods which are circulated by means of it. The revenue of the society consists altogether in those goods, and not the wheel which circulates them" (*WN*, 1: 306).

18 Steven Horwitz (2003: 94) misses this point in Say's explanation, claiming instead the insufficiency of money as a hindrance to production: "Excess demands for money suggest that owners of productive assets are having difficulty selling those assets as potential buyers lack the medium of exchange they need to make their demands effective. If buyers do not have money, they cannot buy and sellers cannot sell, and so forth."

19 Becker and Baumol (1952: 372) miss recognizing Say's employment of Hume's Quantity Theory of money and claim the price level is indeterminate in his analysis.

20 Say (1821a: 218) describes money as "precisely that commodity" whose possession makes it easy to procure one's future needs "without any difficulty," just as Smith (*WN*, 1: 26–7) explains.

21 The so-called Say's Identity version of the law, e.g. Becker and Baumol (1952, 371–5), thus misrepresents Say's own argument.

22 As Adam Smith (*WN*, 1: 373–4), Say (1821b: 334), David Ricardo (*Works*, 1: 363–5, 3: 912), and John Stuart Mill (*Works*, 2: 55; 3: 508–9) well explain, it is not money that is borrowed for production but capital or savings. Say also considers it "a great abuse of words, to talk of the interest of money" (1821a: 353) since "it is value which [is] borrowed, and not any particular sort of metal or of merchandise" (1821a: 352).

23 Marshall (1920: 590–2) discusses the disorganization of industry that results from shaken business confidence resulting in the "enforced idleness" or involuntary unemployment of labor. Mill (*Works*, 3: 356–8) discusses involuntary unemployment that may result from government legislated minimum wage rates.

24 Evelyn Forget (2003) cites Baumol's (1977) interpretation of Say's own argument, "I cannot conceive that the products of the labour of an entire nation *can ever be overabundant* since one good provides the means to purchase the other" (556; italics added). Yet

Forget still claims, "[Say] did recognise the possibility of *general cyclical overproduction*, and attributed this state of affairs to extraordinary circumstances brought about, usually, by inept public administrations that disrupt normal markets" (59–60; italics added). Forget's assertion reflects Keynes's influence regarding the possibility of overall demand deficiency.

25 Hollander (2011: 27) appropriately observes, regarding Keynes's treatment of Say's Law that he "misinterpreted his predecessors disgracefully," citing Ahiakpor (2003a) as illustration.

26 Keynes's version of the same point is, "Consumption—to repeat the obvious—is the sole end and object of all economic activity" (1936: 104).

27 Montesquieu argued the mercantilist money supply and demand theory of interest that Say (1821a: 353) urges the French to ignore in favor of Hume's and Smith's savings supply and demand theory.

28 Patinkin (1965: 649, n. 24) also fails to recognize the interest rate determination mechanism in his discussing Say's Law. He claims, "There are, indeed, hints here and there of an equilibrating mechanism, but these are never developed into a systematic theory."

29 Keynes (1937a: 223) repeats his misunderstanding that classical analysis claims that "every individual spends the whole of his income either on consumption or on buying, directly or indirectly, newly produced capital goods."

30 Baumol (1977: 150) cites Say's having repeated Smith's argument that savings "are consumed; they furnish markets for many producers; but they are consumed reproductively."

31 Yet Forget (2003: 59) also asserts: "in his correspondence with Malthus, [Say] continued to acknowledge the possibility ... of general gluts caused by poor administration." Say (1821b: 24), in fact, argues the opposite.

32 Say's wording invites a misunderstanding. Savings are the purchases of, or investments in, interest- and/or dividend-earning assets. Part of the capital so acquired remains "in the shape of money" (Say 1821a: 72) or "Capital, at the moment of lending, commonly assumes the form of money" (1821a: 352). Thus, some capital may be held in the form of money rather than being spent on raw materials or hiring labor in times of increased anxiety of making losses in production. But that does not mean savings have not been "invested" in financial assets. See also John Stuart Mill (1874: 55, 58).

33 Kates (1998: 151) also cites, without criticism, Fred Taylor's ([1921] 1925: 203) having made the future Keynesian argument: "If ... the public authorities step in and undertake a large program of road-making or building construction or harbor improvements, this will mean a considerable increase in *total demand* and so an increase in general prosperity" (italics added). But the claim ignores the displacement of private spending by the government's taxation.

34 Fred Taylor (1925) also follows the Smithian tradition of defining saving as an accumulated "fund with which [the saver], or someone else to whom [it is lent], can buy engines or other productive goods" (113).

35 Similarly, Béraud and Numa (2019: 239–40) cite some comments by Say on government spending on public works without also noting their displacement of private sector spending. They then claim, "Say was perfectly clear in his support of stimulating the private sector with the underpinning of a public works program ... In Say's thinking, public infrastructure boosted productivity and spurred economic growth."

36 Mill's third fundamental theorem respecting capital is that "Capital ... the result of saving ... is nevertheless consumed" (*Works*, 2: 70).

37 Remarkably, Kates (1998) does not make some of the above errors in his interpreting Say's Law from J.S. Mill. He there recognizes saving as "individuals placing funds with financial institutions" (1998: 70); he interprets Mill's fourth fundamental theorem as "obviously related to the wages fund doctrine" (71, n. 15); and he distinguishes someone's benefiting the productive laboring classes by directly hiring them instead of purchasing consumption goods or services—"capital that might otherwise have been devoted into payments to labour" (73).

38 Indeed, Béraud and Numa's (2019) latest claim that Keynes and Say shared similar views about the economy's functioning lacks textual support.

39 In fact, Say (1821a: 340) refers to Smith as "a writer of no small experience and singular penetration" on the subject of wages, and mentions the chapter in which Smith notes the rigidity of money wages: "the wages of labour do not in Great Britain fluctuate with the price of provisions … But in many places the money price of labour remains uniformly the same sometimes for half a century" (*WN*, 1: 83).

40 Contrast with Béraud and Numa's (2018b: 286) claim, "Say did not clearly explain the recovery process."

3 Could Keynes have made a legitimate case against John Stuart Mill's statement of the law of markets?

An Illustration of Keynes's Abiding Influence

Introduction[1]

As argued in Chapter 2, John Maynard Keynes rejected the validity of Say's Law mainly because of (a) his having misinterpreted such classical concepts as saving, capital, investment, and money,[2] (b) his incomplete reading of the proposition by John Stuart Mill and Alfred Marshall, and (c) his having incorrectly attributed assumptions, including particularly the existence always of full employment, to classical analysis (James Ahiakpor 1997a; 2003a). Keynes appears not to have read Jean-Baptiste Say's own writings or elaborations of them by James Mill and David Ricardo. Roy Grieve (2016) acknowledges the validity of some criticisms of Keynes's (1936: 18) interpretation of John Stuart Mill's restatement of Say's Law as "supply creates its own demand" by Axel Leijonhufvud (1968), Robert Mundell (1968), and Samuel Hollander (1979), but not because of the above other problems with Keynes's reading of Say's Law.[3] Rather, Grieve claims that the law is fundamentally flawed and Keynes could better have made that point. He charges defenders of Mill's restatement of the law against Keynes's criticisms as having "evidently failed to appreciate just how problematic Mill's analysis … actually is when viewed from a Keynesian perspective" (2016: 330). To Grieve, Mill was not "in the clear on the 'general glut' issue: it is with Mill's handling of the desire to possess—*the will to buy*—that, from the Keynesian perspective, a problem arises" (333; italics original). The crux of Grieve's argument is that the defenders of Say's Law deny "the possibility of deficient demand's causing unemployment" (333–4) in normal economic times, that is, "outside a crisis" (336).

Grieve relies on the following premises to develop his new criticisms of Mill's restatement of the law of markets: (a) contending that "Investment is in fact quite typically envisaged [by John Stuart Mill] as involving simply the purchase of wage goods to maintain labor, rather than the acquisition of durable capital goods" (2016: 336); (b) questioning Mill's explanation that "production in itself guarantees a corresponding demand for goods" (337); (c) believing that increased saving by the rich can "adversely affect employment through a shortage of aggregate demand" (338); and declaring that (d) a reduction in the consumption of luxury goods by capitalists would not necessarily cause the increased production of wage goods (339), (e) the classics assumed the economy's adjustment process to be automatic and quick to assure full employment of labor, and (f) the monetary economy Mill describes is best characterized by the Keynes-Marx schema of M-C-M', in which money (M) is used to acquire goods for production and then sold for more money (M'), rather than the alleged C-M-C', where commodities are sold for money in order to purchase a greater volume of commodities. But none of these bases for Grieve's criticisms of Mill's restatement of Say's Law is correct, and the single-factor model he employs to illustrate them is incapable of correctly representing Mill's restatement of the law. Grieve also appears not to be aware of Keynes's changed definitions of saving, capital, investment, and money that contributed to his difficulties in interpreting correctly the law of markets as stated by John Stuart Mill and Alfred Marshall (Keynes 1936: 18–22). Thus, in his response to my criticism of his defense of Keynes on Say's Law, Grieve (2018: 275; italics original) insists, "what *is* important, but overlooked by [James Ahiakpor] is Mill's characteristic presumption that under (normal, non-crisis) conditions, income saved is automatically put into the production of capital goods." Grieve's criticisms of the law of markets thus illustrate the abiding impediment of Keynes's influence on many analysts' correct interpretation of the classical literature.

Say's law of markets or outlets first explains that the production of a commodity immediately opens a demand, an outlet, or a vent for other produced goods and services, and secondly that productions can only be purchased by or with productions (J.-B. Say 1821a: 133–5; 1821b: 2, 15). The first part of Say's proposition derives from the intentions behind any production, namely, either for one's own consumption[4] or for sale. Mill restates the explanation as, "What constitutes the means of payment for commodities is simply commodities [of which one is money]. Each person's means of paying for the productions of other people consist of those which he himself possesses" (quoted in Keynes 1936: 18). The second part of Say's argument derives from the fact that purchases are the exchanges of one's income—earned from the sale of productions (exchange with money)—for someone else's produced goods and services. As noted in Chapter 2, the law does not claim that everything produced is sold or sold at cost-recovering prices, contra Keynes (1936: 21–2). But when sales are made, Say's Law explains the interconnection between markets for produced goods (including money) and services as well as for credit or capital (savings), both in the short run and in the long run. From such interconnection, the relative prices of produced goods and services are determined, just as are interest rates in credit markets, and the value of money—inverse of the weighted average of commodity prices.

The law says nothing about the labor market. It takes a combination of labor services, machinery, and equipment, as well as the services of land to produce commodities either for consumption or for sale. The relative prices of these factors of production determine the combinations in which they are employed in production, labor and capital equipment being particularly in competition with each other for employment. The wage rate relative to the rental rate of capital equipment importantly determines how much labor is employed relative to capital equipment. Besides, more machinery tends to be employed in production as the level of output increases, leading to increased unemployment.

However, it is nearly impossible to appreciate the logic of the law when employing Keynes's (1936) conceptions of (a) saving as merely the non-consumption of one's income without relating saving to the purchasing of interest- and/or dividend-earning assets; (b) capital as only capital goods without recognizing the term also as referring to loanable funds or savings; (c) investment as only the purchase of capital goods rather than also applying to the purchasing of interest- and/or dividend-earning assets by income earners besides the purchasing of fixed capital and circulating capital in the sphere of production; and (d) money variously as cash or cash plus savings, with banking institutions and sometimes including the purchase of treasury bills instead of money being cash only. Also, Say's Law may not seem applicable in the short run if one accepted as valid Keynes's (1936) attributing to the law the assumptions of there always being full employment of labor or no involuntary unemployment; the instantaneous adjustment in all markets, including that of labor; and a world of certainty about the future. This chapter clarifies the extent to which Keynes's influence has impeded Grieve's correct interpretation of Say's Law as restated by John Stuart Mill.[5]

Flaws in Grieve's criticisms of John Stuart Mill's explanations

(a)   Investment as the purchase of wage goods

Grieve (2016: 336) is mistaken in reading John Sturat Mill to have argued that investment is typically the purchase of wage goods: "Investment is in fact quite typically envisaged [by John Stuart Mill] as involving simply the purchase of wage goods to maintain labor, rather than the acquisition of durable capital goods." Grieve derives this mistaken claim from Mill's employing a "most extreme case conceivable" (*Works*, 2: 67) to illustrate the effect of capitalists and landlords having increased their savings or turned "their income into capital." But Mill did not, by that extreme hypothetical case, argue that investment typically takes the form of purchasing only wage goods. Indeed, in the preceding paragraph, Mill mentions multiple factors of production, besides labor: "I do not mean to deny that the [increased] capital [funds], or part of it, may be so employed as not to support labourers, being fixed in machinery, buildings, improvement of land, and the like" (*Works*, 2: 66). Grieve also incorrectly attributes to Mill the claim that "workers have command not only of the current output of wage-goods, but of everything else produced—the wage bill paid by the employers constitutes purchasing power over all national output" (2016: 340). Upon what would capitalists (and landlords) survive, if that were so?

On the contrary, Mill follows Adam Smith's (*WN*, 1: 358) definition of investment by producers as their employing savings—the residual of disposable income over consumption and cash hoarding—either of their own or borrowed, in the sphere of production.[6] Savings supply investment capital: "A second fundamental theorem respecting Capital, relates to the source from which it is derived. It is the result of saving" (Mill *Works*, 2: 68). The funds are invested in acquiring "fixed capital" or producer's goods of long duration and "circulating capital" that are used up within each production cycle, and include the funds for paying wages (Mill *Works*, 2, Bk 1, Chapter 6). Contrast with Keynes's conception of saving as merely "the excess of income over what is spent on consumption" (1936: 74) or "the negative act of refraining from spending the whole of [one's] income on consumption" (1930, 1: 172), and which could mean cash hoarding (1936, 167). Worse yet, Keynes (1937c: 669) insists, "The investment market can become congested through the shortage of cash. It can never become congested through the shortage of saving. This is the most fundamental of my conclusions in this field."[7]

Mill also explains, "It is of no consequence that a part, or even the whole of [invested capital], is in a form in which it cannot directly supply the wants of labourers" (*Works*, 2: 56). Grieve's misinterpretation of Mill regarding the nature of investment thus leads to his mistaken claim that "All savings, [Mill] contends, will—under normal conditions ... *automatically* pass into the hands of the laboring class" (2016: 337; italics original), and that Mill "argues that without *previous* production of wage-goods it would be impossible to support additional workers in employment" (341; italics original). In fact, Mill (*Works*, 2: 57) allows for the importation of "food," were that to become necessary, in his analysis. Mill indeed discusses the case in which, in the absence of

> any demand for luxuries, on the part of capitalists and landowners ... these turn their income into capital, [but] they do not thereby annihilate their power of consumption; they do but transfer it from themselves to the labourers to whom they give employment ... [And] the production of necessaries for the new population [if there is such an increase], takes the place of the production of luxuries for a portion of the old, and supplies exactly the same amount of employment which has been lost.
>
> (quoted in Grieve, 338)[8]

Mill's argument that borrowed capital or savings will be productively employed follows from the fact that a borrower has to pay back the capital with interest.[9] Thus, both fixed capital and circulating capital have to be devoted to profitable production, without which the investor makes losses and may have to declare bankruptcy: "Nobody willingly produces in the prospect of loss. Whoever does so, does it under a miscalculation, which he corrects as fast as he is able" (Mill *Works*, 3: 471). Note that Mill does not claim an immediate cessation of production upon losses being made. Profit maximization also entails producing at a loss in the short run so long as avoidable or variable costs are being met from revenues. Only in the long run, when contracts come up for renewal, is it wise for a producer to close down, if losses persist; see also Mill (*Works*, 2: 338).

It was also in following Smith's (*WN*, 1: 359–60) explanation that savings provide "a perpetual fund for the maintenance" of productive hands that Mill argues that "a saving once made becomes a *fund* to maintain a number of labourers in perpetuity, reproducing their own maintenance with a profit" (*Works*, 2: 71; italics added). But the wages fund is always a subset of invested capital. As Mill (*Works*, 2: 92) argues, "Another large portion of capital … consists in instruments of production of a more or less permanent character."

(b)   Questioning whether production guarantees demand for goods

Grieve is not persuaded by Mill's explaining in the *Principles*, "Whoever brings additional commodities to the market, brings an additional power of purchase … also an additional desire to consume; since if he had not that desire, he would not have troubled himself to produce" (quoted in Grieve 2016: 337). Mill makes the same point in his essay "Of the Influence of Consumption on Production," noting: "To produce, implies that the producer desires to consume; why else should he give himself useless labour?" (1874: 49). Ricardo (*Works*, 1: 290) earlier draws upon the second edition of Say's *Treatise* to argue:

> No man produces, but with a view [expectation or intension] to consume or sell, and he never sells, but with an intention to purchase some other commodity, which may be immediately useful to him, or which may contribute to future production. By producing, then, he necessarily becomes either the consumer of his own goods, or the purchaser and consumer of the goods of some other person.

Say's original explanation of production being the source of demand for other produced commodities includes, "The mere circumstance of the creation of one product immediately opens a vent for other products" (1821a: 134–5). The logic of the explanation is rather clear. It clarifies why people engage in production. However, Grieve asks, "Could saving cause a problem?" (2016: 337).

Grieve's questioning the explanation of productions constituting the demand for other productions because of saving clearly derives from his failure to recognize that savings are spent by borrowers, as Smith (*WN*, 1: 359) explains: "What is annually saved is as regularly consumed as what is annually spent, and nearly at the same time too; but it is spent by a different set of people." Say (1821b: 39) adopts Smith's explanation, as does James Mill (1808: 68–74). Similarly, John Stuart Mill (*Works*, 2: 70) argues:

> The word saving does not imply that what is saved is not consumed [used up], nor even necessarily its consumption is deferred; but only that, if consumed immediately, it is not consumed by the person who saves it …

if employed as capital, it is all consumed; though not by the capitalist. Part is exchanged for tools or machinery, which are worn out by use; part for seed or materials, which are destroyed as such by being sown or wrought up, and destroyed altogether by the consumption of the ultimate product. The remainder is paid in wages to productive labourers who consume it for their daily wants.

Furthermore, saving is not the same thing as cash hoarding, which withholds incomes from being spent on other produced goods and services. John Stuart Mill (*Works*, 2:70) makes the point: If unspent income is "merely laid by for future use, it is said to be hoarded;[10] and while hoarded, is not consumed at all. But if employed as capital, it is all consumed; though not by the capitalist." In contrast with Keynes's view of saving which Grieve adopts, Mill continues to argue:

> To the vulgar, it is not at all apparent that what is saved is consumed. To them, every one who saves, appears in the light of a person who hoards … saving is to them another word for keeping a thing to oneself; while spending appears to them to be distributing it among others.
>
> (*Works*, 2: 70–1)

Now, money (specie) itself is a produced commodity in Say's Law; see Say (1821a: 218). As Say explains: "almost all produce is in the first instance exchanged for money, before it is ultimately converted into other produce" (1821a: 133–4). And, "to receive money in exchange is called *selling*, and to give it *buying*" (Say 1821a: 220; italics original). Similarly, John Stuart Mill notes, "money is bought and sold like other things, whenever other things are bought and sold *for* money. Whoever sells corn, or tallow, or cotton, buys money" (*Works*, 3: 509; italics original). Therefore, exchanging one's produce for money to be held (hoarding) does not reduce the demand for all produced goods (including money) and services to undermine the validity of Say's Law. John Stuart Mill affirms the point with his clarification of the impossibility of a general glut that Grieve, following Keynes, fears:

> In order to render the argument for the impossibility of an excess of all commodities [general glut] applicable to the case in which a circulating medium is employed, money must itself be considered as a commodity. It must, undoubtedly, be admitted that there cannot be an excess of all other commodities, and an excess of money at the same time.
>
> (1874: 71)

Were more money to be demanded to hold in excess of the quantity supplied, commodity prices would fall while money's value rises, and vice versa. As Mill also explains, regarding the determination of commodity prices by money's supply and demand,

> The supply of money … is the quantity of it which people are wanting to lay out; that is, all the money they have in their possession, *except what they are hoarding*,[11] or at least keeping by them as a reserve for future contingencies. The supply of money, in short, is all the money in *circulation* at the time.
>
> (*Works*, 3: 509; italics original)

This is why in a commercial crisis in which there is an excessive demand for money, prices fall, production decreases, and unemployment rises for as long as the excess demand lasts, as Mill (*Works*, 3: 516) explains,

> If extra currency were not forthcoming to make … payments … money … must be withdrawn from the market for commodities, and prices, consequently, must fall. An increase of the circulating medium, conformable in extent and duration to the temporary stress of business, does not raise prices, but merely prevents this fall.

Note also the time interval Mill includes in the explanation—"the extent and duration"—not the "automatic and quick" adjustment Grieve (2016: 348) misattributes to him.[12] Such was the experience of the Great Depression that Keynes cited as proof of the invalidity of Say's Law in the short run; I elaborate below.

We may acknowledge an ambiguity about the word "consume or consumption," which James Mill (1808: 68–9) clarifies to have a "double meaning."[13] One is the satisfaction of an immediate and personal desire—an "extinction, actual annihilation of property" (69); the other is to employ a commodity reproductively, that is, its being "wrought up"—a "renovation, and increase of property" (69). With such understanding of the word "consumption," there is little difficulty with understanding Smith's explanation that savings are consumed and nearly at the same time too as what are spent by income earners.[14] It is Keynes's distinct failure to recognize savings as being spent reproductively that has given Grieve his doubts about the validity of Mill's restatement of productions (supply) creating demand for other productions.

(c)   Increased saving by the rich adversely affects the employment of labor

Grieve (2016: 337) doubts the validity of Mill's explanation that "the theory of overproduction implies an absurdity" because savings are invested "productively." He thinks there is a need to explain how it could be true that "no matter how large a proportion of their income the wealthy save, demand and employment will not be affected" (ibid.). He neglects Mill's explaining that savings by the wealthy transfer funds from their "unproductive consumption," such as "hiring grooms and valets, or maintaining hunters and hounds" (*Works*, 2: 56), to hiring productive workers.

In making the argument, Mill follows Smith's distinction between productive and unproductive labor, in which expenditure on the latter "does not fix or realize itself in any particular subject or vendible commodity ... [The] services generally perish in the very instant of their performance, and seldom leave any trace or value behind them, for which an equal quantity of service could afterwards be procured" (*WN*, 1: 352). Thus, Mill defines unproductive labor as that "which is employed for the purpose of directly affording enjoyment, such as the labour of a performer on a musical instrument" (1874: 82). Mill describes as productive

> Labour and expenditure, of which the direct object or effect is the creation of some material product useful or agreeable to mankind ... or of which the direct effect and object are, to endow human or other animated beings with faculties or qualities useful or agreeable to mankind, and possessing exchangeable value.
>
> (1874: 84)

See also *Works*, 2: 48–52. Therefore, labor spent on manufacturing a musical instrument is productive labor, whereas the performance of a musician is unproductive labor. It is the reduction in such unproductive expenditures (consumption) in order to save—increasing the supply of capital—that Mill urges against claims by the likes of Malthus, Chalmers, and Sismondi that "the unproductive expenditure of the rich is necessary to the employment of the poor" (quoted by Grieve 2016: 337).

Grieve instead misinterprets Mill's argument to mean a call for the rich to reduce their expenditure on luxury goods, whose production he incorrectly designates as "unproductive employment" (2016: 341). The production of luxury goods is not the same thing as the production of services that, following Smith (*WN*, 1: 352), Mill designates as expenditure on unproductive labor. The sale of such goods, including "plate and jewels" (Mill *Works*, 2: 56–7) normally yields profits to their manufacturers. Also, smartphones, iPads, diamond rings, and yachts may be considered luxury goods, but the labor employed in their production does not fit the classical designation of "unproductive" labor. In fact, Mill expects that the savings (capital) invested in the production of luxury goods would yield profits and promote economic growth: "whatever increases the productive powers of labour, creates an additional fund to make savings from, and enables capital to be enlarged not only without additional privation, but concurrently with an increase of personal consumption" (*Works*, 2: 70).

Grieve employs a two-goods, one-factor (labor) model to illustrate his perceived flaw in Mill's analysis. The model assumes labor to be more productive in wage-goods production, yet be paid the same $1 wage rate in both sectors of the economy. Investment takes the form of only purchasing wage goods, the only goods consumed by workers, while capitalists consume only luxury goods. By implication, capitalists choose to commit suicide by starvation with an "outbreak of thrift" (Grieve 2016: 339). Grieve overlooks Mill's (*Works*, 2: 161) explaining in the hypothetical case that "The capital of the employer forms the revenue of the labourers, and if this exceeds the necessaries of life, it gives them a surplus which they either expend in enjoyments, or save." There is no room for exports in Grieve's model, and the capitalists are then faced with the dilemma of what to do with the extra wage goods produced. There is no money, and there are no markets in which money is exchanged for commodities to determine their prices. There is no market for credit where interest rates are determined by the supply and demand for savings, e.g. Mill (*Works*: 3: 647). Thus, there is no room for income earners to balance their spending decisions at the requisite three margins: utility of consumption, utility of the returns to saving (interest or dividends), and utility of holding money (cash).

In doubting that increased savings benefit workers by enhancing their employment opportunities, Grieve also neglects Mill's affirming Smith's (*WN*, 1: 362–3) explanation that the reason we save is to better our own conditions: "The principle which prompts us to save [invest], is the desire of bettering our condition, a desire which … comes with us from the womb, and never leaves us till we go into the grave." Mill's affirms the principle: "A part of the motive for saving consists in the prospect of deriving an income from savings; in the fact that capital, employed in production, is capable of not only reproducing itself but yielding an increase" (*Works*, 2: 161). Also, argues Mill, "All accumulation [of capital] involves the sacrifice of a present, for the sake of a future good" (*Works*, 2: 162). Furthermore, the decision to save entails "weighing the future against the present" (*Works*, 2: 163).[15] An example of Mill's excellent illustration of the point is the case of someone who skips purchasing velvet and uses the funds to hire bricklayers instead. The bricklayers acquire the means to purchase "bread, beer, labourers' clothing, fuel, and indulgences," while their employer subsequently consumes the services of a house or something else in the future (*Works*, 2: 83–4). That is, saving entails a transfer of present consumption into a future consumption, which contrasts with Keynes's (1936: 210) insistence that saving "is not a substitution of future consumption-demand for present consumption-demand,—it is net diminution of such demand."

Were there a capital-goods production in Grieve's model, and which would also employ some workers, Grieve's puzzles about finding an increased demand for labor and commodities, following an increased saving, might not have arisen. Modern macroeconomics also recognizes capital goods, such as equipment and machinery, as part of aggregate demand since their purchases constitute final demand. Grieve's model simply is incapable of illustrating Mill's restatement of Say's Law.

(d)   Difficulty of producers in adjusting to a changed demand

Employing his model, Grieve claims to demonstrate a difficulty for producers to adjust production towards more wage goods, following a reduction in luxury-goods demand by the rich, contrary to the logic of Say's Law. He

wonders, "Why should it be supposed that labor released from luxury production will *automatically* be deployed to the production of wage goods?" (2016:
339; italics original). Mill, in fact, provides the answer to Grieve's puzzlement
in the "fourth fundamental theorem regarding Capital." The theorem argues
that changing demand for commodities causes the reallocation of capital—both
fixed and circulating, including the wages fund—away from producing less
profitable commodities to producing more profitable ones.

Mill starts his explanation by noting that the wages fund constitutes the
demand for labor:

> What supports and employs productive labour, is the capital [funds]
> expended in setting it to work, and not the demand of purchasers for the
> produce of the labour when completed. Demand for commodities is not
> demand for [current] labour.[16] The demand for commodities determines
> in what particular branch of production the labour and capital shall be
> employed; it determines the *direction* of the labour; but not the more or less
> of the labour itself, or of the maintenance or payment of the labour. These
> depend on the amount of the capital [wages fund], or other funds [such
> as taxes to pay government workers or payments to domestic servants][17]
> directly devoted to the sustenance and remuneration of labour.
>
> (*Works*, 2: 78; italics original)

Mill further clarifies that "The demand for commodities is a consideration of
importance rather in the theory of exchange [law of markets], than in that of
production" (*Works*, 2: 88). The proposition, as Mill's extensive illustrations
(*Works*, 2: 79–88) show, recognizes that changes in the demand for commodities affect future employment of labor (and capital goods) in the affected
consumption-goods production, contrary to Grieve's interpretation of Mill to
have denied. It is also important to interpret "capital" as funds in the proper
context in which Mill uses the term, e.g., "capital, thus withdrawn from the
maintenance of velvet-makers, is not the same *fund* with that which the customer employs in maintaining bricklayers; it is a second *fund*" (*Works*, 2: 82;
italics added). Without that interpretation, Mill's explanations may appear
meaningless or confused.[18]

Once again, Mill's argument follows Smith's (*WN*, 1: 63–5) observations regarding the determination of market prices by supply and "effectual
demand." A reduced demand for luxury goods will reduce the profitability of
their production, relative to the production of necessaries or wage goods. It
is purely from the profit motive of producers—on pain of bankruptcy, otherwise—that they would divert labor and capital (both funds and capital goods)
away from producing goods in less demand. Mill well explains:

> A manufacturer, finding a slack demand for his commodity, forbears to
> employ laborers in increasing a stock which he finds it difficult to dispose
> of; or if he goes on until all his capital is locked up in unsold goods, then at

least he must of necessity pause until he can get paid for some of them. But no one expects either of these states to be permanent; if he did, he would at the first opportunity remove his capital to some other occupation, in which it would still continue to employ labour.

(*Works*, 2: 338)

We also find Mill explaining the adjustment of production to changing demand in his extensive discussions of the migration of capitals (funds) in search of profits (e.g. *Works*, 2: 403–10; 3: 471–2). The explanation follows Ricardo's (*Works*, 3: 102) argument: "It is self-interest which regulates all the speculations of trade, and where that can be clearly and satisfactorily ascertained, we should not know where to stop if we admitted any other rule of action." Indeed, if the cessation of demand were to lead to a loss of capital, it also would destroy the demand for labor, Mill also explains:

If the demand ceases *unexpectedly*, after the commodity to supply it is already produced, this introduces a different element into the question [of how producers adjust employment of capital in accord with changing commodity demands]: the capital has actually been consumed [used up] in producing something which nobody wants or uses, and it has therefore perished, and the employment which it gave to labour is at an end, not because there is no longer demand, but because there is no longer a capital.

(*Works*, 2: 79; italics added)

Mill's argument leads to his conclusion, in contradiction to Keynes's and Grieve's thinking:

Thus the limit of wealth is never deficiency of consumers, but of producers and productive power. Every addition to capital [increased saving] gives to labour either additional employment, or additional remuneration; enriches either the country, or the labouring class. If it finds additional hands, it increases the aggregate produce: if only the same hands, it gives them a larger share of it;[19] and perhaps even in this case, by stimulating them to greater exertion, augments the produce itself.

(*Works*, 2: 68, also quoted in Grieve 2016: 340)

However, Grieve's persistent wondering about the adequacy of aggregate demand because of savings, following Keynes (1936), appears to have led to his ignoring Mill's explanation, following Smith, J.-B. Say, and Ricardo, that savings are "consumed," e.g. "Capital … although saved, and the result of saving, it is nevertheless consumed (*Works*, 2: 70).

Mill's explanations above also show Grieve's error in attributing to him the view that producers expect a guaranteed demand for their productions. Grieve argues,

> We ... are particularly uncomfortable with [Mill's] fourth proposition: it fails to recognize explicitly that not only is capital necessary to "put labour into motion," but that there must be present also—if that capital is actually to be invested—a factor that cannot be guaranteed always to exist; i.e., an appropriate expectation of the profitability of investment (along with a sufficient degree of confidence) on the part of investors.
>
> (2016: 340, n. 12)

Grieve (2016: 343) repeats the mistaken concern: "For Mill, as regards the volume of employment, the critical issue is the availability of resources with which to support labor in employment, not whether there exists demand for the output of that labor. He foresees no problem with respect to the latter [demand]." However, producers always form expectations of demand for what they produce. When they are correct, producers make profits; losses are incurred otherwise: "the *calculations of producers* and traders being of necessity *imperfect*, there are always some commodities which are more or less in excess, as there are always some which are in deficiency" (Mill 1874: 67; italics added). Also underlying Grieve's concern is his employing Keynes's definitions of saving and investment such that "savings may not always be accompanied by an equal volume of intended investment" (2016: 343). But savings are purchases of interest- and/or dividend-earning assets. The assets suppliers (investors) employ the funds they receive reproductively, as the classics, including John Sturat Mill, have explained.

(e)   The economy's adjustment process is automatic and quick

Grieve asserts that Mill assumed an automatic and quick adjustment by producers in order to assure the full employment of labor in no-crisis conditions. He also asserts that Mill claims "full recovery from a commercial crisis [to be] automatic and quick" (348). Thus, he believes "there is no way in which [Mill's] analysis can account for prolonged periods of low activity and high unemployment" (ibid.). Now as Smith explains, the self-interest pursuit of sellers and buyers assures their reaction to changing market opportunities. Therein lies the automaticity view of the adjustment process Grieve draws from Mill's explanations. But the quickness of the adjustment Grieve infers is an exaggeration. Rather, when a producer makes a loss, "he corrects [his miscalculation] as fast as *he is able*," Mill (*Works*, 3: 471; italics added) argues.

Besides, there are some impediments to an economy's normal functioning, including those initiated by government policies, which producers by themselves could not get around. These include "wars, embargoes, oppressive duties [and] dangers and difficulties of transportation" (Say 1821a: 142) and minimum-wage legislation, all of which may result in "some labourers being kept out of employment" (Mill *Works*, 2: 356). Mill also explains that a commercial crisis arising from the public's shaken confidence impairs an economy's functioning and increases unemployment until "the restoration of confidence"

(*Works*, 3: 574); see also Marshall (1920: 590–2). It often takes a government's actions to restore the public's shaken confidence.

These explanations can be related to the Great Depression that started from the United States. The shaken public confidence in the banking system that led to massive withdrawals of savings deposited with banks (Friedman and Schwartz 1963, Chapter 7; Ahiakpor 2019, Chapter 5), the Smoot-Hawley tariffs that constricted free trading, and the adherence to the gold-exchange standard that frustrated the Federal Reserve's ability to meet the currency's demand until March 1933,[20] all contributed to the prolonged period of economic malaise and unemployment in the United States rising from 3% to 25%. Britain's going back to the gold standard at the pre-war parity in 1925 overvalued the pound, which impaired British exports and encouraged imports, and Trade Union resistance to nominal wage rate reductions in the face of business losses all assured that the British economy contracted and unemployment rose. None of these events prove Say's Law's invalidity.[21] In fact, countries that abandoned the gold standard sooner recovered from the world depression earlier than those that held on to the gold standard longer; see Bernanke (2000, esp. Ch. 1). Only by misinterpreting the law of markets, as Grieve does under Keynes's inspiration, can the Great Depression be used to argue otherwise.

Grieve's view of Say's Law as claiming the existence of labor's full employment in non-crisis conditions, following Keynes's (1936: 26) assertion of the same, conflicts with Mill's explanation that not even the capital of a country, let alone its labor, is always fully employed:

> When we have thus seen accurately what really constitutes capital, it becomes obvious, that of the capital of a country, there is at all times a very large proportion lying idle. The annual produce of a country is never anything approaching in magnitude what it might be if all the resources devoted to production, if all the capital, in short, of the country, were in full employment.
>
> (1874: 55)

Mill also explains that

> there are actually at all times producers and dealers, of all, or nearly all classes, whose capital is lying partially idle, because they have not found the means of fulfilling the condition which the division of labour renders indispensable to the full employment of capital,—viz., that of exchanging their products with each other.
>
> (1874: 58)

Mill's argument is similar to Grieve's (2017: 272) observation that "If prospects appear unpropitious, funds may be retained in liquid form rather than committed to specific real assets. Both the volume and direction of production *do* depend on demand" (italics original).

Ricardo (*Works*, 1: 265) also argues that some labor may become unemployed during the period when firms are adjusting to a changed demand for commodities arising from the "commencement of war after a long peace or of peace after a long war." In such circumstance, Ricardo explains,

> much fixed capital is unemployed, perhaps wholly lost, and labourers are without full employment. The duration of this distress will be *longer or shorter* according to the strength of that disinclination, which most men feel to abandon that employment of their capital to which they have long been accustomed.

(ibid.; italics added)

Ricardo further notes that the duration of the disruption in production "is often protracted too by the restrictions and prohibitions, to which the absurd jealousies which prevail between the different States of the commonwealth give rise" (ibid.). Clearly, neither the assumption of full employment of labor always in non-crisis conditions nor a quick adjustment in markets after a crisis is part of Say's Law.

Grieve also misattributes to Mill the view that "The generation of profit ... is the natural and *characteristic outcome* of investment in the employment of productive labor" (2016: 344; italics added). But what Mill argues is that the *expectation* of profits, not their guaranteed outcome, is what motivates investment decisions. Grieve further ignores Mill's (*Works*, 2: 402–3) discussing the risks associated with the investment of capital, for which the rate of profit is expected to compensate, just as Smith (*WN*, 1: 59) explains: "Part of ... profit naturally belongs to the borrower [of capital or 'stock'], who runs the risk and takes the trouble of employing it." Mill makes the point that "in a generally secure state of society, the risks which may be attendant on the nature of particular employments [of capital] seldom fall on the person who lends his capital, if he lends on good security" (*Works*, 2: 403). In states of less security of property, the risks may include confiscation by a tyrannical government or from "its rapacious and ill-controlled officers" or from the "audacious withholding of just rights" (ibid.). Therefore, to entice investment under such uncertainties and risks, the expected compensation in profits "must be something very considerable."

Thus, the Keynesian view that the classical writers, including John Stuart Mill, were not aware of the risks and uncertainties attending to the investment of capital in their explanation of the law of markets is simply false. Grieve, in fact, invokes "the real world of uncertainty," of which Mill allegedly was unaware, to criticize both Kates (2015) and Mill: "What Kates (like Mill) cannot understand is that in the real world of uncertainty, resources are invested to support labour in employment on the basis of expectations—forecasts—as to conditions in the markets for the output which that labour will produce" (2017: 271–2). But, as noted above, Mill did not dispute any of this.

(f)   The nature of the economic process

Keynes (1936) misinterpreted capital in classical analysis to mean only producer's goods, never savings or loanable funds,[22] and also defined investment as only the purchase of capital goods. Keynes (quoted in Grieve 2016: 346) thus sides with Karl Marx's critique of the capitalist production system, which claims that it is money (M) that capitalists use to invest in the production of commodities (C) to be sold for more money (M'), the difference reflecting the exploitation of labor in the sphere of production. This sequence is supposed to counter the alleged classical system in which commodities (C) are sold for money (M) with which to purchase more commodities (C'). Grieve similarly follows the Keynes-Marx argument to interpret investment in Mill's restatement of the law of markets to mean only the purchase of wage goods by capitalists, rather than producers employing savings or loanable funds to acquire fixed and circulating capital, including the wages fund. Grieve (2016: 346) then draws upon John Henry's (2003: 193) employing the Keynes-Marx argument to claim that "the economic world as envisaged by Say and the Mills is 'not the economy that exists.'"

Henry (2003: 193) also incorrectly asserts that "Say's economy is constructed on the basis of a society comprised of petty producers engaged in bartering products of different use values … Money arises more or less spontaneously, simply as a medium to facilitate the more fundamental barter relationships." But Say was describing a 19th-century economy that includes the equivalent of a modern central bank, other banks receiving savers' deposits to lend, businesses producing a variety of goods and services, dealers in credit and produced goods, and a government conducting taxation and trade policies. Besides, the Keynes-Marx critique is not well-founded: the classical explanation of the production process starts with savings or capital (funds) that may be borrowed in the form of money (specie or its substitutes), to be invested in production to yield revenue in excess of the initial value of the borrowed capital.

The term "money" tends to be used loosely in economic discourse (Smith *WN*, 1: 306–7) to mean several things, including cash, credit, savings, or capital. That usage may appear to give the Keynes-Marx alternative description of the production process validity. However, businesses do not invest money (cash) but savings or capital. As John Stuart Mill argues:

> When one person lends to another … what he transfers is not the mere money, but a right to a certain value of the produce of the country … the lender having first bought this right, by giving for it a portion of his capital. What he really lends is so much capital; the money is the mere instrument of transfer.
>
> (*Works*, 3: 508)

Mill here restates Smith's (*WN*, 1: 373) explanation:

> Almost all loans at interest are made in money … But what the borrower really wants, and what the lender really provides him with, is not the

money, but the money's worth, or the goods which it can purchase ... By means of the loan, the lender, as it were, assigns the borrower his right to a certain portion of the annual produce of the land and labour of the country, to be employed as the borrower pleases.

Similarly, Say (1821a: 353), following Smith and Hume, argues that "it is a great abuse of words, to talk of the interest of money; and probably this errone-ous expression has led to the false inference, that the abundance or scarcity of money regulates the rate of interest."

Thus, it is not increases in central bank money (cash) that facilitate sus-tainable investment and production, but increased savings.[23] If the former were true, central banks' money creation would "become powerful [growth] engines indeed ... To what absurdities would not such a theory lead us!" (Ricardo *Works*, 3: 92). The temporary increased production that may result from an increased money creation by a central bank is due to the phenom-enon of "forced saving" or "forced accumulation" (Mill 1874, 118), when price increases lead the growth of nominal wage rates, as the classics, includ-ing Ricardo (*Works*, 3: 318–9) and Mill (1874, 67–8), have argued; Ahiakpor (2009) elaborates. Once again, Grieve fails to interpret the classical literature correctly to appreciate the logic of Say's Law, just as Keynes did.

Summary and conclusions

Say's law of markets simply explains that (a) production opens a market or a vent for other productions and (b) productions can only be purchased by or with productions: to make a purchase, one must have earned income or bor-rowed someone else's. Also, no one produces but with a view to consume or acquire the means to purchase those goods and services they themselves have not produced. That is why production is the basis of demand, rather than the other way around, as Keynes (1936) incorrectly argued. As Smith (*WN*, 2: 179) explains, "Consumption is the sole aim and purpose of all production; ... The maxim is so perfectly self-evident, that it would be absurd to attempt to prove it." Mill's equivalent of Smith's point is:

> Consumption never needs encouragement. All which is produced is already consumed, either for the purpose of reproduction or of enjoy-ment. The person who saves his income is no less a consumer than he who spends it: he consumes it in a different way; it supplies food and clothing to be consumed, tools and materials to be used, by productive labourers.
>
> (1874: 48)

However, if one read Say's Law with the conception of such important eco-nomic concepts as saving, capital, investment, and money, differently than they are supposed to mean in classical analysis, and one also attributed assumptions to the law that the classics did not make, especially the assumption of there being always full employment of labor, one is likely to find its logic unconvincing. Roy Grieve compounds Keynes's errors of interpreting the law by misattributing to John Stuart Mill claims that investment takes the form of purchasing only wage goods; that labor's demand for wage goods constitutes total national output; and that product demand and profits are guaranteed for producers. His interpretive model has no money, no markets on which commodity prices are determined, no credit markets on which interest rates are determined by the supply and demand for savings, and savings not being consumed or spent. The coordinating function between markets that the law argues is performed by changing relative commodity prices, interest rates, and the value of money is thus lost in Grieve's interpretation of the law. Grieve also misidentifies unproductive labor. His misinterpretations and incomplete reading of Mill's restatements of Say's Law therefore leave him puzzled about its logic. His attempt to defend Keynes's criticisms of Say's Law on the basis of there being insufficient consumption demand to keep labor fully employed in non-crises situations thus fails.

It is quite illegitimate to misinterpret or misrepresent an argument, find faults with the resulting product, and then blame the original argument for the faults. That was the problem with Keynes, which Grieve (2016, 2017) repeats.

Notes

1 This chapter elaborates my "Keynes, Mill, and Say's Law: A Comment on Roy Grieve's Mistaken Criticisms of Mill," in the *Journal of the History of Economic Thought* 40, No. 2 (June): 267–73. The published comment is a significantly reduced version of my critique of Grieve's (2016) claims that was judged too long and went beyond pointing out Grieve's errors of interpreting John Stuart Mill's restatement of Say's Law.

2 As Jacob Viner (1936: 147) acutely observes of Keynes (1936), "no old term for an old concept is used when a new one can be coined, and if old terms are used new meanings are generally assigned to them."

3 Hollander (2011: 27) subsequently declares Keynes to have "misrepresented his predecessors disgracefully," citing Ahiakpor's (2003a) explanation of Keynes's success with the law's misrepresentation as evidence on "various aspects of Keynes's [incorrect] treatment of the Classics" (27, n. 10). Grieve (2016: 339, n. 11) instead cites approvingly Hollander's (1985: 374–5; italics original) doubts about the existence of "purchasing power for the *net* flow of output from [an] expanded national capacity once in place," following an increased savings rate. But as Mill (*Works*, 2: 70) explains, following J.-B. Say and Smith, "The word saving does not imply that what is saved is not consumed, nor even necessarily that its consumption is deferred; but only that, if consumed immediately, it is not consumed by the person who saves it."

4 James Mill well explains that it is unnecessary to consider the own-consumption part of the intention behind productions since that does not affect the market: "that part of the annual produce which may be consumed by the producer, as it increases not the demand in the national market, so neither does it increase the stock or supply in that market, because it is not carried to market at all" (1808: 84n).

5 Steven Kates's (2015) defense of Say's Law, but without employing the classical fund concept of capital and the wages fund as constituting the demand for labor, also appears to have motivated Grieve's (2016, 2017) criticisms of the law.

6 Smith explains that "Capitals are increased by parsimony … Whatever a person saves from his revenue he adds to his capital, and either employs it himself in maintaining an

additional number of productive hands, or enables some other person to do so, by lending it to him for an interest, that is, for a share of the profit" (*WN*, 1: 358). Mill (*Works*, 2: 56; italics added) also argues that capital is what constitutes the "*fund* for carrying on fresh production."

7   It was from such misconception of saving that Keynes developed his mistaken paradox-of-thrift proposition, arguing the negative growth consequences of increased saving (Ahiakpor 1995).

8   An anonymous reader for the Journal of the *History of Economic Thought* points to this statement as providing a basis for granting that "Grieve has [a legitimate] basis for his view." But Mill's arguing a hypothetical case in order to illustrate a point—increased savings increases the demand for productive labor, which does not reduce total demand for produced goods by income earners—hardly is good justification for claiming, as Grieve does, that all savings are invested in purchasing wage goods and never capital goods in Mill's analysis.

9   An anonymous reader for the *Journal of the History of Economic Thought* makes the valid point that "Smith, for one, was well aware that capital might be lent at interest for unproductive purposes and Mill presumably agreed." However, even borrowers for "unproductive purposes" must anticipate earning enough income in the future (from production) in order to pay back the loan principal and interest. Borrowers neither for "productive" nor for "unproductive" purposes anticipate becoming bankrupt from taking loans.

10   Grieve incorrectly believes that Mill recognized "a demand for money *per se* could emerge on the occasion of a financial crisis" (2016: 347), as if a financial crisis is the only occasion for that. The quantity of money (H or high-powered money) in an economy is always held: $H = kY$, where k = proportion of income the public wishes to hold in cash, and Y = nominal national income; see John Stuart Mill (*Works*, 3: 509–12) and Marshall (1923: 44–7).

11   Grieve (2016: 334–6) mistakenly believes Mill argues that the public holds money only in periods of commercial crises.

12   In the classical specie money economy, money's quantity may adjust to the increased demand on its own through Hume's price-specie-flow mechanism, although not instantaneously. In a fiat money system, it requires a central bank to adjust money's quantity to the increased demand.

13   The *Webster's New Collegiate Dictionary* (1980: 242) also includes "to use up" among the meanings of "to consume" before "to eat."

14   In fact, as James Mill illustrates, the period of savings being consumed tends to be shorter than the period of income earners' consumption: "that … which is destined for reproduction … is probably all expended in the shortest time" (1808: 76).

15   It is not difficult to recognize in these arguments by Mill the modern explanation of saving as entailing individuals' "calculations about time discount rates" or time preference, as an anonymous reader for the *Journal of the History of Economic Thought* would like to see. Indeed, John Stuart Mill (*Works*, 2: 163) elaborates the same point, just as he does with his explanation of interest being the "real reward for abstinence" and how variations in market interest rates reflect relative intensities of "lending and borrowing" desires (*Works*, 2: 405–6); see also Mill (*Works*, 3: 647–50) on the capital (savings) supply and demand theory of interest, but whose validity Keynes (1936, Ch. 14) firmly denies.

16   Mill's proposition is evidently true, but its meaning may be clearer with the insertion of "current" to qualify "labour." As Mill restates his proposition, "the demand for labour is constituted by the wages which precede the production, and not by the demand which may exist for the commodities resulting from the production" (*Works*, 2: 80). Otherwise, the sentence appears to be inconsistent with experience or firms' behavior. Current sales receipts either justify the previous hire of labor or not. The omission of "current" in the sentence may affirm Marshall's (1920: 681) observation that the statement "expresses [Mill's] meaning badly." Marshall (ibid.) agrees with Mill that "the wages of labour [are] paid, as in practice they commonly are, while the work is proceeding."

17 Mill clarifies this point in his chapter "Of Wages," where he explains the "wages-fund of a country" as constituting the demand for labor: "by capital [is meant] only circulating capital, and not even the whole of that, but the part which is expended in the direct purchase of labor. To this, however, must be added all funds, such as the wages of soldiers, domestic servants, and all other unproductive labourers" (*Works*, 2: 337).

18 Steven Kates (2015, esp. 45–9), regrettably, does not employ the wages fund as constituting the demand for labor in his defense of Mill's fourth fundamental theorem regarding capital. Kates's (2015) defense of Mill's fourth proposition, besides Grieve's own mistaken attribution of a world of certainty to Mill's analysis, also has motivated Grieve's (2017) further criticism of Kates. Grieve there declares Mill's "fourth proposition [to be] simply *wrong*" (271; italics original). Ahiakpor (forthcoming) discusses the mistakes in the arguments of both Roy Grieve and Steven Kates.

19 Note that Mill does not assign "all national output" to labor alone, contrary to Grieve's (2016: 340) misinterpreting Mill to have argued.

20 Federal Reserve money (currency) increased from $6.83 billion to $8.41 billion ($1.58 billion or 23.1%) between the third quarter of 1930 and end of the first quarter of 1933, while checkable deposits decreased by $6.87 billion or 31.6% and time deposits decreased by $6.95 billion or 34.4%—both reflecting the public's increased demand for cash—over the same period.

21 Ahiakpor (2019: 105–7) elaborates the consistency of Say's Law with the experience of the US Great Depression.

22 That misinterpretation of capital is at the heart of Keynes's (1936, Chapter 14, especially appendix 1) failure to recognize that, by the capital supply and demand theory of interest, Marshall meant the supply and demand for savings or loanable funds; Ahiakpor (1990) elaborates.

23 A Keynes-confused referee for the *Journal of the History of Economic Thought* argues that my discussion here misses "significant parts of post-Keynesian discussions about the role of the banking system and the reverse causality between savings and investment." But when one recognizes banks as intermediaries between savers and borrowers (for investment), little is left of Keynes's claim that investment precedes saving or that banks do not depend upon the public's savings (including banks' own equity capital) to lend. The problem with Keynes was his having misinterpreted saving to be the equivalent of cash hoarding, rather than savings being the source of bank credit (see Ahiakpor 1995; 1998b). The post-Keynesians would find clarity in classical analysis, including Say's Law, if they interpreted money, saving, capital, and investment as the classics meant these terms, not as Keynes misinterpreted them to mean.

4 Saving and the relevant Ricardian equivalence theorem

Introduction[1]

John Maynard Keynes's definition of saving as simply the non-consumption of one's income and thus a withdrawal from the expenditure stream of an economy has served modern macroeconomic analysis rather poorly. Robert Barro's (1974) initial effort to undermine belief in the efficacy of Keynesian fiscal policy to expand aggregate demand (total spending) relies on that definition of saving by Keynes. Thus, to Barro, a government that undertakes deficit spending in hopes of boosting aggregate demand and economic expansion would encounter a rational, forward-looking public that would save current incomes against future tax liabilities and frustrate the government's expectation from being realized. Had Barro instead employed the classical (and correct) definition of saving as the purchase of interest- and/or dividend-earning financial assets, and thus merely a transfer of spending power from savers to borrowers, he might have chosen an alternative method of undermining Keynesian fiscalism consistent with David Ricardo's own analysis. That alternative is the recognition that a government's sale of bonds to the public (other than to the central bank) in a closed economy completely displaces private sector spending, leaving total spending unchanged. Thus, there is contemporaneous equivalence between government taxation and debt financing of its spending.

Ricardo indeed discussed two types of equivalence between taxation and bond financing of government expenditures. One is a contemporaneous equivalence and the other, an intertemporal equivalence of the government's borrowed funds being equal to the present value of future taxes to retire the debt. It is the second equivalence that has become familiar in modern macroeconomics, emphasizing the transfer of debt burden onto future generations. Ricardo used the first equivalence to explain the "true cost" or "burden" of government spending as the foregone private sector output, which occurs whether government finances its spending out of taxes or issues debt (bonds).[2] He did not believe that people act according to the second, intertemporal equivalence, and therefore argued against debt financing of government spending. Deficit financing, Ricardo also argued, tends to shift the cost of government financing disproportionately onto a minority of the community—the bond purchasers—and thus impairs the community's savings or capital accumulation and economic growth.[3]

Barro (1974, 1976) and James Buchanan (1976) are responsible for popularizing Ricardo's second equivalence proposition in modern macroeconomics. Barro's (1974) earlier analysis was aimed at contradicting the Keynesian notion that bond-financed government expenditures expand aggregate demand[4] through a wealth effect on the part of bondholders who increase their consumption expenditures, e.g. Alan Blinder and Robert Solow (1973). In Barro's view, even parents anticipating their death before the arrival of the tax liabilities would save enough to make bequests that take care of the higher taxes their heirs would be paying. Thus, for a given level of government expenditures, switching between bond and tax financing would leave aggregate demand unchanged. Barro's proposition turns out to be both inconsistent with Ricardo's own argument regarding people's behavior with respect to the intertemporal equivalence between debt and tax finance, and unnecessary for his intended goal of undermining the effectiveness of deficit financing to change an economy's aggregate demand (total spending).

Referring to Ricardo's own writings, several previous critics have noted the error of Barro's (and Buchanan's) attribution of the intertemporal equivalence behavior of the public to Ricardo. Gerald O'Driscoll (1977) argues that Ricardo might have concluded as Barro does, had he followed the logic of his (Ricardo's) own analysis, but Ricardo did not. Relying partly on O'Driscoll's analysis, Martin Feldstein (1982) also distinguishes what he calls, "pre-Ricardian analysis," from the modern Ricardian equivalence proposition. Giuseppe Tullio (1989: 729) observes that "The equivalence of bond financing and taxation has been wrongly attributed to Ricardo." Mark Blaug (1996) also argues that "there is no real equivalence between paying for government expenditures by taxation or by borrowing, so that the modern 'Ricardian equivalence theorem' that some commentators have read into [Chapter 17 of Ricardo's *Principles*] is yet another misnomer associated with the name of Ricardo" (132). Also following O'Driscoll's interpretation of Ricardo's analysis, Nancy Churchman (2001) argues: "While Ricardo anticipated Barro's reasoning, he came to an opposite conclusion as far as concerns its application" (37), and she describes Barro's analysis as "the unfortunately named 'Ricardian Equivalence'" (115). N. Gregory Mankiw (2010: 484), among textbook authors, also declares: "It is one of the great ironies in the history of economic thought that Ricardo rejected the theory that now bears his name!" For a summary of the empirical literature attempting to demonstrate the error of the modern Ricardian proposition, see John Seater (1993).

However, the refutations of Barro's (and Buchanan's) attribution of the modern Ricardian equivalence proposition to Ricardo have tended to divert attention from Ricardo's contemporaneous equivalence explanation that is more relevant to current debate over government deficit spending. Thus, some of Barro's critics continue to argue or fail to fault the Keynesian belief in the expansionary effect of government deficit spending on the basis of whether government bonds are perceived as net wealth or not, e.g. Feldstein (1982), Tullio (1989), Churchman (2001),[5] and Mankiw (2010).

Barro (1989) defends his having accepted Buchanan's (1976) attribution of his analysis to Ricardo by focusing on Ricardo's intertemporal equivalence explanation rather than on the contemporaneous equivalence explanation. He also invokes in that defense what he terms "Stigler's Law," namely, the proposition that "nothing is named after the person who discovered it." He declares: "as far as I have been able to discover, David Ricardo (1951) was the first to articulate the theory. Therefore, the attribution of the equivalence theorem to Ricardo is appropriate even if he had doubts about some of the theorem's assumptions" (1989: 39n); see also Barro (2010). Relying mostly on Buchanan's (1958) interpretation of Ricardo's analysis, Dennis O'Brien (2004: 317) also endorses the view of Ricardo's parentage of the modern Ricardian equivalence idea, arguing,

> Ricardo ... laid the foundation for what has subsequently become known as "Ricardian Equivalence"—the idea that taxes and debt creation both impose the same burden on the wartime generation. In the hands of latter economists this became the proposition that government deficits would not stimulate the economy because people adjust their consumption in response to the stream of future tax payments.

In this chapter, I emphasize the distinction between Ricardo's contemporaneous equivalence of taxation and bond financing of government expenditures and his explanation of the intertemporal equivalence of current bond finance and the capitalized value of future tax payments, but the latter of which he argued few take into account in their spending decisions. The contemporaneous equivalence in terms of the foregone output from private investment expenditures is what creates the impossibility of deficit financing to increase aggregate demand and economic growth for a closed economy. Were the government to borrow some of its funds from abroad, current aggregate demand would rise from deficit spending, and future generations also would bear some of the tax burden to retire the debt. Ricardo's contemporaneous equivalence analysis also renders unnecessary the invocation of the irrationality assumption on the part of the public to reject Barro's future tax-capitalization hypothesis as some have argued, e.g. Churchman (2001: 38) and Tullio (1989: 729). Rationality or irrationality in consumption decisions has little to do with the opportunity cost of government's spending, however financed. It also turns out that statistical tests of Barro's Ricardian equivalence theorem have so far been improperly designed. They have tested changes in aggregate consumption rather than the intentions behind individuals' consumption or saving behavior as Barro's theorem claims, a point some earlier critics also have noted.

Originating the modern Ricardian equivalence theorem

Robert Barro's (1974) original intertemporal equivalence argument that James Buchanan (1976) subsequently dubbed Ricardian[6] was intended to negate the presumption of "a positive effect on aggregate demand of 'expansionary' fiscal policy" (1974: 1096)—the neutrality of fiscal policy—employing an overlapping-generations model. According to the argument, if the government grants a tax relief to generation 1 (old) and runs a budget deficit financed by new bond issues, the same generation would anticipate a higher future tax burden and thus increase their own saving accordingly rather than spend the tax relief on themselves. Thus, the tax relief would not promote the increased consumption spending that most analysts typically attribute to a net-wealth effect from government bonds, e.g. Blinder and Solow (1973: 323): "it has always been a central tenet of Keynesian macroeconomics that bond-financed government spending has a net expansionary impact on the level of economic activity"; see also Feldstein (1982).[7]

Barro further argues that the increased government debt would not raise the level of interest rates because of the increased demand for government bonds (increased saving rate) prompted by households' capitalization of their future tax liabilities. Also, if members of generation 1 engaged in intergenerational transfers, such as bequests,[8] to members of generation 2 (young), they would increase their current savings enough to relieve the younger generation of the burden of increased future taxes. Subsequently, Barro (1989: 38) presents his Ricardian equivalence proposition to refute the claim "in the language of Franco Modigliani (1961) [that] the public debt is an intergenerational burden that leads to a smaller stock of capital for future generations." Barro bases his argument on a rationality assumption about individuals that some analysts believe to be unassailable, but his critics consider implausible; see Barro (1989) for his reactions to some of the criticisms.

Barro's 1974 analysis also attempts to build upon arguments by James Tobin's (1971) and Martin Bailey's (1962) disputing the alleged expansionary effect of government debt financing. Tobin (1971) questions the possibility that a community would deceive itself about its status of wealth, which Barro (1974: 1096) cites in support of his own argument about individuals' inclination to capitalize their future tax liabilities: "How is it possible that society merely by the device of incurring a debt to itself can deceive itself into believing that it is wealthier? Do not the additional taxes which are necessary to carry the interest charges reduce the value of other components of private wealth?"

Barro next cites Bailey's (1962) explanation of what people would do *if* they considered the tax liabilities of increased government debt to support of his own view that individual government bondholders do not perceive such bonds as net wealth:

> It is possible that households regard deficit financing as equivalent to taxation. The issue of a bond by the government to finance expenditures involves a liability for future interest payments and possible ultimate repayment of principal, and thus implies future taxes that would not be necessary if the expenditures were financed by current taxation ... If future tax liabilities implicit in deficit financing are accurately foreseen, the level at

which total tax receipts are set is immaterial; the behavior of the community will be exactly the same as if the budget were continually balanced.

(quoted in Barro 1974, 1096)[9]

However, neither Tobin's nor Bailey's argument provides a good basis for Barro's claims about individuals' reaction to increased government indebtedness. Society does not decide whether it is richer by its accumulation of government debt, but, rather, individual bondholders do. And, the perception of government bonds as net wealth by their purchasers appears logically consistent, although, for the community as a whole, government bonds are not net wealth. They are merely an instrument for transferring the public's wealth to government for its spending. Such individual perception of government bonds is also consistent with savers' perception of their other financial assets, including corporate bonds and deposits with financial intermediaries, as net wealth even though these financial assets are the liabilities of their issuers.

Bailey's argument also appears to be a weak basis for Barro's claims about individual bondholders' future tax capitalization. First, Bailey argues the possibility that the public regards deficit financing as being equivalent to taxation, but not that people necessarily do so. Even if they did, individual bondholders may not necessarily expect that their future taxes would amount exactly to the portion of the government debt they acquire through their bond purchases. Indeed, for a closed economy, all government expenditures necessarily must be paid for either through borrowed funds or by taxes collected from the community (but ultimately through taxes alone), hence the contemporaneous equivalence. This follows from the government's budget constraint that Barro (1989: 38–9; 2010: 260–3) well notes: $G = T + \Delta B_g$, where G = government expenditure, T = taxes, and ΔB_g = change in the stock of government bonds.[10]

But the reality that, for a closed economy, whatever a government spends must first be taken from the community does not translate into individual bondholders' decision not to regard government bonds as part of their net wealth. Furthermore, Bailey's argument is that of a hypothetical, namely, what would happen "if future tax liabilities implicit in deficit financing are accurately foreseen." He does not claim that the community is, in fact, accurate in its perception. Barro thus appears to have turned hypothetical statements about a possible community behavior into a claim about what every individual in a community actually does: "*each household* subtracts its share of [the expected value of future taxes] from the expected present value of income to determine a net wealth position" (1989: 39; italics added).

It turns out that Buchanan's (1976) attribution of Barro's argument to Ricardo is inaccurate. Buchanan (1958: 44) earlier concluded that, for Ricardo to argue that taxation or government debt must impose contemporaneously the same burden on an economy, he must have assumed that taxpayers immediately capitalize their future tax liabilities whenever governments run deficits: "Ricardo assumes that the creation of the debt, with its corresponding obligation to meet the service charges from future tax revenues, causes individuals to write down the present value of their future income streams"; see also Buchanan (1958: 104). Buchanan thus saw in Barro's future tax-capitalization proposition just a restatement of an old argument. But the textual evidence does not support Buchanan's attribution of that behavioral assumption of individuals to Ricardo. Below, I restate Ricardo's explanation of the contemporaneous equivalence of taxation and government borrowing in terms of the opportunity cost of government spending being the same, a point the modern Ricardian proposition appears to miss.[11]

Ricardo on the equivalence of debt and tax finance

Ricardo's focus in explaining the contemporaneous equivalence between debt and tax finance was to note their "real expense" in terms of the opportunity cost of government spending, not the intertemporal equivalence of the present value of future taxes to the amount currently borrowed. Ricardo also sought to underscore the point already made by others that, for a closed economy or where only domestic residents purchase government bonds, only the debt's principal constitutes a burden, not the interest incurred on it. The principal is what the government spends and is thus withdrawn from the community's capital or savings, whereas the interest is merely a transfer from those who are not the public's creditors—the non-bond purchasers—to the public's creditors through future taxes:

> Taxes which are levied on a country for the purpose of supporting war, or for the ordinary expenses of the State, and which are chiefly devoted to the support of unproductive labourers,[12] are taken from the productive industry of the country; and every saving which can be made from such expenses will be generally added to the income, if not to the capital of the contributors. When, for the expense of a year's war, twenty millions are raised by means of a loan, it is the twenty millions which are withdrawn from the productive capital of the nation. The million per annum which is raised by taxes to pay the interest of this loan, is merely transferred from those who pay it to those who receive it, from the contributor to the tax, to the national creditor. The real expense is the twenty millions, and not the interest which must be paid for it.
>
> (*Works*, 1: 244)

Ricardo also cites with approval, as having been "conceived and expressed in the true spirit of the science," J.-B. Say's paraphrasing the same argument advanced by Jean-François Melon in 1734:

> It is true that the general wealth is not diminished by the payment of the interest on arrears of the debt: The dividends are a value which passes from the hand of the contributor to the national creditor ... The society is

deprived not of the amount of interest, since that passes from one hand to the other, but of the revenue from a destroyed capital.

(*Works*, 1: 244n)

David Hume (1752: 96) also cites Melon's argument, but with a stinging rebuke that it derives from "loose reasoning and specious comparisons." Hume recounts the argument:

We have, indeed, been told, that the public is no weaker upon account of its debts; since they are mostly due among ourselves, and bring as much property to one as they take from another. It is like transferring money from the right hand to the left; which leaves the person neither richer nor poorer than before.

(ibid.)[13]

He wonders whether Melon's argument is not likely to "be carried to a length that is ruinous and destructive" (97)—this after Hume has discussed five reasons debt finance is likely not benign to the well-being of a nation. His reasons include (1) debt finance's encouraging an excessively large capital city relative to the rest of a nation; (2) its stimulating the circulation of money and raising prices; (3) the taxes raised to pay "the interests of these debts, [being] apt either to heighten the price of labour, or be an oppression on the poorer sort"; (4) its subjecting the nation to foreign influence because of their funding a part of the debt; and (5) the interest payment to "idle people, who live on their revenue, our funds," giving "great encouragement to an useless and unactive life" (1752: 95–6).

Ricardo also argues that the same transfer of interest expense would have occurred had the government raised the loan amount through taxes instead. Those who would have been unable to pay their share of the tax out of their own incomes would borrow from some others in the community. The borrowers subsequently would pay their creditors their loan principal and interest. Thus the main difference between borrowing to pay one's tax obligations and paying future taxes to service the public debt is that the former entails a private debt settlement, whereas the latter entails a loan intermediation by the government, Ricardo explains:[14]

Government might at once have required the twenty millions in the shape of taxes; in which case it would not have been necessary to raise annual taxes to the amount of a million. This, however, would not have changed the nature of the transaction. An individual instead of being called upon to pay 100*l.* per annum, might have been obliged to pay 2000*l.* once and for all. It might also have suited his convenience rather to borrow the 2000*l.*, and to pay 100*l.* per annum for interest to the lender, than to spare the larger sum from his own funds. In one case it is a private transaction between A and B, in the other Government guarantees to B the payment of interest to be equally paid by A.

(*Works*, 1: 244–5)

Clearly, then the equivalence between bond and tax finance of public expenditure is in the amount the government spends, net of interest on the debt. Ricardo elaborates the point in the article "Funding System":

> In the case of a loan, A advances the money, and B pays the interest, and everything else remains as before. In the case of war-taxes, A would still advance the money [to some taxpayer B], and B pay the interest, only with this difference, he would pay it directly to A; now he pays it to government, and government pays it to A.
>
> (*Works*, 4: 188)

Nowhere in Ricardo's arguments does he claim that individuals capitalize their future tax liabilities when governments resort to debt financing in order to determine their consumption expenditures or saving. Indeed, Ricardo goes to a great length to argue that, although paying a large lump-sum tax is economically equivalent to paying small amounts over a long period of time—the intertemporal equivalence—people do not act in accordance with that equivalence:

> In point of economy, there is no real difference in either of the modes [of financing]; for twenty millions in one payment [of taxes], one million per annum forever, or 1,200,000*l.* for 45 years [to service a twenty million debt], are precisely of the same value; but the people who pay the taxes *never so estimate them*, and therefore do *not* manage their private affairs accordingly.
>
> (*Works*, 4: 186; italics added)

Not only do people not act in accordance with the intertemporal equivalence that Ricardo explains above, he also anticipates the main reason why it would be difficult to convince taxpayers of it. He notes that they would think someone else would be paying the future taxes: "It would be difficult to convince a man possessed of 20,000*l.*, or any other sum, that a perpetual 50*l.* per annum was equally burdensome with a single tax of 1000*l.* He would have some vague notion that the 50*l.* per annum would be paid by posterity, and would not be paid by him" (*Works*, 4: 187).[15] And, in contrast to the future tax capitalization by individuals claimed in the modern Ricardian equivalence proposition, Ricardo (ibid.; italics added) declares: "That an annual tax of 50*l.* is *not deemed* the same in amount as 1000*l.* ready money, must have been observed by every body."

It was because Ricardo believed that few act in accordance with the equivalence of a large lump-sum tax to a long series of small taxes that he judged tax finance of government expenditures to be economically more defensible than bond finance. Bond finance, Ricardo (*Works*, 1: 247) argues, "is a system which tends to make us less thrifty—to blind us to our real situation."[16] It encourages savings by individuals only "to the amount of the interest of such expenditure, and therefore the *national capital is diminished* in amount" (*Works*,

4: 188; italics added). Tax finance, on the other hand, forces every taxpayer to increase their saving up to their tax liabilities and thus preserves the nation's capital (savings) for productive private investment, Ricardo insists.

Ricardo's argument above is in clear contradiction to Barro's Ricardian equivalence proposition that "a decrease in the government's saving (that is, a current budget deficit) leads to an offsetting increase in *desired* private saving, and hence to no change in desired national saving" (1989: 39; italics added).[17] Similarly, Ricardo's argument appears to conflict with O'Brien's (2004: 316) view that Ricardo accepted the modern Ricardian equivalence proposition "on the grounds that individuals wrote down the capitalized value of their income streams to allow for future payments of debt-service taxes." O'Brien partly bases that interpretation on Ricardo's argument in (*Works*, 1: 247–8), cited below.

Indeed, besides some taxpayers anticipating posterity to pay a part of their future tax liabilities, Ricardo also argues that some may even yield to the temptation to emigrate to a lower-tax country rather than to bear the burden of higher taxes in their own country of birth:

> A country which has accumulated a large debt, is placed in a most artificial situation; ... it becomes the interest of every [tax] contributor to withdraw his shoulder from the burthen, and to shift this payment from himself to another; and the temptation to remove himself and his capital to another country, where he will be exempted from such burthens, becomes at least irresistible, and overcomes the natural reluctance which every man feels to quit the place of his birth, and the scene of his early associations.
>
> (*Works*, 1: 247–8)

In modern times, Swiss Bank accounts or tax havens may substitute for an actual emigration to a lower-tax jurisdiction. In the US, it is not uncommon for some high-income earners to move from high income-tax states to zero or low income-tax states.

Thus, rather than having argued that all taxpayers increase their current saving rate in anticipation of their higher future tax liabilities, Ricardo's point was that some tax payers do not increase their saving rate while others may remove their capitals or savings from the country in order to avoid paying higher future taxes on income. And, since the government's expenditures must be financed mostly by funds collected from the community, Ricardo considered it a matter of unfairness to burden disproportionately one class of the society, namely, the government bondholders, to the relative relief of some others, the non-bondholders, by resorting to debt financing:

> It is by the profuse expenditure of Government, and of individuals, and by loans, that the country is impoverished; every measure, therefore, which is calculated to promote public and private economy, will relieve the public distress; but it is error and delusion to suppose, that a real national difficulty

can be removed, by shifting it from the shoulders of one class of the community, who justly ought to bear it, to the shoulders of another class, who, upon every principle of equity, ought to bear no more than their share.

(*Works*, 1: 246)

My interpretation of Ricardo's arguments differs from O'Driscoll's (1977) supporting Barro's conclusion about individuals' behavior that has been influential with some analysts. O'Driscoll believes that Ricardo considered "taxation and public debt are equivalent 'in point of economy,' though not in point of fact" (1977: 208). He appears to interpret "in point of fact" to mean the public's failure to act in accordance with the intertemporal equivalence—a large lump-sum tax being equal to the capitalized value of small future taxes—for which Ricardo cites taxpayers' expectation of passing the future taxes on to posterity. He does not appear to recognize Ricardo's treatment of the burden of government spending in terms of the withdrawal of funds from the community's capital, whether through taxation or borrowing, hence the contemporaneous equivalence. Thus, O'Driscoll credits Ricardo with less analytical consistency than Barro: "Ricardo, the nineteenth-century theorist of equilibrium, could not carry over to this problem his usual assumption of perfect foresight; Barro, the twentieth-century Ricardian, is undoubtedly the more consistent on this point" (209).

It is unclear in what context O'Driscoll reads Ricardo to have employed the assumption of "perfect foresight." Ricardo (*Works*, 3: 318–9; 4: 36–7), for example, recognizes the phenomenon of lagged adjustment of wage rates after commodity prices in response to changes in the quantity of money and credit, an argument that underlies the classical forced-saving mechanism; Ahiakpor (2009) elaborates. That phenomenon is the result of a lack of perfect foresight in contracting for wages. Similarly, Ricardo (*Works*, 3: 316) argues that

It may be laid down as a principle of universal application, that every man is injured or benefited by the variation of the value of the circulating medium in proportion as his property consists of money, or as the fixed demands on him in money exceed those fixed demands he may have on others.

The injury would not occur if wealth owners acted with perfect foresight regarding future variations in the value of money (price level). Ricardo's (*Works*, 1: 290–2) contributions to Say's law of markets also contradict the claim that he employed Keynes's alleged "perfect foresight"; see Chapter 1. Thus, O'Driscoll's attribution of the perfect foresight assumption to Ricardo appears to be unfounded. Also, when one interprets Ricardo's "in point of economy" to mean the contemporaneous equality of the burden of taxation and government debt in the amounts spent by government or the opportunity cost for a closed economy, O'Driscoll's treatment of Ricardo's analysis turns out to be inaccurate.

Fiscal policy neutrality without the modern Ricardian equivalence

Indeed, one can explain fiscal policy neutrality or the complete crowding-out of private sector spending by government spending for a closed economy or where government debt is sold only to domestic residents without resort to the modern (Barro's) Ricardian equivalence proposition or future tax capitalization. One just needs to recognize the government's budget constraint, $G = T + \Delta B_g$, as Barro (1989) himself does, as well as invoke the total expenditure constraint, $TE = Y - \Delta(H^d - H^s) = C + I + G$. That is, government expenditure (G) has to be financed by tax revenues (T) and/or the sale of government bonds (ΔB_g), and total expenditure (TE) equals income (GDP) less the change in the public's excess demand for money (currency, $\Delta(H^d - H^s)$); C = private consumption spending, I = private gross investment spending $= \Delta FA_p$ $(FA_p =$ private sector financial assets or IOUs). Given the excess demand for money, variations in government spending must be fully offset by variations in private sector spending since the public's savings are used to purchase government $(\Delta B_g = \alpha Y)$ and private sector bonds or financial assets $(\Delta B_p = \Delta FA_p = \phi Y)$. And taxes do not have to be lump sum for the neutrality to occur since all taxes must be paid out of income $(T = tY)$.[18] Thus, we can trace the process of government spending displacing private sector spending without resort to speculations about people's motives for purchasing government bonds or their degree of rationality. Also, taking note of the fact that, for a closed economy, all expenditures, except those financed by a central bank's money creation, depend upon current income helps us to recognize that the government expenditure multiplier effect, upon which belief in the expansive power of fiscal policy is based, does not exist.[19]

The main problem with the modern Ricardian equivalence proposition is its presumption that all individuals capitalize their future tax liabilities as government debt increases and, therefore, leave their consumption expenditures unchanged. The proposition appears quite unrealistic since few individuals react to changes in government indebtedness that way, even if capitalizing future tax liabilities may appear to be a rational course of action. So far, empirical investigations of the proposition have not tested that presumption directly—determining the reasons for changes in individuals' saving rates. Rather, there have been indirect tests of the effect of government debt on aggregate consumption spending. A statistically insignificant coefficient of government debt in a consumption function model has tended to be interpreted as supporting the Ricardian equivalence hypothesis; see, for example, John Seater (1993: 172–3). Yet the estimated zero effect could be explained by at least two alternative factors that do not derive from individuals' future tax capitalization.

One explanation is that aggregate consumption demand may not change even as bond holders consider government bonds as net wealth. Saving is the acquisition of interest- and/or dividend-earning financial assets out of income $(S = \Delta FA^d = \Delta B_g + \Delta FA_p)$. Thus, having purchased government bonds, the bondholders have no other means by which they could purchase more goods and services for consumption unless they borrowed. Feeling wealthier does not by itself enable one to engage in more purchases. Thus, the claim that bondholders increase their consumption spending because of a wealth effect, without also noting that they would have had to reduce their own savings in order to increase consumption, cannot be correct.

Secondly, although some taxpayers may not anticipate having to pay higher future taxes because of increased government indebtedness and therefore do not save more currently, the government's expenditures would still have to be financed by funds acquired from the public in a closed economy. Thus, the failure of some in the community to increase their saving, following a tax cut, would have to be matched either by increased saving by others (induced by higher interest rates on government bonds) or by a shifting of some funds away from private borrowers toward purchasing more government bonds. Such shifting of savings may leave total community savings, and thus consumption, unchanged, even as the government's indebtedness has increased. Neither the displacement of private sector borrowing by government borrowing nor the disproportionate increased saving by some in the community is what the modern Ricardian equivalence theorem claims. But they are the consequences that Ricardo himself noted as resulting from increased government debt.

Barro also claims the failure of interest rates to rise in the US during the early 1980s in the presence of increased government deficits as proof of the validity of the modern Ricardian equivalence proposition. But a tax cut by the government increases disposable incomes and, thus, increases the flow of savings or increases the demand for financial assets $(S = Y(1 - t) - C - \Delta H_h = \Delta FA^d$, where ΔH_h = change in households' demand for cash) at existing interest rates—a shift of the savings–supply curve to the right (see Figure 4.1).[20] In the absence of an increase in government debt to be financed by increased borrowing (increased supply of bonds), such a rightward shift of the savings–supply curve (increased demand for financial assets) would have lowered equilibrium interest rates (raised the price of bonds or financial assets), all else given.[21] But the increased government borrowing may shift the economy's credit demand curve to the right (moving along the upward-sloping, increased savings–supply curve) by the same amount as the excess supply of credit (increased demand for financial assets) resulting from the tax cut, therefore leaving equilibrium interest rates unchanged.

That is, the increased demand for credit by the government (increased supply of bonds) raises the level of interest rates (decreases price of bonds) beyond the equilibrium level to which they would have declined (risen). If the increased supply of savings (increased demand for financial assets) is less than the increased government demand for credit (increased supply of bonds), equilibrium interest rates would rise (price of bonds fall). Interest rates would fall (price of bonds or financial assets would rise) if the increased supply of savings (increased demand for bonds or financial assets) exceeds the increased government demand for credit (increased supply of bonds). Because of the numerous other factors that

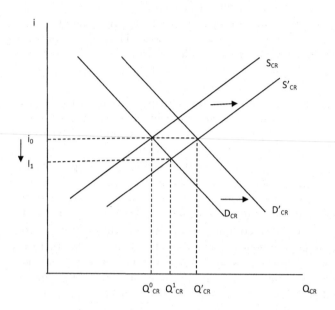

Figure 4.1 A tax cut shifts the savings/credit supply curve, creating an excess supply $(Q^0_{CR} Q'_{CR})$ at i_0 and decreasing the equilibrium interest rate to i_1. Increased budget deficit increases the demand for credit and raises the equilibrium interest rate.

affect equilibrium interest rates (inverse of the price of bonds or financial assets), besides changes in the government's budget deficit, the level of interest rates is quite an unreliable indicator of the effect of changes in government debt.

Moreover, aggregate data on savings and consumption expenditures do not tell us much about individuals' reactions to increased government debt. Thus far, the econometric tests using aggregate data, including Levis Kochin's (1974)[22] that Barro (1976) cites in support of his Ricardian equivalence proposition, have missed accurately evaluating individuals' reactions, hence the theorem. Seater (1993) almost accepts my conclusion. He notes that "An initial reading of [the aggregate consumption studies] literature is both confusing and disheartening, suggesting that such tests are uninformative about Ricardian equivalence and that aggregate data are *inherently unilluminating*" (174; italics added). But he is, nevertheless, convinced that when the problems he notes about the studies he reviewed are corrected, "the aggregate consumption data almost always fail to reject Ricardian equivalence"[23]—this even though his own attempted corrections do not test individuals' reactions to variations in the level of government debt.

Implications and conclusions

Barro often limits his Ricardian equivalence proposition to arguing about a change in government financing toward more debt and less taxation while keeping the level of government spending unchanged. The modern Ricardian equivalence theorem thus presumably avoids dealing with whether increased government spending hurts an economy's growth or not. But the effect of government spending on an economy was Ricardo's principal concern in his discussing the nature of financing government expenditures. Ricardo argued that (for a closed economy) whatever the government spends must first be taken from the public, and that impairs the community's capital (savings) accumulation and economic growth, particularly when financed by borrowing. That is why he considered reductions in the level of government spending a surer way to promote economic prosperity than raising taxes in order to reduce public debt. Ricardo's argument is, thus, very relevant to current debate on public debt.

By limiting the modern Ricardian equivalence proposition mainly to a switching of the modes of financing, Barro's argument misses addressing the more relevant issue. If increased government indebtedness has neutral effects on the economy because the public presumably increases its saving in anticipation of increased future taxes, it legitimately may be argued that increased government spending imposes no negative growth effects on an economy. That would be the exact opposite of Ricardo's concerns and that of other classical writers, including Adam Smith, on the need to restrict government spending to the spheres that may not be left safely to private enterprise; see also Levy (1986) and Tullio (1989). Indeed, Barro (1989: 37) downplays concerns about the negative economic consequences of budget deficits in the US, arguing:

> This crisis scenario has been hard to maintain along with the robust performance of the U.S. economy since late 1982. This performance features high average growth rates of real GNP, declining unemployment, much lower inflation, a sharp decrease in nominal interest rates and some decline in expected real interest rates, high values of real investment expenditures, and (until October 1987) a dramatic boom in the stock market.

Surely, the tax cuts and regulatory reforms of the Reagan administration must be considered far ahead of budget deficits in explaining the positive economic performance in the US during the early 1980s. Similarly, it would be misleading to cite the coincidence of lower nominal interest rates in the US and rising federal government deficits between 2008 and 2010 as proof of the Ricardian equivalence proposition's validity without considering the significant increase in Federal Reserve purchases of US Treasury securities, the sharp recession between 2008 and 2009, and the shaken business confidence during the same period.

The Federal Funds rate declined sharply from 2.00% in August 2008 to 0.11% by January 2010 and rose to 0.17% by January 2011, while the four-week US Treasury rate fell from 1.65% to 0.14% over the same period. The credit market debt owed by the federal government rose from $6361.5 billion at the end of 2008 to $9385.6 billion at the end of 2010, a 47.5% increase. The credit market assets of the Federal Reserve also increased from $986.0 billion by the end of 2008 to $2,259.2 billion by the end of 2010, a 129% increase in credit extension by the Fed. On the other hand, the household sector's credit market assets rose from $3,966.2 billion at the end of 2008 to $4,354.7 billion at the end of 2010, barely a 10% increase (data from Federal Reserve Statistical Series).[24]

Barro (1989: 48, 52) also appears puzzled by the reluctance of "most macroeconomists" and "most analysts" to accept his proposition as being relevant to a modern economy. But most analysts know that they themselves do not increase their own saving as a result of having capitalized their higher future tax liabilities as government indebtedness increases. Nor do they believe that they change their consumption spending in response to changes in government indebtedness.

Besides, the variations in the public's aggregate saving that the modern Ricardian equivalence proposition is supposed to show can be explained in alternative ways that are more convincing. It is also not irrational not to curb one's consumption spending because of increased government indebtedness if one expects (a) to die soon, (b) not to leave any bequests, or (c) to be able to escape the burden of higher future tax liabilities through emigration or by shifting savings to tax havens. The modern Ricardian equivalence proposition's claim of future tax capitalization by all individuals as the only rational response to increased government debt thus appears to be unwarranted.

All of government spending has to be financed either through taxation and/or through bond issues. Either form of financing draws funds from the public's savings in a closed economy. The burden of government spending for a closed economy or when government debt is bought by domestic residents only is thus concurrent with its amount, not deferred into the future, Ricardo argued. Future interest payments on the debt are merely transfers from non-bond holders to the public creditors. Emphasizing that point, instead of the government debt burdening future generations, almost ignoring the current opportunity cost to the economy, as recently has been asserted regarding the rising deficit spending in the US, is more consistent with Ricardo's analysis.

Besides being the exact opposite of what Ricardo himself wrote about taxpayers' behavior in response to increased government indebtedness, the modern Ricardian equivalence proposition misses the essence of Ricardo's (and other classicals') criticism of government deficit financing. Finally, increased saving does not reduce total spending in an economy, as Keynes's treatment of saving suggests. Paying attention to the classical definition of saving as the purchasing of financial assets might have alerted Robert Barro to an alternative means of arguing the futility of fiscal policy to promote an economy's growth.

Notes

1   The chapter draws heavily on my article "The Modern Ricardian Equivalence Theorem: Drawing the Wrong Conclusions from David Ricardo's Analysis," in the *Journal of the History of Economic Thought* 35, No. 1 (March): 77–92.

2 R. O. Roberts earlier emphasized the contemporaneous equivalence argument in Ricardo's analysis, but mainly in terms of the relative productivity of private versus government spending: "Ricardo's theory of public loans then was based on an emphasis of the fact that the primary burden to the community was derived from the *wasteful* nature of public expenditure itself rather than from the methods adopted to finance such expenditures" (1942: 257; italic added). However, the wastefulness of government spending is not a prerequisite for recognizing the opportunity cost or contemporaneous nature of the equivalence between taxation and debt financing for a closed economy. Both methods of financing immediately withdraw all the funds from the public for government to spend.

3 An anonymous referee of my original article observes that my argument overlaps with David Levy's (1986). However, the focus of Levy (1986) is to explain the classical economists' dim view of a sinking fund being a remedy for the negative economic growth consequences of deficit financing. Levy does not address Robert Barro's Ricardian equivalence proposition, let alone mention Barro (1974 and 1976) or dispute James Buchanan's (1976) and Gerald O'Driscoll's (1977) attributions of Barro's argument to David Ricardo.

4 The term "aggregate demand" may be alien to the language of David Ricardo's macroeconomic analysis, as a referee of my article observed, urging me to drop it. But it is that concept Robert Barro's analysis addresses. My argument thus cannot avoid its use. See my direct quotes from Barro (1974) below.

5 Churchman's (2001) discussion of Ricardo's alternative forms of public financing in a "full employment, price and wage flexibility, and a long-term" (121) framework appears to miss recognition of Ricardo's contemporaneous equivalence analysis. Ricardo, indeed, adopted both the short run and the long run modes of analysis and he did not assume full employment or complete wage flexibility; see, e.g. Ricardo (*Works*, 1: 160; 3: 318–9; 6: 233). Ahiakpor (1985) elaborates.

6 In making the attribution, Buchanan evidently draws upon his own earlier claim that Ricardo's analysis "was, in fact, based upon his assumption that future tax payments would be fully capitalized in a world of rational individuals. If taxpayers living during the period of debt creation fully capitalize future tax payments, the interest payments do become mere transfers which involve no 'sacrifice' on the part of future generations" (1958: 104).

7 The claim has been a standard macroeconomic argument, following the Ando-Modigliani aggregate consumption function specification; see, e.g. William Branson (1972: 192–5) and Robert J. Gordon (2006: 63–4, 506–7).

8 Barro (1989) includes parents' expenditures on their children's education among the intergenerational transfers. Ricardo (*Works*, 4: 187) indeed refers to the tax implications for a bequest but not that a parent necessarily recognizes it: "if he leaves his fortune to his son, and leaves it charged with [a] perpetual tax [of 50*l*. per annum], where is the difference whether he leaves him with 20,000*l*., with the tax, or 19,000*l*. without it?"

9 Bailey (1971: 156, 158) restates the argument.

10 Barro (2010: 260–1) employs only the stock of government bonds rather than the change in the stock of bonds.

11 Buchanan (1958: 18–9, 44–6, 116–7) recognizes this argument in Ricardo's analysis but considers it to be erroneous. The principal basis for Buchanan's disagreement with Ricardo's analysis is that bond purchasers do so voluntarily. He therefore concludes that they must not be presumed to bear any "burden" of government debt-financed expenditure (1958: 34–5). But volition or involution has nothing to do with the opportunity cost of government spending that Ricardo explains.

12 In the classical language, labor is unproductive if its employment leaves behind nothing that can be sold—a "vendible commodity" (Smith *WN*, 1: 351). Such labor includes the services of the "sovereign with all the officers both of justice and war who serve under him, the whole army and navy, churchmen, lawyers, physicians, men of letters of all

kinds; musicians, opera-singers, opera-dancers" (1: 352), although their labor has "value, and deserves its reward as well as that of the [manufacturer]" (1: 351).

13 Buchanan (1958: 4–20, 102–113) well summarizes the modern Keynesian view of national debt being owed to ourselves as being similar to the mercantilist right-hand, left-hand argument, against which Hume, as well as Adam Smith, reacted.

14 Ricardo's argument appears similar to Barro's (1974: 1111–12) observation that "the government bond issue amounts to effecting a loan from … low-discount-rate (savers) to … high-discount-rate individuals (non-bond purchasers). On the other hand, this sort of transfer could already have been accomplished privately, except that the transaction costs … made this transfer marginally unprofitable."

15 Some analysts incorrectly have treated Ricardo's comment as his referring to the "irra-tionality" of some taxpayers, e.g. Churchman (2001: 38). As I explain in the concluding section, such thinking to which Ricardo refers does not necessarily constitute irra-tionality.

16 Ricardo's argument is similar to the modern public choice proposition, articulated by Buchanan (1976), that it is much easier for politicians to resort to debt financing than raising taxes to fund projects they advocate, but an argument Barro (1976) disputes. See also Levy (1986).

17 An increase in desired saving implies a greater amount saved at the same rate of interest; a shift of the savings–supply curve, which Barro argues. But an increased quantity of sav-ings may be induced by the rise of interest rates, which appears to be a more plausible argument. See below.

18 Barro (1989: 45) allows departures from his Ricardian equivalence proposition if taxes are not lump sum, "for example, with an income tax."

19 With a zero excess demand for money, $\Delta(H^d - H^s) = 0, Y = C + I + G = \beta Y + \phi Y + tY + \alpha Y$. $C = \beta Y$ since there can be no consumption in the aggregate for a closed economy without current production (income). Thus, $Y(1 - \beta - \phi - t - \alpha) = 0, Y = [1 / (1 - \beta - \phi - t - \alpha)].0 = 0$, and there is no government expenditure multiplier effect; Ahiakpor (2001) elaborates.

20 We also may illustrate the interest rate (inverse of the price of bonds or financial assets) determination by changes in financial assets supply (ΔFA^s) and demand (ΔFA^d) leading to changes in the price of financial assets ($P_{FA} = \$X/i$, not drawn. I, therefore, disagree with a journal referee's view that "Market interest rates are strictly nominal but the supply of savings in [the following] context only makes sense if we are thinking about investible resources … that is, the supply of real productive assets." Interpreting "the supply of sav-ings" as "the demand for bonds or financial assets" is equally meaningful, as I explain in brackets below.

21 Interest rates are determined by a host of factors, including the public's expectation of inflation or deflation, the public's changing time preference or degree of impatience to consume, changes in the public's disposable income, changes in the public's demand for money (cash) to hold, changes in business profit expectations, past and present variations in a central bank's money (currency) creation, and changes in the government's demand for credit.

22 Kochin actually finds that the level and variations in aggregate consumption expen-ditures, variously measured, are negatively related to the level and variations in federal government deficits in the US. He also finds a close relation between the ratio of saving to disposable income and the ratio of deficit to disposable income and considers these as "consistent with the hypothesis that consumers discount implicit tax liabilities involved in deficit finance" (1974: 389).

23 Seater (1993: 171n) also reports others' observation that "aggregate data do not have enough variation to evaluate the [Ricardian equivalence] theory or much else of inter-est," but he "very much" disagrees with the observation.

24 As noted earlier, interest rates are determined by a multiplicity of factors rather than being limited to the state of government borrowing or deficit spending.

5 Milton Friedman's permanent income hypothesis

A distraction from Keynes's misrepresentation of saving as non-spending

Introduction

John Maynard Keynes (1930: 1, 172–4, 1936: 74, 210) defines saving merely as not spending one's income on consumption and that saving is a withdrawal from the expenditure stream. Keynes (1936: 166–7), in fact, treats saving as being equivalent to cash hoarding: "It should be obvious that the rate of interest cannot be a return to saving or waiting as such. For if a man hoards his savings in cash, he earns no interest, though he saves just as much as before." He did not employ Adam Smith's (*WN*, 1: 358–9) definition of saving as the purchase of interest- and/or dividend-earning financial assets, let alone savings being spent by borrowers, a definition that was followed by subsequent writers in the classical tradition, including Alfred Marshall (1920: 192–3; 1923: 46).[1] However, it is from Smith's definition of saving that we readily can understand his declaration, "What is annually saved is as regularly consumed[2] as what is annual spent, and nearly at the same time too; but it is consumed by a different set of people" (*WN*, 1: 359). Furthermore, having designated the expected level of consumption spending as the principal determinant of the demand for labor by businesses, Keynes (1936, Ch. 8) laments the fact that individuals do not devote all of their additional incomes to consumption but save some. Worse yet, in Keynes's view, the additional consumption declines whereas the additional saving increases as income increases. This is Keynes's "fundamental psychological law" (1936: 96) of individuals' spending behavior, represented in the now-familiar aggregate consumption function.

But in the above argument, Keynes commits the fallacy of composition by projecting his otherwise accurate description of an individual income earner's behavior regarding consumption and saving to the behavior of consumption and saving in the aggregate or at the national level.[3] At the aggregate level, government transfer payments that are financed by taxes as well payments to retirees out of pension plans affect aggregate consumption and saving. It thus should not have been such a significant puzzle when Simon Kuznets (1952) found that "the period since 1899 revealed no rise in the percentage of income saved during the past half-century despite a substantial rise in real income ... the percentage of income saved was much the same over the whole of the period" (quoted in Friedman 1957: 3–4). Failing to observe a rising savings ratio as national income increased in the US, Elizabeth Gilboy also declares, "Mr. Keynes seems to have propounded a theorem which may be applicable to particular groups at particular times, not a general psychological law which may be relied upon to describe the actions of all men (or even most men) at all times" (1938: 140). She firmly concludes, "There is no clear evidence that [Keynes's] psychological law is a fundamental law of human nature" (ibid.).

The apparent conflict between aggregate data and Keynes's description of an individual's consumption and saving behavior also could have been explained by other factors that tend to suppress the aggregate savings ratio as incomes rise, including the sorts of income redistribution policies adopted by governments. Also, most researchers, including James Duesenberry (1949), Franco Modigliani and Richard Brumberg (1954), and Milton Friedman (1957), have tended to omit Keynes's own elaborate discussion of other determinants of consumption spending besides real income, particularly those Keynes classified as "Subjective Factors" in Chapter 9 of the *General Theory*. These other determinants include "the institutions and organization of the economic society ... and ... the prevailing distribution of wealth and the established standards of life" (1936: 109). Instead, the researchers have attempted to explain the apparent conflict between aggregate data and an individual's consumption and savings behavior differently by the relative income hypothesis, by the inclusion of wealth in the consumption function,[4] and ultimately, by Milton Friedman's (1957) permanent income hypothesis. According to Friedman, his "new hypothesis seems potentially more fruitful and is in some measure more general than either the relative income hypothesis or the wealth–income hypothesis taken by itself" (1957: 6). In fact, Friedman's analysis only partly repeats Keynes's own elaborate description of the determinants of individuals' consumption spending, although he draws different conclusions from Keynes's.

Moreover, none of these attempts empirically to evaluate the validity of Keynes's consumption function focuses on his incorrect treatment of saving simply as non-consumption and that increased saving contracts total spending in an economy and causes increased unemployment. They also do not appear to recognize the fallacy of composition entailed in Keynes's treatment of the aggregate consumption function. Thus, the influence of Friedman's permanent income hypothesis as the more accurate description of the consumption function has served to sustain the distraction of the early evaluations of Keynes's consumption function from recognizing his incorrect treatment of saving. Both Keynes and Friedman have been wrong on saving and its role in a monetary economy.

Savings are consumed (spent or used up) by borrowers, most of whom are businesses. Therefore, the fact that most people may save the greater proportion of incomes they may consider transitory is not the reason traditional Keynesian aggregate demand management policies such as temporary tax cuts or stimulus spending do not succeed, as has become the standard implication drawn from Friedman's permanent income hypothesis.[5] Rather, it is because, for a closed economy and other than borrowing from the central bank, whatever the government spends must be taken from the public, creating a 100% crowding out in total spending.

This chapter explains the error of Keynes's treatment of saving and the misleading nature of the consumption function studies that have followed his work. We begin with Milton Friedman's (1957) attempt to resolve the apparent conflict between budget studies that appear consistent with Keynes's description of an individual's consumption function and the aggregate data that suggest the constancy of consumption– and saving–income ratios.

Friedman's permanent income hypothesis

Milton Friedman was not the first major analyst to have missed Keynes's failure to recognize savings as being spent by borrowers. He developed his permanent income hypothesis to reconcile Kuznets's (1952) study that finds the ratio of aggregate consumption to aggregate income in the US to have been constant for several decades with several budget and time series studies that evaluated Keynes's (1936) description of individuals' consumption behavior. Keynes's (1936) description of the consumption function argues a "fundamental psychological rule of any modern community that, when its real income is increased, it will not increase its consumption by an equal absolute amount" and that "as a rule … a greater proportion of income … (is) saved as real income increases" (quoted in Friedman 1957: 3).[6] The studies include (1) Dorothy Brady and Rose Friedman's (1947) arguing a relative income explanation of individuals' consumption behavior such that a consumer unit's consumption depends upon "its position in the distribution of income among consumer units in its community" (quoted in Friedman 1957: 4); (2) James Duesenberry's (1949) elaborating the relative income hypothesis by explaining the dependence of lower income consumers' spending upon the quality of goods consumed by higher income earners in a community as well as its depending upon the ratio of current income to the highest level of income previously attained; (3) Franco Modigliani's (1949) affirming Duesenberry's conclusion regarding the significance of a consumer unit's position within the distribution of income; (4) James Tobin's (1951) affirming the greater consistency of current real income in explaining the level of consumption over the relative income hypothesis, but also adding the role of wealth to explain "the rough constancy over time in the fraction of income saved" (quoted in Friedman 1957: 5); and (5) Gottfried Haberler's (1941) and A.C. Pigou's (1943) also invoking the role of individuals' wealth in determining the ratio of their consumption to income.[7]

Friedman's review of the early literature does not take into account some early doubts about the validity of Keynes's description of the consumption function, including their assigning its relevance to 19th-century society, e.g. Elizabeth Gilboy (1938).[8] Gilboy also declares, "Not only has the economic philosophy of spending [consumption] superseded that of thrift [saving] in general popularity, but constant emergence of new commodities allied with pressure advertising makes spending very attractive to the average individual" (1938: 138–9).

Like Keynes, Friedman argues his permanent income hypothesis first as descriptive of an individual's behavior and then generalizes it for the community as a whole. He states: "if a consumer unit knows that its receipts in any one year are unusually high and if it expects lower receipts subsequently, it will surely tend to adjust its consumption to its 'normal' receipts rather than to its current receipts" (1957: 10).[9] The consumption consistent with "normal" receipts Friedman terms permanent real consumption, $c^p = k(i, w, u)y^p$ where k = ratio of real consumption to real permanent income, i = interest rate, w = ratio of nonhuman wealth to income, u = utility factors, such as age and family composition, and y^p = permanent real income. From that reasoning, Friedman classifies consumption into permanent (c^p) and transitory (c^t) components, similarly for income, $y = y^p + y^t$. Friedman then extends the same account of an individual's consumption behavior to the community: "In order to use this equation in interpreting group behavior, we must take the additional step of regarding the same equation as applicable to all members of the group—not merely the same form of equation, but the same functional relation" (1957: 18).

Plausible though Friedman's argument may appear, and it has motivated subsequent empirical work,[10] he acknowledges the difficulty of its precise measurement and testing. He admits, "The magnitudes termed 'permanent income' and 'permanent consumption' ... cannot be observed directly for any individual consumer unit" (1957: 20).[11] Moreover, the permanent components of his consumption function do not "correspond to average lifetime values and the transitory components as the difference between such lifetime averages and the measured values in a specific time period" (1957: 23). Equally troubling is his claiming, "it seems neither necessary nor desirable to decide in advance the precise meaning to be attached to 'permanent'" (1957: 23). Also, "The precise line to be drawn between permanent and transitory components is best left to be determined by the data themselves, to be whatever seems to correspond to consumer behavior" (ibid.). Furthermore, the permanent income component "is to be interpreted as the mean income at any age regarded as permanent by the consumer unit in question, which in turn depends on its horizon and foresightedness" (1957: 93).

On the other hand, Friedman argues,

> It is easy to confuse our [permanent income] hypothesis with the very different one that the appropriate time unit for studying consumption behavior is the individual's horizon, whether it be his lifetime or a shorter period, and that the individual is to be regarded as making and, more important, carrying out successfully, plans for that period—what might be called a "planning period" hypothesis.
>
> (1957: 213)

Friedman also declares: "The concept of permanent income is easy to state in ... general terms, hard to define precisely" and "Permanent income cannot be observed directly, it must be inferred from the behavior of consumer units. And this is equally true of permanent consumption and its relation to permanent income" (1957: 221). Now data do not speak for themselves, and it is hard to ascertain from the population what individuals considered their permanent incomes separately from their transitory incomes.[12] Moreover, individuals are continually making decisions to consume and to save (invest) at any point in time without knowing exactly the permanence or sustainability of their future income streams.

Nevertheless, it is from such imprecise specification of the consumption function on the basis of his permanent income hypothesis that Friedman sought to explain Kuznets's estimated constancy of the ratio (k) of aggregate consumption to aggregate income. He also acknowledges that statistical estimates of permanent income and permanent consumption are not consistent with his theoretical specification of the consumption function: "measured consumption turns out to be a smaller fraction of measured income for high than for low measured incomes even for groups of consumer units for whom it does not seem reasonable to attribute this result to difference in the values of i, w, or u" (Friedman 1957: 20). Friedman could have interpreted the differences in the consumption–income ratios of high and low income earners as affirming Keynes's description of the consumption function for individuals.

Modigliani and Brumberg (1954: 408) interpret the data from budget studies as showing that "the proportion of income saved, far from being constant, tends to rise from a very low or even negative figure at low levels of income to a large positive figure in the highest brackets," which accords with Keynes's argument for most individuals. Instead, Friedman employs his permanent income hypothesis to interpret such data somewhat differently, even as he acknowledges that the permanent component of actual income is hard to estimate:

> The [permanent income] hypothesis asserts that planned savings are the *same fraction* of permanent income at all income levels and have the same relative dispersion as permanent income. But equally, it asserts that the actual savings of any unit equal its planned savings plus the transitory component of income, positive or negative, minus the transitory component of consumption, positive or negative. The result is that the absolute dispersion of measured savings is necessarily higher than that of planned savings.
>
> (1957: 210; italics added)

Had Friedman defined saving as purchasing interest- and/or dividend-earning financial assets as in Adam Smith (*WN*, 1: 358–9), he might have recognized the impossibility of individuals in all income classes having the same planned ratio of savings to their "permanent" incomes.[13] Rather, Friedman included cathedrals built in the Middle Ages and hoarded precious metals in India among forms of saving: "Savings may well have been at least as large a fraction of income in the Middle Ages as in modern times: they then in considerable measure ... took the form of cathedrals ... The East was for long regarded as a 'sink' for the precious metals" (1957: 236). He thus, argues, "Perhaps the crucial role that has been assigned to the savings ratio in economic development should be assigned instead to the factors determining the form in which wealth is accumulated; to the investment rather than saving process, as it were" (ibid.). But savings, correctly understood, take the form of purchasing or investing in interest- and/or dividend-earning assets, e.g. Marshall (1920: 192; 1923: 46) and John Stuart Mill (*Works*, 2: 70). Cathedrals and hoarded precious metals yield no interest or dividends; they are not savings in the economic sense.

Clearly, low income earners do not have the same means to purchase financial assets (save) as do middle and higher income earners; see e.g. Marshall (1920: 190). Even as purchases of consumer durables tend to increase with the level of households' incomes,[14] purchasers of such durable goods still tend to have larger proportions of their incomes (savings) in bank accounts, stocks and bonds, and pension funds than lower income earners. Modigliani and Brumberg (1954: 426, n. 54) appear to confirm this when they argue: "There is ample evidence of a very pronounced correlation between assets and income, at least as far as liquid assets are concerned." Low income earners may have negative savings (being net borrowers) because middle and high income earners are more able to save, making the funds available for their borrowing. Nevertheless, Modigliani and Brumberg (1954: 430) also insist, "We depart from Keynes ... on his contention of 'a greater *proportion* of income being saved as real income increases' (p. 97, italics his). We claim instead that the *proportion of income saved is essentially independent of income*." They explain their contention by arguing as Friedman does: "systematic deviations of the saving ratio from the normal level are largely accounted for by the fact that short-term fluctuations of income around the basic earning capacity, may cause accumulated savings to get out of line with current income and age" (Modigliani and Brumberg 1955: 430).

However, carefully considered, data in Table 7, p. 82 in Friedman (1957), showing a lower ratio of consumption to mean income for Whites than Blacks, while Blacks earn significantly lower incomes than Whites, appear to confirm Keynes's description of his consumption function.[15] It is also the intra-community subsidization of consumption at a point in time that yields the positive intercept for the estimated aggregate consumption function; no one can consume if there is no production (and income earned). But resorting to the possibility of such borrowers earning higher incomes in the future to retire their indebtedness, similar to Modigliani and Brumberg's (1954) life-cycle hypothesis, rather inhibits that realization. Thus, Friedman claims, "Their negative savings are financed by large positive savings in years when their incomes are abnormally large, and it is these that produce the high ratios of savings to measured income at the upper end of the measured income scale" (1957: 39–40). Clearly, those drawing upon their past savings to sustain their current consumption because their current incomes have fallen must exhibit a higher consumption to income ratio than those whose current incomes have not fallen:

a lower saving–income ratio as incomes fall and a higher savings–income ratio as incomes rise, just as Keynes describes an individual's consumption function.

Instead of the above recognition of the differences between different income earners regarding their consumption and savings behavior, Friedman's employing his permanent income hypothesis to interpret Kuznets's estimated constancy of the aggregate consumption–income ratio in the US for more than half a century[16] has resulted in his most influential conclusion: "consumers adapt their expenditures to longer-run income status as measured by permanent income rather than to their momentary receipts. The effects of changes in measured income on consumer expenditures can all be accounted for in this way" (1957: 228). But the positive "momentary receipts" are increases in income. And if more of these incomes are saved, they represent a declining marginal propensity to consume, which is consistent with Keynes's formulation of his consumption function. In any case, since all savings are consumed (spent) by borrowers, it really does not matter what proportion of measured income constitutes permanent income and what proportion of measured consumption constitutes permanent consumption.

In his attempt to reconcile Kuznets's finding of a constant ratio of aggregate consumption to aggregate income (k^*), Friedman (1957: 229) also advances three factors that appear to blur recognition of an individual's consumption–income behavior. The factors include: (i) "the declining relative importance of farming, which would raise k^*"—farmers have a higher propensity to save or have a lower propensity to consume because of the greater uncertainty of their incomes; (ii) "the declining size of family, which would tend to lower k^*"—a large family size tends to increase consumption as a proportion of income; and (iii) "the changing role of the state in the provision of [financial] security, [which] has itself had offsetting effects on k^*"—saving against retirement and old age is an alternative to the state's provision of old age financial payments or social security in the US. But Friedman does not advance these explanations as creating a conflict between Keynes's "psychological law" of consumption behavior at the individual level and the behavior of aggregate consumption to aggregate income. Indeed, to argue that individuals save a lot more of increases in their incomes they consider to be transitory is not that much of a contradiction of Keynes's observation that the savings rate increases with increases in people's incomes.

Freidman's failure to interpret savings as the purchasing of interest- and/or dividend-earning assets also has led to his drawing some unhelpful conclusions from his permanent income hypothesis for the less developed countries. One is that, according to the hypothesis, "the savings ratio is independent of the level of income. Relative income, as measured, is empirically related to the savings ratio within a country not because of emulation or the demonstration effect but because relative measured income is a biased index of relative permanent income status" (1957: 234). Surely, if the demonstration effect of high-quality consumption goods raises the consumption to income ratio of lower income earners, it must reduce the aggregate savings ratio. Another is, "Insofar as [income] inequality is attributable to differences in permanent income status, it has no effect on the savings ratio. Insofar as it is attributable to differences in transitory components, it does" (1957: 235). Thus, Friedman argues that uncertainty is what would promote a higher savings ratio in the less developed countries, so long as it is "uncertainty of a kind that does not reduce the average rate of return on capital" (ibid.). These arguments provide little guide to sound policymaking to increase the savings rate in the less developed countries to enhance their economic growth. The savings-enhancing policies include low taxation of income, low inflation rates, political stability, and minimizing the transactions cost of saving or purchasing financial assets. Increased uncertainty about the future rather may cause income earners to increase their cash hoarding than to save. Stock market behavior in response to increased uncertainty in the more developed countries well illustrates the point.

Friedman's partial replication of Keynes's consumption function

Milton Friedman proposed his permanent income hypothesis to be a more useful and complete statement of the consumption function. He contrasts his hypothesis with both the absolute income hypothesis that argues a stable relation between aggregate consumption to real aggregate income and the relative income hypothesis that argues the relevance of a consumer unit's position in the distribution of income in determining its consumption–income ratio. Friedman judges these other hypotheses to be inferior to his; and his permanent income hypothesis has achieved considerable influence in macroeconomic analysis. However, Keynes's description of the consumption function in Chapters 8 and 9 of the *General Theory* shows that the absolute income hypothesis derives from a rather limited interpretation of his explanations of the determinants of consumption spending beyond real income while the relative income hypothesis emphasizes just one of Keynes's own listed determinants. Friedman's description of his consumption function rather amounts to a formalization of Keynes's more elaborate description of the consumption function, but drawing the opposite of Keynes's conclusion from it. While Keynes used his concerns over the declining marginal propensity to consume or rising marginal propensity to save to argue for the increasing role of government spending, Friedman used his permanent income hypothesis to argue the ineffectiveness of fiscal stimulus not considered to be permanent because it will not much affect aggregate consumption or demand.

Keynes's discussion of the determinants of aggregate consumption classifies them under "objective" and "subjective" factors:

> The amount that the community spends on consumption obviously depends (i) partly on the amount of its income, (ii) partly on the other objective attendant circumstances, and (iii) partly on the subjective needs and the psychological propensities and habits of the individuals composing

it and the principles on which the income is divided between them (which may suffer modification as output is increased).

(1936: 90–1)

Even as Keynes makes "the aggregate income measured in terms of the wage unit [real income] ... as a rule, the principal variable upon which the consumption-constituent of the aggregate demand function will depend" (1936: 96), he lists six (6) elements of the "objective" factors determining consumption behavior. They include:

(1) "*A change in the wage-unit*" (91), including "the distribution of a given real income between entrepreneurs and rentiers" (92; italics original);
(2) "*A change in the difference between income and net income*" (92; italics original);[17]
(3) "*Windfall changes in capital-values not allowed for in calculating net income.*— These are of much more importance in modifying the propensity to consume, since they will bear no stable or regular relationship to the amount of income. The consumption of the wealth-owning class may be extremely susceptible to unforeseen changes in the money-value of its wealth. This should be classified amongst the major factors capable of causing short-period changes in the propensity to consume" (92–3; italics original);[18]
(4) "*Changes in the rate of time-discounting, i.e. in the ratio of exchange between present goods and future goods*"; Keynes approximates this factor to the rate of interest, although he also argues, "The influence of this factor on the rate of spending out of a given income is open to a good deal of doubt" (93; italics original);[19]
(5) "*Changes in fiscal policy* ... If fiscal policy is used as a deliberate instrument for the more equal distribution of incomes, its effect in increasing the propensity to consume is, of course, all the greater ... We must also take account of the effect on the aggregate propensity to consume of Government sinking funds ... For these represent a species of corporate saving, so that a policy of substantial sinking funds must be regarded in given circumstances as reducing the propensity to consume" (94–5; italics original).
(6) "*Changes in expectations of the relation between the present and the future level of income* ... But, whilst it may affect considerably a particular individual's propensity to consume, it is likely to average out for the community as a whole. Moreover, it is a matter about which there is, as a rule, too much uncertainty for it to exert much influence" (95; italics original).

Nevertheless, Keynes argues the existence of a "fairly stable" functional relation between consumption and changes in real income, windfall changes in capital values, and substantial changes in the rate of interest and fiscal policy. However, he adds: "the other objective factors which might affect [consumption], whilst they must not be overlooked, are not likely to be important in ordinary circumstances" (96). Keynes's ultimate conclusion is that "the aggregate income measured in terms of the wage-unit is, as a rule, the *principal* variable upon which the consumption-constituent of the aggregate demand function will depend" (96; italics added). It could not be otherwise; income is the principal source from which people acquire consumption goods. Even gifts and tax revenues can only derive from incomes earned by gift givers and taxpayers. Loans also derive principally from saved incomes.

Keynes's "subjective factors" determining the propensity to save he lists in Chapter 9 include the decision (i) "To build up a reserve against unforeseen contingencies"; (ii) "anticipated future needs ... [such as] old age, family education, or the maintenance of dependents"; (iii) "To enjoy interest[20] and appreciation, i.e. because a larger real consumption at a later date is preferred to a smaller immediate consumption"; (iv) "To enjoy a gradually increasing expenditure"; (v) "To enjoy a sense of independence and the power to do things, though without a clear idea or definite intention of specific action"; (vi) "To ensure a *masse de manoeuvre* to carry out speculative or business projects";[21] (vii) "To bequeath a fortune"; and (viii) "To satisfy pure miserliness, i.e. unreasonable but insistent inhibitions against acts of expenditure as such" (1936: 107–8). Keynes summarizes these subjective factors under "Precaution, Foresight, Calculation, Improvement, Independence, Enterprise, Pride and Avarice."

In contrast to the above motives for saving, Keynes's subjective "motives to consumption" include "Enjoyment, Shortsightedness, Generosity, Miscalculation, Ostentation and Extravagance" (1936: 108). Keynes further complicates the influence of these subjective factors on individuals' behavior by noting that their strength tends to

> vary enormously according to the institutions and organisation of the economic society which we presume, according to habits formed by race, education, convention, religion and current morals, according to present hopes and past experiences, according to the scale and technique of capital equipment, and according to the prevailing distribution of wealth and the established standards of life.
>
> (1936: 109)

None of the modern formalizations of the consumption function, including those founded upon the relative income hypothesis, life-cycle hypothesis, and Friedman's permanent income hypothesis, captures the full extent of Keynes's description of the determinants of individuals' consumption and saving behavior. But what is more important for understanding and policy formulation is their failure to critique Keynes's incorrect treatment of increased saving as being a detriment to an economy's growth, especially in Chapter 8 of the *General Theory*.

Keynes's mistaken treatment of saving as non-spending

Keynes's principal motivation for his elaborate discussion of the consumption function was to argue that extant macroeconomic analysis, derived from the classical economists, overlooks the crucial role consumption plays in determining the level of employment. Keynes declares, "The ultimate objective of our analysis is to discover what determines the volume of employment" since "it is the part played by the aggregate demand function which has been overlooked" (1936: 89)—thanks to Say's law of markets.[22] Keynes mostly denies that savings supply the funds borrowed for investment spending or acquiring capital goods. Implicitly assuming a fixed labor-output coefficient in all productions, Keynes defines the aggregate demand function as relating "any level of employment to the 'proceeds' which that level of employment is expected to realise. The 'proceeds'... [being] the sum which will be spent on consumption when employment is at a given level, and the sum which will be devoted to investment" (1936: 89–90). However, because Keynes separates savings from investment spending, he considers people's tending to save proportionally more as real incomes rise a major obstacle for sustaining the growth of output and employment.[23] To him, investment is only the purchase of capital goods: "we must mean by [investment] the current addition to the value of capital equipment which has resulted from the productive activity of the period" (1936: 62). In his *Treatise*, Keynes declares, "the increase or decrease of capital [goods] depends on the amount of investment and not on the amount of saving" (1930, 1: 173).[24] Also, Keynes believed that the funds for investment spending depend "on the terms on which the banks are prepared to become more or less liquid" (1937c: 668), having earlier argued that banks do not depend upon the public's savings to lend (1930, 1: 24–6).

Keynes's separating savings from banks' loanable funds also inhibits his correctly inferring the effects upon consumption spending or savings from adjustments in market interest rates. Thus, drawing upon his liquidity preference theory of interest rates, Keynes argues, "a rise in the rate of interest must have the effect of reducing incomes to a level at which saving is decreased in the same measure as investment ... [therefore] saving and spending will *both* decrease" when the rate of interest rises (1936: 110–1; italics original). Therefore, "The more virtuous we are, the more determinedly thrifty, the more obstinately orthodox in our national and personal finance, the more our incomes will have to fall when interest rises relatively to the marginal efficiency of capital" (1936: 111).

It is also from Keynes's failure to link savings directly with supplying loanable funds or his deriving any effects from changing market interest rates on consumption or savings that Keynes argues his negative consequences from the public's not increasing their consumption spending to match increases in real income—declining marginal propensity to consume—in the short run. The same reasoning underlies Friedman's permanent income hypothesis in which only long-run or permanent changes in income affect consumption spending in any significant way in the short run. Keynes argues:

A man's habitual standard of life usually has the first claim on his income, and he is apt to save the difference which discovers itself between his actual income and the expense of his habitual standard; or, if he does adjust his expenditure to changes in his income, he will over short periods do so imperfectly. Thus a rising income will often be accompanied by increased saving, and falling income by decreased saving, on a greater scale at first than subsequently.[25]

(1936: 97)

Had Keynes linked saving with funding investment spending, rather than investment spending creating additional income from which savings emerge simply as a residual, he could have avoided his fearing an emerging gap between total income and total spending as real income increases. Instead, he was left with arguing, "Since consumers will spend less than the increase in aggregate supply price when employment is increased, the increased employment will prove unprofitable unless there is an increase in investment to fill the gap" (1936: 98).

Furthermore, Keynes's failure to link savings with funding investment spending extends to his treatment of depreciation charges and sinking funds. He argues that sinking funds cause increased unemployment because they reduce consumption spending without increasing "new investment" and therefore reduce aggregate demand. Regarding depreciation allowances, Keynes argues:

When the financial provision *exceeds* the actual expenditure on current upkeep ... this excess neither directly gives rise to current investment nor is available to pay for consumption. It has, therefore, to be balanced by new investment, the demand for which has arisen quite independently of the current wastage of old equipment against which the financial provision is being made.

(1936: 99)

Rather than recognizing that the excess funds being held in bank accounts or some financial instruments, whose suppliers spend them, Keynes reasons that those funds diminish income creation and employment: "the new investment available to provide current income is correspondingly diminished [by the financial provision] and a more intense demand for new investment [purchasing capital goods] is necessary to make possible a given level of employment" (1936: 100).

Thus, Keynes incorrectly concludes: "Sinking funds, etc., are apt to withdraw spending power from the consumer long before the demand for expenditure on replacements (which such provisions are anticipating) comes into play; *i.e.* they diminish the current effective demand and only increase it in the year in which the replacement is actually made" (1936: 100). Keynes further insists, "Aggregate demand can be derived only from present consumption or from present provision for future consumption ... We cannot, as a community, provide for future consumption by financial expedients [savings] but only by current physical output" (1936: 104). Keynes also repeats his *Treatise* (1930: 1, 176–7) paradox of thrift proposition,[26]

The larger our income, the greater, unfortunately, is the margin between our incomes and our consumption. So, failing some novel expedient, there is ... no answer to the riddle, except that there must be sufficient unemployment to keep us so poor that our consumption falls short of our incomes by no more than the equivalent of the physical provision for future consumption which it pays to produce to-day.

(1936: 105)

In his *Principles*, Marshall explains,

The accumulation of wealth [savings] is governed by a great variety of causes: by custom, by habits of self-control and realizing the future, and above all by the power of family affection. Security is a necessary condition for it, and the progress of knowledge and intelligence furthers it in many ways.

(1920: 196; see also 443)

Marshall connects saving with interest rates by noting that interest is saving's demand price: "A rise in the rate of interest offered for capital [loanable funds], *i.e.* in the demand price for saving, tends to increase the volume of saving." Marshall also links his long discussions of capital and interest to the principles that have been explained since Adam Smith and David Ricardo:

The scientific doctrine of capital [and interest] has had a long history of continuous growth and improvement ... during the last three centuries. Adam Smith appears to have seen indistinctly, and Ricardo to have seen distinctly, almost everything of primary importance in the theory, very much as it is known now: and though one writer has preferred to emphasize one of its many sides, and another another, there seems no good reason for believing that any great economist since the time of Adam Smith has ever completely overlooked any side ... Scarcely anything done by any great thinker has had to be undone, but something new has constantly been added.

(1920: 484)[27]

However, Keynes does not appear to recognize Adam Smith's explanation:

What is annually saved is as regularly consumed as what is annually spent, and nearly in the same time too; but it is consumed by a different set of people. That portion of his revenue which a rich man annually spends, is in most cases consumed by idle guests, and menial servants, who leave nothing behind them in return for their consumption. That portion which he annually saves, as for the sake of the profit it is immediately employed as a capital, is consumed in the same manner, and nearly in the same time too, but by a different set of people, by labourers, manufacturers, and artificers, who reproduce with a profit the value of their annual consumption.

(*WN*, 1: 359)[28]

Neither does Keynes appear to recognize Smith's explaining,

By what a frugal man saves, he not only affords maintenance to an additional number of productive hands, but like the founder of a public workhouse, he establishes as it were a *perpetual fund* for the maintenance of an equal number in all times to come … No part of it can ever afterwards be employed to maintain any but productive hands, without an evident loss to the person who thus perverts it from its proper destination.

(*WN*, 1: 359–60; italics added)

But it is from understanding Smith's explanation of savings being reproductively spent, and thus being more conducive to employment and economic growth than consumption, that Jean-Baptiste Say, David Ricardo, and John Stuart Mill emphasized the importance of saving.[29] Thus, Mill instructively argues,

The word saving does not imply that what is saved is not consumed, or even necessarily that its consumption is deferred … To the vulgar, it is not at all apparent that what is saved is consumed. To them, every one who saves, appears in the light of a person who hoards: they may think such conduct permissible, or even laudable, when it is to provide for a family, and the like; but they have no conception of it as doing good to other people: saving is to them another word for keeping a thing to oneself; while spending appears to them to be distributing it among others.

(*Works*, 2: 70–1)

Rather than savings disappearing into some "black hole," as Keynes's typical treatment of saving suggests, Marshall also explains that savings are borrowed by some "to meet a pressing need, real or imaginary … Some to obtain machinery, and other 'intermediate' goods, with which they may make things to be sold at a profits; some to obtain hotels, theatres and other things which yield their services directly, but are yet a source of profit to those who control them" (1920: 482). Keynes (1936: 19) quotes a similar explanation of savings being spent from Alfred Marshall's *Pure Theory of Domestic Values* but fails to interpret it correctly. The quote is, in part,

But it is a familiar economic axiom that a man purchases labour and commodities with that portion of his income which he saves just as much as he does with that he is said to spend. He is said to spend when he seeks to obtain present enjoyment from the services and commodities which he purchases. He is said to save when he causes the labour and the commodities which he purchases to be devoted to the production of wealth from which he expects to derive the means of enjoyment in the future.

Instead, Keynes incorrectly laments that the role played by consumption in sustaining "aggregated demand" has been overlooked in macroeconomic analysis. The modern focus on elaborating aspects of Keynes's consumption function, including those of Milton Friedman and Franco Modigliani, without a hint of his incorrect treatment of savings as not being spent, has served macroeconomic analysis rather poorly.

Implications and conclusions

Keynes argues the necessity of increased government spending to bridge an increasing gap between consumption and a growing national income because of an increasing propensity to save as real income increases. Friedman's permanent income hypothesis, mostly derived from Keynes's own description of the consumption function, has now attained the common usage as explaining why government tax relief, unless perceived to be permanent, would not achieve its anticipated stimulus to consumption spending in order to cure a depressed aggregate demand and to revive an economy from a slump. Much, if not most, of the tax relief would be saved and thus would not stimulate aggregate demand, so goes the incorrect argument that also renders Keynes's policy conclusion moot. However, in the process of developing his argument, Friedman missed identifying Keynes's real analytical flaw, namely, that of treating savings as not being consumed or spent. Franco Modigliani's formulation of his life-cycle hypothesis of saving, without explicitly recognizing that financial assets accumulated out of savings provide the funds concurrently for investment spending, also has helped to divert attention from the correct treatment of savings.

The diversion also has inhibited most analysts' recognizing the fallacy of composition entailed in attempting to infer the behavior of aggregate consumption levels from the behavior of individuals. The diversion furthermore has inhibited our noting Keynes's error of attributing increased unemployment of labor to increased savings or to businesses or households' setting aside funds toward depreciation expenditures or "sinking funds." Thus, a review of some studies of the consumption function summarized in *Wikipedia* (November 2019) merely concludes: "The PIH (permanent income hypothesis) helps explain the failure of transitory Keynesian demand management techniques to achieve its policy targets"—this because of the marginal propensity to consume being less than one and only permanent changes in income entice significant changes in consumption spending.[30] *Wikipedia* further reports, "A comprehensive meta-analysis of 3000 tests of the permanent income hypothesis reported in 144 studies found that many rejections of the PIH are due to publication bias and that, after correction for publication bias, the PIH is consistent with data."

But were saving correctly understood as purchasing interest- and/or dividend-earning assets and thus providing the funds for borrowers to spend, a temporary tax relief's failure to stimulate aggregate demand would be explained differently—that is, not by income earners' matching their consumption spending only to their permanent income levels. Rather, the correct explanation would be that a tax relief financed by government's borrowing from the public to meet its deficit spending creates a 100 percent crowding out. Only financing of such deficit by borrowing from a central bank—increased quantity of (high-powered) money—or from savers abroad would increase the total domestic spending or "aggregate demand" anticipated from the tax relief.

Keynes's incorrect treatment of saving merely as non-consumption without connecting savings with the purchase of financial assets and his defining investment as only the purchase of capital goods has served modern macroeconomic analysis rather poorly. Milton Friedman's partial formulation of Keynes's description of the consumption function to derive his permanent income hypothesis has served mostly to divert many analysts into econometric tests of that hypothesis, overlooking the fact that savings (not cash hoarding) are consumed or spent.

Notes

1 In Chapter 23, Keynes refers to Adam Smith's views on interest rates and capital accumulation but does not link savings with consumption or spending by borrowers. Thus, he paraphrases Smith's proposition that "capitals are increased by parsimony [savings], that every frugal man is a public benefactor, and that the increase of wealth depends upon the balance of produce above consumption" and observes its being "true to a great extend [and] perfectly unquestionable" (1936: 363). But he adds, "it is quite obvious that [these propositions] are not true to an indefinite extent, and that the principles of saving, pushed to excess, would destroy the motive to production" (ibid.). Keynes here appears to be repeating Thomas Malthus's fears of too much saving being detrimental to economic growth that David Ricardo (*Works*, 2: 326, 449) explains to be incorrect; see also Ahiakpor (2019: 175–6). From the classical theory of interest rates, increased saving lowers equilibrium interest rates and motivates increased borrowing to spend.

2 Consumption here means not only eating but also "using up." Thus, *Webster's Dictionary* (1980: 242) gives the second meaning of "to consume" as "a: to spend wastefully: SQUANDER b: to use up" before "3: to eat or drink." John Stuart Mill also uses "consumption" in the sense of "using up": "if [saving] is employed as capital, it is all consumed: though not by the capitalist. Part is exchanged for tools or machinery, which are worn out by use; part for seed or materials, which are destroyed as such by being sown or wrought up, and destroyed altogether by the consumption of the ultimate product" (*Works*, 2: 70). In his *Treatise on Money*, Keynes uses "consumption" in the "using up" sense too: "technical methods change and different types of investment, even where they consume iron and steel, consume them in widely varying proportions" (1930, 2: 99).

3 Gottfried Haberler (1960) also questions the legitimacy Keynes's claiming a "simple and unique relationship" between individual marginal propensities to consume and the "marginal propensity to consume of *society as a whole*" (231; italics original).

4 The treatment of wealth in the consumption function also tends to vary among researchers. Some include durable goods as wealth separately from consumption while some appropriately recognize accumulated financial assets as the relevant wealth that could be employed to smoothen consumption over time. Modigliani and Brumberg (1954) include both durable goods and financial assets, which can be misleading.

5 See, for example, Costas Meghir (2004) and Greg Mankiw (2013: 484–7).
6 Friedman selects these statements from Keynes's *General Theory*, pp. 96 and 97. He does not address the mistaken output and employment implications Keynes draws from his consumption function in Chapter 8.
7 Friedman (1957: 6, n. 12) notes that he completed his study before encountering Modigliani and Brumberg's (1954) making arguments similar to his permanent income hypothesis, but which develop "its implications in a rather different direction." That direction is the now familiar life-cycle hypothesis of an individual's consumption and saving behavior.
8 See Gilboy's review of other studies critical of Keynes's formulation of the consumption function.
9 An equivalent argument by Modigliani and Brumberg (1954: 406) is that "a household whose current income unexpectedly rises above the previous 'accustomed' level … will save a proportion of its income larger than it was saving before the change and also larger than is presently saved by the permanent inhabitants of the income bracket into which the household now enters." Both Friedman's and Modigliani and Brumberg's statements mirror Keynes's explanation of consumption according to one's "habitual standard of life" (1936: 97).
10 *Wikipedia* (November 2019) includes a summary of these empirical studies of the permanent income hypothesis, including Robert Hall (1978), Marjorie Flavin (1981), Ben Bernanke (1984), Greg Mankiw and Matthew Shapiro (1985), Nicholas Souleles (1999), Melvin Stephens, Jr (2003), and Costas Meghir (2004).
11 Similarly, Modigliani and Brumberg (1954: 419) acknowledge: "information on the permanent component of income and the degree of adjustment to it is not available [and] it is impossible to locate a sample fulfilling exactly our specifications."
12 A temporary tax relief, mistakenly aimed at promoting consumption spending, may well be considered "transitory income." But there are other changes in business and farming incomes the extent of whose transitory nature may be hard for their recipients accurately to judge at the time of their receipt.
13 Appropriately disputing Keynesian concerns over "secular stagnation" because of increased savings, Friedman yet argues, "Acceptance of the permanent income hypothesis removes completely one of the pillars of the 'secular stagnation' thesis; there is no reason to expect the savings ratio to rise with a secular rise in real income" (1957: 236–7).
14 Gilboy (1938) bases part of her disputing Keynes's description of the consumption function on such purchases, arguing: "For non-farmers with incomes above $2,500, automobiles, furnishings, education, gifts, miscellaneous expenditures, recreation and travel usually have an elasticity as high as, or higher than savings" (137).
15 The consumption–income ratio is even greater than unity for Blacks in some cases.
16 From Kuznets's work, Friedman reports, "The ratio of aggregate consumption to aggregate income for the United State ($k\star$) has remained roughly constant for more than a century at about .88 for a definition of consumption that excludes expenditures on major consumer durable goods and includes their estimated use value" (1957: 228–9).
17 Keynes defines "net income" as "consumption *plus* net investment" (1936: 98). He nevertheless argues, "Save in exceptional circumstance … I doubt the practical importance of this factor" (1936: 92).
18 Specification of the consumption function to include the role of wealth, like Modigliani and Brumberg's (1954) and Friedman's (1957), appear to follow Keynes's argument here.
19 Friedman's consumption function includes the level of interest rates. Friedman's specification gives the impression of the rate of interest as the opportunity cost of present consumption, implying that a higher level of interest rates may induce greater savings. But Keynes (1936: 93) argues the opposite: Higher interest rates reduce the level of investment, income, and thus the level of savings—this because Keynes denies that interest is

a reward for saving (1936: 166–7), in contrast with Marshall's explaining that interest is the reward for abstinence or waiting (1920: 192–3, 487–8).

20 Keynes here contradicts his insistence that interest is not the reward for saving; see note 19 above.

21 Here is another self-contradiction by Keynes as he connects savings with providing the means to engage in business projects.

22 As explained in Chapter 2, Say's Law clarifies that the incidence of producing a commodity immediately opens a vent or a market for other produced goods and services, and that productions can only be purchased with or by productions. However, Keynes misrepresents Say's Law as having claimed that "supply creates its own demand" and that there are no obstacles to labor finding full employment; see Keynes (1936: 16–22, 25–6, 32–3).

23 This is the secular stagnation hypothesis Friedman (1957: 236–7) disputes as an implication of his permanent income hypothesis by arguing the constancy of aggregate permanent consumption to aggregate real permanent income.

24 By 1937, Keynes firmly declares that savings have nothing to do with making investment possible: "The investment market can become congested through the shortage of cash. It can never become congested through the shortage of saving. This is the most fundamental of my conclusions within this field" (1937c: 669).

25 Modigliani and Brumberg (1954: 406) also draw on this argument by Keynes in deriving their life-cycle hypothesis of saving behavior.

26 Keynes (1936: 29–31) also restates his paradox of thrift argument.

27 Marshall in a footnote (1920: 484, n. 2) goes on to explain the source of Eugene Böhm-Bawerk's confusion, leading to the latter's criticisms of the classical theory of interest. For a more elaborate discussion of Marshall's inheritance of the theory of interest on "capital" from the classics and Keynes's misinterpretation of that theory, see Ahiakpor (1990).

28 With reference to Smith's *Wealth of Nations*, Keynes acknowledges that Smith "was well aware that individual savings may be absorbed either by investment or by debts, and that there is no security that they will find an outlet in the former" (1936: 352).

29 Mill summarizes the classical position thus: "Saving, in short, enriches, and spending impoverishes, the community along with the individual; which is but saying in other words, that society at large is richer by what it expends in maintaining and aiding productive labour, but poorer by what it consumes in its enjoyments" (*Works*, 2: 72).

30 Some of the studies summarized in *Wikipedia* (2019) include those disputing the validity of Friedman's permanent income hypothesis. They include Marjorie Flavin (1981) and Melvin Stephens, Jr (2003).

6 The classical heritage of monetary theory and policy at Chicago and Harvard before the Keynesian conquest

Introduction[1]

Both the 1932 Harvard and Chicago recommendations for dealing with the Great Depression include vigorous open market purchases by the Fed, federal government deficit spending, including public works, financed by newly created money, reduction in tariffs, and the cancellation of inter-allied debts. The similarities are no coincidence because both documents draw mostly from well-known classical and early neoclassical monetary analysis and free-trade principles, and partially from Keynes's pre-1936 work. The classical principles are embodied in then familiar economics texts such as John Stuart Mill's *Principles of Economics*, Alfred and Mary Marshall's *The Economics of Industry*, Alfred Marshall's *Principles of Economics*, and Frank Taussig's *Principles of Economics*. However, such has been the influence of Keynes's *General Theory* with some analysts, it would appear, that they find considerable originality in the Harvard memorandum and its influence on the authors of the Chicago proposals. This chapter restates the classical principles underlying both antidepression proposals.

I illustrate the point with David Laidler and Roger Sandilands's (2002a) article. They argue that the 1932 antidepression memorandum, written by Lauchlin Currie, P.T. Ellsworth, and Harry D. White of the economics department at Harvard, deserves much more attention than it previously has been accorded. They base their contention on the fact that the Harvard document's contents are very similar to the recommendations contained in the 1932 Chicago Harris Foundation document, which Milton Friedman (1974) cites as evidence of a modern "Chicago tradition" in macro-monetary analysis. Rather than mainly the same classical tradition in monetary analysis that was commonplace by the early 1930s being the basis of the documents' similarities in terms of monetary policy, Laidler and Sandilands offer an account in which Lauchlin Currie appears to emerge as the principal formulator of specific solutions that most likely had been seen by John H. Williams, his 1931 doctoral dissertation supervisor and a participant at the Chicago conference:

The similarities between the two documents are so great that we find it hard to believe that they are coincidental. Moreover, there is a direct connection between these two documents, in the person of John H. Williams. He was beyond doubt familiar with Currie's earlier work, having supervised his thesis.

(2002a: 527)

Besides, they argue, Currie's dissertation contains a similar diagnosis of the monetary cause of the depression as well as the monetary solutions. This view of Currie's influence on John Williams is consistent with Laidler's (1993a) earlier description of Currie as a "creative ... thinker" (1071n) and of Williams as "a transmitter of ideas" (1078).

Further to support their view of Currie as having been the principal source of ideas that were carried to the Chicago conference by Williams, Laidler and Sandilands cite a 1992 remark by Currie, claiming, "I [Currie] probably had more influence on his [Williams's] thinking than he had on mine" (2002a: 520, n. 9); Laidler (1993a: 1091n) also quotes this remark by Currie. And, rather than noting that Currie and his co-authors mostly just applied the monetary analysis that was then current at the Harvard economics department, particularly as in the third edition of Frank Taussig's *Principles of Economics* (1921),[2] Laidler and Sandilands describe the quality of opinions held by some otherwise distinguished members of that department as mediocre: "There is ... no question that Harvard's reputation for mediocrity and policy pessimism in the early 1930s is well founded in fact" (2002a: 518; see also 521).

Laidler (1993a: 1077) applies the same description of "mediocrity" to the quality of opinion in the Harvard economics department during the early 1930s. He invites "Anyone who doubts this [designation] ... to peruse the 1934 commentaries on *The Economics of the Recovery Program* (Brown et al. 1934) prepared by members of the department, most of which verge on the incoherent and do no credit to their distinguished authors" (1077–8). But that assessment appears unwarranted. Rather than advancing solutions to the Great Depression, authors of the essays in that 1934 book were mainly evaluating arguments in support of the New Deal. Thus they note in the introduction, "It was no part of our plan to suggest measures of remedial policy. We do not see any force in the question: What remedies have you yourselves to offer? Analysis and criticism have their place quite independently of the existence or nature of alternative proposals" (1934: xii). Douglas Brown, for example, makes the point very well: "To the extent that the preceding discussion has been adversely critical of official policies of the last year, the quarrel is rather with the methods pursued than with the aims envisaged" (88)—this after having criticized proposals for work-sharing to minimize unemployment; having noted the displacement of funds for private investment by government borrowing; and after having employed the classical inverse wage–profit principle to warn that "An increase in the wages of the employed is secured at the expense of greater unemployment" (82).

Nevertheless, Laidler and Sandilands (2002a) explain the sweep of modern (post-1936) Keynesian ideas at Harvard mainly by the departure or easing out from the Harvard economics department Currie, Ellsworth, and White, who had taken "the more radical and intellectually coherent position" of the New Deal, and by the migration to Harvard of "a new crop of graduate students who had studied with [Keynes] at Cambridge" (522). But Currie (1972: 139, 141) himself claims that his "theoretical approach had been influenced by Keynes since [his] London School of Economics days in 1922–25, and at Harvard throughout the Depression [he] had bootlegged [Keynes's] heretical views on fiscal policy … [and] considered [himself] a Keynesian from way back," that is, before the publication of Keynes's *General Theory*. Laidler and Sandilands (2002a: 516) also note that Ellesworth "was … a very early (December 1936) but hitherto unrecognized discoverer of what came to be called the IS–LM model as a means of elucidating issues raised by Keynes's (1936) *General Theory*." However, Taussig (1936) and Wassily Leontief (1936) at Harvard gave quite favorable reviews of Keynes's *General Theory*, in contrast with the critical reviews of Henry Simons (1936), Jacob Viner (1936) and Frank Knight (1937) at Chicago. Joseph Schumpeter's (1936) review also was mostly negative except for his praising Keynes's liquidity (cash) preference theory of interest rates. And Harry Dexter White was disposed to collaborating with Keynes at the 1944 Bretton Woods conference. It thus would appear that the adoption of Keynesianism at Harvard might little have been impaired had the three Harvard memorandum authors remained there.

Laidler and Sandilands further claim that the 1929 premature death of Allyn Young, whom they designate as the leading monetary economist, "left a vacuum in the field of what we would now call macroeconomics among the senior ranks at Harvard that Joseph Schumpeter was soon to fill" (519). But, besides international trade theory, Frank Taussig also was internationally known as a monetary economist. For example, F.A. Hayek cites Taussig's monetary analysis in his 1928 and 1929 publications written in German, but not Young's; see Hayek ([1939] 1969: 254, and 1984 117, n. 26). Keynes (1930, 1: 186; 1936: 176) also lists Taussig among the leading exponents of the modern "classical" analysis.

Indeed, while not unanimously accepted by all the prominent economists at the time, including some of those who participated at the Chicago conference, a central bank's vigorous expansion of the quantity of money, if possible,[3] during a financial crisis accompanied by a falling level of prices was a well-known policy prescription by the 1920s. The recommendation follows a correct application of the classical Quantity Theory of money that embodies the forced-saving mechanism—the lagged adjustment of wage rates, interest rates, and rental rates behind changes in the price level—that produces the short-term effects on output and employment from variations in the quantity of money and credit.[4] Some of the neoclassicals couched that analysis under the rubric of "business cycles," hence Currie's (1934b: 4) subsequent declaration that "The logic of practically all monetary theories of the business cycle called for an energetic expansion of money in 1930–33." Indeed, Seymuor E. Harris, whose 1934 essay Laidler includes among the representatives of intellectual mediocrity at Harvard during the early 1930s, goes a step further in pointing out that "Open market operations are not the most effective method of dealing with the problem of bank failures" (104). Rather, "Direct advances either by the [Reconstruction Finance Corporation] or the reserve banks [to failing banks] are the only sensible method of coping with [the] problem," since cash released through open-market operations tend to go to "the stronger banks" while the weaker ones "continue to lose" deposits (105). He was not opposed to monetary action to deal with the bank failures experienced in the early 1930s.

In their introduction to the memorandum, the Harvard authors also note that, rather than pessimism about the possibility of ending the depression through policy action being the norm,

> A great number of economists ... believe with Dr. Persons that "the depression will not cure itself and requires prompt, intelligent, and vigorous action"; they believe that recovery can and should be hastened thru the adoption of proper measures. The recommendations recently made by Dr. Persons and signed by a number of eminent economists are a first step towards a vigorous grappling with the situation.
>
> (Laidler and Sandilands 2002b: 534)

Dr. Persons, a former member of the Harvard economics faculty, was familiar with the classical and early neoclassical monetary analyses of Adam Smith, David Ricardo, John Stuart Mill, Alfred Marshall, Irving Fisher, R.G. Hawtrey, A.C. Pigou, and D.H. Robertson, besides Taussig's; see Persons (1931, esp. Ch. 15, originally published in 1926). He regarded Marshall's *Principles of Economics* as "the leading treatise on economic theory of its time and remains the outstanding representative of the English classical school" (1931: 266). Chapter 4 of Person's book, *Forecasting Business Cycles*, contains his own views regarding actions needed from the Federal Reserve and other banks to promote economic recovery from the depression. They include urging "the adoption of liberal credit policies" by the Federal Reserve banks (55).

Thus, the Harvard authors saw their own contribution as being more specific and comprehensive than those of Dr. Persons. That is why their recommendation of a vigorous expansion of the quantity of Federal Reserve Bank money to deal with the depression was not such a "radical policy program" as Laidler and Sandilands (2002a: 516) claim, neither did it need to have been taken to the Chicago conference by John Williams to be adopted. It is also noteworthy that Jacob Viner and John Williams both wrote their doctoral dissertations under the supervision of Frank Taussig at Harvard. Taussig also supervised the dissertations of P.T. Ellsworth and H.D. White, co-authors of the Harvard document with Currie. Indeed, Currie's subsequent publications contain references to both the classical and some of these early neoclassical authors, including to Taussig's text.[5]

The use of budget deficits financed by money creation by a central bank as a means of sustaining the level of prices and to deal with fluctuations in unemployment also had been argued prominently by R.G. Hawtrey and A.C. Pigou, and was common knowledge by the early1930s; see comments to that effect by William Leiserson, Harold Moulton, and Jacob Viner, quoted in J. Ronnie Davis (1971: 16–18). Also, the dangers to economic prosperity created by protective tariffs had long been argued by Adam Smith and had been pretty much accepted by most trained economists. Finally, Keynes's (1919) arguments for dealing with international indebtedness and war reparations were common knowledge by the time of both the Harvard and Chicago documents' writing. Thus, besides some specifics in the Harvard document, there was little that was new or could be classified as "an original and provocative element in ... macroeconomic thought" (Laidler and Sandilands 2002a: 516) that "Currie did not develop ... in isolation" (521), and that was conveyed by John Williams to the January 1932 Chicago conference.

Milton Friedman had the occasion to point to the common theoretical heritage of the Harvard and Chicago documents, but did not. He appears not to have been much keen on the history of monetary thought.[6] In his reaction to the Laidler and Sandilands piece, Friedman notes, "I have no doubt, as you suggest in your introductory comments, that more than coincidence explains the similarity of the views expressed by the Harvard trio and the recommendations coming out of the Harris conference" (quoted in Laidler and Sandilands 2002a: 518n). This chapter aims to fill the gap Friedman left in not having pointed out the common theoretical heritage of the two documents. I subtitled an earlier version of my original paper "An Alternative Explanation." A referee for the *History of Political Economy* objected to it, arguing:

> The [Laidler and Sandilands] argument to which this essay is put forward as an "alternative explanation" appears to be an exceptionally weak one, that focuses on the presence of a particular individual, John Williams. Like many, I have understood that the Chicago and Harvard recommendations both drew upon the classical tradition that Ahiakpor outlines ... What do we gain from the pretence of making an "alternative explanation"? Precious little.

The referee thought I must have a "hidden agenda" behind my essay, namely, drawing attention to my work on Keynes's economics. Would that Laidler and Sandilands had presented the Harvard document as representing a shared theoretical tradition with the Chicago document; see also note 9.

The Quantity Theory and antidepression policy in early neoclassical analysis

Alfred and Mary Marshall's (1879) *The Economics of Industry* well restates the classical Quantity Theory of money, the forced-saving mechanism explaining the short-run output and employment fluctuations that result from changes in the quantity of money and credit, and the need for taking confidence-restoring measures to deal with a financial crisis. They employ that analytical framework to explain the commercial crisis of 1857 as having arisen from a significant contraction of credit even as the quantity of money (cash) continued to increase: "many trading firms were unable to pay their debts, credit was violently contracted, and prices fell, although the store of precious metals [money] in the country was growing as rapidly as ever" (1879: 151–2). They point out,

> The chief cause of the evil [commercial disorganization and the accompanying increased unemployment] is a want of confidence. The greater part of it could be removed almost in an instant if confidence could return, touch all industries with her magic wand, and make them continue their production and their demand for the wares of others.
>
> (155)

Alfred Marshall repeats the argument in the *Principles* (1920: 591–2). The Harvard document also refers to the problem of shaken confidence at the start of the depression: "With confidence as badly shaken as it is at present, and with prices continuing to fall, there is little in the current outlook to make it attractive for business men to borrow in amounts sufficient to stimulate recovery" (2002b: 540). Also, they argue, "Hoarding took place [in 1931], but it was the hoarding of paper money, not gold, and indicated a *loss of confidence* in the banks, not in Government" (543; italics added).

The Marshalls (1879: 156–7) also point to the lagged adjustment of wages behind product prices—the forced-saving mechanism—as a principal factor amplifying economic fluctuations, thus requiring monetary measures to stabilize the price level. Marshall's (1920) *Principles*, which also served as an economics textbook in many universities around the world before the 1930s, restates the above explanations; see especially pages 493–4 and 515. Taussig (1921) provides detailed restatements of classical and early neoclassical monetary analysis and antidepression policies in the two-volume *Principles of Economics* (first published in 1911). The book makes references to works by Adam Smith, David Ricardo, John Stuart Mill, Alfred Marshall, Irving Fisher, R.G. Hawtrey, John Maynard Keynes, and A.C. Pigou. Taussig considers Fisher's (1911) treatment of money and prices as "excellent, at once conservative and constructive," and Hawtrey's (1919) as "able, discriminating, and in several respects novel, but somewhat clumsily written" (Taussig 1921: 442). Drawing on insights from John Stuart Mill and Adam Smith, Taussig (ibid. 237, 244–6) discusses the Quantity Theory of money in volume 1, Chapter 18.

In Chapter 22, especially sections 5 and 6, Taussig explains the lagged adjustment of wages behind changes in the level of prices following changes in the quantity of money that accounts for increases in output and employment when prices are rising and decreases in output and employment when prices are falling—the forced-saving mechanism:

That wages go up more slowly than prices is one of the best-attested facts in economic history … To the extent that prices of commodities advance faster than expenses for the labor [employers] buy, the payers of wages gain … Conversely, the business class as a whole commonly loses in periods of falling prices. Then, since the same forces tend to keep wages stable, a fall in prices brings loss.

(Taussig 1921: 298, 299)

The 1932 Harvard document also argues that "with prices continuing to fall … a policy of waiting for [recovery on its own] involves us in a continuation of the present unemployment and business losses for an indeterminate period" (Laidler and Sandilands 2002b: 540). On the basis of Taussig's above discussion, Hayek (1935: 25n) lists Taussig's text among exponents of the classical forced-saving doctrine in the US, besides Frank Knight, D. Friday, and A.H. Hansen. Robertson (1926: 52) also refers to Taussig's text in his own discussion of forced saving, attesting to the book's international reputation.

In chapter 28, titled "Crises," Taussig (1921) employs the classical quantity theory framework to discuss business cycles as well as the failure of some major financial institutions in the US between 1857 and 1907. Regarding the role of a central bank to deal with a financial crisis, Taussig in chapter 29 writes:

The central public bank has a conscious duty toward the public, and, rightly conducted, is prepared for the performance of its duty in times of stress. By providing cash from its own ample holdings; by making loans itself, not least by bolstering up the other banks so that each of them is encouraged to take care of its own customers—the great central bank can certainly mitigate a panic, and can probably prevent the stage of general collapse from being reached. The Bank of England has learned by long and hard experience, but has thoroly [*sic*] learned, that free offering of accommodation of all sorts is the way to meet a panic … Such is the policy which the banks of the United States should adopt—boldness and liberality.

(Taussig 1921: 403)

Further, to emphasize the need for increasing the quantity of money (currency) during a commercial crisis as a means of restoring business and public confidence, Taussig explains:

The generic feature of an acute crisis, whether in the mercantile community or as regards the banks, is loss of confidence … The scarcity of cash and the high rates of discount are a result and a symptom, not a cause. The *remedy* must be one that will *restore confidence*. Only so far as an increase in the supply of cash does this is it a remedy. More effective than anything else is a bold and liberal policy by the banks: free offering of loans and free offering of cash to all who want it.

(1921: 410; italics added)

Taussig appears to have drawn upon that insight during the Great Depression to support "careful and discriminating federal expenditure on public works" as a means of releasing more cash to stimulate spending and halt the declining level of prices (Davis 1971: 19).

Similar monetary analyses and antirecession or antidepression policy prescriptions as those of the Marshalls and Taussig are contained in other well-known pre-1930s works, such as those of Irving Fisher (1913 and 1926), R.G. Hawtrey (1913 and 1919), and A.C. Pigou (1912, 1913, and 1927). Analysts familiar with these sources could draw upon them to discuss the specifics of the Great Depression, which appears to have been the case with the drafting of both the 1932 Harvard and Chicago recommendations.

Indeed, presentations by some of the participants at the Chicago conference, especially Jacob Viner, Gottfried Haberler, H. Parker Willis, and Lionel Eddie, both for and against expansionary monetary policy during the Great Depression, refer to the classical principles. In objecting to the recommendation of monetary expansion to stabilize the level of prices as a cure for the depression, Haberler made the "Austrian" argument that the general price level is "frequently a misleading guide to monetary policy and that its stability is no sufficient safeguard against crises and depressions" (1932: 53)—this after giving a good account of the classical forced-saving analysis, but without naming it, and acknowledging the work of "Professor Cassel, R.G. Hawtrey, and Irving Fisher" as the exponents of this "traditional monetary theory" (50). Willis followed his recounting the forced-saving analysis and noted it is "a view of the matter which has become quite general" (1932: 103), but rejected the monetary stimulus solution to the depression. He believed that advocates of that analysis had "only the most slender of statistical or other support and that the data put forward in [the doctrine's] behalf are of a wholly unconvincing character" (103–4). He feared the "Prospect that this new [central bank] credit will do harm rather than good by being used where it is not needed" (106).

On the other hand, Viner, after recounting the history of the gold standard's operation and acknowledging his "respect for traditional doctrines and ancient institutions" (1932: 38), drew upon Fisher's recommendation of price-level stability as the proper goal of monetary policy. Thus, he called for "co-operation by the federal government and the Federal Reserve System in formulating objectives, making them known to the public, and making unquestionable their determination to carry out all the steps—expansionary at this time, contractionist at other times, when circumstances are different—necessary to attain those objectives" (ibid.). Edie also put the blame for the depression partly on domestic hoarding of cash, resulting in "an excess contraction of credit" (1932: 127). Noting that the Federal Reserve Act at the time did not permit the kind of monetary expansion required to deal with the situation, he recommended changes, including the purchasing of government bonds in order to inflate the currency. He chided those "friends of the [gold] standard in official and private circles who are advocating liquidation and deflation to the bitter end [as] the real forces tending to undermine the standard" (128).

In oral discussions at the 1932 Chicago conference, Irving Fisher employed the lagged adjustment of wages behind prices—the forced-saving mechanism—to argue for increases in the quantity of money to restore the level of prices. Otherwise, he explained, there would continue a vicious circle of deflation and unemployment:

> You have the discharge of employees and increase of unemployment, and as a consequence of the bankruptcies and the unemployment and the losses there comes, of course, psychologically a state of pessimism and distress, a lack of confidence, and that starts up another vicious circle, one of the consequences of which is hoarding, first in the banks, because the distress leads to getting rid of risky securities and substituting cash, which is one thing people in fear of bankruptcy want.
>
> (Fisher, quoted in Davis 1971: 126)

Harold Moulton of the Brookings Institution, along with Viner, also argued vigorously for the use of public works as the more immediate means of injecting new money (currency) into the economy than any other means Fisher had proposed at the conference (Davis 1971, 127–9).

The above arguments largely explain the expansionary monetary policy aspects of the Chicago recommendations to President Hebert Hoover, including (1) that the Fed "systematically pursue open-market operations with the double aim of facilitating necessary government financing and increasing the liquidity of the banking structure," (2) that "the Reconstruction Finance Corporation vigorously and courageously ... give aid to banks by making loans on assets not eligible for rediscount with the Federal Reserve banks," and (3) that "the federal government maintain its program of public works and public services at a level not lower than that of 1930–31" (Wright 1932: 162).

The same principle—the lagged adjustment of costs to product prices in the short run—was a basis for another 1932 memorandum signed by 12 Chicago economists recommending activist government deficit spending as a cure for the depression.[7] The memorandum argues that such spending would bring about a quicker recovery "by injecting enough new purchasing power so that much larger production will be profitable at existing costs" (Davis 1971: 26). Reliance on the economy's automatic adjustment process, they feared, would involve "tremendous losses, in wastage of productive capacity, and in acute suffering" (1971: 25). Thus, Robert Dimand's (1990: 46) view that "While many American economists supported increased public works in the early 1930s, they did so without having a theory on which to base their support" is incorrect.[8] Of course, in arriving at this judgment, Dimand considers reliance on the Keynesian multiplier analysis as the only relevant theory upon which to advocate public works as a cure for depressions.[9]

With the exception of Paul Douglas, all of the signatories to that other document also participated in a 1931 Harris Foundation Round Table in Chicago at which antidepression policies, including the use of public works as the most immediate means of releasing new money (cash) into the economy, were discussed. There, both Lloyd Mints and Henry Schultz recommended the use of public works over interest rate reductions or wage cuts as a means of quickly dealing with the depression; see Davis (1971: 108, 121–22). Thus, the familiarity of classical monetary analysis, including the forced-saving mechanism, was not in question by the early 1930s.[10] It was rather a matter of whether a policy advocate accepted its logic enough to adopt the policy implications—contract the quantity of money when the price level is rising and expand the quantity when the price level is falling.

In the following section, I summarize the classical quantity theory analysis and the accompanying antidepression policy from which the neoclassical analysis derives, beginning with David Hume's, although few of the neoclassical writers, including Marshall and Marshall, Fisher, and Taussig, mentioned Hume's work. The neoclassicals tended to reference John Stuart Mill and David Ricardo, who drew upon Hume's monetary analysis. A referee thinks that the section might "even [be] deleted altogether without much loss" because

> the importance of prior quantity theoretic influences in both Chicago and Harvard by the early 1930s of which Ahiakpor makes so much has not been in question for a long time. Incidentally, that such work itself derived from a body of literature going back to Hume is well known to all historians of monetary thought, and hence to readers of *HOPE* who have a particular interest in this topic.

Would that two earlier referees, particularly the one cited in note 9, were so convinced. It is also noteworthy that neither Laidler and Sandilands (2002a) nor Laidler (1993a) refers to the monetary analyses of David Hume, Henry Thornton, David Ricardo, and John Sturat Mill, very much relevant to their discussions.

The classical Quantity Theory of money and antidepression policy

A monetary antidepression policy can be inferred from David Hume's 1752 statement of the quantity theory in the essay "Of Money." Hume explains that variations in the excess demand or supply of money cause less than proportional variations in the level of prices in the short run, and hence variations in output and employment. While the level of prices, output, and employment rise from an excess supply of money (specie or currency), they fall from an excess demand for money:

> Alterations in the quantity of money, either on one side or the other, are not immediately attended with proportionable alterations in the price of commodities. There is always an interval before matters be adjusted to their new situation; and this interval is pernicious to industry, when gold

and silver [money] are diminishing, as it is advantageous when these metals are increasing.

(Hume 1752: 40)

Hume does not clearly specify the mechanism that produces the short-run output and employment variations in the same direction as money and prices, but it can be recognized as the delayed adjustment of nominal wages rates, interest rates, and rental rates to changes in the level of prices that follow changes in the quantity of money—the forced-saving mechanism.[11]

Thus, a nation "whose money decreases [becomes] weaker and more miserable than another nation, which possesses no more money, but is on the increasing side" (Hume 1752: 40). An insufficient quantity of money creates the condition in which "The workman has not the same employment from the manufacturer and merchant; though he pays the same price for everything in the market. The farmer cannot dispose of his corn and cattle; though he must pay the same rent to his landlord. The poverty, and beggary, and sloth, which must ensue, are easily foreseen" (ibid.). Until nominal wage rates, interest rates, and rental rates decrease to restore profitability to manufacturing and agricultural production, or the quantity of money increases to restore the level of prices, there must be economic contraction. Thus, to avoid the pernicious consequences of an excess demand for money or money's inadequate supply, Hume recommends an increasing quantity of money in a growing economy: "The good policy of the magistrate consists only in keeping [the quantity of money], if possible, ... encreasing: because by that means, he keeps alive a spirit of industry in the nation, and encreases the stock of labour, in which consists all real power and riches" (39–40).

Hume's analysis above provides the basic framework for a remedial policy formulation in case of a commercial crisis of the type experienced during the Great Depression. It can be seen in works by such subsequent classical writers as Henry Thornton, David Ricardo, and John Stuart Mill. Thus, employing Hume's quantity theory framework to discuss a 1795 commercial crisis, Thornton argues:

> That ... a reduction of the quantity of paper [money] causes a fall in the price of goods, is scarcely necessary to be proved ... I understand, that at the time of the great failure of paper credit in 1795, the price of corn fell, in a few places, no less than twenty or thirty per cent. The fall arose from the necessity of selling corn under which some farmers were placed, in order to carry on their payments. Much of the circulating medium being withdrawn, the demand for it was in those places far greater than the supply; and the few persons, therefore, who were in possession of cash, or of what would pass as cash, having command of the market, obliged the farmers to sell at a price thus greatly reduced. It was a *new and sudden scarcity of cash*, not any new plenty of corn, which caused the price of corn to drop.

(1802: 196; italics added)

Thornton (1802: 197n) similarly discusses a hypothetical crisis of public confidence:

> In the event of any great public alarm, such, for instance, as that which might be occasioned by the landing in this county of any considerable body of enemies, it is likely that the price of Bank of England notes, compared with that of stocks, or other articles for which there is a ready market, would ... rise [i.e. the level of commodity prices falls], even though the quantity of paper should continue the same: this would happen in consequence of that encreased demand for bank notes, to which it has been repeatedly observed that a state of consternation always gives occasion. Many bankers, at such a time, would feel a doubt whether they might not be drawn upon more largely than usual by some of their more timid customers; and whether, also, they might not be subjected to more than common difficulty in selling government securities, an article which, in ordinary times, they are used to turn into cash on the shortest notice.

For the remedy, Thornton argues: "Some encrease of the bank issues seems very justifiable at such a time; such an encrease, I mean, as should be sufficient only to prevent what may be termed an unnatural rise in the value of bank notes" (197 n). In the case of the US, the quantity of paper money did not merely "continue the same," but the Federal Reserve actually increased it by about 25%, from 4 to 5 billion dollars, between 1930 and 1933 (Fisher 1935: 5). Of course, the increment was not nearly enough to counter the 8-billion-dollar contraction in demand deposits and prevent the level of M1 (total means of payment) from falling.

In his *Principles*, David Ricardo notes the contraction in spending that results when a financial panic of the sort experienced during the Great Depression afflicts an economy, creating an almost insatiable demand for money (cash) unless its quantity quickly were increased. His argument deserves an extensive quotation:

> On those extraordinary occasions, when a general panic seizes the country, and when every one is desirous of possessing the precious metals [modern high-powered money] as the most convenient mode of realizing or concealing his property ... Banks have no security, *on any system*; from their very nature they are subject to them, as at no time can there be in a [central] Bank, or in a country, so much specie or bullion as the monied individuals of such country have a right to demand. Should every man withdraw his balance from his banker on the same day, many times the quantity of Bank notes now in circulation would be insufficient to answer such a demand. A panic of this kind was the cause of the crisis in 1797; and not, as has been supposed, the large advances which the Bank [of England] had then made to Government ... it was the contagion of the unfounded fears of the timid part of the community, which occasioned the run on

the Bank, and it would equally have taken place if they had not made any advances to Government, and had possessed twice their present capital. If the Bank had continued paying in cash, probably the panic would have subsided before their coin had been exhausted.

(Ricardo *Works*, 1: 358–9; italics original)

In the absence of an adequate means of payment, the level of prices would fall, creating a decline in production and increased unemployment until nominal wages sufficiently decline. As Thomas Malthus also wrote to Ricardo: "We know from repeated experience that the money price of labour never falls till many workmen have been for some time out of work" (quoted in Ricardo *Works*, 9: 20). Ricardo includes such unemployment among the "evil consequences which might ensue from a sudden and great reduction of the circulation" (*Works*, 1: 359).

John Stuart Mill also describes the effect of shaken confidence or a commercial crisis on the demand for money (specie or currency) that causes price-level deflation and economic dislocation:

[At such times] no one likes to part with ready money, or to postpone his claim to it. To these rational considerations there is superadded, in extreme cases, a panic ... money is borrowed for short periods at almost any rate of interest, and sales of goods for immediate payment are made at almost any sacrifice. Thus general prices, during a commercial revulsion, fall as much below the usual level, as during the previous period of speculation they have risen above it: the fall, as well as the rise, originating *not in anything affecting* [the quantity of] *money*, but in the state of credit; an unusually extended employment of credit during the earlier [boom] period, followed by a great diminution, never amounting however to an entire cessation of it, in the later.

(*Works*, 3: 542–3; italics added)

Mill further reiterates the point, very much relevant to conditions during the Great Depression:

At such times there is really an excess of all commodities above the money demand: in other words, there is an *under-supply of money*. From the sudden annihilation of a great mass of credit, every one dislikes to part with ready money, and many are anxious to procure it at any sacrifice. Almost everybody therefore is a seller, and there are scarcely any buyers: so that there may really be, though only while the crisis lasts, an extreme depression of general prices, from what may be indiscriminately called a glut of commodities or a dearth of money. But it is a great error to suppose ... that a commercial crisis is the effect of a general excess of production ... its immediate cause is a contraction of credit, and the *remedy* is, not a diminution of supply, but the *restoration of confidence*.

(*Works*, 3: 574; italics added)[12]

To prevent the harmful consequences of the falling level of prices, Mill reiterates the need for an increased quantity of money: "An increase of the circulating medium, conformable in extent and duration to the temporary stress of business, does not raise prices, but merely prevents this fall" (*Works*, 3: 516). Mill's argument is similar to Thornton's (1802: 197n) cited above and to Keynes's cited by the Harvard authors: "To bring up the bogy of Inflation as an objection to capital expenditures at the present is like warning a patient who is wasting away from emaciation of the dangers of excessive corpulation" (Laidler and Sandilands 2002b: 538).

It appears to be quite clear that there were ample and common sources from which drafters of both the Chicago and Harvard antidepression recommendations could draw their guidelines. The specifics of the Harvard recommendations may have been more detailed than those of the Chicago recommendations. But John Williams's participation at the Chicago conference, including the drafting of its recommendations, does not appear to have been a crucial determining factor for the similarities between that document and the Harvard recommendations.

Other similarities between the Harvard and Chicago recommendations

Both the Harvard and Chicago documents recommended a reduction in tariffs by the US as well as inter-allied indebtedness and war reparations as a means of promoting greater international trade and the easing of debt burden among countries. According to the Harvard authors, "Heightened tariff barriers, by rendering more difficult the adjustments of international accounts, have magnified the problem of debt settlements, both private and public" (Laidler and Sandilands 2002b: 546). And since the US had been "in the forefront in building up of tariff walls[,] it is only fitting that she take the lead in the downward revision so necessary to a return to economic sanity" (546), they argue. The memorandum also endorses "that portion of the tariff bill ([then] before Congress) calling for the creation of a commission to confer with European governments with the express intent of securing the scaling down of tariff schedules" (547). On reparations and inter-allied debts, the Harvard authors argue that "Reparations are the chief obstacle to European prosperity" which was crucial to an easier "business recovery in the United States" (548). Thus, the document declares that "the quickest, most equitable, and most effective way to settle the problem of reparations is thru a complete cancellation of interallied debts and reparations" (549).

In his presentation at the Chicago conference, Viner (1932: 21) also pointed to the American tariff, subsidies to American shipping, and "the increasing payments to this country on account of the inter-Allied debts" among the obstacles to the proper functioning of the gold standard and a hindrance to America's recovery from the depression. Thus, he suggested the "reduction or cancellation of reparations and inter-Allied debts … An increase in the volume and elasticity of international trade resulting from a progressive reduction of tariff and other barriers to commerce" (31–2) among the remedies. It thus should not be surprising that the Chicago recommendations include "the reduction or cancellation of the intergovernmental debts as an essential step toward recovery or world industry and trade" and "that the Government enter into negotiations with other countries, leading toward a reciprocal and substantial lowering of tariffs and other barriers to world trade" (162).

The criticisms of US protective tariffs and recommendations for removing them in both documents follow familiar Hume-Smith-Ricardo free-trade arguments, also restated in Taussig (1921), Ch. 36. The views on inter-allied debts and reparations in both documents follow closely those in chapter 7 of Keynes's famous 1919 book, *The Economic Consequences of the Peace*. Allyn Young's (1927, Ch. 2) book also may have had a similar influence on both the Harvard and Chicago recommendations. Once again, common theoretical roots would appear to account for the similarities in the recommendations of the Harvard and Chicago documents rather than a borrowing from the former by the latter through John Williamson's participation, important though his participation at that conference may have been.

Summary and conclusions

Laidler and Sandilands have sought to highlight the contributions of Lauchlin Currie to macroeconomic policy analysis in the US. In so doing, they appear to have overlooked the classical and early neoclassical sources from which Currie and his co-authors drew their insights, especially John Stuart Mill's *Principles*, Alfred Marshall's *Principles*, Irving Fisher's *The Purchasing Power of Money*, and Frank Taussig's *Principles* that were in common usage as textbooks in economics in the 1920s. Thus, they find the similarities between the Harvard and Chicago recommendations of activist monetary policy to deal with the Great Depression a curiosity. They seek to account for the similarities by the participation of John Williams, Currie's doctoral thesis advisor, at the January 1932 Chicago conference, an explanation that Milton Friedman failed to dispute. But, as explained above, the influence that Laidler and Sandilands attribute to the Harvard document over the formulation of the Chicago recommendations because of John Williams's participation at that conference appears to have been overdrawn.

Indeed, Currie's subsequent work on macroeconomic policy after leaving Harvard deviates from classical monetary analysis; see, for example, Byrd Jones (1978) and Currie (1978). It relies more on fiscal stimulus, albeit supported by monetary accommodation, regardless of the direction of the level of prices, to promote economic activity—"pump priming." Such deviation very much follows John Maynard Keynes's abandonment of his original reliance, however uneasily (see Keynes 1939, esp. xxxiv), on the classical quantity theory framework for policy formulation after 1936. Thus, the conquest of Keynesian macroeconomics at Harvard after 1936 could hardly have been due to the departure of Currie or any of his other memorandum co-authors from that economics department, as Laidler and Sandilands suggest: "The Harvard memorandum may be read, then, as giving some indication of the character and quality of an alternative intellectual tradition that might have developed at Harvard in the 1930s, had the department's promotion and tenure policies been different" and the "authors of the memorandum [who] took the more radical and intellectually coherent position [the New Deal] epitomizes" had stayed (2002a: 522).

Laidler and Sandilands's designation of the quality of academic opinion at Harvard in the early 1930s as mediocre, on the basis of the 1934 publication by some members of that department, as compared with the views of Currie, Ellsworth, and White, also appears unwarranted. Besides Joseph Schumpeter,[13] who found no grounds for monetary expansion to halt the declining level of prices during the depression, none of the other contributors to that volume opposed an activist role for the Federal Reserve System at the time. Their contributions were mainly to point out contradictory or theoretically unsound propositions underlying aspects of the New Deal.

Thus, for example, Edward Chamberlin questions the meaningfulness of the Industrial Recovery Act's declaration to have Congress "increase the consumption of industrial and agricultural products by increasing purchasing power" (1934: 22), without relating such to economic "recovery itself" (25). He also explains the error of emphasizing consumption spending as a cure for the depression as if savings were equivalent to cash hoarding (29–31), an analytical confusion that continues to plague modern macroeconomic analysis because of Keynes's changed meaning of saving.[14] Edward Mason criticizes the goal of "increased purchasing power" in the Recovery Act to mean "an increase in wage costs" (1934: 38). He also criticizes aspects of the National Recovery Act, noting, "The provisions for limitation of output and the raising of prices, if effective, can result only in the further curtailment of our already seriously reduced national income" (62). Douglas Brown criticizes efforts at helping labor, arguing that "improvement in the conditions of employment may be secured only at the expense of an increase in the numbers unemployed" (1934: 65). Furthermore, "An increase in the wages of the employed is secured at the expense of greater unemployment" unless labor were being exploited previously or the higher wages were to be counted on to remedy inefficient management (82). He also employs extensively the principle of crowding-out to caution against the displacement of private sector investment as well as funds for state and county expenditures by the massive federal government spending envisaged under the New Deal (66, 76–7).

Seymour Harris notes the stimulative effect of rising prices on profits— through the forced-saving mechanism—but warns that efforts to raise labor and material costs under the National Recovery Act will "nullify the effects of increased spending by the public as a stimulus to business activity" (1934: 96). Thus, "if the temper of the administration and of labor precludes any reduction in real wages (that is, makes it necessary to raise money wages along with

prices), higher prices may be ineffective" in increasing employment and production (97).[15] Harris also was quite optimistic about government programs,
when properly designed, to promote economic recovery: "The whole process
is one in which the responsibility of the Government becomes one of spending
more and inducing more employment as the business situation becomes worse.
It is a race between the diminution of private expenditure and the increase of
effective public expenditure" (114; italics original).

Wassilly Leontief points out the conflict between the goals of industrial policy under the National Recovery Act and some actions under the Agricultural
Allotment Plan, including the bounties and subsidies aimed at raising farmers'
incomes (1934: 154). He notes that "the [planned] curtailment of the agricultural output automatically reduces the size of the total national income and this
reduction evidently imposes an additional burden on the industrial population without diminishing by the same amount the suffering of the farmers"
(156). He also questions the meaningfulness and desirability of the goal of the
Agricultural Adjustment Act to reestablish economic "parity" between industry and agriculture (156–9).

Overton Taylor well summarizes the economic content of his Harvard colleagues' evaluations of the New Deal, while urging economists to take into
account the political dimensions of policymaking: "the criticisms have been
based upon the economic realism which insists that policies aiming to promote
recovery will, in fact, retard recovery if and where they fail to take account
correctly of stubborn facts in the existing economic situation and of the arith-
metic of business as it must be carried on in the economic system we are trying
to revive" (1934: 160). In defense of his appeal to economists for some com-
promise, he argues: "Complete or prefect adaptation of policy to economic
facts alone is never possible, because the conflict of human interests, ideals and
wills, which is politics, forever makes this impossible" (165). It is thus hard to
see how the criticisms of aspects of the New Deal proposals by some members
of the Harvard faculty justify their designation as mediocre by Laidler and
Sandilands.

Laidler and Sandilands (2002a: 517) also cite the Harvard memorandum as
a counter to any claims of "a unique 'Chicago tradition' in monetary analysis"
during the 1930s: "The first mention of this Chicago tradition seems to have
been by Milton Friedman (1956), and its nature and claim to uniqueness were
subsequently discussed by, among others, Don Patinkin (1969, 1973), Thomas
Humphrey (1971), and Friedman (1974)" (517n). Now Friedman (1956: 3;
italics added) himself writes, "Chicago was *one of the few* academic centers at
which the quantity theory continued to be a central and vigorous part of an
oral tradition throughout the 1930's and 1940's," an observation he buttresses
with listing "Henry Simons and Lloyd Mints directly, Frank Knight and Jacob
Viner at one remove," among those who taught the quantity theory tradition
at Chicago.

Patinkin (1973: 457) indeed writes as if Friedman had claimed that "the
Chicago school of that time [could] be represented as an isolated center of

monetary studies and of belief in the importance of money," or "in some important respects [Chicago] behaved as if it were," and George Tavlas (1998) also actually claims uniqueness to the quantity theory tradition at Chicago. But Patinkin is there complaining about the failure of some members of the Chicago school to "refer in either their writings or their lectures … to the work of their contemporaries." Tavlas (1998: 216) uses a dispute over the mechanics of increasing the quantity of money at the 1932 Chicago conference between Irving Fisher, on the one hand, and Harold Moulton and Jacob Viner, on the other, as illustrating the distinctiveness of the Chicago approach. None of these constitutes a claim of uniqueness of Chicago in employing the Quantity Theory of money. It would thus appear unnecessary to argue against Friedman's observation by citing the Harvard document as proof of the existence of monetary analysis elsewhere since Friedman did not claim uniqueness to the quantity theory tradition at Chicago. Perhaps, it is worth noting Laidler's (1993a: 1099) own argument that "Friedman is surely right also in claiming that, *after* 1936, Chicago was unique among major centers in preserving and developing further the analytic tradition … deriving from the quantity theory" (italics original).

The Harvard memorandum is indeed an impressive testament to how much classical and early neoclassical monetary analysis its young Ph.D. authors learned at Harvard. At the same time, its authors' subsequent embrace of the New Deal and "Keynesian fiscalism" may be said to reflect the limited depth to which they ascribed to the classical principles. That monetarism developed from Humean monetary analysis at Chicago (see Mayer 1980) while Harvard became dominated by Keynesian anti-classical monetary principles is thus perhaps the more remarkable puzzle, rather than the similarities between the 1932 Harvard and Chicago recommendations.

Notes

1 This chapter draws heavily on my 2010 article, "On the Similarities between the 1932 Harvard Memorandum and the Chicago Antidepression Recommendations," in the *History of Political Economy* 42, No. 3 (Fall): 547–71.
2 Laidler and Sandilands (2010: 580) subsequently note, "Laidler (1999, pt. 3) was surely remiss in ignoring [Taussig] in his discussion of macroeconomic thought in the interwar United States."
3 Adherence to the gold standard was known to limit the ability of a central bank to respond adequately to an increased demand for money in a banking or financial crisis. That is why central banks typically suspended currency redemption into gold in order to deal with such crises (Jacob Viner 1932).
4 Apparently, owing to Keynes's influence, some modern analysts tend to separate the lagged wage adjustment behind product prices from the classical forced-saving doctrine, e.g. Humphrey (1982a), Hansson (1987), and Laidler (1991; 1993a; and 1999). Also, see Hayek (1933: 218–19n) for some identifications of the equivalence.
5 See Currie (1933 and 1934a). Furthermore, Currie (1934b: 12) considers "Mill's chapter on credit in his *Principles* still the most exhaustive treatment of the whole topic"; he quotes from Marshall's *Money, Credit and Commerce* (1923) the argument that "with every expansion and contraction of credit prices rise and fall" (47); and

refs to Pigou's 1927 text in prescribing management of bank credit to stabilize the price level (47).

6 Friedman would have had a much different stance on Keynes's macro-monetary analysis otherwise, including his claiming, "Keynes's discussion of the demand curve for money in the *General Theory* is for the most part a continuation of earlier quantity theory approaches, improved and refined but not modified" (1970a: 168); see also Friedman (1967, 1968b, 1997) and Chapter 9 below.

7 The signatories include Garfield V. Cox, Aaron Director, Paul H. Douglas, Harry D. Gideonse, Frank H. Knight, Harry A. Mills, Lloyd W. Mints, Henry Schultz, Henry C. Simons, Jacob Viner, Chester W. Wright, and Theodore O. Yntema. See also Davis (1968) on the adherence to classical monetary analysis by some Chicago economists during the early 1930s.

8 I thank a referee for the *History of Political Economy* for bringing Dimand's 1990 article to my attention, although it was cited in apparent approval of Dimand's criticisms of J. Ronnie Davis's account of American economists' monetary policy views during the 1930s.

9 The Keynesian multiplier argument as a basis for aggregate demand management is a dud. On the criticisms of the multiplier argument by the likes of A.C. Pigou, R.G. Hawtrey, and D.H. Robertson, and other significant flaws in the analysis, see Ahiakpor (2001 or 2003b, Chapter 12).

10 Yet a referee for the *History of Political Economy* contends otherwise: "[Ahiakpor] argues that the classical quantity theory tradition that [Currie, Ellsworth, and White] drew upon was essentially a commonplace by 1931. Perhaps it should have been, but it was not. The Austrians—represented at the Harris conference by Haberler—were explicitly opposed to the QTM, as were the American disciples of Laughlin—represented at the same conference by Willis, and it was the latter who dominated US monetary policy thinking and decisions in the early 1930s." Surely, one must be familiar with a theory to oppose it!

11 Some analysts, including a referee for the *History of Political Economy*, do not recognize the forced-saving mechanism in Hume's monetary analysis. I here follow David Ricardo's (*Works*, 4: 36) lead in doing so. See also F.A. Hayek (1935: 9) and Eric Roll (1938: 103).

12 See also Mill (1874: 72). Note the similarity between Mill's identification of confidence restoration as the key to dealing with a commercial crisis and Marshall and Marshall's (1789: 155), Marshall's (1920: 592), and Taussig's (1921: 410) references to the same.

13 Reflecting his "Austrian" economics background, Schumpeter argues: "our story provides a *presumption* against remedial measures which work through money and credit. For the trouble is fundamentally *not* with money and credit, and policies of this class are particularly apt to keep up, and add to, maladjustment, and to produce additional trouble in the future" (1934: 21–2; italics original).

14 A referee for the *History of Political Economy*, retaining the modern confusion of saving with cash hoarding, reacts negatively to this point: "I am likewise unimpressed by [Ahiakpor's] endorsement of Chamberlin's views in Brown (1934). He reckoned that savings were not equivalent to cash hoarding. True for normal times; but for 1933 when he was writing?? Chamberlin (p. 30) even seems to ignore the fact that people really were *saving money by withdrawing it from circulation*. When confronted with incoherence like this, [Ahiakpor] ought to [be] applauding, not deprecating CEW" (italics added). No, there is no incoherence in Chamberlin's analysis, only evidence here of the referee's failure to recognize the difference between saving and hoarding, as the classics explained, e.g. Smith (*WN*, 1: 358–9) and Mill (*Works*, 2:70); Ahiakpor (1995 or 2003b, Chapter 9) elaborates. Dimand (1990: 44) also criticizes Chamberlin for having held that savings are spent, just as the classics taught. Dimand further argues that savings constitute a "leakage" from spending (45), reflecting Keynes's (1936: 166–7) confusion of saving as cash hoarding, a confusion that also drives the Keynesian multiplier analysis Dimand regards

as relevant for effective aggregate demand management. Ahiakpor (2001) explains the mythology of such argument.

15 Apparently believing Keynes's (1936: 80) incorrect claim that the forced-saving mechanism applies only under the condition of full employment, a referee for the *History of Political Economy* also argues, "Whatever may be true of forced savings, following on inflation in time of *full employment*, can hardly be applied mechanically to monetary and fiscal expansion in conditions of mass unemployment" (italics added). In fact, the forced-saving mechanism relies not upon the condition of full employment but on the lack of concurrent adjustment of wage rates, interest rates, and rental rates as the level of prices changes in response to changes in the quantity of money or credit.

7 100% money

A harmful proposal appropriately ignored

Introduction

In their determination to prevent a repeat of the financial collapse experienced during the Great Depression (1930–3) in the US several analysts focused on the fractional-reserve banking system as the principal culprit rather than the shaken public confidence in banking institutions that resulted in the withdrawal of about $15 billion in checkable and savings deposits. Their solution was to prescribe a 100% reserve banking system instead to replace the extant fractional-reserve system. Prominent among advocates of the 100% reserve system was Irving Fisher, whose 1935 book, *100% Money*, claims the advantages of that system over the fractional-reserve system he dubbed the "10% system." The principal advantages Fisher claimed for the proposal, also listed in the book's subtitle, include (a) "to keep checking banks 100% liquid"; (b) "to prevent inflation and deflation"; (c) "largely to cure or prevent depressions"; and (d) "to wipe out much of the National Debt." That item "a" had been rendered practically moot by the institution of the Federal Deposit Insurance Corporation in June 1933, to start operating from January 1934,[1] and none of the other claims is true appears to have been lost on a long list of bankers and economists in the book's preface (pp. vii–x).[2] They include such highly regarded university professors as Frank Knight, Henry Simons, Henry Schultz, Paul Douglas, Lloyd Mints,[3] Frank Graham, and John R. Commons. Lauchlin Currie of Harvard University, later at the Federal Reserve, and an early proponent of the 100% principle as a means for controlling the quantity of money, also features among the listed supporters.[4] The institutions represented among the list of supporters include the Universities of Chicago, Princeton, and Wisconsin, and the Brookings Institution. Fisher considered it

> well said in a memorandum written by some of the economists of the University of Chicago favoring the 100% system: "If some malevolent genius had sought to aggravate the affliction of business-and-employment cycles, he could hardly have done better than to establish a system of private deposit banks in the present form."
>
> (1935: 40)

Rollin Thomas (1940) also notes that "Six well known economists, in February 1939, invited other economists to join them in approving the 100 per cent reserve plan with the aim of submitting recommendations to the President and members of Congress as a basis for reform of the banking and monetary mechanism" (1940: 315, n. 1).[5] James Tobin (1985) and some economics Nobel Laureates, including George Akerlof, Robert Fogel, Robert Lucas, Edmund Phelps, and Edward Prescott, and a host of other notable economists have supported the call for a 100% reserve banking in Laurence Kotlikoff's *Jimmy Stewart Is Dead* (2010).[6]

However, backing demand deposits 100% with currency may prevent a successful run on solvent banks,[7] but it will deprive an economy of its capacity to generate and utilize a much larger amount of savings for productive investment, and from which to derive economic growth and increased employment. Fisher arrived at his accepting the 100% reserve banking proposition from incorrectly believing (a) that banks create "check-book money" or deposits "out of thin air"; (b) that check-book money or checkable deposits are a part of the circulating medium; (c) that variations in bank deposits directly cause inflation or deflation; (d) that a monetary authority under the 100% system can better control the level of prices than under a fractional-reserve (10%) system; (e) that banks would extend a greater volume of loans under the 100% system than under the 10% system; and (f) that equilibrium interest rates would be more easily attained under the 100% system than under a fractional-reserve system. Several of these claims by Fisher have become a part of modern macro and monetary analysis, very much in sharp contrast with the classical monetary and banking analyses that derive from David Hume, Adam Smith, J.-B. Say, David Ricardo, Henry Thornton, and John Stuart Mill; Alfred Marshall (1920, 1923) carries the classical analyses into the 20th century. Indeed, Fisher cites none of the classical writings on money, credit, and banking in his 1935 book.[8]

Fisher declares, "My chief object [in writing the book] is to make every possible relationship of the plan so clear that any intelligent and open-minded reader may be fully convinced as to its soundness and practicability" (1935: xiii). Also, "The essence of the 100% plan is to make money independent of loans: that is to divorce money from banking" (xiii).[9] This because Fisher believed the plan, "properly worked out and applied, is incomparably the best proposal ever offered for speedily and permanently solving the problem of depressions; for it would remove the chief cause of both booms and depressions, namely, the instability of demand deposits tied, as they now are, to bank loans" (1935: xiv). Fisher notes: "Already several bills have been introduced into Congress to create a 100% reserve system. I refer, in particular, to the Bill of Senator Cutting and Congressman Patman, that of Congressman Goldsborough and that of Senator Nye and Congressman Sweeney" (1935: xii). Moreover, the bill by Nye and Sweeney had been endorsed "in March 1935 by the National Monetary Conference, constituted in January, 1935, and representing 16 organizations, said to embrace the American electorate" (1935: xii–xiii).

It is rather fortunate that no countries have as yet adopted the misconceived and harmful 100% reserve proposal and ruined their prosperity as a result, beginning with the US Congress's failure to adopt the proposal in 1930s and 1940s. The Swiss in June 2018, by 76% of the vote, had the good sense to reject 100% reserve banking proposal at the ballot box. Scarcely are appropriate remedies prescribed for problems or diseases without first obtaining their correct diagnosis. This chapter explains the erroneous foundations for Fisher's proposal.

Banks create money (deposits) out of thin air

Easily the starting point of Irving Fisher's erroneous claims regarding the fractional-reserve banking system is his belief that banks create check-book money or checkable deposits out of "thin air" rather than their lending depositors' savings.[10] John Maynard Keynes (1930, 1: 25–6) also makes this claim, which derives from the recognition that, to extend credit to a borrower, banks create or credit an account in the name of the borrower. But Keynes never linked savings with the purchase of interest- and/or dividend-earning assets or savings supplying banks with loanable funds. Keynes (1937c: 668) indeed declares that "the supply [of 'liquid resources'] depends on the terms on which the banks are prepared to become more or less liquid … saving does not come into the picture at all." Now banks earn most of their revenues from loans: the difference between the loan rate and the deposit rate, multiplied by the volume of loans. If banks did not have to attract deposits with interest payments,[11] their revenue from loans would be even much greater.

But the fact is that banks can only lend other people's savings or "capital." Harry Brown correctly notes this fact in his critique of Fisher's proposal: "What banks do is to bring borrowers and lenders together. And the lenders are the bank depositors [savers]" (1940: 309). In contradiction to Fisher's claim, Brown explains that "the banks could not … lend more than they have on hand and have the lending mean anything, if the recipient of their checks drawn on this credit were, every one of them, to insist at once upon taking the money out of the banks" (ibid.). And even though a loan may be extended in the form of money (or checkable deposits), the money is only an instrument for conveying savings to a borrower. Thus, Brown instructively asks, "If all the borrowers of all the banks failed to repay, is it not clear that depositors, even with our present limited deposit guarantee law, must lose?" (ibid.: 309-10). Adam Smith (*WN*, 1: 374; italics added) makes the point clearly:

> Money is, as it were, but the deed of assignment, which conveys from one hand to another those capitals [savings] which the owners do not care to employ themselves. Those capitals may be greater in almost any proportion, than the amount of the money which serves as the *instrument of their conveyance*, the same pieces of money successively serving for many different loans, as well as for many different purchases.[12]

J.-B. Say (1821a: 352) repeats: "Capital, at the moment of lending, commonly assumes the form of money; whence it has been inferred that abundance of money is the same thing as abundance of capital; and, consequently, that abundance of money is what lowers the rate of interest." Also, Say explains, "The article lent is not any commodity in particular, or even money ... it is a value accumulated and destined to beneficial investment" (ibid.). Furthermore, like Smith, Say argues, "The value lent has but for a moment assumed the form of money ... passing through the same temporary form; the identical pieces of money serving perhaps a hundred times in the course of a year, to transfer equivalent portions of income" (ibid.). John Stuart Mill (*Works*, 3: 508; italics added) similarly clarifies,

> Money, which is so commonly understood as the synonyme of wealth, is more especially the term in use to denote it when it is the subject of borrowing. When one person lends to another ... what he transfers is not the mere money, but *a right* to a certain value of the produce of the country, to be selected at pleasure; the lender having first bought this right, by giving for it a portion of his capital. What he really lends is so much capital [savings]; the money is the mere *instrument of transfer*. But the capital usually passes from the lender to the receiver through the means either of money, or of an order to receive money [like a check], and at any rate it is in money that the capital is computed and estimated.

Remarkably, in Fisher's attempt to illustrate his claim that banks create checkbook money or deposits out of thin air, he refers to a bank drawing upon its "capital consisting of actual money in vault" (1935: 30). Such "capital' is the bank owners' savings. It is also common knowledge that a bank's capital (equity or net worth) is typically a rather small proportion of its overall liabilities, matched by the value of its cash reserves, buildings, and equipment. Fisher also understood that there are three sources of funds for banks' loans, including "(1) from [banks'] own money (their capital); (2) from the money received from customers and put into savings accounts ([but] not subject to check); and (3) from the money repaid on maturing loans" (1935: 16). Fisher also correctly notes, "The Savings Bank does not create its deposits. It lends the funds deposited in it" (1935: 38). It was only checkable deposits that Fisher failed to recognize savings as their source of funds.[13]

Furthermore, in Fisher's illustration of a bank's generating check-book money out of its own capital, he fails to take into account the effect of a borrower's spending the loaned-out money. This is how Fisher came by the claim that, under the 10% reserve system, a bank can lend ten times the same amount of money from its capital or reserves. Had Fisher taken into account the withdrawal of money from the bank's vault when the borrower's check clears, he would have recognized that the checkable deposit of the borrower disappears from the "circulating medium" (M1); only currency (money) in circulation increases by the loan's amount.[14] The same result occurs if the loan (or bank credit, BC) is made out of a saver's prior deposit into a checkable account (D). I illustrate below the bank checkable-deposit expansion process.

A bank lends a proportion of its checkable-deposit customer's savings (D_0), keeping a small fraction (reserve, $R_e < R_0 = D_0$) in readiness to meet the depositor's future expected withdrawal demand. Upon lending to a customer, the bank credits the borrower's checkable-deposit account with the loan amount (D_{t+1}, t = 0, n), which is balanced with a similar amount entered as bank credit (BC_t) in the assets column of the bank's balance sheet. But the deposit ($BC_t = D_{t+1}$) so "created" is always going to be a smaller proportion of the prior deposited saving (D_t), listed under the bank's liabilities and matched by the amount of the deposited cash (or reserves, R_t). Otherwise, a check drawn on the borrower's account to make purchases, about the same time that the depositor also wants a fraction of their deposited saving in a checkable-deposit account, would not clear. That is, a banks' reserves ($R_t = r_t D_t$) against a saver's deposit (D_t) must equal the subsequent expected withdrawal demand of the saver ($R_e < R_t$) plus the loan amount the bank "creates" ($BC_t = D_{t+1}$). Thus, $BC_0 = (1 - r_e)D_0 = D_1$, where r_e = excess reserve to deposit ratio (R_e/D). Now a borrower no sooner is credited with a loan amount than they write a check to spend it. When the check clears, the bank's balance sheet again becomes $D_0 = R_e + BC_0 < D_0 + D_1 = R_0 + BC_0$.[15]

The loan expenditure becomes someone else's income. If all of that income is deposited in the same bank or into the banking system, the consolidated banks' balance sheet becomes $D_0 + D_1$ (liabilities) matched by $R_e + 2BC_0$. That is, the bank's balance sheet would show total reserves being equal to $R_e + D_1 = R_e + BC_0$. The next loan the bank extends would also be a fraction of the new deposit (D_1), such that $BC_1 = (1 - r_e)D_1 = (1 - r_e)^2 D_0 < BC_0 < D_0$. Taking into account the more realistic probability that the income earner from the first loan expenditure would not save all of it in a checkable-deposit account but would keep some in cash—"currency drain"—the resulting deposit (new saving) would be $D_1 = (1 - cu)BC_0 = (1 - cu)(1 - r_e)D_0$. The next loan extended would then be equal to $BC_1 = (1 - r_e)D_1 = (1 - r_e)(1 - cu)BC_0 = (1 - cu)(1 - r_e)^2 D_0 < D_0$. But when the borrower writes a check to spend the loan amount (BC_1), the bank's or consolidated banks' balance sheet would revert to $D_0 + D_1$ under liabilities backed under assets by cash reserves held against the deposited savings, $r_e(D_0) + r_e(D_1)$, plus the loan amounts, $BC_0 + BC_1$. Successive savings (D_t) deposited into the banking system out of the incomes earned from loan expenditures would yield the familiar geometric summation, $\Box D_t = [(1/cu + r_e)]D_0$, where $[1/(cu + r_e)]$ is the deposit-expansion multiplier.[16] Considering the existence of required reserves, the deposit multiplier becomes, $d = 1/(cu + r_d + r_e)$; see also Ahiakpor (2019: 96–7, 173).

Even in Fisher's hypothetical case of a bank lending some of its own "capital," the loan amount credited to the borrower's account (D_t) would be an entry in the bank's liabilities column, with no changes in the bank's net worth. There also would be an increase in loans (or bank credit, BC) in the assets column to match the increase in the bank's deposit liabilities; M1 = C + D thus increases. But when the borrower writes a check to spend the funds, the liabilities column (D) shrinks exactly by the amount of cash withdrawn. Only currency in circulation increases, not "check-book" money or deposits (D) included in M1.

Fisher is thus incorrect when he contrasts the 10% system with his preferred 100% system claiming, "it is not a healthy situation when banks lend money without being sure there is already money to lend ... [whereas] under the 100% system ... the banks could not lend money unless they had money in hand to lend—either their own or that of somebody else wishing to lend it" (1935: 122). The savers holding checkable-deposit accounts value the liquidity of their savings, the relief from default risk from directly investing their own funds, the guaranteed income (interest) on those deposits, and the facility to meet their debt obligations easily and cheaply by issuing checks (orders to pay money) on their accounts rather than sending money (currency, H) some other ways.[17] And when people say that they have "money in the bank," they are referring to their savings (wealth), not necessarily physical cash as Fisher (1935: 7) misrepresents such statement to mean.[18] Besides, it is savings—titles to produced goods—that may be loaned out in the form of money.[19] Smith (*WN*, 1: 306–7) discusses the "ambiguity of language" associated with "money," from which modern monetary analysts can benefit:

> When, by any particular sum of money, we mean not only to express the amount of the metal pieces of which it is composed, but to include in its signification some obscure reference to the goods which can be had in exchange for them, the wealth or revenue which it in this case denotes, is equal only to one of the two values which are thus intimated somewhat ambiguously by the same word, and to the latter more properly than to the former, to the *money's worth* more properly than to the money.
>
> (307; italics added)

However, so impressed was Robert Hemphill, a former credit manager of the Federal Reserve Bank of Atlanta, GA, with Fisher's claims of banks being able to create check-book money out of thin air that he incorrectly asserts in the book's forward,

> Neither the banker nor the borrower ordinarily realize[s] that a loan just completed is putting into circulation that much new money, or, as our reactionary friends would say, "inflating the currency," by the amount of the loan. Neither the banker nor the borrower ordinarily realizes that he is starting an *endless* chain of successive transactions which will continue as long as this credit substitute for money remains in circulation.
>
> (1935: xvii; italics added)[20]

The important point, missing in Fisher's analysis, is that loans are not the driver of increases in the demand deposits that are included in the modern definition of money, M1 = C + D. Loans are incurred to be spent quickly. Rather, increased savings expand the checkable deposits or "check-book money." But influenced by Keynes's view of the checkable-deposit expansion process, Fisher laments that

> our circulating medium [is] at the mercy not merely of 14,500 private mints but also of millions of individual borrowers; and Mr. Platt [former vice-governor of the Federal Reserve Board] quotes the English economist Keynes as saying that it is "most unfortunate that depositors [borrowers] should be able to take the initiative in changing the volume of the community's money."
>
> (1935: 37)

Fisher also cites approvingly Mr. Pratt's arguing in the *New York Herald Tribune* of January 2, 1935, that "The banks are powerless if because of lack of confidence or for any other reason borrowers fail to come forward" (ibid.). But interest rates would fall to zero if no one wanted to borrow, which was not the case during the Great Depression.[21] Fisher was also wrong in interpreting the Great Depression as "the situation for several years [when] everybody [was] *waiting for somebody else to go into debt* to the banks in order to supply the public with circulating medium which *all* needed" (1935: 105; italics original). However, so persuasive was Fisher's claiming that the expansion of the money supply depends upon loans that he cites a congressman's having asked him, "Can't you find a system such that to have the money of the Nation adequate does not require somebody going into debt at a bank?" (1935: 50).

Furthermore, unlike private bank notes that were issued to extend loans and could circulate until they were returned to their issuers before the establishment of the Federal Reserve System, checks or checkable deposits do not circulate. They settle payments typically once only. Fisher's including "deposit money" in the circulating medium, as if they were bank notes, is thus incorrect and misleading. Fisher himself recognizes this: "It is true that a check is not 'lawful money' nor legal tender. It *does not circulate* from hand to hand except with the special consent of the person receiving it. It is, therefore, not—like a National Bank note—of equal use to any and every bearer" (1935: 47; italics added).

Banks destroy money by recalling loans or when loans are repaid

The second major error in Fisher's treatment of the 10% or fractional-reserve banking system is his claiming that there occurs a "contraction of check-book money, as bank loans are paid off" (1935: 108) or "liquidation of bank loans destroys check-book money" (1935: 111; see also 120 and 153). The claim appears to follow logically from Fisher's incorrect claim that bank loans expand the "D" in the "money supply," M1. But when a loan is repaid (or recalled) nothing changes in the liabilities (D) column of the bank's balance sheet. As explained above, a bank's liability to the borrower disappears once the borrower writes a check to spend the loan amount. Rather, when a loan is repaid the bank's reserves (cash) increase while the bank's entry of loans (BC) decreases by the loan's amount. Thus, in terms of the modern definition of money, $M1 = C + D$, the deposits in checkable accounts remain unchanged.[22] What decreases is currency in circulation (C): a return from its previous increase when the loan amount was spent and the bank's cash reserves decreased. Put differently, $M1 = C + D$; therefore, $M1 = C + R + BC = H + BC$, since $D = R + BC$. Since commercial banks cannot change H, only BC changes. The expansion in M1 occurs when bank credit (BC) increases and currency in circulation increases, but not D, "check-book money." The contraction in M1 occurs when bank credit or loans contract and currency in circulation decreases, but not D.

Yet, this erroneous claim by Fisher has endured even among some analysts who have rejected all other arguments he advanced in favor of the 100% reserve proposition, e.g. Rollin Thomas (1940).[23] Depriving commercial banks their alleged ability to destroy a large portion of the public's means of payment, namely, checkable deposits, also underlies the 1930s Chicago economists' (see Albert Hart, 1935)[24] and Lauchlin Currie's (1934b) advocacy of the 100% banking system Fisher (1935) promotes. It also should strike us as unimaginable or strange that a bank would pay interest to acquire a liability in the form of savings deposited in a checkable account but would subsequently destroy such savings.[25] The bank would rather value that source of funds for earning interest income by extending loans than to destroy that means. The bank's depositors also would not tolerate the destruction of their savings (wealth). In fact, in the case of a checkable deposit's contraction, the initiative again must come from savers, not borrowers. I illustrate this below.

If a saver writes a check to withdraw an amount ($D = \$100$) greater than the reserves ($R_e = \$10$) the bank holds in readiness to pay money (cash) on demand, the bank sells some of its assets, say bonds, or recalls some loans. Assuming the bank was fully loaned up, which is ever hardly the case, the bank's balance sheet would show a reduction in its liabilities by the amount of deposit withdrawn ($D = \$100$), matched by a contraction of assets mostly in the bank's loans and investments ($BC = \$90$) and partly by a reduction in the bank's cash reserves ($R_e = \$10 = r_e D$), that is, $-D = -[r_e D + (1 - r_e)D] = -[R_e + BC]$. The total amount of currency ($H = C + R$) remains unchanged: a reduction in the amount held as bank reserves (R_e) plus the increased amount in circulation (C) because of the deposit's withdrawal. Thus, the contraction in modern M1 results from a contraction in deposited savings, not from the banks having initiated the destruction of "check-book money."[26]

Recognition of the above may be obscured when we use the deposit-expansion formula associated with determining the modern money supply, $M1 = C + D$, namely, $d = 1/(cu + r_d + r_e)$, where r_d = required reserve ratio and r_e = excess or economic reserve ratio. Increases in r_d and r_e contract the multiplier and thus $M1 = C + D = [(cu + 1)/(cu + r_d + r_e)]H$, where there are no reserves held against time deposits (Ahiakpor 2019, Chapter 5 elaborates). But what really happens is that the banks simply extend a smaller amount of loans on the basis of new deposits they receive or they liquidate some of their investments (loans). The banks do not destroy the savings they already received as checkable deposits (D_c).

The Federal Reserve Board's doubling the required reserve ratio in three steps between August 1936 and May 1937 and the behavior of demand deposits and bank reserves somewhat illustrate the point that only savers can contract the bank deposits included in M1, not the banks. Within that period, high-powered money increased by $0.899 billion or 7.1% from $12.729 billion to $13.628 billion while total commercial bank reserves also increased by $0.569 billion or 7.6% from $7.451 to $8.020 billion (Friedman and Schwartz 1963: 804). Rather than contracting, demand deposits also increased slightly by $0.08 billion or 0.3% from $25.14 billion to $25.22 billion while currency in circulation also increased by $0.34 billion or 6.4% from $5.30 billion to $5.64 billion.[27] Thus, in terms of absolute dollar amounts the doubling of reserve requirements affected mostly banks' reserves.

Fisher thus misrepresents the fractional-reserve banking system when he argues that the proposed 100% reserve system "would actually stop the *irresponsible creation* and *destruction* of circulating medium by our thousands of commercial banks which now act like so many private mints" (1935: vii; italics added) or that it will deprive banks "of their present power virtually to mint checkbook money and to destroy it" (ibid.: 12–13). Fisher was also incorrect to claim that the fractional-reserve banking system acts worse than someone who robs Peter to pay Paul when banks recall loans: "they rob Peter of $10 on the average to pay Paul $1. That is, for every dollar of cash which the public gets it loses $10 in deposits because of the 10-fold lending of each dollar" (1935: 68).[28] But the reverse is true. When a bank recalls a loan to meet a saver's withdrawal demand for, say, $10, it takes a maximum of $9 contraction of cash from the public (sale of assets, if the bank had been fully loaned up) to meet the saver's demand. The other $1 comes out of a bank's reserves under a 10% reserve system. Thus, the net currency in circulation increases by $1; in the case of 100% reserve banking, the change in currency in circulation would be zero.

Loan repayments cause depressions under the 10% system

Another of Fisher's praises for the 100% reserve system is that it would prevent economic depressions that are endemic to a fractional-reserve system: "the 10% system is largely responsible for the development of depressions. For, under a 100% system, the liquidation of bank loans could not ... reduce the quantity of money by a single dollar" (1935: 120).[29] Fisher's conclusion follows from his debt-deflation theory of depressions: debt liquidation causes a contraction of "check-book money," falling prices and economic contraction along with increased unemployment and an increasing real burden for debtors.[30] This is because, in Fisher's reasoning, "*the very effort of individuals to lessen their burden of debt increases it, because of the mass effect (of the stampede to liquidate) in swelling each dollar owed"* (1935: 111; italics original). Thus, the irony that the *"more the debtors pay, the more they still owe* in terms of real commodities" (1935: 111; italics original). It is as though Fisher believed that debtors would be better off not paying their debts and going bankrupt instead. But as explained above, debt repayments do not contract checkable deposits, only savers' withdrawals from their deposits do. Fisher's debt-deflation theory of depressions turns out to be missing its crucial causal link between his so-called "over-indebtedness" and price deflation that generates an economic contraction.

Fisher's argument also appears more relevant to a situation of panic or a bursting of a financial bubble rather than the normal course of loan repayments by businesses. He describes the start of the cycle as being characterized by "over-indebtedness" and *"new opportunities to invest at a big prospective profit,* as compared with ordinary profits and interest" (1935: 116; italics original). The new opportunities may include "new inventions, new industries, development of new resources, [and] opening of new lands or new markets" (ibid.). These, in fact, look like typical ventures for entrepreneurs.

Indeed, economists, since the time of Adam Smith, have blamed over-confidence in some entrepreneurs who borrowed to pursue anticipated profitable ventures but caused economic ruin when they failed. That is why Smith preferred banks to lend to "sober undertakers" rather than to "prodigals and projectors." That way, "A great part of the capital [funds] of the country would ... be kept [in] the hands which were most likely to make a profitable and advantageous use of it [instead of being] thrown into those which were most likely to waste and destroy it" (*WN*, 1: 378; see also 1: 362).[31] Jean-Baptiste Say also blamed bankers' easy lending to business speculators that led to economic recessions (Say 1828–9 cited in Alain Béraud and Guy Numa 2018a: 234–5), besides "times of jobbing and speculation, when the sudden fluctuations caused by gambling in produce, make people look for a profit from every variation of a rise, and money in prospect of a fall" (1821a: 142), similarly David Ricardo (*Works* 3: 134–5; 5: 385). John Stuart Mill (*Works*, 3: 540–4) also gives a vivid account of speculative bubbles, started by "over-confidence" when "money is borrowed for short periods at almost any rate of interest, and sales of goods for immediate payment are made at any sacrifice" (*Works*, 3: 542) that are followed by commercial revulsions. The invitation to such speculative bubbles may be "expectations of rising prices, such as the opening of a new foreign market, or simultaneous indications of a short supply of several great articles" (ibid.).

But the classics did not blame fractional-reserve banking for it. Mill (*Works*, 4: 348), for example, points to such occurrences in France that did not have note-issuing banks as compared with England that did. Thus, Mill sees the rise and fall of prices associated with such speculative bubbles "originating not in anything affecting money, but in the state of credit; an unusually extended employment of credit during the earlier period, followed by a great diminution, never amounting however to an entire cessation of it, in the later" (*Works*, 3: 543). Mill, therefore, observes:

An evil common to all commercial countries, in the ratio of the extent of their transactions, cannot depend upon a cause peculiar to England and the United States. What a currency actually metallic does not prevent, it is impossible that making the paper conform exactly to the variations of a metallic currency can cure.

(*Works*, 4: 348)

Alfred Marshall also blames the "reckless inflations of credit" (1920: 591) for economic fluctuations, accompanied by unemployment in recessions. Moreover, credit is not extended only on the basis of checkable deposits; they are extended out of time deposits too.

Nevertheless, the experience of the Great Depression (1930–3), when the public's shaken confidence in the security of their bank deposits caused many to rush to withdraw their savings, illustrates the opposite of Fisher's claim that banks "irresponsibly" destroy the public's checkable deposits. Some investors who lost their fortunes in the October 1929 stock market crash did default on their bank loans. Later, some other real estate and agricultural loans also went bad; see Elmus Wicker (1996). Many of the banks that did not have readily sellable securities or were unable to borrow from the Federal Reserve Banks because they were not operating within the Federal Reserve System also failed because they could not redeem their depositors' demands for money (cash)— 9,000 banks in total between January 1930 and March 1933; see Friedman and Schwartz (1963) and John Walter (2005). The bank failures also meant that many customers lost their savings rather than the banks having destroyed their checkable deposits from recalling loans.[32]

It was both the rush to withdraw deposits and bank failures that led to demand deposits in commercial banks having contracted by 35.6% or $8.22 billion from $23.12 billion at the end of the fourth quarter of 1929 to $14.90 billion by the end of the first quarter of 1933 at the same time that currency in circulation rather increased by 40.4% or $1.56 billion from $3.86 to $5.42 billion. But Fisher incorrectly characterizes the episode as

> This loss, or destruction, of 8 billions of check-book money [that] has been realized by few and seldom mentioned. There would have been big newspaper headlines if 8 thousand miles out of 23 thousand miles of railway had been destroyed. Yet such a disaster would have been a small one compared with the destruction of 8 billions out of 23 billions of our main monetary highway. That destruction of 8 billion dollars of what the public counted on as their money was the chief sinister fact in the depression from which followed the two chief tragedies, unemployment and bankruptcies.
>
> (1935: 6)[33]

The public's withdrawal of savings affected time deposits too. They decreased by 33.0% or $6.52 billion from $19.75 billion at the end of the fourth quarter of 1929 to $13.23 billion by the end of the first quarter of 1933. Over the same period high-powered money (H) increased by 20.5% or $1.43 billion from $6.98 billion to $8.41 billion. On the other hand, banks' vault cash declined by 10% or $0.087 billion from $0.874 billion at the end of the fourth quarter of 1929 to $0.787 billion by the end of the first quarter of 1933 while bank reserves with Federal Reserve Banks increased by $0.601 billion or 26.1% from $2.304 billion to $2.905 billion.[34]

Clearly, the $1.43 billion increase in high-powered money against the $8.22 billion decrease in demand deposits and $6.52 billion decrease in time deposits easily indicates an excess demand for money (H), about $15 billion, to hold by the public. From the Cambridge-equation version of the classical Quantity Theory, we can derive the level of prices as $P = H/ky$, where k = the proportion of income the public desires to hold in cash and y = real GDP, and anticipate that the level of prices would decrease. That is, $\%\Delta P = \%\Delta H - \%\Delta(ky) < 0$ when $\%\Delta(ky)$ dominates $\%\Delta H$. And such it was between 1930 and 1933 when the level of prices decreased at an annual average of 6.3%: −6.4% in 1930, −9.3% in 1931, −10.3% in 1932, and 0.8% in 1933. The monthly price deflation actually stopped by April 1933.[35]

And, as classical monetary analysis explains, price deflation generates the opposite of the forced-saving mechanism by contacting profits or increasing losses for businesses. Firms react by laying off workers and reducing the level of their productions, a proposition Fisher (1926: 787) repeats: "when prices are falling, expenses … lag behind and reduce profits … Consequently, during periods of falling prices … bankruptcies are increased, concerns shut down entirely or in part, and men are thrown out of work"; see also Alfred and Mary Marshall (1879: 156–7), Marshall (1920: 493–4, 515), and Frank Taussig (1921: 299). The only real cure is to restore the level of prices by restoring the public's confidence in banking institutions in order to reduce their demand for money (cash) to hold and to restore the flow of savings; see Walter Bagehot (1873: 101), Marshall (1920: 591–2, Taussig (1921: 410); Ahiakpor (2019, Chapter 5) elaborates.

Thus, following the confidence restoration policies of the federal government, including (a) assuring the public that only solvent banks were being allowed to reopen from March 13, 1933, (b) the US going off the gold standard that permitted the Federal Reserve System easily to respond to the public's demand for money (H), and (c) President Roosevelt signing in June 1933 the bill to establish the Federal Deposit Insurance Corporation, the public started to return their savings into checkable- and time-deposit accounts with commercial banks. Between the end of the first quarter of 1933 and the end of the fourth quarter of 1935, checkable deposits increased by $7.72 billion or 51.8%, from $14.9 billion to $22.62 billion while time deposits increased by only $0.22 billion or 1.7% from $13.23 billion to $13.25 billion. Currency in circulation decreased by $0.5 billion or 9% from $5.42 billion to $4.92 billion, and banks' vault cash increased by $0.168 billion or 23.9% from $0.702 billion to $0.870 billion, banks' deposits at Federal Reserve Banks increased by $3.711 or 175.2%

from \$2.118 billion to \$5.829 billion. High-powered money (H) also increased by \$3.17 billion or 37.7% from \$8.41 billion to \$11.58 billion, but which was less than the increase in banks' reserves (vault cash and deposits with Federal Reserve Banks), amounting to \$3.879 billion. The \$3.17 billion increase in high-powered money was also considerably less than the \$7.72 billion increase in demand deposits. Again, we can see that money (cash) merely serves as a means of conveying the public's savings to banks, and it is not money we borrow but savings. Checks are money's substitute for transferring such savings to others. Our account is the exact opposite of Fisher's (1935) account of what happened during the Great Depression, especially in Chapter 10, pages 155–9.

Bank lending under the 10% system creates an economic boom and inflation

There is little dispute that by transferring the public's non-consumed incomes saved in checkable deposits banks enable borrowers to acquire both fixed and circulating capital, including funds for hiring more labor services, for increased production. This underlies Adam Smith's and other classical writers' praising the flow of savings as enabling "reproductive consumption"—to earn enough revenue to be able to pay back the loan principal and interest. Smith clarifies bankers' role in that process thus:

> The judicious operations of banking, by providing, if I may be allowed so violent a metaphor, a sort of wagon-way through the air; enable the country to convert, as it were, a great part of its highways into good pastures and cornfields, and thereby to increase very considerably the annual produce of its land and labour.
>
> (*WN*, 1: 341)

Were banks to lock up savers' deposits in faults, as Fisher envisions under the 100% reserves for demand deposits, banks would be turning a large portion of the community's savings into "dead stock":

> It is not by augmenting the capital of the country, but by rendering a greater part of that capital active and productive than would otherwise be so, that the most judicious operations of banking can increase the industry of the country. That part of his capital which a dealer is obliged to keep by him unemployed, and in ready money for answering occasional demands, is so much dead stock, which, so long as it remains in this situation, produces nothing either to him or to his country. The judicious operations of banking enable him to convert his dead stock into active and productive stock.
>
> (Smith *WN*, 1: 340–1)[36]

Indeed, with the return of confidence in the banking system and the return of savings mostly in checkable-deposit accounts, the US economy started to recover. Real GDP grew at 10.8% in 1934, 8.9% in 1935, 12.9% in 1936, and 5.1% in 1937. The Federal Reserve's raising the required reserve ratio against demand deposits—first by 50% in August 1936 and further in March and May, 1937—merely restricted the proportion of savings in checkable deposits banks were able to lend, which curbed the economy's recovery.[37] Even so, demand deposits still increased by $1.39 billion or 5.7% from $24.3 billion at the end of the second quarter of 1936 to $25.69 billion by the end of the second quarter of 1937. Demand deposits then declined by $1.43 billion or 5.6% to $24.26 billion by the end of the fourth quarter of 1937, but then increased again by $2.13 billion or 8.8% to $26.39 billion by the end of 1938.

Between January 1934 and December 1938, high-powered money increased by $7.621 billion or 95.9% from $7.947 to $15.568 billion, but less than the $11.28 billion or 74.7% increase in demand deposits from $15.11 billion at the end of the fourth quarter of 1933 to $26.39 billion by the end of the fourth quarter of 1938. Time deposits increased by only $3.01 billion or 25.3% from $11.90 billion to $14.91 billion over the same time period (data on high-powered money from Friedman and Schwartz 1963, Table B-3, p. 804 and data on demand and time deposits from Friedman and Schwartz, 1970, Table 2, p. 68). Thus, increased savings in demand deposits, not high-powered money or savings deposits, drove the economy's expansion. Under a 100% reserve system savings in demand deposits could not have expanded in excess of the growth of high-powered money, which appears a demerit for that system.

Moreover, Fisher erred in attributing rising prices or inflation to increases in demand deposits. He appears to have arrived at that claim by extending David Ricardo's restatement of the Quantity Theory of money's explanation of the level of prices (P) via the exchange equation by including checkable deposits and their velocity.[38] Ricardo (*Works* 3: 311) indeed argues that putting "the mass of commodities of all sorts on one side of the line,—and the amount of money multiplied by the rapidity of its circulation on the other [is] in all cases the regulator of prices."[39] This may be represented as HV = Py, from which we can derive the level of prices as P = HV/y, where V = money's velocity. But Ricardo, in fact, drew upon David Hume's (1752) earlier explanation:

> It is also evident, that the prices do not so much depend on the absolute quantity of commodities and that of money which are in a nation, as on that of the commodities which come or may come to market, and of the *money which circulates*. If the coin be locked up in chests, it is the same thing with regard to prices, as if it were annihilated; if the commodities be hoarded in magazines and granaries, a like effect follows.
>
> (42; italics added)

However, money in Hume's analysis is specie; in Ricardo's, money is equivalent to a modern fiat money, not bank deposits. Smith (*WN*, 1: 378), J.-B. Say (1821a: 273), and John Stuart Mill (*Works*, 3: 512–3; 538–40, 346) also restate the same argument. Thus, it is the circulating money (specie or H) relative to the flow of produced goods and services that determines the level of prices; see also Francis Walker (1895).

Hume (1752: 35) complained about the introduction of paper money or "paper-credit" causing the increased circulation of money itself and raising the level of prices: "there appears no reason for encreasing [the] inconvenience [of inflation] by a counterfeit money, which foreigners will not accept of in any payment, and which any great disorder in the state will reduce to nothing." Even so, it is the reduction in the demand for money to hold by the use of bank notes to which Hume's complaint refers, not to bank deposits. However, Hume (1752: 68, n. 1) also acknowledges the short-term output and employment growth effects of the use of paper credit.

Furthermore, unlike bank notes that circulated from hand to hand in competition with specie or fiat money (Marshall 1923: 13), the classical Quantity Theory does not employ bank deposits or Fisher's "check-book money" to explain the level of prices. As Marshall argued before the 1886 Gold and Silver Commission, checks are not included in stating the Quantity Theory "because a cheque requires the receiver to have formed some opinion for himself as to the individual from whom he receives it" (1926: 35).[40] Fisher also employs the same description of checks as Marshall (1926: 35) does as the reason for not including them in stating the Quantity Theory's explanation of the level of prices. Fisher argues: "a check is not 'lawful money' nor legal tender. It does *not circulate* from hand to hand except with the special consent of the person receiving it" (1935: 47; italics added).

Francis Walker's (1878: 405) warning about the analytical confusions that may arise from the inclusion of bank deposits in the definition of money appears quite relevant:

> Money is that which passes from hand to hand in final discharge of debts and full payment for goods. The bank-deposit system allows the mutual cancellation of vast bodies of indebtedness which would, without this agency, require the intervention of an actual medium of exchange; but deposits, like every other form of credit, save the use of money; they do not perform the functions of money. *Money is what money does.*
>
> (italics original)[41]

However, Fisher's extended version of the Quantity Theory from Ricardo's restatement is $MV + M'V' = PT$, where M = currency (our preferred H), M' (checkable deposits), V = transactions velocity of currency, V' = velocity of checkable deposits, P = average level of prices, and T = the volume of transactions, representing the quantity of goods produced. Fisher thus appears to have been led to impute an increased level of prices to the use of checkable deposits and their presumed velocity: $P = (MV + M'V')/T$. But since checks do not circulate, let alone bank deposits, whose velocity thus can hardly be greater than unity, Fisher's extended version of the Quantity Theory appears illegitimate and quite misleading.[42]

Furthermore, the increased production that arises from the transformation of savings into business loans under the 10% banking system tends to decrease the level of prices, given the quantity of money (H). Also, not all of the incomes saved in a checkable-deposit account are spent on making purchases at any point in time. Less is spent than had been withdrawn from consumption expenditures by savers when the deposits were made. The use of transferable bank deposits, credit cards, and other non-cash media to make purchases also reduces the public's demand for money (H) to hold. Their usage thus increases money's velocity and increases the level of prices than would otherwise have occurred. That is why there is no legitimate basis for including the velocity of any other means of payment, such as demand deposits (V'), besides money's own velocity (V) in the price-level equation. On balance then, only the variations in the supply of money (H) relative to variations in money's demand to hold provide a reliable basis for explaining the level of prices or inflation.

As John Stuart Mill declares, regarding the determination of prices, "I apprehend that bank notes, bills, or cheques, as such, do not act on prices at all. What does act on prices is Credit, in whatever shape given, and whether it gives rise to any transferable instruments capable of passing in to circulation, or not" (*Works*, 3: 538–9). Milton Friedman's several failures to predict inflation rates based upon the growth rates of M1 in the early 1980s well illustrate the misleading nature of Fisher's Quantity Theory formulation.[43] The Quantity Theory is the application of classical value theory—determination of commodity market prices by supply and demand—to money (specie or currency), not to credit (loans) or savings. The theory of value's application to the latter explains the level of interest rates.

Fisher's view that we will better be able to determine the equilibrium level of interest rates when checkable deposits are backed 100% by currency is thus misconceived. He claims, "Under the 10% system, the borrowing and lending do not usually come into equilibrium at the proper rate of interest to clear the market" (1935: 124) and that only the 100% system would facilitate "normal loan operations, with supply and demand balanced, and with loans always available *at a price*" (ibid.; 136; italics original). Fisher also refers to his *Theory of Interest* (1930) where "the rate of interest is said to be 'determined by impatience to spend income and opportunity to invest it'" (1935: 132), as if that is the most complete theory of interest rate determination rather than the classical supply and demand for "capital" or savings theory.[44]

Fisher's focus on MV + M'V' = PT also appears to have inhibited his taking directly into account variations in the public's demand for money (currency) to hold in his explaining variations in the level of prices. That consideration appears more evident in the Cambridge version of the Quantity Theory, H = kPy, from which we drive the level of prices as P = H/ky and inflation as %ΔP = %ΔH − %Δk − %Δy; see also Marshall (1923: 45). Thus, Fisher argues, "These changes in the quantity of money [M1] were somewhat aggravated by like changes in velocity. In 1932 and 1933, for instance, not only was the circulating medium small, but its circulation was slow—even to the extent of widespread hoarding" (1935: 5). In fact, it was rather the widespread increase in the demand for money (currency) to hold (k = 1/V) or increased hoarding, resulting in money's decreased velocity that caused the decrease in both demand and time deposits in those years, as noted above; see also Ahiakpor (2019, Chapter 5).

Other relevant classical economic principles Fisher missed or ignored

In advancing his perceived benefits of the 100% reserve proposal, Fisher missed the following other relevant classical economic principles. Easily the most important of these is the classical designation of money as an economy's unit of account or standard of value. Until the late 19th century, the unit-of-account function was the first the classical economists cited before money's serving as a medium of exchange. Thus, David Hume (1752: 37) explains that "money is nothing but the representation of labour and commodities, and serves only as a method of rating or estimating them." This besides acknowledging money as "not, properly speaking, one of the subjects of commerce; but only the instrument which men have agreed upon to facilitate the exchange of one commodity for another" (ibid.: 33). Adam Smith argues, "At the same time and place … money is the exact measure of the exchangeable value of all commodities" (*WN*, 1: 42), and in the *Lectures in Jurisprudence*, Smith states: "In treating of opulence I shall consider … Money as 1st The measure by which we compute the value of commodities (as a measure of value) [and] 2nd The common instrument of commerce or exchange" (1978: 353). Henry Thornton, David Ricardo, and John Stuart Mill, among the major classical economists, all followed Hume and Smith in recognizing money first as a measure or standard of value before money's serving as a medium of exchange; see Ahiakpor (2003b: Chapter 3). Although Alfred Marshall adopted the reverse ordering of standard of value and medium of exchange, he nevertheless recognized the "*standard of value*" function being "admirably discharged by gold and silver and paper based on them" (1923: 16; italics original). Marshall there also recognizes money as "a material thing carried in purses, and 'current' from hand to hand, because its value can be read at a glance."

Fisher's (1913), however, adopted the definition of money as "Any property right which is generally acceptable in exchange" or "*what is generally acceptable in exchange for goods*" (5, 8; italics original), without regard for the unit-of-account characteristic.[45] That definition appears to have made Fisher amenable to accepting the 100% reserve proposal from the Chicago economists and Lauchlin Currie as the necessary remedy against bouts of inflation and depression.[46] The Chicago economists were concerned to regulate the quantity of "money" as a means of stabilizing the level of prices. Similarly, Currie widened the meaning of money "so as to make it synonymous with means of payment" (1935: 10) and listed "demand deposits or deposits subject to check" as the "second constituent of money" (ibid.: 12) that needed to be controlled, taking his cue from Keynes (1930). Invoking the US constitutional requirement that "The Congress shall have power … to coin money [and] regulate the value thereof" (1935: 18), Fisher correctly assigned the performance of that task to the government. But because he included checkable deposits in the "circulating medium," Fisher charged banks with having usurped a power granted to government, not to private entities:[47] "Virtually, if not literally, every checking bank coins money; and the banks, as a whole, regulate, control, or influence the value of all money" (1935: 18–19); see also (1935: 183–6).

However, checks are not a unit of account; no one measures the value of commodities by bank deposits or checks. Even as a means of payment, checks are orders to pay money, whose settlements are conducted through deposits (reserves) at the central bank. Fisher previously argued, "Real money is what a payee accepts without question, because he is induced to do so by 'legal tender' laws or by established custom" (1912: 149). He also noted,

> One degree more exchangeable than a government bond is a time bill of exchange; one degree more exchangeable than a time bill of exchange is a sight draft; while a check is almost as exchangeable as money itself. Yet no one of these is really money, for none of them is "generally acceptable."
>
> (ibid.: 148)

It thus was not helpful that Fisher switched to treating checkable deposits as "money" rather their being substitute means of payment only.

Fisher also could have learned from David Hume's (1752) essay, "Of Money," that it is variations in modern central bank notes, the equivalent of classical specie, that are needed to meet variations in their demand to sustain the level of prices, and not changes in the public's savings in checkable deposits. Hume prescribed "the good policy of the magistrate [as consisting] only in keeping [money], if possible, still encreasing [in a growing economy]; because, by that means, he keeps alive a spirit of industry in the nation, and encrease the stock of labour, in which consists all real power and riches" (1752: 39–40). Hume qualified his policy prescription with "if possible" because he was dealing with specie money whose inflow depended upon a country's net exports, not "counterfeit money" or "paper-credit" (1752: 35):

> The alterations in the quantity of money, either on one side or the other, are not immediately attended with proportionable alterations in the price of commodities. There is always an interval before matters be adjusted to their new situation; and this interval is as pernicious to industry, when gold and silver are diminishing, as it is advantageous when these metals are encreasing.
>
> (Hume 1752: 40)

Alfred Marshall makes the same point: "If an inconvertible currency is controlled by a strong Government, its amount can be so regulated that the value of a unit of it is maintained at a fixed level" (1923: 50). Since its being delinked from gold in March 1933, control over the quantity of Federal Reserve notes supplied has been completely under the Federal Reserve System. There is thus no need for imposing 100% reserve on checkable deposits in order to achieve the monetary control that the Chicago group, Currie, and Fisher wanted.

Fisher also misinterpreted the 1844 Banking Act of England that imposed the 100% reserve of bullion on Bank of England notes as a legitimate precedence for the 100% reserve proposal for US commercial bank checkable deposits. In fact, the banking division of the Bank of England did not have to back its deposits 100% with currency (Walter Bagehot 1873: 97). Thus, the point of Bagehot's 1873 book was to urge the banking division of the Bank of England to hold more reserves than it did to be able to lend sufficiently upon the threat of bank runs in order quickly to stem them. In Bagehot's view, "The best palliative to a panic is a confidence in the adequate amount of the Bank reserve, and in the efficient use of that reserve" (ibid.: 101). However, Bagehot believed that "the reserve in the Banking Department of the Bank of England [had become] the banking reserve, not only of the Bank of England, but of all London, and not only of all London, but of all England, Ireland, and Scotland too" (ibid.: 16), and therefore not being enough.

Rather than focusing on banks' lending actual money instead of savings in checkable deposits with them, Fisher also could have benefited from Adam Smith's explaining the real essence of bank loans. Such loans are the transfers of claims or titles to portions of produced commodities that savers have lodged with the banks. As Smith clarifies,

> Almost all loans are made in money, either of paper, or of gold and silver. But what the borrower really wants, and what the lender really supplies him with, is not the money, but the *money's worth*, or the goods which it can purchase. If he wants it as a stock for immediate consumption, it is those goods only which he can place in that stock. If he wants it as a capital for employing industry, it is from those goods only that the industrious can be furnished with the tools, materials, and maintenance, necessary for carrying on their work. By means of the loan, the lender, as it were, assigns to the borrower his *right to a certain portion* of the annual produce of the land and labour of the country, to be employed as the borrower pleases.
>
> (*WN*, 1: 373; italics added)

Such understanding makes it unnecessary to back checkable deposits 100% with currency, whether of the Federal Reserve System or Fisher's proposed Currency Commission. Other than the cash reserves banks keep in readiness to redeem their deposit customers' redemption needs; banks are simply record keepers of the amounts (titles) deposited with them and the loans and investments the banks make out of those deposits. Thus, the greater their reserve ratios, the smaller the bank loans, resulting in less production and employment. Fisher is simply wrong in his belief that under the fractional-reserve banking system "the bankers cannot help destroying money when it should be created, namely in a depression; while in a boom they create money when it should be destroyed" (1935: 68).[48]

Had Fisher been attentive to the criticisms of government deficit spending by David Hume, Adam Smith, and David Ricardo, he also likely might not have touted the 100% reserve scheme as having the benefit of reducing the national debt. Fisher arrived at that conclusion from envisioning his proposed Currency Commission buying up all federal government bonds from the commercial banks, thus saving on interest payments. The classical criticism of government deficit spending is that it encourages a level of profligate spending that otherwise would not occur if budgets were financed through taxes (Ahiakpor 2013). However, Fisher believed that, freed from its obligation to retire the debt, the Currency Commission's money creation, would end federal taxes and "money would be given by the people to the people, to supply the needs of growing business and prevent the fall of the price level which such growth would otherwise cause" (1935: 191).[49] Several early commentators on Fisher's argument have declared it an illusion, e.g. Hart (1935), which indeed it is.

As explained above, money is not what businesses need to invest but savings—earned titles to produced goods. The Currency Commission's purchasing government bonds merely would raise the level of prices more than they otherwise would have been. Fisher's acceptance of the classical theory of interest rates also might have led him to recognize that the government's payment of interest to the public amounts mostly[50] to the transfer of funds from tax payers to the public creditors—purchasers of the government bonds—within the economy; see Hume (1752: 96), Smith (*WN*, 2: 463), and Ricardo (*Works*, 4: 188). Nevertheless, it is best for an economy's efficient growth that the government should curb its level of spending, whether financed with taxes or with debt, e.g. Ricardo (*Works*, 1: 246); see Chapter 4. Fisher also could have benefitted from Ricardo's warning against regarding a central bank's printing of money to lend at low interest rates as a reliable source of economic growth. If that were the case,

> [central] Banks would ... become powerful engines indeed. By creating paper money, and lending it at three or two per cent under the present market rate of interest, the Bank would reduce the profits on trade in the same proportion ... no nation, but by similar means, could enter into competition with us, we should engross the trade of the world. To what absurdities would not such a theory lead us!
>
> (*Works*, 3: 92)

Implications and conclusions

The Great Depression was the most severe and longest lasting in Fisher's time. Having ventured his debt-deflation theory of depressions as its explanation since 1932, Fisher adopted the 100% reserve proposal at Chicago and by

Lauchlin Currie, meant to control the quantity of money (M1), to lead a vigorous campaign for its adoption, including revising his 1935 book twice, making speeches, writing articles, and testifying before Congress (Allen 1993). But in that quest, Fisher made some fundamental errors. First, he drew little from the classical literature on economic recessions, just as was the case with the Chicago economists and Lauchlin Currie. Fisher could have learned that, since the time of Adam Smith, economists have identified the alternation between business euphoria about profitable investments and panic disinvestments as a common source of business fluctuations. He then could have recognized that, other than his peculiar sequencing of events, his debt-depression theory of depressions was not new. More importantly, he would not have blamed the occurrence of business fluctuations mainly on the fractional-reserve banking system.

Another of Fisher's fundamental errors was attributing to commercial banks the ability to create checkable deposits "out of thin air," almost as Keynes (1930) argues, rather than the banks' lending deposited savings in those accounts. From that error arose Fisher's view of thousands US banks having acted as "private mints" and controlled the quantity of money. Thus, Fisher's declaration, repeating Henry Simons's mistaken claim: "we must denounce the notion that bankers, because they deal in money, have any right whatever to control money—to manufacture and destroy money and so to lower or raise the value of the monetary unit of our nation" (1935: 197).

Fisher's understanding that most savers prefer short-term lending through holding checkable-deposit accounts—Harry Brown calls it "convenience waiting" (1940: 313)—also could have led to his appreciating that turning banks into warehouses and making such depositors "pay a small service and warehouse charge to the [banks] for keeping [their] money and for keeping track of its transfers by check" (Fisher 1935: 137–8) would decrease the supply of loanable funds to the banks.[51] The total volume of loans would contract, to the detriment of the economy's growth and employment creation. Fisher's expectation that the 100% system would generate "increased lending of longer-term money on the basis of time, or savings, deposits, not to mention increased investment" (ibid.: 139) presumes that the decrease in demand deposits would be more than compensated for by increases in time deposits. That is a rather doubtful supposition.

The institution of federal deposit insurance (FDIC) and eliminating the previous restrictions on branch banking in the US, including the McFadden Act (1927), have gone a long way to improve the functioning of the banking system. As Fisher acknowledged, "the United States [was] the only country which, in this depression, suffered from *general* bank failures, and accordingly we suffered more than any other country from contraction of check-book money" (1935: 147; italics original). He also correctly recognized that "The risk of bank failures could be nearly eliminated if we were willing to adopt the banking methods of other countries—especially branch banking" (1935: 177). However, the most Fisher credited the FDIC was "As a temporary expedient, deposit insurance was a helpful measure designed to get us out of the depression" (1935: 144). Thus, he argued, "Deposit insurance is at present adding safety, but that safety may yet turn into danger, if we retain the already inherent dangerous 10% system" (ibid.: 145). The history of US commercial banking has not affirmed his fears. Indeed, regulating banking firms according to the CAMELS (Capital, Assets, Management, Earnings, Liquidity, and Sensitivity to market risk; see R. Glenn Hubbard and Anthony O'Brien, 2018: 416–7) criteria has gone a long way to secure the safety of the US banking system.

Fisher also failed to recognize that the depression had ended in 1933 and the economy was well under way to its full recovery when his 1935 book was published. The sharp 1937–8 recession that followed the doubling of the reserve requirement also did not impress Fisher of the unhelpfulness of his 100% reserve proposal. It also appears to have been a significant hindrance to Fisher, just as it was to the Chicago proponents,[52] that the 100% reserve scheme was supposed to save capitalism from a socialist take-over. Fisher (1935: 200) declares: "the bankers, as long as they insist on operating or are permitted to operate their 10% system, will be playing with fire. The best available safeguard against the overthrow of capitalism is the 100% system, combined with money management, to give us a stable dollar." But the 100% proposal is a significant interference in the business of banking and the public's choice regarding the forms in which they hold their short-term savings and choice between alternative means of payment, based mainly upon misconceptions of money, money's substitute means of payment, and savings as the source of loanable funds.

Monetary theorists and macroeconomists may not have sufficient clarity about the institution of banking. Thus, for example, to determine the appropriate compensation to banking firms for the government's replacing their earning assets with currency, Fisher called for banking "experts … to work it out" (1935: 140). However, by including checkable deposits in "money," the variation of whose quantity constitutes monetary policy, many economists are inclined to accept the imposition of 100% reserve requirement as a legitimate policy tool. But checks and checkable deposits do not circulate, even as they may be the dominant means of payment in a modern economy. The evolution of modern banking, from the goldsmiths' custodial services to money depositors of old into their lending most of the public's savings, has served to promote economic growth, just as Adam Smith explained. Only by failing to appreciate the economic harm that the imposition of 100% reserve on checkable deposits would cause that many economists,[53] including some Noble Prize laureates, have supported the proposal.

Remarkably, even as John Maynard Keynes's (1930) treatment of banking and money influenced the conception of the 100% reserve proposal, he declined being its advocate when Fisher asked for his support in 1944: "I am satisfied that in British conditions anyhow … we can obtain complete control over the quantity of money by means much less capable of exciting unfavorable comment and opposition" (July 7, 1944, letter from Keynes to Fisher, quoted in Allen 1993: 715, n. 49).[54] One hopes that the public's sensitivity to their potential losses from the disappearance of fractional-reserve check-able deposits in terms of (a) the greater liquidity of their short-term savings in checkable deposits, (b) the cheaper means of making payments with checks rather than money, (c) their being spared the cost of gathering information on borrowers of funds held in checkable deposits by the banks, and (d) the elimi-nation of income risk by specified interest on their checkable deposits rather than their investing the funds themselves would keep the 100% proposal from being accepted at the ballot box.

Notes

1 Albert Hart (1935: 104) notes, "All immediate interest in [the Chicago 100% Plan] is removed by the advent of the Federal Deposit Insurance Corporation." Hart, neverthe-less, supported the plan because of its enabling a "truly effective monetary control" (ibid.: 105). Similarly, Milton Friedman (1960: 20–1) observes that "establishment of federal insurance of bank deposits ... renders banking panics all but impossible ... by eliminat-ing any reason for runs to begin." Friedman and Anna Schwartz (1963: 11) also argue that "the enactment of federal deposit insurance ... probably has succeeded, where the Federal Reserve Act failed, in rendering it impossible for a loss of public confidence in some banks to produce a widespread banking panic involving severe downward pres-sure on the stock of money." Yet Friedman (1960: 65–6) still endorses the 100% reserves proposal as an instrument of monetary control, not for price-level stability. Fisher did not fully recognize the assurance provided savers by the FDIC. He argued, "As a tem-porary expedient, deposit insurance was a helpful measure designed to get us out of the depression ... Deposit insurance is at present adding safety, but that safety may yet turn into danger, if we retain the already inherent dangerous 10% system" (1935: 144). The willingness of many economists to trade economic growth from increased savings under a fractional-reserve system for "monetary control" has been quite remarkable. Keynes's (1930) inclusion of savings deposited with commercial banks in "money" has played a considerable role in this, e.g. Lauchlin Currie (1935, esp. Ch. 2).

2 Fisher notes that "At one state in its evolution the book was mimeographed and sent to one hundred and fifty persons for criticism" (1935: x). Perhaps he just disregarded argu-ments by those included in the list who opposed his proposal, believing them simply to have failed to understand it. He treated mostly the bankers who objected to his scheme as worth regarding as "ignorant, indifferent, or even malicious malefactors" (1935: 197). He also believed, "One reason why bankers in general will oppose the 100% system is that they do not realize the fool's paradise in which they are now living because of the 10% system. They are blissfully unaware of the risks they carry" (1935: 154). The subse-quent pointed criticisms by Harry Brown (1940), his assistant in writing the *Purchasing Power of Money* (1911), and Rollin Thomas (1940) also had little influence on Fisher's belief in the desirability of the scheme. Benjamin Higgins of Harvard also disagreed with Brown's explaining that savers in checkable deposits are the real lenders. Higgins argues, it "is surely not the case [that] demand depositors are the true lenders" (1941: 92, n. 5). Similarly, Frank Graham of Princeton describes Brown's clarification as "sheer casuistry" (1941: 338), that is, a "false application of principles" (*Webster's Dictionary* 1980: 172). For a review of the literature on Fisher's 100% proposal, see Robert Dimand (1993b). For a very informative account of Fisher's promotion of the program till his death in 1947, see William Allen (1993).

3 Fisher credits a group at the University of Chicago from whose "memorandum" on the 100% proposal he "originally obtained many of the ideas embodied in this book. Professor Simons, in particular, has given generously of his time in personal consultation, as well as in going over parts of the manuscript" (1935: ix). For a good account of the

Chicago economists' formulation of their monetary and banking policies in the 1930s, see George Tavlas (2019).

4 Fisher acknowledges Currie's *The Supply and Control of Money in the United States* as also having "treated of this subject" (1935: ix).

5 Allen (1993) documents Fisher's efforts to recruit mostly economists to support his 100% reserve program. In a letter to President Roosevelt in January 1941, Fisher claimed the support of "some 400 economists" for the program (Allen 1993: 714).

6 Kotlikoff terms his 100% reserve banking "Limited Purpose Banking," seeking to separate the business of deposit-taking and its transfer to make payments from the business of investing people's savings. That was exactly Fisher's (1935) intent. Fisher wanted "the replacement of demand deposits by time deposits [so that] Commercial banking would gradually tend to become investment banking in all of its forms … instead of what the bankers, in their 10% straight jacket, now need" (1935: 136). However, the US financial crisis of 2008 really involved investment banks, such as Lehman Brothers, that invested in mortgage-backed securities, not commercial banks. Kotlikoff thus misapplied the 100% reserve remedy.

7 Depending upon the kind of contract banks have with their time-deposit customers, a bank could be driven into bankruptcy if such depositors demanded repayment of their deposits in cash when the bank's investments have failed. Fisher (1935: 197–8), in effect, concedes the point.

8 Currie ([1934b] 1935) has spotty references to John Stuart Mill and Alfred Marshall, mainly with respect to their treatment of credit. His references to John Maynard Keynes there are quite extensive.

9 Lauchlin Currie's version of the same argument is: "The merit of the proposal here set forth lies … in the fact that it divorces the supply of money from the loaning of money" (1935: 152).

10 Fisher (1935) makes this erroneous claim repeatedly, including on pages 17, 34, 38, 81, 84, 121, and 130, or that "check-book money is … created by a sort of sleight of hand" (36). Even the Bank of England repeats the claim on its 2014 website. Martin Wolf, chief economic commentator for the *Financial Times*, is there quoted to have argued that "the essence of the contemporary monetary system is the creation of money, *out of nothing*, by private banks' often foolish lending" (italics added).

11 Until its prohibition in Regulation Q in August 1933, commercial banks paid interest on checkable or demand deposits. The prohibition lasted until July 2011 when banks were again allowed to pay interest on demand deposits.

12 Fisher expresses a similar view of money (cash) being employed to extend multiple loans, but he incorrectly limits that understanding to time deposits only: "the volume of loans can exceed the volume of money just as sales do. The same money can negotiate one loan after another just as it can negotiate one sale after another. It can even come back to the same savings bank and be relent so long as the loans are made out of real money" (1935: 79–80). A qualifying point, however, is that smaller units of money (savings) are returned at each successive deposit. I elaborate below.

13 George Robinson (1937: 447) appropriately objects to Fisher's "erroneous distinction of character and origin between demand deposits and time deposits." William Hackett (1945) similarly disputes Fisher's treatment of demand deposits, mentioned in Dimand (1993b).

14 Robert Hemphill yet repeats Fisher's mistaken argument in the book's foreword (1935: xiii).

15 As Harry Brown well describes the process, "The borrowing accomplishes nothing for those who receive the deposits until they use their newly acquired credit for the purchase of goods, by writing checks on this credit. When they have done this, they no longer have claims on the lending banks" (1940: 309). That is, the "D" in M1 decreases to its previous level after a loan is spent.

16 The typical textbook exposition of the deposit-expansion process tends to neglect the fact that the deposits are the public's savings into checkable accounts, e.g. Gregory

Mankiw (2013: 88–91) or James Gwartney et al. (2018: 260–2). Lauchlin Currie's illustration of the deposit-expansion process is also quite misleading. He starts with an initial deposit of $1,000, assumes a 10% reserve against deposits at all banks, and then proceeds to generate diminishing redeposits as banks purchase bonds. The end result is $10,000 in checkable deposits, $9,000 generated loans, and $1,000 in accumulated reserves. He does not reckon that the initial and subsequent borrowers (bond sellers) spend the funds rather than leave them with their banks to lend (buy bonds); see Currie (1935: 65–6).

17 Smith includes securing "from fire, robbery, and other accidents" (*WN*, 1: 503) among the reasons for keeping bank deposits rather than currency.

18 Fisher claims that "at present, there is a confusion of ownership. When money is deposited in a checking account, the depositor still thinks of that money as his, though legally it is the bank's. The depositor owns no deposit; he is merely a creditor of a private corporation" (1935: 11). But Fisher recognizes deposits as belonging to savers under his 100% plan: "A full 100% reserve has the status of a *trust fund*, the real owners of which are the depositors. A 99% reserve would have to be considered, like a 10% reserve, as belonging to the banks" (1935: 177; italics original). Of course, a saver's deposit is a bank's liability and an asset (wealth) for the saver, be it a checkable or time deposit.

19 Douglas Diamond and Phillip Dybvig (1986) regrettably use "liquidity" as what banks transfer in their lending activity rather than savings or loanable funds. Almost like Keynes (1930), they even reverse the order of the transaction: banks converting "illiquid loans [assets] into liquid deposits [liabilities]" (1986: 58) instead of banks converting their liquid liabilities (deposits) into illiquid assets (loans). Otherwise, their analysis of banking and the danger to an economy from the 100% reserve proposal is very informative. "In conclusion," they declare, "100% reserve banking is a dangerous proposal that would do substantial damage to the economy by reducing the overall amount of liquidity [loanable funds]" (ibid.: 66).

20 A loan extended with a private bank note in a most unusual instance of its not ever being redeemed may fit Hemphill's description, but not a loan credited to a checkable-deposit account.

21 In fact, short-term (3 months) Treasury bill rates rose from 0.95% in January 1931 to 3.25% by December 1931 before declining to their lowest of 0.08% in December 1932. The rates then rose to 2.20% by March 1933, declined to 0.10% by September 1933, and then rose again to 0.69% by December 1933. See Federal Reserve (federalreserve.g ov) Table 1. 3-Month Treasury Bill Rates.

22 This is the exact opposite of Robert Hemphill's claim in the book's foreword: "If all bank loans are paid, no one would have a bank deposit, and there would not be a dollar currency or coin in circulation" (1935: xiii).

23 Thomas argues, "The only legitimate claim which can be made for the 100 per cent reserve plan is that it furnishes a better way to introduce control over the supply of money than any which might reasonably be provided under the existing banking set-up" (1940: 315–6); "under no circumstances can the 100 per cent plan do more than free the economy from forced credit liquidation imposed by the banks" (320–1); and "monetary shrinkage arising from forced liquidation of credit may be eliminated under the 100 per cent plan" (ibid.).

24 Hart thinks the 100% plan would abolish what Senator Gore remarks of the Federal Home Loan Banks as their being engaged in the "free and unlimited coinage of debt" and he also entertained the view that "Bankers could … call more loans than they made" (1935: 106). This is why the plan was needed to control the money supply.

25 Fisher (1935: 140) recognizes that banks paid interest on checkable deposits.

26 Currie (1935: 67) does not derive the same conclusion because he reasons that the cash received to retire the debt comes from the banking system, not from currency in circulation.

27 Data on currency in circulation and demand deposits are from Friedman and Schwartz (1970: 68), Table 2, and data on banks' reserves at Federal Reserve Banks are from Friedman and Schwartz (1963: 740), Table A–2.

28 Fisher (1935: 165) repeats the mistaken claim: "in a depression the public increases its *pocket-book* money [cash] by withdrawing it from the banks, being led to do so by the fear that the 10% reserves will not hold out. But for every dollar added to *pocket-book* money about ten dollars of check-book money has to be destroyed" (italics original). Friedman and Schwartz (1963: 346) repeat Fisher's claim: "It was the necessity of reducing deposits by $14 in order to make $1 available for the public to hold as currency that made the loss of confidence in the banks so cumulative and so disastrous. Here was the famous multiple expansion process of the banking system in vicious reverse."

29 Fisher's argument repeats his debt-deflation theory of depressions in his 1933 *Econometrica* article, itself a summary of his arguments in *Booms and Depressions* (1932).

30 Even as they correctly reject the usefulness of the 100% reserve proposal, Diamond and Dybvig (1986) also accept Fisher's tying loans to the money supply: "unanticipated deflation causes higher than expected loan losses. Higher loan losses lead to more bank failures and decrease in the money supply, adding to unanticipated deflation" (63).

31 Smith also observes, "The speculative merchant exercises no one regular, established, or well known branch of business … He enters into every trade when he foresees that it is likely to be more than commonly profitable, and he quits it when he foresees that its profits are likely to return to the level of other trades … A bold adventurer may sometimes acquire a considerable fortune by two or three successful speculations; but is just as likely to lose one by two or three unsuccessful ones" (*WN*, 1: 127).

32 For example, the Bank of the United States in New York "ultimately paid off [only] 83.5 per cent of its adjusted liabilities at its closing on December 11, 1930" (Friedman and Schwartz 1963: 311).

33 In the third edition of the book, Fisher uses a similarly dramatic but misleading description of the episode: "Deposits are the modern equivalent of bank notes. But bank deposits may be created and destroyed invisibly, whereas bank notes have to be printed and cremated. If eight billion bank notes had been cremated between 1929 and 1933, the fact could scarcely have been overlooked" (Fisher 1945: 8; quoted in Dimand 1993b: 63).

34 Data from Friedman and Schwartz, 1970, Table A–2, pages 739, 740, and Friedman and Schwartz 1963, Table 2, pages 803–4.

35 We may infer from the 40% increase in currency in circulation plus the net 16% increase in bank reserves (10% decrease in vault cash plus 26.1% increase in reserves held at Federal Reserve Banks) that money's transactions velocity decreased over the period by about 56%. We need an estimate of the behavior of transactions (T) to employ the equation-of-exchange version of the Quantity Theory, HV = PT, from which to derive $\%\Delta P = \%\Delta H + \%\Delta V - \%\Delta T$. The volume of business transactions (T) evidently decreased over the period but would likely not have overcompensated for the decline in velocity (V = 1/k) to have prevented the level of prices from falling in spite of the 21% increase in currency (H).

36 Thus, Smith's warning about the dangers to the commerce and industry of a country when "suspended upon the Daedalian wings of paper money" rather than being founded "upon the solid ground of gold and silver" (*WN*, 1: 341) may not be read as his advocating no loan extensions by paper money, the modern equivalent of bank deposits.

37 The doubling of the required reserve ratio against demand deposits is widely credited with having produced the sharp recession between May 1937 and June 1938 when real GDP fell by 19%; see Friedman (1960: 14, 20), and Richard Timberlake (1999), and Michael Bordo and Joseph Haubrich (2017). The recession ended after the Federal Reserve reversed the increase in required reserves.

38 Fisher (1913: 25–6, n. 2) credits David Ricardo with "probably [deserving] chief credit for launching the [quantity] theory" which explains the level of prices by "the amount of money, rapidity of circulation, and the amount of trade."

39 Marshall (1923: 48) acknowledges that proposition as "almost a truism."
40 Keynes (1983: 693) considers Marshall's testimony before the 1886 Gold and Silver Commission and 1899 Indian Currency Committee the "best and clearest statements of the [Quantity] theory."
41 Walker here well restates Mill's (*Works*, 3: 539–40) argument. Marshall (1923: 13, n. 2) acknowledges Walker's distinction between money and non-monies (money substitutes) on the basis of money's use fully to discharge debts as having "won its way to general acceptance." Fisher (1913: 11) also acknowledges Walker's argument. But Keynes (1930) appears to be the principal source of the current inclusion of savings in bank deposits as "money."
42 Keynes (1930, 1: 233–9), however, praises the "genius of Professor Fisher" for his statement of the equation of exchange to include checkable deposits, but faults him for not including "overdraft facilities" as well. Ralph Hawtrey (1950), David Laidler (1969, 1993b), and Milton Friedman and Anna Schwartz (1970) all have followed Keynes's and Fisher's inclusion of checkable deposits in "money."
43 For example, in December 1980, Friedman predicted that because of "the rapid monetary growth [M_{1-B}, "currency and all checking account"] of the past six months, we would be heading for inflation in the neighborhood of 20 percent by the end of 1981 or early 1982" (1983: 268). But the inflation rate in 1981 turned out to be 10.32%; the rate was 6.16% in 1982. Michael Brady (1986) and Edward Nelson (2007) detail Friedman's incorrect predictions of inflation in the US between 1981 and 1985. I thank Jeffrey Hummel for alerting me to Friedman (1983) and George Selgin for helping me locate Edward Nelson's (2007) article.
44 Fisher in that book, in fact, argues, "The student should … try to forget all former notions concerning the so-called supply and demand for capital as the causes of interest" (1930: 32). Ahiakpor (2003b, Ch. 8) elaborates Fisher's unhelpful views on capital and interest theory.
45 Dennis Robertson ([1922] 1957; italics original) also appears to have encouraged the neglect of the unit-of-account characteristic of money by arguing, "It is not necessary that everything which is used as a medium of exchange should itself be also a standard of value, but only that it should be expressed in terms of something which *is* a standard of value. For instance, John Smith's cheques may be widely accepted in discharge of his obligations, and are therefore rightly regarded … as money" (3)."
46 As Allen (1993: 706–7) explains, it took about eight months of persuasion from the Chicago group, mostly from Henry Simons, for Fisher to embrace the 100% proposal by the end of 1933.
47 Fisher's claim follows closely the opening sentence in the November 1933 Chicago memorandum prepared by Henry Simons: "Our government has, in a significant sense, allowed the commercial banks to usurp its primary function of controlling the currency" (quoted in Allen 1993: 707). Currie (1935: 155–6) also invokes the same constitutional argument for demanding that the government control all money, "both notes and deposits subject to check" (151).
48 The claim repeats a statement in the opening paragraph of Henry Simons's 1933 memorandum: "Money is created [by commercial banks] when it should be destroyed, and destroyed when it should be created" (quoted in Allen 1993: 707).
49 Currie (1935: 154–5) similarly envisions tax reduction benefits to the public from the government's buying up its bonds from the banks.
50 Payments to foreign holders of a nation's debt represent a leakage from the left-hand to the right-hand conception of such interest payments.
51 Currie's 100% reserve proposal also includes banks imposing "a service charge on depositors" for acting as "middlemen or forwarding agents" between the depositors and borrowers. Rather than "a small service charge," as Fisher believed, Albert Hart (1935: 105, 113, 115) anticipates the checkable-deposit account holders paying "heavy service charges."

52 The Chicago group called their plan, "*A Positive Program for Laissez-Faire*," although it entailed significant restrictions on the public's freedom to make short-term deposits with commercial banks and the banks' making most of those funds available to borrowers at interest, some of which they share with the depositors.

53 Clearly, understanding what banks do requires serious study. Macroeconomics is taught to all students of economics but banking is a specialized subject to which most students tend not to be exposed. The bank-deposit expansion process, for example, tends to be explained as banks magically creating deposits without their reliance on the public's deposited savings. That banks "create money" by extending loans (Keynes 1930) is the typical explanation.

54 However, rather being inflationary, as we noted above, Keynes thought the 100% money "would, certainly in England, have a highly deflationary suggestion to a great many people" (quoted in Allen 1993: 715, n. 49).

8 Keynes's liquidity trap is impossible

Classical monetary analysis helps to explain

Introduction[1]

Modern macro and monetary economists' adoption of Keynes's changed and inconsistent definitions of money, sometimes as central bank currency and at other times to include bank deposits, and their acceptance as legitimate his liquidity-preference (cash) theory of interest rates have enabled his impossible liquidity-trap proposition to endure in modern macroeconomics for far too long. Not even such acute macro and monetary theorists as Milton Friedman (1970a) and David Laidler (1993b) deny the proposition's possibility; they only doubt its empirical significance or verification.[2] But the proposition is badly flawed when carefully examined in light of the classical economic principles to which Keynes (1936) failed to adhere.

Keynes's (1936) liquidity trap argues that an economy could get stuck in a depression when

> after the rate of interest has fallen to a certain level, liquidity-preference [demand for cash] may become virtually absolute in the sense that almost everyone prefers cash to holding a debt which yields so low a rate of interest. In this event the monetary authority would have lost effective control over the rate of interest.
>
> (207)[3]

It would then require government deficit spending, financed by borrowing from the central bank, to stimulate aggregate demand and achieve economic recovery.

Keynes was arguing against the generally accepted view at the beginning of the Great Depression that an increased rate of money creation by central banks was a requisite to cure the price deflation that was depressing business investment and production, a conclusion that derives readily from the classical Quantity Theory of money; see J. Ronnie Davis (1971) and Ahiakpor (2010).[4] R.G. Hawtrey (1933) prominently canvassed the monetary expansion view, but which Keynes (1936) does not mention. According to Hawtrey,

A moderate trade depression can be cured by cheap money. The cure will be prompter if a low bank rate is reinforced by purchases of securities in the open market by the central bank. But so long as the depression is moderate, low rates will of themselves suffice to stimulate borrowing.

(29)

Hawtrey also insists, "The only satisfactory way to escape from [a] trade depression is by restarting the normal process by which the banks lend, and generate incomes and demand ... The *only* real remedy is the expansion of credit by the central bank" (127; italics original).

Keynes's changed view on the potency of monetary policy in a depression is illustrated in modern macroeconomics with a horizontal LM curve in the IS–LM model (Hicks 1937; Branson 1972: 129–30),[5] whose analytical usefulness Hicks (1980/81) no longer believed. The liquidity-trap proposition lost currency from about the mid-1970s,[6] mostly following publications by Milton Friedman's (1960, 1968a, 1970a, 1970b) and Friedman and Anna Schwartz (1963, 1970). These succeeded in persuading most of the economics profession that the Great Depression rather demonstrated the potency of monetary policy: reduce the money supply, and the economy contracts; increase the money supply, and the economy expands. In easily his most well-known form, the 1967 Presidential address to the American Economic Association, Friedman (1968a: 3; italics added) declares,

> The Great Contraction in the United States occurred ... [because] the U.S. monetary authorities followed highly deflationary policies. The quantity of money in the United States fell by one-third in the course of the contraction ... because the Federal Reserve System forced or permitted a sharp reduction in the *monetary base*.

In fact, the monetary base or "high-powered money" actually increased by 20.49%, from $6.98 billion in January 1930 to $8.41 billion by March 1933 when the US went off gold (Friedman and Schwartz 1963: 803–4; see also Fisher 1935: 5–6).

However, Friedman and Schwartz demonstrated their claim about the potency of monetary policy, not with money defined as cash, as Keynes (1936: 174, 207) himself argued, but with M1 or M2, which partly obscures recognition of a flaw in Keynes's argument. Keynes had turned the Quantity Theory into a theory of interest rates. Friedman's (1956: 3) "restatement" of the Quantity Theory of money, as a theory not of the price level but of the demand for money, also appears to have obscured effective evaluation of Keynes's liquidity-preference theory of interest. It also appears to have deflected critical examination of Keynes's claim that the demand curve for money (currency) is capable of changing shape to become horizontal at some low level of interest rates, contrary to the curve's representation as a rectangular hyperbola (Marshall 1923: 39–43, 282; Pigou 1912: 423; 1917).[7] The experience of stagflation in the late 1970s, during which interest rates rose along with increases in M1 and M2, also may have undermined the seriousness with which macroeconomists took the liquidity-trap proposition until its revival by Paul Krugman (1998).

Krugman (1998) cites the persistence of economic recession in Japan in the 1990s as evidence of Keynes's liquidity trap's return. Kathryn Dominguez (1998) agrees with Krugman's analysis but questions his prescription of an "irresponsible" monetary policy to the Bank of Japan. Kenneth Rogoff (1998) expresses skepticism about Krugman's prescription of a 15-year, 4% inflation policy pursuit and doubts his diagnosis of a liquidity trap for Japan, but describes his analysis as "a stunning piece of work" (199). Other than Edmund Phelps, none of the commentators on Krugman's (1998) analysis expresses doubt about the relevance of Keynes's liquidity-trap proposition to the experience of Japan. Lars Svensson (2003) follows Krugman in affirming the existence of liquidity traps; see also Eggertsson (2006; 2008). Following the US financial crisis of 2008, Krugman and several others have invoked the proposition to explain the failure of the Federal Reserve quickly to jump-start the economy with its massive purchases of financial assets under the so-called Quantitative Easing (QE1, QE2, and QE3) programs. Abel, Bernanke, and Croushore (2014: 561), Arias and Wen (2014), and Mishkin (2015: 277) are among those who have accepted that diagnosis for the US economy. Arias and Wen further argue that the low inflation rate experienced in the US since 2009 is due to the liquidity trap.

Most adherents to Krugman's claim also have changed Keynes's definition of a liquidity trap that focuses on a central bank's inability to reduce long-term interest rates below some (unspecified) low level to claiming its existence when central banks operate within a "zero lower bound" or when they appear unable to stimulate economic recovery. The claim has spawned literature that treats short-term interest rates close to zero as if they had the same effects as actual zero interest rates. Krugman (2013) updates his 1998 view thus:

> America and Japan (and core Europe) are all in liquidity traps: private demand is so weak that even at a zero short-term interest rate spending falls far short of what would be needed for full employment. And interest rates can't go below zero (except trivially for very short periods), because investors always have the option of simply holding cash.

But this is not Keynes's (1936) liquidity trap frustrating monetary policy; see below. It also must be a strange investor indeed who prefers holding cash that pays no interest to holding a bank account, mutual fund shares, or short-term government treasury bills that pay some low interest rate. The inflation tax at zero interest is higher than the tax at a non-zero interest on a financial asset. That partly explains why the fall of interest on 9-month CDs from more than 4% in 2008 to less than 0.1% by 2013 in the US did not cause their holders to redeem them to hold in cash at home. Besides, holding such financial assets also promotes increased borrowing and spending. The data too contradict Krugman's supposition about savers' behavior at near-zero interest rates; I elaborate below.

However, the appeals to Keynes's liquidity trap to explain persistent recessions fail to examine the legitimacy of his liquidity-preference theory of interest rates from which it derives.[8] In fact, the liquidity-preference theory of interest rates misrepresents the process of interest rate determination;[9] it gives an undue influence to a central bank's money creation, misrepresents the role of the public's savings, and minimizes or almost ignores the role of business and government's demand for credit in the determination of interest rates; neither Japan nor the US has experienced a liquidity trap, according to Keynes's own definition; and a liquidity trap is impossible, given the nature of an economy's demand curve for money (cash) that should be downward sloping throughout, not with respect to interest rates but with respect to the value of money— inverse of the level of prices ($V_m = 1/P$).

With the value of money on the vertical axis, money's nominal demand curve shifts with changes in interest rates, income, expectations, and other factors. Moreover, income is the means by which money is demanded to hold, which is thus limited at any point in time, and money's demand curve cannot keep shifting out endlessly upon a fall in interest rates. Several of Keynes's contemporaries, including Hawtrey (1937), Frank Knight (1937), Robertson (1936, 1940), and Jacob Viner (1936), criticized his pessimism over the potency of monetary policy in a depression but did not dwell on his misrepresentation of the nature of money's demand curve. Rather, they sought to reconcile his liquidity-preference theory of interest with the classical theory and emphasized his exaggeration of cash hoarding's effect; see Laidler (1999: 283–7) and Ahiakpor (2003b: 92–5).

Recent criticisms of the application of Keynes's liquidity trap to the experience of Japan, including Sumner (2002), Laidler (2004), and Sandilands (2010), have not addressed the above fundamental flaws in Keynes's proposition. They rather have noted Keynes's own downplaying the significance of his speculated phenomenon, besides criticizing the Bank of Japan for having failed to expand its monetary base adequately to deal with the price deflation. Laidler and Sandilands also suggest instead the relevance of Hawtrey's "credit deadlock" explanation for the alleged failure of monetary policy in Japan.

The failure to deal with Keynes's fundamental problems with the classical Quantity Theory have encouraged elaborations of his liquidity-trap argument with such analyses as Eggertsson's (2006; 2008) intertemporal stochastic general equilibrium model that shed little light on the proper role of a central bank. That role is to maintain the purchasing power of money or zero inflation (Hume 1752: 39), not central banks to be "irresponsible, to seek a higher future price level" (Krugman 1998: 139) or to manipulate the level of interest rates, short-term or long-term, let alone pursuing negative real interest rates. The rest of the chapter elaborates, employing classical monetary analysis.

Keynes's liquidity-preference theory of interest rates

Keynes's speculation about the possibility of a central bank's increased rate of money creation failing to reduce long-term interest rates below some unspecified low level derives from his cash (liquidity) supply and demand theory of interest rates. He advanced this theory in place of the classical Quantity Theory's explanation of the average level of prices and its growth rate—inflation or deflation—from variations in the supply of money relative to variations in money's demand by the public. To Keynes, the classical Quantity Theory's explanation is founded on the "assumptions that there is no propensity to hoard and that there is always full employment" (1936: 209), neither of which is true (Ahiakpor 1997a). He argues that the "primary effect of a change in the quantity of money ... is through its influence on the rate of interest" (298),[10] and in general, "instead of constant prices in conditions of unemployment, and of prices rising in proportion to the quantity of money in conditions of full employment, we have in fact a condition of prices rising gradually as employment increases" (296), following increases in the quantity of money.[11] Keynes elaborates the claim in his 1939 Preface to the French edition of the *General Theory*:

> The quantity of money determines the supply of liquid resources, and hence the rate of interest, and in conjunction with other factors (particularly that of confidence) the inducement to invest [purchasing producer's goods],[12] which in turn fixes the equilibrium level of income, output and employment and (at each stage in conjunction with other factors) the price level as a whole through the influences of supply and demand [for output] thus established.
>
> (1974: xxxv)

Money in Keynes's (1936) liquidity-preference theory refers to cash, which is thus exogenous: "it is impossible for the actual amount of [cash] hoarding to change as a result of decisions on the part of the public ... and the quantity of money is not determined by the public" (174). The public's desire to hold money depends upon the level of income, the level of interest rates, and expectations regarding future interest rates, according to Keynes. The familiar illustration of this theory of interest as the intersection of the supply and demand for money, but money defined as M1 or M2, derives from Keynes's argument that

> The rate of interest is not the "price" which brings into equilibrium the demand for resources to invest with the readiness to abstain from present consumption [savings]. It is the "price" which equilibrates the desire to hold wealth in the form of *cash* with the available quantity of *cash*;—which implies that if the rate of interest were lower, i.e. if the reward for parting with *cash* [interest] were diminished, the aggregate amount of *cash* which the public would wish to hold would exceed the available supply, and that

if the rate of interest were raised, there would be a surplus of *cash* which no one would be willing to hold. If this explanation is correct, the quantity of money is the other factor, which, in conjunction with liquidity-preference, determines the actual rate of interest in given circumstances.

(1936: 167–8; italics added)

Thus, according to Keynes's argument, an increase in the quantity of money (cash) would reduce the level of nominal interest rates, given money's demand, while a decreased quantity would increase their level. There is no upper limit to the level of interest rates, but zero is the lower bound: "the rate of interest is never negative" (1936: 168) or "in practice interest cannot be negative" (217).[13]

Increases in money's demand would increase the level of interest rates, given the exogenous supply, while decreases in the demand would decrease interest rates. However, if the demand for money increased at the same rate as the quantity increased, interest rates would be left unchanged. This defines the mechanism of Keynes's liquidity-trap proposition, although he limits its occurrence to some unspecified low (non-zero) level of long-term interest rate. The condition would arise if current holders of debt instruments (savers) expected future interest rates to rise; higher rates would cause a fall in the price of debt instruments (bonds), resulting in capital loss for their holders. They and prospective buyers of debt instruments would rather add to their cash balances instead, Keynes claims.

It is noteworthy that Keynes claims not to have observed the above phenomenon:

> But whilst this limiting case [of a liquidity trap] might become practically important in future, I know of no example of it hitherto. Indeed, owing to the unwillingness of most monetary authorities to deal boldly in debts of long term,[14] there has not been much opportunity for a test.
>
> (1936: 207)

This statement appears to have been a significant distraction for several scholars of Keynes's monetary analysis from examining the validity of his claim, e.g. Leijonhufvud (1968: 158, 161), Friedman (1970a: 25–6), and Patinkin (1976: 111–4).

But, in the very next paragraph, Keynes (1936) cites "certain dates in 1932" when the US experienced the "liquidity function flattening out … —a financial crisis or crisis of liquidation, when scarcely anyone could be induced to part with holdings of money on any reasonable terms" (207–8).[15] However, interest rates did fluctuate during 1932, contradicting Keynes's claim of their having got stuck at some low level (Table 8.1; see also Chart 35, p. 454 in Friedman and Schwartz 1963 for rates on US government bonds "not due or callable for 12 years or more." These fell below 3.5%, rose above that, and then declined to about 3.2% between 1930 and 1933).

Table 8.1 Three-Month US Treasury Bill Rates

Month	1931	1932	1933
January	0.95	2.68	0.21
February	1.21	2.65	0.48
March	1.46	2.08	2.29
April	1.31	0.77	0.56
May	1.01	0.43	0.42
June	0.63	0.41	0.27
July	0.48	0.42	0.37
August	0.60	0.44	0.21
September	1.22	0.23	0.10
October	2.47	0.18	0.16
November	2.22	0.18	0.42
December	3.25	0.08	0.69

Source: US Federal Reserve (federalreserve.gov).

Hawtrey (1950: 101), on the other hand, argues that England and the US experienced a "credit deadlock" between 1932 and 1939 when "an uninterrupted application of cheap money of unprecedented duration failed ever to induce a return of full activity." Hawtrey's argument is that businesses may not be enticed to increase borrowing at low interest rates if price deflation dampens their profit expectations. Hawtrey (1913: 186) also speculates about a possible "vicious circle" of declining prices and declining interest rates, owing to reductions in business demand for loans, but without relating that to a central bank's having initiated the decline in interest rates. However, a more direct argument seems to be that rising *real* interest rates, because of declining prices, discourage business borrowing even as nominal interest rates fall.

But, following the US going off gold in March 1933, the government assuring the public that only solvent banks were being allowed to reopen after the national banking holiday, and President Franklin Roosevelt signing in June 1933 the bill establishing the Federal Deposit Insurance Corporation (FDIC), the bank runs and price deflation ended, and real GDP grew at rates of 10.8%, 8.9%, 12.9%, and 5.1% between 1934 and 1937, along with continuing increases in the monetary base (federalreserve.gov); recall our discussion in Chapter 7 earlier.

The fundamental flaws in Keynes's liquidity-trap proposition

The first fundamental flaw in Keynes's liquidity-trap proposition is his having treated the rate of interest as the "reward for parting with liquidity [cash] for a specified period" (1936: 167), while denying that interest rates are the reward for saving. The claim follows from his inclusion of cash hoarding in his conception of saving: "if a man hoards his savings in cash, he earns no interest though he saves just as much as before" (167); see also Keynes (1937c: 668–9; 1938: 321). But the rate of interest is the cost of credit, made possible principally by the public's savings; and cash hoarding is not saving (purchasing interest- or dividend-earning assets), e.g. Smith (*WN*, 1: 358). Furthermore, it is not money (cash) that is borrowed; money merely serves as the loan's conveyance. Credit (loans) may be extended in the form of cash, a check, a bank draft, or an electronic transfer. As Smith (*WN*, 1: 373–4) explains:

> Almost all loans are made in money, either of paper, or of gold and silver. But what the borrower really wants, and what the lender really supplies him with, is not the money, but the money's worth, or the goods which it can purchase ... the money is, as it were, but the deed of assignment, which conveys from one hand to another those capitals [savings] which the owners do not care to employ themselves. Those capitals may be greater in almost any proportion, than the amount of the money which serves as the instrument of their conveyance, the same pieces of money successively serving for many different loans, as well as for many different purchases.

An approximation to Smith's explanation is the ratio of high-powered money (H) to M2, most of which is loaned out (bank credit).

Thus, interest rates are determined by the supply and demand for credit, of which changes in the quantity of a central bank's money are often a minor part. A central bank's money creation may influence the level of interest rates by affecting the supply of credit, as it lends directly to banks or purchases securities. The stock of central bank money relative to its demand determines the average level of prices, $P = H/ky$, using the Cambridge version of the Quantity Theory of money, where H = high-powered money, k = proportion of the public's income held in cash, and y = real income (GDP).

In the absence of a central bank's changed quantity of money (H), the flow of credit (S_{CR}) for a closed economy equals the savings rate, $S_{CR} = S_c = Y(1 - t) - C - \Delta H_h = \Delta FA^d$, where S_c = supply of "capital," Y = income, t = taxes, C = consumption spending, ΔH_h = change in households' cash holding, and ΔFA^d = savers' acquisition of financial assets, including bank deposits, money market mutual fund shares, pension funds, annuities, bonds, corporate paper, and stocks. Some savings may go into the bonds market, raise bond prices, and lower their yields; some may go into the stock market and raise stock prices. In the loanable-funds market, the credit supply curve slopes upward with respect to the rate of interest while the credit demand curve slopes downward. In equilibrium, market interest rates must equal bond yields and the dividend-price ratio, adjusting for default and liquidity risks. Saving is thus the act of acquiring interest- and/or dividend-earning assets by income earners, rather than merely the passive or "negative act of refraining from spending the whole of [one's] income on consumption" (Keynes 1930, 1: 172). As Mill (*Works*, 3: 647) explains,

The rate of interest will be such as to equalize the demand for loans with the supply of them. It will be such, that exactly as much as some people are desirous to borrow at that rate, others shall be willing to lend. If there is more offered than demanded, interest will fall; if more is demanded than offered, it will rise; and in both cases, to the point at which the equation of supply and demand is re-established.

Following a central bank's money creation, the flow of credit is, $S_{CR} = S_c + \Delta H$; a decrease in the quantity of central bank money decreases the flow of credit to $S_{CR} = S_c - \Delta H$. In the short run, before the level of commodity prices has reacted to the changed quantity of money, interest rates would fall (bond prices rise) when the quantity of money increases (see Figures 8.1a and 8.1b) or interest rates

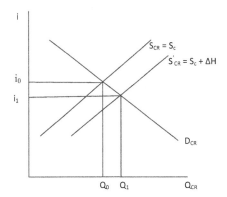

Figure 8.1a Increased central bank money creation ($\Delta H > 0$) increases the supply of credit ($S'_{CR} > S_{CR}$) and lowers equilibrium average interest rates ($i_1 < i_0$) before commodity prices rise.

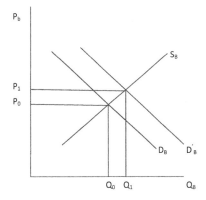

Figure 8.1b Increased central bank purchase of bonds increases the price of bonds ($P_1 > P_0$) and lowers bond yields before commodity prices rise.

rise (bond prices fall) when the quantity of money decreases—the liquidity effect (Gibson 1970; Friedman 1972). Interest rates would be restored to their original level after the level of commodity prices has reacted to the changed quantity of money—the price-level or income effect. In the case of an increased quantity of money, "The whole money may still be in the state, and make itself felt by the encrease of prices: But not being now collected into any large masses or stocks, the disproportion between the borrowers and lenders is the same as formerly, and consequently the high interest returns" (Hume 1752, "Of Interest," 58). Hume's argument is in respect to metallic money, but it applies to fiat, paper money as well. Marshall (1923: 257) restates the same principle, which Robertson (1936: 178, n. 2) and Hicks (1937: 151) quote: "The new currency, or the increase of currency, goes, not to private persons, but to the banking centers; and therefore, it increases the willingness of lenders to lend in the first instance, and lowers the rate of discount. But it afterwards raises prices; and therefore it tends to increase discount. This latter movement is cumulative."

The inflation (deflation) expectation effect moves equilibrium interest rates in the opposite direction of the liquidity effect; see also Friedman (1972) and Gibson (1970). Mill (*Works*, 3: 656) argues well the inflation expectation effect:

> Depreciation, merely as such, while in process of taking place, tends to raise the rate of interest: and the expectation of further depreciation adds to this effect; because lenders who expect that their interest will be paid and the principal perhaps redeemed, in less valuable currency than they lent, of course require a rate of interest sufficient to cover this contingent loss.

Marshall (1923) restates the classical principle:

> As a general rule, interest rises in consequence of a greater willingness of borrowers to borrow, or of a greater unwillingness of lenders to lend: the first generally indicates increased confidence, and perhaps increased prosperity; the latter generally indicates the opposite ... a fall in the purchasing power of money tends, after a while, to raise the rate of interest on investments, whether for long periods, or short.
>
> (73; see also 254–8)

Discussions of Keynes's liquidity trap that fail to take into account the price-level and expectations effects of changes in central bank money creation are thus incomplete.

Keynes (1936, Ch. 13), in effect, restates the classical determination (theory) of interest rates by the demand and supply of savings when he argues that "the rate of interest [depends] on the interaction of the schedule of the marginal efficiency of capital [profitability of investment in producer's goods] with the psychological propensity to save" (165). But, as is evident in the appendix to chapter 14 of the *General Theory*, Keynes's main obstacle to recognizing the classical theory's validity is his having misinterpreted "capital" to mean capital goods rather than savings or loanable funds.[16]

Keynes's focus on income earners' liquidity preference relative to a central bank's supply of liquidity (cash) as the determinant of interest rates also significantly blurs the impact of variations in business loans-demand in determining the level of interest rates. Interest rates may fall because of a reduced business demand for loanable funds or "capital," following shaken confidence in their expectation of profits or fears of losses. Similarly, interest rates may rise from an increased business demand for loanable funds, spurred by an increased expectation of profits, rather than from an increase in the public's liquidity preference or a reduced savings rate.

The second fundamental flaw in Keynes's liquidity-trap proposition derives from his having changed income earners' decision-making over spending from concurrently involving three margins, namely, consumption, acquisition of financial assets (saving), and cash holding (hoarding), to only two. Keynes first separates an individual's decision to hold money and to purchase debt instruments (or making bank deposits) from the decision to purchase consumption goods (time preference). Only afterwards do people make the money-debt split decision, Keynes argues: would the non-consumed income be held

> in the form of immediate, liquid command (i.e. money or its equivalent)? Or is [one] prepared to part with immediate command for a specified or indefinite period, leaving it to future market conditions to determine on what terms [one] can, if necessary, convert deferred command over specific goods into immediate command over goods in general?
>
> (1936: 166)

But people's decisions over income spending entail equalizing concurrently at three margins: (a) the utility of consumption, (b) the utility of the returns to saving (interest or yield on debt instruments), and (c) the utility of money's liquidity services, including the convenience and certainty of making future purchases; see Marshall (1923: 44–7).[17] Were the marginal utility of money's liquidity services to rise above those of consumption and the yield from investing in debt instruments or interest on bank deposits, income earners would increase their demand for money and cut back on both consumption purchases and the acquisition of financial assets. Given the available quantity of money, prices of consumption goods and debt instruments would fall (rise of yields or interest rates).[18] But were the marginal utility of money's liquidity services to fall below those of consumption and the yield from holding debt instruments or interest on deposits, the demand for money would fall while consumption spending and purchases of financial assets would increase. Product prices would rise, along with the price of debt instruments (yields or interest rates fall). The state of employment is thus irrelevant to the price-level effects of these changes in money's demand, or the Quantity Theory—determining the level of commodity prices by money's supply and demand.

Also, an increase in the public's time preference or impatience to consume would cause a reduction in the demand for debt instruments or holding bank deposits as well as a decrease in the demand for money to hold. Prices of consumption goods would rise along with a fall in the price of debt instruments (increased yield or interest rates). On the other hand, a decrease in time preference would decrease consumption demand, decrease consumption-goods prices, increase the demand for debt instruments or bank deposits (increased saving), and raise the price of debt instruments (reduce yields), or lower interest rates. An increase in savers' expectation of inflation would decrease the demand for money to hold, increase consumption spending, and reduce the savings rate (decreased demand for debt instruments or bonds), causing a rise of interest rates. On the other hand, a decrease in savers' expectation of inflation or the expectation of price deflation would decrease consumption demand, increase the demand for money as well as increase the savings rate (increased demand for financial assets), and lower interest rates (raise the price of financial assets).

Interest rates are thus determined by a host of factors, of which a central bank's rate of money creation is just one. Keynes thus was over-optimistic about the power of central banks to control interest rates with his assertion, "The short-term rate of interest is easily controlled by the monetary authority, both because it is not difficult to produce a conviction that its policy will not greatly change in the very near future, and also because the possible [capital] loss is small compared with the running yield (unless it is approaching vanishing point)" (1936: 202–3). But short-term interest rates have been known to rise even as a central bank increased its rate of money creation. For example, interest rates rose in the US between 1975 and 1980 while the Fed increased its rate of money creation above 5.9% each year; see Table 8.2. In a high inflation environment, the inflation expectation effect of monetary expansion may negate the liquidity effect. For example, in Argentina the monetary base increased at percentage rates of 99.3, 491.2, 369.7, 466.2, and 413.9 between 1981 and 1985. The inflation rate, measured as the GDP deflator, increased at percentage rates of 106.5, 201.9, 383.1, 609.3, and 618.2 in those years, while interest rates on deposits also rose along with the monetary increases: 157, 127, 283, 397, and 520% (*source: International Financial Statistics Yearbook 1995*).

The ultimate fundamental flaw in Keynes's liquidity-trap proposition is his claim that "the liquidity function flatten[s] out in one direction or the other … in very abnormal circumstances" (1936: 207) or the demand curve for money becomes horizontal at some low level of nominal (long-term) interest rates. The demand for money (cash) is for an asset to hold towards achieving some future real value function—purchase of goods and services: "A country's demand for [money] is not for a certain amount of metallic (or other) currency; but for an amount of currency which has a certain purchasing power" (Marshall 1923: 39). Therefore, more of the nominal quantity is demanded when prices rise (value falls) and a smaller quantity is demanded when prices fall (value rises); Keynes (1924: 83–5) repeats the point, citing its exposition by Marshall (1923, I, iv) and Pigou (1917). Pigou (1912: 423) earlier writes: "The

Table 8.2 US Money Growth, Interest Rates, and GDP Growth

	1975	76	77	78	79	80	81	82	83	84	85
H Growth	5.9	5.9	6.6	9.8	8.7	7.2	3.7	4.8	7.0	5.7	8.1
TBR	5.82	4.99	5.27	7.22	10.04	11.62	14.08	10.72	8.62	9.57	7.49
FFR	5.82	5.05	5.54	7.93	11.20	13.36	16.38	12.26	9.09	10.23	8.10
G Bond Y(M)	7.49	6.77	6.69	8.29	9.71	11.55	14.44	12.92	10.45	11.89	9.64
G Bond Y(L)	7.99	7.61	7.42	8.41	9.44	11.46	13.91	13.00	11.11	12.52	10.62
GDP Def	9.9	6.3	6.7	7.4	8.8	9.1	9.6	6.4	3.9	4.0	2.8
GDP Growth	−1.0	4.8	4.6	5.2	2.1	−0.2	2.0	−2.5	3.7	6.8	3.8

Note: TBR = Treasury bill rate; FFR = Federal Funds rate; G Bond Y(M) = medium-term government bond yield; G Bond Y(L) = long-term government bond yield.
Source: IMF, *International Financial Statistics Yearbook 1995.*

elasticity of demand for money is, as is well known, equal to unity." See also Frank Taussig (1921: 234). That is why the money demand curve, properly drawn, has a unitary elasticity with respect to the value of money (1/P)—a rectangular hyperbola—and not with the interest rate on the vertical axis.

Changes in the level of interest rates shift the money demand curve: money's demand increases when interest rates fall, and decreases when interest rates rise. But the primary means for acquiring money (besides borrowing) is income, which is fixed at any point in time. If money is borrowed, it is meant to be spent rather than held or hoarded. Moreover, money's velocity (V = Y/H) cannot fall below 1. That is, the proportion of income that the public chooses to hold in cash (k) cannot reach 1; all monetary exchanges would cease, if that happened. Besides, if everyone tried to sell their existing financial assets for money, asset prices sharply would fall, raising their yields or nominal interest rates enormously. The rise of interest rates would thus put the brakes on the increasing demand for money, as income earners balance at the margin the utility of money's liquidity services, the return on holding financial assets, and the utility of consumption spending. It is therefore inconceivable for the money demand curve to keep endlessly increasing at some low level interest rate, as Keynes claims. It is also unnecessary to invoke bond suppliers' behavior to deny Keynes's claim as Patinkin (1965: 349) argues: "the amount of money demanded cannot become infinite unless the supply of bonds does so." The supply of bonds is a demand for credit to spend, not for money to hold.

Keynes (1936: 167, n. 1) did shift from defining money as cash only to including other financial assets, such as bank deposits and treasury bills. But that changed definition only confuses his analysis.[19] If money is defined to include anything other than cash, its quantity is no longer fixed by a central bank. Money's supply curve would then be positively sloped with respect to the rate of interest: more funds offered on loan as interest rates rise. Keynes's argument that "the quantity of money is not determined by the public" (1936: 174) would no longer hold. However, even if money were defined broadly, its increased holding (by savers) need not decrease spending on commodities because banks lend most of the public's deposits (both demand and time) at interest, to be spent by borrowers.

Patinkin could have helped to end the propagation of Keynes's liquidity-trap proposition sooner, but did not. Patinkin (1965: 28–30) switches from representing nominal money demand curve as a rectangular hyperbola to one that is not, although still negatively sloped, "as soon as the increase in money prices is *not* accompanied by an equiproportionate increase in nominal money holdings" (29; italics original). Instead, he derives a "market-equilibrium curve" for money's demand that is a rectangular hyperbola by conducting a "conceptual market-experiment" (48–50) in which an increase in the money supply immediately increases money's demand at existing prices; Blaug (1996: 153–5) adopts Patinkin's reasoning.

Fisher (1913: 242–4), for example, gives a detailed refutation of that reasoning. A more plausible argument is that an increase in money's supply may lower interest rates and shift rightward the rectangular hyperbola money demand curve that Patinkin's (1965: 605–9) survey of neoclassical monetary analysts, including Marshall and Pigou, shows they argued. When prices rise and an increased demand for credit causes interest rates to rise, the demand for money (to hold) would fall back to its original position. Patinkin (1965: 349) also argues that "when due account is taken of the individuals' planned behavior in all markets, [the money demand] curve must retain its negative slope throughout." Nevertheless, he argues the possibility of monetary policy's failure to reduce market interest rates below some low level "no matter the shape of the demand curve for money" (352), thus continuing to affirm the possibility of Keynes's liquidity trap.

Ascertaining the occurrence of a liquidity trap

Keynes's liquidity trap can be shown to be impossible on theoretical grounds; empirical evidence also fails to support it. As noted above, interest rates were not stuck at some low level, in spite of the US Fed's (base) money creation in 1932,[20] as Keynes claimed. Recent Japanese data (Table 8.3a) also do not confirm Keynes's proposition. The high-powered money's growth rate was erratic, varying between 2.9% and 8.5% between 1993 and 1998, reaching 44.5% in 1999, then declining by a negative rate of −19.9% in 2000. The growth rate was reversed almost by the same magnitude in 2001, and then it declined to 12.0% in 2003. These money growth rates were accompanied by a steady decline in government bond yields, from 3.693% in 1993 to 1.097% in 1998, rising to 1.748% in 2000 before declining steadily to 1.013% in 2003. Lending rates, on the other hand, declined steadily from 4.410% in 1993 to 1.767% in 2004 (*International Financial Statistics Yearbook* 2005). With the exception of 1993, 1994, 1997, and 1998 when the inflation rate, measured by the GDP deflator, was positive or zero, there was deflation that attained its highest rate of −2.6% in 2003. Thus, nominal interest rates did not fail to decline in Japan while money's growth rate averaged 9.4% over 11 years. But claiming that "The short-term nominal interest rate in Japan collapsed to zero in the second half of the 1990s" (Eggertsson 2008: 155) is an exaggeration.

The price deflation, however, means that Japan's money growth rate over the period had been less than the growth of money's demand. The deflation also means that real interest rates had risen, discouraging business borrowing. It thus should not be surprising that Japan's unemployment rate increased steadily from 2.5% in 1993 to above 5.0% between 2001 and 2003, even as the GDP's volume growth rate was negative only in 1998 and 2002. It is well known that price deflation causes business losses and increased unemployment; see Marshall and Marshall (1879: 156–7), Marshall (1920: 493–4, 515), Taussig (1921: 299), and Fisher (1926). On the other hand, Japan's money growth rate averaged only 2.8% between 2004 and 2012 while the deflation averaged −1.2%; see Table 8.3b. Bond yields also tended to decline over the period while the discount rate rose from 0.10% to 0.75% in 2007, then declined to

Table 8.3a Some Relevant Japanese Data

	1993	94	95	96	97	98	99	00	01	02	03
H Growth	5.8	2.9	7.8	8.5	7.3	3.7	44.5	-19.9	19.4	11.8	12.0
3-M DR	3.00	2.31	1.27	0.63	0.63	0.71	0.22	0.28	0.15	0.08	0.06
Disc Rate	1.75	1.75	0.50	0.50	0.50	0.50	0.50	0.50	0.50	0.10	0.10
G Bond Y	3.693	3.714	2.532	2.225	1.688	1.097	1.771	1.748	1.334	1.251	1.013
GDP Def	0.6	0.1	-0.5	-1.0	0.3	–	-1.6	-2.0	-1.5	-1.1	-2.6
GDP Growth	0.2	1.13	1.88	3.62	1.82	-1.16	0.19	2.88	0.40	-0.49	2.57
UER	2.5	2.9	3.2	3.4	3.4	4.1	4.7	4.7	5.0	5.4	5.3

Note: H Growth = growth rate of Reserve money; 3-M DR = three-month deposit rate; Disc Rate = discount rate; G Bond Y = government bond yield; GDP Def = GDP deflator; GDP Growth = GDP volume growth rate; UER = unemployment rate.
Source: International Financial Statistics Yearbook 2005.

Table 8.3b Recent Japanese Data

	04	05	06	07	08	09	10	11	12	13
H Growth	3.8	0.9	-18.7	1.3	5.5	4.5	3.5	14.2	10.7	45.8
Disc Rate	0.10	0.10	0.40	0.75	0.30	0.30	0.30	0.30	0.30	0.30
G Bond Y	1.499	1.360	1.731	1.653	1.449	1.343	1.151	1.118	0.839	0.700
GDP Def	-1.4	-1.3	-1.1	-0.9	-1.3	-0.5	-2.2	-1.9	-0.9	-0.6
GDP Growth	2.4	1.3	1.7	2.2	-1.0	-5.5	4.7	-0.5	1.4	1.5
URE	4.4	4.4	4.1	3.8	4.0	5.1	5.1	4.6	4.4	4.0

Note: H Growth = growth rate of Reserve money; Disc Rate = discount rate; G Bond Y = government bond Yield; GDP Def = GDP deflator; GDP Growth = GDP volume growth rate; UER = unemployment rate.
Source: IMF, *International Financial Statistics 2014.*

0.30% throughout the period. Clearly, the Bank of Japan was not consistently aggressive with its monetary expansion to deal with the deflation.

Recent US data (see federalreserve.gov) also show varying but declining long-term and short-term interest rates, along with the Fed's Quantitative Easing, especially between 2008 and 2012. Starting from 3.94% in January 2008, the federal funds rate declined to an average of 1.76% for the year, 2008, and further sharply to an average of 0.15% in 2009. The average rose slightly to 0.16% in 2010 and fell to 0.09% in 2011. It rose to 0.13% in 2012, and fell to 0.10% in 2013, and further to 0.08% in 2014. The average rate on 3-month Treasury bills declined steadily from 3.69% in 2008 to 3.23% in 2009 then rose to 3.21% in 2010. It decreased to 2.79% in 2011, and further significantly to 1.80% in 2012, before rising to 2.35% and 2.54% in 2013 and 2014, respectively. The average rate on 30-year Treasury bonds declined from 4.28% in 2008 to 4.07% in 2009, rose to 4.25% in 2010 and declined to 3.91% in 2011, then sharply declined to 2.92% in 2012 before rising to 3.45% in 2013; it declined to 3.34% in 2014. Between January and April 2015, the average rate on 30-year Treasuries was just 2.57%. Meanwhile, real GDP growth rate was negative in 2008 and 2009 (−0.3% and −2.8%, respectively; see Table 8.4a) but turned positive in subsequent years: 2.5% in 2010, 1.8% in 2011, 2.8% in 2012, and 1.9% in 2013.

The sharp decline in yields on financial assets from 2008 also did not result in households completely substituting cash for them, as Keynes's liquidity trap argues. Between 2008 and 2014, holdings of time and saving deposits by households and nonprofit organizations rather increased by 28.53%, from $6118.8 billion to $7864.2 billion (see Table 8.4b). Purchases of Treasury securities also increased by 337.04% over the same period. What declined were purchases of money market fund shares, municipal securities, and corporate and foreign bonds.

Krugman's (1998, 2013) claims that Japan and the US have experienced liquidity traps rather stem from his having omitted the downward rigidity of (long-term) nominal interest rates as the key identifier of a liquidity trap in Keynes's own proposition to, "conventional monetary policies have become impotent, because nominal interest rates are at or near zero: injecting monetary base into the economy has no effect, because base and bonds are viewed by the private sector as perfect substitutes" (1998: 141) or "increases in the money supply seem to have no effect" (180).[21]

Krugman also claims that a liquidity trap results from the public not believing a central bank's commitment to cure a deflation with monetary expansion: "A monetary expansion that the market expects to be sustained (that is, matched by equiproportional expansions in all future periods) will always work, whatever structural problems the economy might have; if monetary expansion does not work—if there is a liquidity trap—it must be because the public does not expect it to be sustained" (1998: 142). He therefore argues that the liquidity trap "involves a kind of credibility problem." Now, a deflation lowers the level of prices. An increased rate of money creation to end

Table 8.4a US Reserve Money Growth, Interest Rates, Inflation, Output Growth, and Unemployment

	2004	05	06	07	08	09	10	11	12	13
H Growth	4.4	4.7	3.0	1.4	106.7	15.4	1.5	35.8	0.2	38.6
H	0.745	0.780	0.803	0.814	1.683	1.942	1.970	2.675	2.680	3.714
CC	0.719	0.758	0.783	0.792	0.850	0.890	0.944	1.035	1.125	1.195
CC/H	0.965	0.972	0.975	0.973	0.505	0.458	0.479	0.387	0.420	0.322
Disc Rate	3.15	5.16	6.25	4.83	0.86	0.50	0.75	0.75	0.75	0.75
G Bond Y(M)	2.78	3.93	4.77	4.34	2.24	1.43	1.11	0.75	0.38	0.54
G Bond Y(L)	4.27	4.29	4.79	4.63	3.67	3.26	3.21	2.79	1.80	2.35
GDP Def	2.7	3.2	3.1	2.7	2.0	0.8	1.2	2.0	1.7	1.5
GDP Growth	3.8	3.4	2.7	1.8	−0.3	−2.8	2.5	1.8	2.8	1.9
UER	5.5	5.1	4.6	4.6	5.8	9.3	9.6	9.0	8.1	7.4

Note: H = high-powered money or monetary base (trillions of dollars); CC = currency in circulation (trillions of dollars); Disc Rate = discount rate; G Bond Y(M) = medium-term government bond yield; G Bond Y(L) = long-term government bond yield; GDP Def = GDP deflator; UER = unemployment rate.
Source: IMF, *International Financial Statistics Yearbook 2014*.

Table 8.4b Balance Sheet of Households and Nonprofit Organizations Billions of Dollars; Amounts Outstanding End of Period, Not Seasonally Adjusted

	2007	2008	2009	2010	2011	2012	2013	2014
ChD and Currency	160.2	349.6	373.6	423.7	724.1	887.4	1008.1	1115.7
TD and SD	5914.6	6118.8	6231.9	6450.8	6820.1	7187.1	7393.2	7864.2
MM Fund Shares	1346.7	1581.8	1313.1	1131.0	1109.9	1110.2	1135.7	1102.1
Treasury Securities	202.0	204.9	762.3	1127.3	707.3	908.7	960.3	895.5
Municipal Securities	1698.2	1737.0	1866.5	1871.5	1805.8	1661.0	1605.2	1538.0
Corp and Fgn BDs	2118.1	2062.7	2227.0	1374.5	1331.7	1184.2	814.4	680.4

Note: ChD = checkable deposits; TD = time deposits; SD = savings deposits; MM = money market; Corp = corporate; Fgn = foreign; BDs = bonds.
Source: U.S. Federal Reserve (federalreserve.gov).

the deflation does not require a subsequent monetary contraction to sustain the price level, as Krugman argues with a two-period model. A central bank's matching the growth of its money supply to the growth of the demand in future is all that is requisite to maintain the level of prices (zero inflation).

Moreover, the public acts on the experience of past and present inflation (deflation) in allocating income between consumption, saving (purchase of financial assets), and holding cash balances, rather than mainly on what a central bank promises. Krugman's belief in the ability of a central bank to change the public's inflationary expectations, "despite the absence of any direct traction on the economy by means of current monetary policy" (1998: 180), is mistaken. Krugman also treats the alleged liquidity trap as a mystery: "what happens when an economy is *trying* to have deflation—a deflationary tendency that monetary expansion is *powerless to prevent* ... and the reason why structural explanations, in a fundamental sense, cannot by themselves resolve that *mystery*" (1998: 141; italics added). The claim shows little appreciation for the relevance of the Quantity Theory as an explanation of the level of prices and from which to derive the appropriate price-level policy.

It is also relevant to understand why the growth of the public's demand for money exceeds the growth of money's supply, unrelated to the growth of real output, and to have generated price deflation. Such an understanding helps in devising appropriate remedy. The cause in the US during the Great Depression was the public's shaken confidence in the banking firms that resulted in the run on banks. That led to the failure of 9,000 banks and $8 billion contraction of demand deposits as well as a $7.85 billion contraction in time deposits between 1930 and 1933; see also Chapter 7. The US government's actions to restore the public's confidence in the security of their bank deposits halted the runs. Friedman and Schwartz (1963) thus would have been consistent with classical monetary analysis by acknowledging that the more than $1 billion increase of currency by the Fed between January 1930 and December 1933 (currency in circulation also increased from $3.78 billion to $5.57 billion in March 1933; see also Friedman and Schwartz 1970: 24−9) had been overwhelmed by the increased demand for cash, as reflected in bank (demand and time) deposits withdrawals. Their choice of the M2 measure of money, rather than the monetary base, instead led to their accusing the Fed of having caused the Great Depression. They argue that the Fed could have prevented the one-third contraction of the "money stock," but a variable the Fed cannot control, a fact Friedman (1960) also acknowledges; Ahiakpor (2019, Ch. 5) elaborates.

However, Friedman (1960: 31; italics added) acknowledges that "The Federal Reserve cannot currently affect the currency-deposit ratio directly ... In the main ... the Reserve System must regard the currency-deposit ratio as determined by *forces outside its control* which shape the preferences of the public about the form in which it wants to hold its cash balances." While urging a continuous attempt by the Fed to counter movements in the public's currency-deposit ratio and banks' reserve-deposit ratio in order to stabilize the "money stock," Friedman also admits, "In practice, this is easier said than done" (68). Furthermore, Friedman acknowledges that "Under present circumstances, even the stock of money is not directly controlled by the System. The System controls directly its own earning assets" (88–9). Indeed, no central bank can compel the public to hold deposits with banks to be counted as M1 or M2. The classical unit-of-account definition of money excludes bank deposits, e.g. Hume (1752) "Of Money" and Smith (*WN*, 1: 36, 42, 310); see also Fisher (1913: 11) and Marshall (1923: 13–5).[22]

Problems with Japanese banks in the late 1980s and early 1990s also have been noted as a principal reason for the public's distrust in the security of their bank deposits, and the resort to increased cash hoarding. Dealing directly with those problems, along with increasing the quantity of (base) money, could have helped Japan's economy recover quickly. Krugman (1998) minimizes the significance of such explanation with a cash-in-advance constrained consumption model, which misses the point that consumption is constrained not by cash availability but rather by income or access to credit.

The IS-LM model gives the impression that increases in a central bank's money would increase real output and employment in the short run, unless the economy were experiencing a liquidity trap. Hicks (1937: 149) follows Keynes's claim to have turned the classical Quantity Theory from explaining the level of prices into a theory of interest and therefore a theory of output and employment with his argument that, from the "Cambridge Quantity equation [$M = kI$] ... as soon as k and M are given, I [income] is completely determined." The failure of the US economy to recover quickly from the severe contraction of 2008 through 2009, in spite of the massive increases in the Fed's money (H)—106.7% in 2008, 15.4% in 2009, 35.8% in 2011, and 38.6% in 2013 (see Table 8.4a)—thus has led some to conclude that the economy has been in a liquidity trap. But the conclusion is mistaken.

First, Keynes's liquidity trap is about the public's excess demand for money (cash) preventing (long-term) interest rates from falling below some low level to stimulate total spending. However, interest rates rather have fluctuated, not got stuck at some constant low level. Besides, the quantity of high-powered money increased by 356% between 2007 and 2013 (from $0.814 trillion to $3.7 trillion), but currency in circulation rose only by 51% (from $0.792 trillion to $1.2 trillion). The ratio of currency in circulation to high-powered money that stood above 90% in the earlier years decreased to 50% in 2008, and below that in subsequent years. This may be explained by the Fed's paying banks 0.25% interest on their required and excess reserves since October 2008 (more than the federal funds rate until December 2015) and the Fed having engaged in currency swaps with some foreign central banks (Ben Bernanke 2009), thus restraining the increased currency's domestic circulation. Furthermore, the US currency has been adopted as a means of payment in some other countries, including Zimbabwe (from 2009), which provides a vent to the currency from affecting US domestic prices. As Hume (1752: 42) explains, only the circulating money affects prices: "If the coin be locked up in chests, it is the same thing with regard to prices, as if it were annihilated." Nevertheless, the positive US rate of inflation still means that the Fed's rate of money creation has exceeded the growth of its demand.

Secondly, even though Keynes claimed to have been advancing Hume's positive view of money on output and employment during the transition between money's increase and the rise of prices, he left out Hume's warning against attributing economic growth to the abundance of money: mistaking, "as is too usual, a collateral effect for a cause" (1752: 41). Among trading nations employing commodity money (specie) as a means of payment, increased production in a country may reduce its level of prices, increase exports, and draw money in from abroad. Otherwise, an increased quantity of money would only raise domestic prices, reduce exports, increase imports, and cause the outflow of money; see also Hume (1752), "Of the Balance of Trade." Rather, "industry and refinements of all kinds ... a change in the manners and customs of the people" (45, 46), Hume argues, are the causes of economic growth. Thus, Hume opened his essay with:

> Money is not, properly speaking, one of the subjects of commerce; but only the instrument which men have agreed upon to facilitate the exchange of one commodity for another. It is none of the wheels of trade: It is the oil which renders the motion of the wheels more smooth and easy.
>
> (33)

See also Smith (*WN*, 1: 313) and Ricardo (3: 92) for affirmations of Hume's point.

That is why Hume's "good policy" advice to the "magistrate" (meaning the sovereign in old English; see *Oxford English Dictionary* 1989: 189) is, if possible, only to keep money increasing in a growing economy in order to sustain the level of prices from falling (Hume 1752: 39). Hume did not prescribe seeking constantly to depreciate money's value by targeting a positive rate of inflation, as the US Fed currently has pledged to do—a 2% inflation target. A modern central bank, issuing fiat paper money, should attempt to replicate what the more resource-costly commodity money system would achieve, namely, a constant level of prices overtime; see also Marshall (1923: 50).

In a commercial crisis that has shaken business and savers' confidence, resulting in increased hoarding of money, price deflation, and increased unemployment, John Sturt Mill called for "the restoration of confidence" (*Works*, 3: 574) as the cure; Walter Bagehot (1873: 101) also considers confidence restoration the "best palliative to a [banking] panic." So does Marshall (1920: 592):

> The chief cause of the evil [commercial disorganization] is a want of confidence. The greater part of it could be removed almost in an instant if confidence could return, touch all industries with her magic wand, and make them continue their production and their demand for the wares of others.

Dealing with the busted US housing bubble, including allowing quick foreclosures on delinquent borrowers, and letting investors in mortgage-backed securities bear their losses, might have speeded up recovery from the financial crisis. Having instead the Fed purchase securities under the Quantitative Easing programs, significantly depressing interest rates; the government promoting new automobile purchases, while having used but functional ones destroyed; and Congress extending the unemployment compensation period from 26 to 99 weeks have not been helpful in promoting the requisite business confidence.

Summary and conclusions

Keynes reversed his earlier preference for monetary expansion to lower interest rates as a stimulant to economic recovery, arguing that the demand for money (cash) is capable of becoming insatiable at some unspecified low level of (long-term) interest rates or the money demand curve changing shape from a rectangular hyperbola to becoming horizontal at its lower end. The argument provided Keynes the theoretical basis for urging increased government spending, even if "wasteful" (1936: 128–31), financed by borrowed central bank money, as the more reliable means of restoring economic prosperity. Keynes derived the possibility of a liquidity trap from having turned the classical Quantity Theory of money from a theory of the level of prices into a theory of interest rates. He reached that conclusion from having mistaken "capital" in the classical theory of interest to mean capital goods rather than savings. Contemporaries who criticized Keynes's liquidity-trap proposition focused not on this aspect of his argument but rather on his having exaggerated the importance of cash hoarding. They also did not explicitly deny the legitimacy of his new view of money's demand curve and thus the impossibility of his liquidity trap's occurrence. Subsequent monetary analysis, mostly led by Milton Friedman, rather has adopted Keynes's broad money demand curve.

But money is acquired with income to hold (or borrowed at interest), which imposes a limit on its demand by the public at any point in time. It is thus impossible for money's demand curve, properly construed, to keep endlessly increasing after (long-term) interest rates have fallen to some low level. Income earners also optimize their spending concurrently along three margins: consumption, saving (acquiring interest-yielding financial assets), and cash holding (hoarding), not just two, as Keynes (1936) argues. The three-margin analysis helps to appreciate the impossibility of his liquidity trap. People have other useful things to do with their incomes than to turn them all into cash hoarding when interest rates have fallen to some low level.

Besides, an increased money demand may raise nominal interest rates, as it reduces the flow of savings. It also may generate price deflation and decrease business profits. The resulting decreased business demand for credit would thus reverse the rise of interest rates, assuring that the increased money demand cannot permanently prevent interest rates from falling. Keynes's interest theory thus gives an undue influence to a central bank's money creation, misrepresents the role of the public's saving, and minimizes or almost ignores the role of business demand for credit in the determination of interest rates.

Keynes's claim to have turned the Quantity Theory into a theory of output and employment and Hicks's (1937) incorporation of that argument into the IS-LM model have encouraged neglect of the classicals' warnings about the limited role of money creation in an economy. Friedman's and Friedman and Schwartz's interpretations of US monetary statistics during the Great Depression also have exaggerated the potential of money creation for an economy's growth and diverted attention from effectively evaluating Keynes's liquidity-trap proposition. Krugman's revival of the proposition presents an opportunity for its more careful evaluation.

Interest rates have not behaved as Keynes alleged in a liquidity trap. The classical theory of interest and the Quantity Theory of money help to explain the impossibility of his liquidity-trap proposition even without statistical testing. There is little legitimacy to declaring the occurrence of a liquidity trap just because a central bank's increased money creation has failed to spur an economy's quick recovery from a recession.

Notes

1 This chapter draws upon my 2018 article, "On the impossibility of Keynes's Liquidity Trap: Classical Monetary Analysis Helps to Explain," in the *History of Economic Ideas* 36 (1): 31–58.

2 See interview of Friedman in Brian Snowdon and Howard Vane (1997: 196). David Laidler (1993b) concludes from econometric tests: "Most evidence goes against the liquidity trap hypothesis ... however, the conclusion to which I subscribe, that the liquidity trap hypothesis is of no empirical significance, rests on some degree of personal judgment" (152). Laidler (2004) also does not reject the proposition's possibility.

3 Dennis Robertson (1936: 190) describes this as the liquidity preference becoming a "trap for savings" being unable to depress interest rates. Robertson (1940: 45) subsequently questions the possibility that "the existence of the liquidity trap for thrift ... [hampers] the banking system in its long-run task of" credit intermediation. He did not explicitly reject the nature of Keynes's money demand curve.

4 At the 1931 Harris Foundation Meetings, Keynes also favored expansionary monetary policy: "central bank action [is] on the whole rather more important than government action" (cited in Davis 1971: 122).

5 Hicks (1937: 155) also argues that it is "the rate for loans of indefinite duration," rather than short-term rates, that Keynes always had in mind as not falling "very near zero." Hawtrey (1939) follows Hicks in interpreting Keynes to have meant the long-term rate of interest; see also Friedman (1970a: 22).

6 Krugman (1998: 138) observes that, modern macroeconomists since 1975, have concluded "basically that a liquidity trap cannot happen, did not happen, and will not happen again."

7 Friedman (1970a: 168) yet argues that "Keynes's demand curve for money in the *General Theory* is for the most part a continuation of earlier quantity theory approaches, improved and refined but not basically modified."

8 In his 1939 Preface to the French edition of the *General Theory*, Keynes explains: "I am here returning to the doctrine of the older, pre-nineteenth century economists. Montesquieu, for example, saw this truth with considerable clarity ... The following analysis registers my final escape from the confusions of the Quantity Theory, which once

entangled me ... in the theory of interest it is a return to the doctrines of Montesquieu" (1939: xxxiv, xxxv). David Hume's (1752) essay, "Of Interest," explains the error of this mercantilist view of interest rate determination, but to which Keynes (1936) does not refer. See also J.-B. Say's discrediting Montesquieu, among others, over the theory of interest: "It is a great abuse of words to talk of the interest of money; and probably this erroneous expression has led to the false inference, that the abundance or scarcity of money regulates the rate of interest. Law, Montesquieu, nay, even the judicious Locke, in a work expressly treating of the means of lowering the interest of money, have all fallen into this mistake; and it is no wonder that others should have been misled by their authority" (1821a: 353). Say further observes, "The theory of interest was wrapped in utter obscurity, until Hume and Smith dispelled the vapour" (1821a: 353–4).

9　Keynes (1936) arrived at this theory of interest mainly from having misinterpreted "capital" in the classical theory of interest as restated in Marshall (1920) to mean capital goods; see Ahiakpor (1990). This is a major blind spot, not mentioned, in scholarship on Keynes's macro-monetary analysis, e.g. Patinkin (1965, 1976), Leijonhufvud (1968), Friedman (1970a), Blaug (1996), and Laidler (1999).

10　Friedman's (1956, 1970a) adoption of this view of the Quantity Theory has helped to obscure recognition of the error of Keynes's argument. Friedman (1956: 4) declares that the "quantity theory is in the first instance a theory of the *demand* for money. It is not a theory of output, or of money income, or of the price level" (italics original).

11　Keynes (1936: 343, n. 3) draws upon Hume's (1752) explanation in "Of Money" that "between the acquisition of money and the rise of prices, ... the increasing quantity of gold and silver is favourable to industry" for this view. Keynes argues, "It is in the transition that we actually have our being." An eagle-eyed referee for the *History of Economic Ideas* notices that Keynes substituted in his quotation from Hume (1752: 40), "state of labour" for Hume's "stock of labour" and "increasing trend" for "encreasing hand" in Eugene Rothwein's (1955) edited version. Eugene Miller's (1985) edited version of Hume's essay is consistent with Rothwein's wording. Keynes thus appears to have altered Hume's statements.

12　Keynes (1936: 62; italics original) defines investment as the purchase of capital goods only: "the definition of *current investment*. ... [means] the current addition to the value of the capital equipment." Similarly, in his *Treatise*, Keynes defines investment as "the increased production of material wealth in the shape of capital-goods" (1930, 2: 207). Hawtrey (1950: 43) appropriately contrasts Keynes's definition with its ordinary meaning: "acquisition of income-yielding securities or property, not Keynes's sense of the accumulation of capital assets and unconsumed goods." Keynes's definition of investment is one reason he failed to appreciate the validity of the classical explanation that the supply of savings (demand for income-yielding securities) and investment-demand (supply of income-yielding securities) determine interest rates (inverse of the price of income-yielding securities). Besides, the funds employed in production (investment) include the classical wages fund and cash-on-hand, or "circulating capital."

13　Boianovsky (2004: 93) thus credits Hicks (1937) with too much originality with his claim that "Hicks based his formulation of the liquidity trap on the notion that the short-run nominal interest rate cannot be negative."

14　Keynes's reference to debts of "long term" justifies Hicks's explanation that Keynes always had the long-term rate of interest in mind in the liquidity-trap proposition. Current discussions of the liquidity trap in term of the US Fed's operating in an environment of a zero lower bound of short-term rates and Boianovsky (2004) cited above thus appear to be inconsistent with Keynes's own proposition.

15　As Hawtrey (1933: 140) notes, "The currency in circulation in the United States rose [about one billion] from \$4,598,000,000 in February, 1931, to \$5,627,000,000 in February, 1932, while the depression was rapidly growing worse and the price level falling." During this period three-month US Treasury bill rates actually rose: from 1.21% in February 1931 to 3.25% in December before falling to 2.65% in February 1932. The rate thereafter declined sharply to its lowest level of 0.08% in December 1932, rising again to 2.29% by March 1933 before declining to 0.10% in September. It rose to 0.69% in December 1933; see Table 8.1.

16 Rather than recognizing this problem with Keynes, Robertson (1936: 183) argues: "Ultimately, therefore, it is not as a refutation of a common-sense account of events in terms of supply and demand for loanable funds, but as an alternative version of it, that Mr. Keynes' account as finally developed must be regarded"; see also Robertson (1937: 431; 1966: 151). Hicks (1937: 157), on the other hand, treats Keynes's argument as his having explained the determination of the "investment rate of interest" differently from the money rate.

17 Keynes (1924: 85–6) states the three-margin analysis and cites Marshall's (1923, I: iv, 3) version as its best summary. Hicks (1937: 151) also cites the three-margin decision analysis by Lavington (1921: 30) and "Pigou (1922: 179–81)" but does not employ it to reject Keynes's two-margin argument as Robertson (1936: 189–90; 1940: 27) does. Hicks's citation of 1922 for Pigou's work may be a typo. The first edition was in 1923; second edition in 1924.

18 The credit (savings) supply curve would shift to the left causing interest rates to rise unless countered by a fall in business credit demand as product prices fall. As Hicks (1937: 155, n. 6) acknowledges, "the short term [interest] rate may rise, either because trade improves, and income expands; or because trade gets worse, and the desire for liquidity increases."

19 Mainly following Friedman's lead, most monetary analysts have estimated the interest elasticity of the demand for money defined as M1 or M2, rather than H. Nevertheless, they typically have not found an infinite interest elasticity of such money's demand (Laidler 1993b: 138).

20 The growth rate of high-powered money is the relevant data for ascertaining the existence of Keynes's liquidity trap, not M1 or M2, as nearly all previous analysts have done. These other measures of "money" include the public's deposits (savings) with banks, which central banks cannot control.

21 Eggertsson's (2008: 154) version is: "A liquidity trap is defined as a situation in which the short-term nominal interest rate is zero."

22 Friedman and Schwartz (1970) ignore the classical unit-of-account definition of money, arguing instead: "The problem of definition has received much attention—in our opinion far more than it deserves. So far as we can see, no issue of principle is involved, and no single definition need be 'best'" (1). Smith (*WN*, 1: 306–7) cautions against the "ambiguity of language" involved in using "money" to mean the unit of account, income, and wealth, a point Friedman (1972) later makes, cautioning against confusing money and credit. But Friedman's "money stock," M, commingles high-powered money (H) with bank credit (BC). Ignoring traveler's checks, $M1 = C + DD = C + R_1 + BC_1 = H(1 - \alpha) + BC_1$, where C = currency in circulation, DD = demand deposits = $R_1 + BC_1$, R_1 = reserves against demand deposits, BC_1 = bank credit based upon demand deposits, and $\alpha = R_2/H$, the fraction of high-powered money held against time deposits (TD). Then $M2 = C + DD + TD = C + R_1 + R_2 + BC_1 + BC_2 = H + BC_1 + BC_2$, where R_2 = reserves against time deposits, and BC_2 = bank credit based on time deposits.

9 The classical roots of the Phillips curve analysis

Introduction[1]

The Phillips curve analysis is now employed to demonstrate the neutrality of money on real output and employment in the long run, but also money's non-neutrality in the short run when changes in the quantity of money are unanticipated. The analysis is consistent with the classical Quantity Theory of money's explanation of the short-run versus long-run effects of increases in the quantity of money (cash), except that the Phillips curve analysis focuses on the stickiness of wage rates. Indeed, before Keynes's economics took hold in modern macroeconomics, employing the forced-saving explanation was commonplace, e.g., Alfred and Mary Marshall (1879), Alfred Marshall (1920), Irving Fisher (1912, 1913), A.C. Pigou (1913, 1927, 1933), R.G. Hawtrey (1913, 1919), Frank Taussig (1921), and Dennis Robertson (1926), although without explicit reference to the name. Pigou, for example, used "forced levies," while Robertson used "imposed lacking"; see F.A. Hayek (1933: 218 9n) for some equivalent references to the classical forced-saving doctrine.

The classical forced-saving doctrine argues that rising prices, generated by increasing quantities of money (or credit), cause wage-, interest-, and rental-income earners to suffer a reduction in real consumption while profit rates increase in the short run because of the lagged adjustment of producers' costs (wages, interest, and rentals). The explanation has tended to be traced to Jeremy Bentham or Henry Thornton in the literature, but David Ricardo (*Works*, 4: 36–7; italics added) recognizes the analysis in David Hume:

> Mr. Malthus notices an observation, which was *first made by Hume*, that a rise of prices, has a magic effect on industry: he states the effects of a fall to be proportionally depressing … It is said to be beneficial, because it betters the situation of the commercial classes at the expense of those enjoying fixed incomes;—and that it is chiefly in those classes, that the great accumulations are made, and productive industry encouraged.

Thornton's (1802: 239) discussion of forced saving was in reaction to Hume's (1752) essay on money just as it was Bentham's (1951, 1954, 1: 270–1) on

Hume's essays, "Of the Balance of Trade," "Of Interest,' and "Of Money." Mises (1934, 1963) and Hayek (1935) also trace the forced-saving doctrine to Hume. But Hume's discussion of the sequence of wage rate and adjustment of the level of prices, following an increase in the quantity of money in "Of Money," a discussion Rotwein (1955: lxv) aptly describes as an "unresolved ambiguity," has tended to create problems for many readers in interpreting his analysis as being consistent with forced-saving in respect to wages; Ahiakpor (2019, Chapter 4) elaborates. Cantillon's (1755) essay, "Of the Increase and Decrease in the Quantity of Hard Money in a State" (esp. 163–7), describing the differential impact of changes in the quantity of money on wage, rental, and profit earners, which Hayek (1935: 9) suspects Hume must have read before publishing his own essays, gives a clearer sequence of wage and price-level adjustments consistent with the forced-saving mechanism.

A.W. Phillips's (1958) original analysis does not employ the classical Quantity Theory of money as a theory of the level of prices nor the forced-saving doctrine derived from it. Fisher (1926) explains the phenomenon of rising prices along with a falling rate of unemployment in the short run, followed by rising nominal wages, and interest and rental rates because of increases in the quantity of money or credit (and vice versa), drawing upon the classical principle. However, he only notes that "the principle underlying this relationship is, of course, familiar" (1926: 787).[2] Some recent analysts also have made the connection between Phillips's work and Hume's monetary analysis. But they have cast Hume among believers in a downward sloping, long-run Phillips curve, e.g. Charles Nelson (1981a) and Thomas Humphrey (1982a, 1985), a claim Jacob Frenkel (1981) appropriately disputes.[3]

In fact, several major classical economists frowned upon the injustice of the inflationary tax imposed on fixed-income earners by an excessive money creation intended to create the short-run positive effects on output and employment. That is why they did not recommend the forced-saving mechanism as a growth-promoting tool. Discussion of the forced-saving doctrine now tends to be consigned to texts in the history of economic thought, with hardly any mention in modern macroeconomics. Austrian macroeconomists who discuss the concept employ it rather to explain the changing structure of production, and thus do not relate it directly to the Phillips curve analysis, e.g., Roger Garrison (2004). This chapter bridges that gap in modern macroeconomics.

Keynes's influence in modern macroeconomics appears responsible for the absence of the doctrine's mention. Thus, instead of explaining fluctuations in the price level with the Quantity Theory of money, Phillips (1950) assigns to that theory the determination of interest rates and investment, just as Keynes (1936) did; see also Phillips (1961). Richard Lipsey (1960) mostly elaborates Phillips's excess demand/supply of labor theory of wage rates, besides refining Phillips's estimation technique. We may trace Keynes's influence as follows. First, Keynes (1936: 80) argues that the concept of forced saving is relevant only to an economy operating at full employment, but which is mistaken. The lagged adjustment of wages, interest, and rental rates to a changing level of prices occurs because of the existence of contracts and/or lack of full anticipation of the behavior of prices. And this may take place whether or not an economy is at full employment; Ahiakpor (1997a or 2003b, Chapter 10) elaborates. Secondly, Keynes thinks little of the concept because, he argues, "the new money is not 'forced' on anyone" (1936: 328), as if saving meant the hoarding of cash, but which it does not; Ahiakpor (1995) elaborates. Thirdly, Keynes (1930, 1: 171n) attributes the forced-saving doctrine mainly to "German writers" or Austrian economists, a tendency some analysts, including Frank Steindl (1995) and David Laidler (1991, 1999), to a considerable extent, still follow.[4] Ironically, Austrian economists, such as Ludwig von Mises (1934, 1963), F.A. Hayek (1935, 1932, 1933), and Gottfried Haberler (1932), trace the forced-saving doctrine to the classical Quantity Theory of money.

Thus, Milton Friedman (1968a, 1977) could have employed the classical forced-saving doctrine to make his point about the illusion of attempting to reduce unemployment below its natural rate by money creation and the need rather to regulate the quantity of money so that its variations do not become the source of economic fluctuations. The classical forced-saving phenomenon also could have assisted the research efforts of the new classicals in the 1970s and 1980s; see Robert Lucas (1996). Indeed, one really does not need "the equipment of modern mathematical economics" to explain the short-run, non-neutrality of money on output and employment from the phenomenon of lagging factor prices behind changes in the level of prices as Lucas (1996: 669) suggests. All one needs is a lack of full anticipation of changes in the quantity of money and the level of prices, which the classical explanation entails.[5]

Furthermore, the fruitless efforts during the 1960s and 1970s to estimate reliable trade-off coefficients between rates of inflation and unemployment to guide macroeconomic policy (see Robert Leeson 1997) might have been spared had analysts sooner made the connection between the Phillips curve analysis and the classical forced-saving doctrine. The doctrine explains the non-permanency of any short-run trade-off between inflation and unemployment. Besides, the period of short-run lags that produces the trade-off cannot be expected to be the same within a country over different inflationary (or deflationary) epochs since people do learn over time and the institutional features that generate the factor price rigidities do change as well. Even now, the search for a "new Keynesian Phillips curve" continues, e.g. Nicoletta Batini, Brian Jackson, and Stephen Nickell (2005)—this in spite of Robert Solow's (2002: 74) disavowal that he and Paul Samuelson meant to encourage the search for "a menu of choice" with the Phillips curve. How much wasteful research effort could be saved by learning from monetary history!

The essence of the Phillips curve analysis

Phillips (1958) reveals a fundamental pattern of behavior between the rate of unemployment and changes in money wage rates. For eight business cycle periods between 1861 and 1913 he finds that, on average, nominal wage rates rose faster in the United Kingdom during periods of low rates of unemployment and rose less fast or fell during periods of high rates of unemployment. Phillips explains the observed pattern by (1) the tendency of employers to bid up wages in times of business boom and to demand wage rate reductions during recessions, (2) the tendency of labor unions to demand cost of living adjustments during periods of rising product prices, and (3) a lag in the adjustment of wage rates behind changes in the rate of unemployment. A combination of these factors leads to the non-linear negative curve he fits for the 1861–1913 period. He also notes a counter-clockwise movement of pairs of wage rate changes and rates of unemployment over the business cycles. Subsequent period data, especially for 1913–48, that include the two World Wars and Britain's return to the gold standard, are less "well-behaved."

Indeed, one could draw a series of non-linear, downward-sloping curves through the pairs of wage rate changes and unemployment rates above and below Phillips's fitted curve. Similarly, one could connect points of high and low (or negative) growth rates of nominal wages above and below the same unemployment rate to depict a vertical long-run Phillips curve. The same short-run curves could be drawn through the scatter diagram Samuelson and Solow (1960: 188) produce using data on hourly earnings in manufacturing and rates of unemployment in the US. Such depiction of the data has become the norm in subsequent analyses, with changes in the nominal wage rate replaced by rates of inflation on the vertical axis, following Samuelson and Solow (1960), Edmund Phelps (1967), and Friedman (1977).

Phillips's explanations leave out the crucial factors determining changes in business activity that cause changes in the demand for labor. His approach was merely to infer changes in the demand for labor from changes in business conditions (1958: 283). Among the relevant determinants of changes in the demand for labor Phillips left out are (1) changes in the quantity of money (currency) or credit supplied by a central bank and (2) changes in the extension of credit by financial intermediaries, a reflection of their own demand for money to hold as reserves. Indeed, changes in the quantity of central bank money act directly on the supply of credit. Open-market purchases or reductions in the discount rate increase the excess reserves of financial intermediaries which then expand their loans or credit beyond the savings deposited with them ($S_{cr} = S_c +/- \Delta H$, where S_{cr} = supply of credit, S_c = supply of "capital" or savings = $Y(1 - t) - C - \Delta H_h$, $Y(1 - t)$ = disposable income, C = consumption, and H = currency or high-powered money, and H_h = households' hoarding of cash). Interest rates fall below the level determined by the supply of savings relative to the demand for "capital" or investment funds—what the classicals called the "natural rate," e.g., Ricardo (*Works*, 1: 91–2) and Mill (*Works,* 3: 648).[6] In fact, the "cumulative process" analysis, derived from deviations of the market rate of interest from the natural rate and commonly associated with Knut Wicksell, originates with the classics, e.g., Ricardo (*Works*, 1: 363–4; 3: 91), which Wicksell (1935: 79–80) himself acknowledges.

The increased supply of currency (H) increases the level of prices ($P_1 = H_1/k_0y_0 > P_0 = H_0/k_0y_0$, where k = proportion of income held in cash and y = real output or income), and while wage, rental, and interest rates are yet to rise, salaried workers, savers, and property owners suffer a diminution in their real consumption. That is why the classics described the phenomenon as "forced saving." (Some analysts fail to identify the lagged adjustment of wages, interest, and rentals behind the rise of product prices with the classical forced-saving doctrine, e.g., Humphrey (1991: 6–9), perhaps because they identify the "capital accumulation" in the doctrine with only capital goods instead of with funds, e.g., Björn Hansson (1987); see also note 4.) A decrease in banks' excess or economic reserves in order to extend more credit amounts to a decrease in the economy's total demand for cash, $H^d = kPy$, which also raises the level of prices. In the absence of a central bank's credit expansion, the increased quantity of "capital" or investment funds would have been obtained only at a higher rate of interest.

On the other hand, a central bank's contraction of currency through an open-market sale of securities reduces the reserves of financial intermediaries, causing them to contract their lending or supply of credit ($S_{cr} = S_c - \Delta H < S_c$). This causes interest rates to rise besides creating an excess demand for money. The latter causes a fall in the level of prices and a slowing down in business activity. In the face of wage, interest, and rental contracts keeping factor costs from falling immediately, businesses incur reduced profits or losses. They lay off some workers and reduce production. A contraction of credit by financial institutions also has the same short-run deflationary effect on prices, output, and employment as a central bank's contraction of currency. Thus, it is the lagged adjustment of factor costs behind changes in product prices that generates the observed inverse relation between changes in nominal wage rates and rates of unemployment, not differences in perceptions of the level of prices between employers and workers as Friedman (1987: 14) argues.

Fisher (1926) relies on the above explanation to interpret his estimated relation between price-level changes and employment:

> Changes in the purchasing power of the dollar may very largely explain changes in employment. The principle underlying this relationship is of course familiar. It is that when the dollar is losing value, or in other words when the price level is rising, a business man finds his receipts rising as fast, on the average, as this general rise of prices, but not his expenses, because his expenses consist, to a large extent, of things which are contractually fixed, such as interest on bonds; or rent, which may be fixed for five, ten, or ninety-nine years; or salaries, which are often fixed for several years; or wages, which are fixed sometimes, either by contract or custom, for at least a number of months. For this and other reasons, the rise in expenses is slower than the rise in receipts when inflation is in progress and the price level is rising or the dollar falling … Employment is then stimulated—for a time at least …

On the other hand, when prices are falling, expenses likewise lag behind and reduce profits, for exactly the same reason turned about. Consequently, during periods of falling prices profits are reduced, bankruptcies are increased, concerns shut down entirely or in part, and men are thrown out of work.

(Fisher 1926: 787)

Thus, Fisher concludes:

Changes in the price level do definitely foreshadow or anticipate changes in employment ... as the economic analysis already cited certainly indicates a causal relationship between inflation and employment or deflation and unemployment, it seems reasonable to conclude that what the charts show is largely, if not mostly, a genuine and straightforward causal relationship; that the ups and downs of employment are the effects, in large measure, of the rises and falls of prices, due in turn to the inflation and deflation of money and credit.

(Fisher 1926: 792)

Fisher (1926: 788) also notes that the effects are temporary:

It is not a high price level that makes for full employment or a low price level that makes for unemployment. Whether a price level is high or low has, in the long run, nothing whatever to do with employment ... But if we sink from one [price] level to another, then during the time of falling, we do produce depression of trade and unemployment. Reversely, if we rise from one level to another, then during the period of rising we do for a time produce more employment.

Fisher's *Elementary Principles of Economics* (1912), especially in Chapter 10, as well as his *Purchasing Power of Money* (1913), especially in Chapter 4, also employs the above analysis. In the latter work Fisher refers to "the salaried man, or the laborer, most of whom are silent but long-suffering,—paying higher prices, but not getting proportionally higher incomes" (1913: 61–2)—to illustrate the forced saving imposed on wage earners. He also notes, "It is the lagging behind of the rate of interest which allows [business] oscillations to reach ... great proportions" (71). Fisher further draws upon Marshall's (1907) explanation that rising prices lower real interest rates and encourage increased business spending because "those working on borrowed capital pay back less real value than they borrowed, and *enrich themselves at the expense of the community*" (1913: 72; italics added); Marshall (1920: 493–4) restates the argument.

Pigou (1927: 196) is an example of the familiarity of this type of macroeconomic analysis before Keynes's *General Theory* took hold. He interprets his own chart relating rates of inflation to changes in employment with some lag as being in "close accord" with Fisher's earlier work. And, referring to the redistributive effects of unforeseen inflation, especially on wage earners and savers, Pigou (1927: 157) observes that "price changes wrench the terms of contracts for loans and wages away from the terms that were intended when these contracts were made." Similarly, Hawtrey (1919: 262) considers the real wage reductions caused by the lagged adjustment of nominal wages as "one of the most serious evils of inflation." Hawtrey (1913: 265–6) also explains fluctuations in output and unemployment by the lagged adjustment of nominal wages:

> In a sense all the mischief of trade fluctuations arises from the tendency of changes in wages to lag behind changes in the value of money. The unemployment during bad trade is mainly the consequence of wages remaining on a level too high for the reduced stock of money. The fall of real wages during good trade is the consequence of delay in the increase of money wages corresponding to the increase in the stock of money. If the working classes would accept an early reduction of wages when a period of bad trade begins and if the employers would give an early increase of wages when a period of good trade begins, not only would the harmful consequences of a trade fluctuation be avoided, but the fluctuation itself might even be prevented.

Alfred and Mary Marshall (1879: 156–7) earlier employed the lagged adjustment of factor costs to explain fluctuations in business profits and production as well:

> When prices are rising, the rise in the price of the finished commodity is generally more rapid than that in the price of the raw material, always more rapid than in the price of labour [wage rate]; and when prices are falling, the fall in the price of the finished commodity is generally more rapid than in the price of the raw material, always more rapid than in the price of labour. And therefore when prices are falling the manufacturer's receipts are sometimes scarcely sufficient even to repay him for his outlay on raw materials, wages, and other forms of Circulating capital; they seldom give him in addition enough to pay interest on his Fixed capital and Earnings of Management for himself.
> … a fall in prices lowers profits and impoverishes the manufacturer: while it increases the purchasing power of those who have fixed incomes … it impoverishes those who have to make, as most business men have, considerable fixed money payments for rents, salaries, and other matters.

Marshall (1920: 515) repeats the explanation, noting that rising prices and profits enable employers to pay higher wages, but "experience shows that (whether they are governed by sliding scale or not) [wages] seldom rise as much in proportion as prices." Even as Keynes (1936) rejects the meaningfulness of the forced-saving doctrine, he makes a similar observation with respect to wage rate changes:

In addition to the final critical point of full employment at which money-wages have to rise, in response to an increasing effective demand in terms of money, fully in proportion to the rise in the prices of wage-goods, we have a succession of earlier semi-critical points at which an increasing effective demand tends to raise money-wages though not fully in proportion to the rise in the price of wage-goods; and similarly in the case of a decreasing effective demand.

(1936: 301)

Taussig (1921: 298–9) gives the same explanation as the Marshalls:

That wages go up more slowly than prices is one of the best-attested facts in economic history. It holds good of almost all sorts of hired persons. ... It is due mainly to the force of custom, which is especially strong as to wages; ... Of the fact there can be no question; when prices rise, the wages of hired workers do not rise as fast ... The business man who is nearest the ground, so to speak ... profits from the relative stability of wages. Conversely, the business class as a whole commonly loses in periods of falling prices. Then, since the same forces tend to keep wages stable, a fall in prices brings loss. Probably wages feel the effect of falling prices less slowly than they do those of rising prices.

Fisher's (1913) reference to the "long-suffering" salaried man or the laborer and Marshall's (1920) to the delayed rise in wages also reflect the sentiments of several classical economists about forced-saving being unjust to fixed-income earners. Similarly, Taussig (1921: 294) observes that a "different question of justice between debtor and creditor arises from the fact that money wages and other money incomes do not necessarily move in the same way as the prices of commodities." The modern Phillips curve analysis is silent on the undesirability of the income or wealth redistribution effects of price level changes, a neglect worth reversing. We next take up the major classicals' discussion of the forced-saving doctrine. This will be followed by noting the equivalent analysis in modern macroeconomics.

The classical forced-saving doctrine

Henry Thornton (1802) takes his cue in discussing the phenomenon of forced saving imposed on fixed-income earners from Hume's (1752) essay "Of Money." He first agrees that national income may increase, following an increase in the quantity of money (specie), adding, "We may presume an encrease of paper to have exactly the same effect" (238). He then argues:

It must also be admitted that provided we assume an *excessive* issue of paper to lift up, as it may for a time, the costs of goods though not the price of labour, some augmentation of stock [i.e. "capital"] will be the consequence; for the labourer according to this supposition, may be *forced* by his necessity *to consume fewer articles*, though he may exercise the same industry. But this *saving*, as well as any additional one which may arise from a similar defalcation of the revenue of the unproductive members of the society, will be attended with a proportional *injustice* and hardship.

(Thornton 1802: 239; italics added)[7]

Jeremy Bentham, following Hume's monetary analysis, decries the injustice and hardships that are inflicted upon fixed-income earners through the forced-saving mechanism. He first considers the case of full employment: "If all were fully employed, [the increase of money] could not encrease industry" (*Economic Writings*, 1: 270). Next, he considers the case of less than full employment, where both employment and real output may increase from an increase in the quantity of money or bank credit: "If any were unemployed, or not fully employed, [the increased quantity of money] might encrease industry *pro tanto*" (ibid.). Noting that the "consequence would be the same if, instead of coin, paper money were added (if not in such excess as to destroy its credit)," Bentham lists the effects of an increase of money as:

1. A tax upon capital, i.e. upon the capital of moneyed men whose money is placed out at interest, in so far as their debtors are able to pay them off.
2. In [another] respect it is a tax on consumption, in so far as it raises the price of all commodities. Meantime it actually is productive of an *addition* to the mass of *national wealth*, in as far as it gets *extra hands*, or sets them to work at extra hours.

(*Economic Writings*, 1: 271; italics added)

But the increased output derives from "*forced frugality* ... at the expense of national comfort and national *justice*" (*Economic Writings*, 3: 349; italics added).

Bentham relies on the non-anticipation of increases in the quantity of money and the resulting inflation to argue the increase in output and employment: "If the accession was universally known and the principles of economy under this head universally known likewise, the money prices of things would be doubled" (*Economic Writings*, 1: 270) from a doubling of the quantity of money—a new classicals' rational expectations argument. Thus, claims that Bentham assumed only full employment, according to which "the supply of output as a whole ceases to be elastic, i.e. where a further increase in the effective demand will no longer be accompanied by an increase in output" (Keynes 1936: 26; also 80–1) as well as Hollander (1987: 270) and Humphrey (1991: 9) are inaccurate.

David Ricardo's monetary analysis draws insights from Hume's "Of Interest" and "Of Money," e.g. Ricardo (*Works*, 3: 90; 4: 36–7; 5: 12). He also makes similar points as Thornton and Bentham regarding forced saving: "Depreciation of money ... augment[s] riches by diminishing happiness ... and it [is] advantageous only by occasioning a great pressure on the labouring classes and on those who live on fixed incomes" (*Works*, 6: 233). In his "Notes on Bentham," Ricardo (*Works*, 3: 318–9; italics added) explains:

> There is but one way in which an increase of money no matter how it be introduced into the society, can augment riches, viz. at the expense of wages of labour; till the wages of labour have found their level with the increased prices which the commodities will have experienced, there will be so much additional revenue to the manufacturer and farmer they will obtain an increased price for their commodities, and can whilst wages do not increase employ an additional number of hands, so that the *real riches* of the country will be somewhat *augmented*. A productive labourer will produce something more than before relatively to his consumption, but this can be only of momentary duration.

Ricardo is here cautioning against Bentham's argument that, as long as there is some unemployment, increases in the quantity of money or bank credit will increase the rate of output and employment, as if permanently; see also Ricardo (*Works*, 6: 16–7). It is thus incorrect to insist that Ricardo saw no way by which the rise of prices could increase real output and employment in the short run, as Joseph Schumpeter claims: "the Ricardian or strict type of quantity theory so steadfastly denied [the] existence of relations between the circulating medium and output" ([1954] 1994: 723, n. 16). Cory (1962: 55) repeats the claim, as does Humphrey (1991: 6). Humphrey (ibid.) also invokes Ricardo's dismissal of C.C. Western's misapplication of Hume's analysis to the condition of England in 1822 as "An erroneous view of Mr. Hume" (Ricardo *Works*, 5: 524) in support of the claim, as does Hollander (1987: 270). But the error to which Ricardo refers appears not to be Hume's own analysis but Western's application of it.

Ricardo also considers the increase in the real riches of the country through the forced-saving mechanism as being brought about by "a violent and unjust transfer of property" (*Works*, 3: 93), and "It must be accompanied with a degree of injustice to individuals which requires only to be understood to excite the censure and indignation of all those who are not wholly insensible to every honourable feeling" (*Works*, 3: 123).[8] Thus he insists that "the augmentation of goods is the only legitimate cause of an increase of money" (*Works*, 3: 302, n. 3; see also 3: 139–40).

Like Hume (1752: 40), who considered an inadequate supply of money being "pernicious to industry" and employment in the short run, Ricardo was concerned about the short-run negative output and employment effects of an inadequate supply of money because of the forced-saving mechanism's operation in the reverse. Thus, to avoid "the most disastrous consequences to the trade and commerce of the country" (*Works*, 3: 94), he prescribed a gradual contraction of the currency in an attempt to restore the value of the depreciated pound in terms of specie. A gradual contraction would be easier to adapt to or even anticipated than a large, sudden contraction.

Ricardo was well aware that nominal wages do not immediately adjust downwards when the level of prices falls, producing increased unemployment, as Malthus also pointed out to him: "We know from repeated experience that the money price of labour never falls till many workmen have been for some time out of work" (quoted in Ricardo *Works*, 9: 20).[9] Thus, Ricardo (*Works*, 1: 359–60) declares: "when I contemplate the evil consequences which might ensue from a sudden and great reduction of the circulation, as well as from a great addition to it, I cannot but deprecate the facility with which the State has armed the Bank [of England] with so formidable a prerogative." Also, "I consider any Variation in the Value of the Currency as an Evil, from producing a Variation in the Prices of all Articles" (*Works*, 5: 442). Therefore, to secure a stable level of prices and avoid the evil, Ricardo (*Works*, 1: 356) prescribed the regulation of paper money by its convertibility into gold.

Ricardo's arguments above appear to contradict Viner's (1937: 195) view that he had a "temperamental reluctance to explore the short-run and intermediate phases of economic process" and D.P. O'Brien's (1975: 164; 2004: 196) claim that "Ricardo, focusing as usual on successive periods of long-run equilibriums, denied the damage of deflation, and the stimulating effect of rising prices." Some also have interpreted Ricardo's views on the forced-saving mechanism as his having minimized its significance, e.g. Blaug (1996: 159). Such interpretation would be correct only if intended to convey Ricardo's cautioning against attempts to promote long-term growth with increases in the quantity of money.

Unlike Ricardo, Thomas Malthus's discussion of the output and employment stimulating effect of inflation from increases in the quantity of money focuses unduly on the short run. Production and employment are increased if more of the new money goes into the hands of producers than fixed-income earners:

> On every fresh issue of notes, not only is the quantity of the circulating medium increased, but the distribution of the whole mass is altered. A larger proportion falls into the hands of those who consume and produce, and a smaller proportion into the hands of those who only consume ... [working] to increase the national capital [and] to lower the rate of interest.
> (1811: 96–7)

Although Malthus acknowledges the "manifest injustice" to fixed-income earners by inflation as "unjust transfers of property," he argues that the "evil" would be "more than counterbalanced ... by the advantage which the country derives from it" (97).[10]

Malthus believes that "a rise of prices is generally found conjoined with public prosperity; and a fall of prices with national decline" (1811: 97). He even suggests that the "increased command of the produce transferred to the industrious classes by the increase of prices" would so increase production as to restore "prices ... to their former level" (97–8). His argument misses consideration of the subsequent increase in nominal wages, interest, and rental rates that would eliminate the initial advantage to producers. Thus, Ricardo (*Works*, 3: 120–3) criticizes Malthus's argument, particularly the presumption that fixed-income earners do not save, and that inflation necessarily increases overall "capital" or savings. Malthus (1836: 314) subsequently relies on voluntary savings as promoting long-term economic growth.

John Stuart Mill, who also draws insights from Hume's monetary analysis in "Of Money," e.g. Mill (*Works*, 3: 511, 564–5), expresses as much indignation at the income and wealth redistribution by unanticipated inflation as Thornton, Bentham, and Ricardo did. He regards the "substitution of paper for metallic currency [as] a national gain: any further increase of paper beyond this is but a form of robbery" (*Works*, 3: 565). He considers the relief obtained by borrowers whose real interest costs are diminished by inflation an "unjust gain" for their having had a "part of the property of their creditors ... gratuitously transferred to them" (565). Mill argues,

> The depreciation of the currency, when effected [through the excessive money creation], operates to a certain extent as a *forced accumulation*. This, indeed, is no palliation of its iniquity. Though A might have spent his property unproductively, B ought not to be permitted to rob him of it because B will expend it on productive labour.
>
> (1874: 118; italics added)

Mill also discusses the short-run, expansionary effect of unanticipated increases in the quantity of money on output, a phenomenon he ascribed to "delusion":

> The commonest cause of such delusion is some general, or very extensive, rise of prices (whether caused by speculation or by the currency) which persuades all dealers that they are growing rich. And hence, an *increase of production* really takes place during the progress of depreciation, as long as the existence of depreciation is *not suspected*; and it is this which gives to the fallacies of the currency school, principally represented by Mr. Atwood, all the little plausibility they possess. But when the delusion vanishes and the truth is disclosed, those whose commodities are relatively in excess must diminish their production or be ruined: and if during the high prices they have built mills and erected machinery, they will be likely to repent at leisure.
>
> (1874: 67–8; italics added)[11]

Clearly, employment and probably wage rates would increase during the period of rising prices, while employment would decrease when production decreases as the "delusion" vanishes.

Austrian business cycle theorists may find similarity between their prediction of idle productive capacity at the end of a boom with Mill's reference to builders of mills and erectors of machinery repenting at leisure when the expansionary phase comes to an end. However, for Mill, as for other classicals, the forced accumulation refers first to funds, and not necessarily to capital goods, as the Austrian theory argues, e.g., Hayek (1935).

The above views of Thornton, Bentham, Ricardo, Malthus, and Mill on the forced-saving mechanism appear to conflict with David Laidler's (1999: 89) claim that the forced-saving idea "never played more than a peripheral role in" the English classical tradition.[12] Although most classicals did not advocate use of the mechanism to promote economic growth, they recognized its operation from unanticipated variations in the quantity of money or bank credit. Viner (1937: 185–200) includes discussions by lesser-known classical economists, including Thomas Atwood, Thomas Joplin, Lord Lauderdale, and John Wheatley. Viner (1937: 188), however, describes a situation in which "commodity prices do not rise immediately or do not rise in as great proportion as the increase in money, and the money left over is available for additional expenditures and consequently for the employment of additional labor" as another form of forced saving that Hume believed. But that phenomenon does not explain how and from whom the saving is forced. See also Ricardo's interpretation of Hume earlier above or Hayek's (1935: 9–10).

From the above classical and early neoclassical arguments we can envision a leftward movement along a short-run Phillips curve from unanticipated increases in the level of prices and a fall in the rate of unemployment, but a rightward (upward) shift of the whole curve as wage rates adjust to the rise of prices and the rate of unemployment returns to its original position. Similarly, their arguments depict a rightward movement along a short-run Phillips curve from an unanticipated decrease in the level of prices and an increase in the rate of unemployment, but a leftward (downward) shift of the whole curve when nominal wage rates or their rate of growth declines in line with the fall of prices, and the unemployment rate returns to its original position. Only an increased flow of savings or "capital," consistent with the natural rate of interest, would increase production and permanently reduce the (natural) rate of unemployment.

The forced-saving doctrine and modern macroeconomics

Modern macroeconomists, in effect, employ the classical forced-saving doctrine when they argue the non-neutrality of money and credit on output and employment in the short run because of the existence of contracts or lack of full expectations of inflation or deflation, but money's neutrality in the long run. Friedman (1968a, esp.: 7–11) pretty much restates the classical argument, partly in criticism of Phillips's original analysis, and concludes: "there is always a temporary trade-off between inflation and unemployment; there is no permanent trade-off. The temporary trade-off comes not from inflation per se, but from unanticipated inflation" (11). He comes close to acknowledging the classical origin of his argument when he explains that an increase in monetary growth lowers interest rates and increases aggregate demand, to which producers respond by "increasing output, employees by working longer hours, and the unemployed, by taking jobs now offered at former nominal wages. This much is pretty standard doctrine" (10). Indeed, Patinkin (1969) affirms that the lagged adjustment of factor prices behind product prices—the mechanism that generates the forced saving when prices are rising—was a standard principle taught at Chicago by the likes of Henry Simons and Frank Knight. See also Simons, et al., cited in Laidler (1993a: 1094).

Friedman (1968a: 7), however, thanks Knut Wicksell for our being "acquainted with the concept of a 'natural' rate of interest and the possibility of a discrepancy between the 'natural' and the 'market' rate." The discrepancy is the basis upon which Friedman develops his argument of a "natural rate of unemployment," which could not permanently be altered by a central bank's money creation. But, as noted above, the explanation of the "natural rate" of interest comes from Adam Smith and was picked up by Ricardo (see Mill *Works*, 3: 648). Wicksell (1935: 79–80) himself also acknowledges Ricardo's precedence in the "cumulative process" analysis of price-level changes generated by deviations of the market rate of interest from the natural rate. That analysis, being part of the classical forced-saving argument, also was discussed by Alfred Marshall before Wicksell; see Patinkin (1965: 631–2) and Ahiakpor (1999).

Hicks (1967: 162–3; italics original) also notes:

> Inflation does give a stimulus [to production], but the stimulus is greatest when inflation starts—when it starts from a condition that has been non-inflationary. If the inflation continues, people get adjusted to it. But when people are adjusted to it, when they *expect* rising prices, the mere occurrence of what they had expected is no longer stimulating. Nor can the fade-out be prevented by accelerating the inflation; for acceleration of inflation can be expected too.

Hicks offers this argument as what he thinks the classics would say about the short-run effect of money on output: "some such short-period theory, somewhere at the back of their minds, though [the classicals] preferred not to emphasize it" (1967: 162). The classical views presented above argue what Hicks suggests. Indeed, in an April 9 letter to Keynes, Hicks acknowledges that he "made a practice of restraining [his] interest in the history of economic theory at 1870" (Keynes 1973, 14: 81).

Similarly, the new classicals argue that only unanticipated changes in the quantity of money affect real output and employment in the short run (Lucas 1996). Were changes in the quantity of money fully anticipated and acted upon by the general public, nominal wages and rental rates would rise with the expected rate of inflation. There would then be no tendency for real wage rates to fall and for more workers to be hired for increased production. That is, the short-run Phillips curve would immediately shift rightward in anticipation of an increased rate of inflation. Also, the saving rate would immediately decline and/or the demand for credit increase to match an anticipated increase in the supply of central bank credit, and thus keep nominal interest rates from falling. Conversely, an anticipated decrease in central bank money (credit) creation would have no effect on production and employment because nominal wage and rental rates would immediately fall and thus keep their real rates unchanged. This is the equivalent of a leftward shift of the short-run Phillips curve in anticipation of a fall in the rate of inflation or a deflation. There also would be increased saving and/or decreased demand for loans to match a central bank's credit contraction, which would keep nominal interest rates from rising.

Such emphasis on the non-anticipation of a central bank's monetary actions as the key to the short-run, non-neutrality of money reflects the mechanism underlying the classical forced-saving doctrine. Instead, Lucas (1996: 679) thinks, "The discovery of the central role of the distinction between anticipated and unanticipated money shocks resulted from the attempts, on the part of many researchers, to formulate mathematically explicit models that were capable of addressing the issues raised by Hume." There may only have been a re-discovery with the mathematical models. An interpretation of Hume's (1752: 38) argument that an increase in the quantity of money enables "a set of manufacturers or merchants" to hire "more workmen than formerly, who never dream of demanding higher wages, but are glad of employment from such good paymasters" as indicating the non-anticipation of rising prices on the part of the workmen hitherto unemployed would fit that explanation. But, as mentioned above, Hume's own narrative of the price-level and wage rate adjustment during the transition appears to create problems for a consistent interpretation for some readers; see also Perlman (1987) and Wennerlind (2005).[13]

However, the version of forced saving argued by Austrian economists does not lend itself readily to a representation by the Phillips curve analysis. They disagree on the process by which forced saving occurs. Rather than a rise in the level of prices reducing the purchasing power of fixed-income earners, hence their real consumption, the Austrians argue that it is principally the fall in the nominal rate of interest induced by an increased supply of bank credit that enables producers to bid resources away from consumption goods into capital goods production.[14] The reduced availability of consumption goods and the subsequent rise of their prices is what constitutes the forced saving in the Austrians' account. Thus, all categories of income earners may bear some forced saving in that version.[15]

The Austrians also do not necessarily argue a subsequent rise in the real wage, interest, and rental rates, following the revision of contracts to reflect the increased rate of inflation or the higher level of prices, as the process that terminates the initial positive effects of credit or monetary inflation. Their strict designation of producer's goods from consumption goods also assures them a longer impasse in the economy's adjustment process than the classical analysis suggests. Besides, their version appears unable to deal with the case of falling prices from a decreased money or credit creation or from an increased demand for money (currency), as occurred during the Great Depression. Thus, instead of endorsing calls for increased money creation to deal with the ongoing depression, the Austrians advocated against doing anything of the sort. Their stance cost them significant following, much to the advantage of Keynes's revolution in macroeconomic analysis.

Summary and conclusion

The classical forced-saving doctrine was an integral part of their monetary analysis. It explains the mechanism by which unanticipated increases in the quantity of money or credit increase the rate of production and employment in the short run but not in the long run. It also explains why unanticipated decreases in the quantity of money or credit decrease the rate of production and employment in the short run but not in the long run. Significant in their explanation is the lagged adjustment of nominal wage, interest, and rental rates behind changes in product prices. The modern Phillips curve analysis is thus an illustration of the doctrine with respect to wage rates only.

Phillips's original diagram illustrates this lagged relationship between wage rates and the level of prices through changes in the rate of unemployment, but without relating the phenomenon to changes in the quantity of money or credit. He had little use for the classical Quantity Theory of money as a theory of the level of prices or the price level, following Keynes's (1936) influence. Fisher's (1926) analysis correctly has been recognized as explaining the same phenomenon Phillips sought to illustrate. Since Phelps (1967) and Friedman (1968a), modern macroeconomists essentially have been restating the classical doctrine, but without its explicit acknowledgment. Instead, some analysts increasingly have been associating the doctrine mainly with Austrian business cycle theory, while minimizing its analytical significance in classical macromonetary analysis or sometimes even denying that the classics employed that doctrine, e.g. Laidler and Sandilands (2010).

A greater appreciation of the classical heritage of the Phillips curve analysis as outlined above may lead to a more general acceptance of the classical view with respect to monetary policy: changes in the quantity of money (currency) should be directed at meeting changes in money's demand so as to sustain the level of prices, a view also argued ardently by Fisher (1913). He considers "the evils of a variable monetary standard [to be] among the most serious economic evils with which civilization has to deal" (1913: ix). A referee for the article on which I base this chapter thinks, "Inflation targeting appears to be a better alternative, one that recognizes the monumental role played by the huge, sophisticated, credit system." Indeed, the price-level raising effect of the increased use of credit (checkable deposits, electronic transfers, or credit cards in modern times) as a means of payment was well known to the classical writers. Hume (1752: 36) describes it as credit "encreasing money beyond its natural proportion to labour and commodities, and thereby heightening their price to the merchant and manufacturer"; he repeats the point in "Of the Balance of Trade" (68–73), and in "Of Public Credit" (95n). See also Ricardo (*Works*, 3: 90) and Mill (*Works*, 3: Chapters 8, 11, and 12). Thus reducing the rate of currency (H) creation to match its declining demand (H^d = kPy), because of the development of the modern credit system, achieves the constant price-level or zero inflation goal: $\%\Delta P = \%\Delta H - \%\Delta k - \%\Delta y$.

Following the classical logic, interest rates should be left alone to be determined in the various "capital" or credit markets by the supply and demand for voluntary savings. Policies encouraging increased voluntary saving would then promote increased rates of investment, production, and employment at the "natural" rate of interest. Monetary inflation does not promote long-term growth because there are forces constantly working to reverse its initial positive effects, the classics taught. There is also room for re-emphasizing in modern macroeconomics the classical moral outrage over the redistribution of real incomes from wage, interest, and rental earners to the benefit of profit earners that the short-run inflation-unemployment trade-off entails.

Notes

1 This chapter draws on my article, "The Phillips Curve Analysis: An Illustration of the Classical Forced-Saving Doctrine," in the *Journal of the History of Economic Thought* 31, No. 2 (June): 143–60.

2 Recognizing that Fisher's (1926) statistical analysis precedes that of Phillips's, the *Journal of Political Economy* in 1973 republished Fisher's article with the preceding title, "I discovered the Phillips Curve." Humphrey (1985) also lists Hume, Henry Thornton, Thomas Atwood, Fisher, Jan Tinbergen, Lawrence Klein and Arthur Goldberger, A.J. Brown, and Paul Sultan among earlier Phillips curve analysts. However, Don Mathews (2019) disputes Fisher's (1926) work being recognized as a Phillips curve analysis since Fisher there deals with changes in the level of prices rather than Phillips's focus on changing wage rates.

3 Nelson (1981b: 495; italics original) argues that Hume's analysis clearly describes "a process of adjustment from one [price] *level* to another, not from *one rate of change* to another." Humphrey (1991: 6) also interprets Hume as having argued that "Continuous money growth combines with sluggish price adjustment to keep money forever marching a step ahead of prices, perpetually frustrating the latter's attempts to catch up. The gap between money and prices persists indefinitely, thus producing a permanent change in the level of real activity." In Hume's monetary analysis, in which money was specie, the scenario Humphrey envisages would not occur. The flow of money between trading nations stabilizes their price levels: "The same causes, which would correct ... exorbitant inequalities [of money in nations], were they to happen miraculously, must prevent their happening in the common course of nature, and must for ever, in all neighbouring nations, preserve money nearly proportional to the art and industry for each nation. All water, wherever it communicates, remains always at a level" (Hume 1752: 63).

4 A journal referee's comment (*Journal of the History of Economic Thought*) on the original manuscript well reflects this confusion on the part of some analysts: "[Ahiakpor's] use of the phrase 'forced saving' to characterize the classical quantity theory analysis of short-run adjustment mechanisms is eccentric and misleading. The quantity theory is about the effects of variations in the money supply on the price level, and the forced saving doctrine (as analyzed by Hayek and Mises, but also D.H. Robertson), deals with the

effects of bank lending on the allocation of resources between the production of consumption and investment goods. These factors are related to one another, of course, [but] they are not the same thing—indeed Hayek and Mises were quite explicit in treating the quantity theory as an invalid alternative to *their version* of the forced saving doctrine" (italics added). The referee forgets that the Austrians were reacting to an existing classical argument, as also well explained in Hudson (1965). Like the referee, David Laidler and Roger Sandilands (2010: 581–3) also object to my use of the term "forced saving," calling the analysis instead, a "wage-lag hypothesis."

5 Lucas (1996: 676) finds that "unexplained errors of judgment or ignorance [of individuals] … lie at the center of Hume's" account of the short-run non-neutrality, but long-run neutrality of money. A different reading of Hume that recognizes his employment of incomplete information or differences in expectations on the part of traders, as Mill (*Works*, 3: 564) does, would correct that ambiguity.

6 On the classics' use of "capital" or "stock" to mean savings or investment funds, see Ahiakpor (1990; 1997b). Failure to recognize such usage of the term has led to misinterpretations of their work, including the forced-saving analysis, in which "capital accumulation" refers first to funds, not necessarily to capital goods as Austrians and some earlier referees have insisted. Laidler (2006: 45) attributes the market rate versus natural rate analysis rather to Knut Wicksell. But Mill (*Works*, 3: 648) explains, "there must be, as in other cases of value, some rate which (in the language of Adam Smith and Ricardo) may be called the *natural rate*, some rate about which the market rate oscillates" (italics added).

7 Thornton's argument is an elaboration of Hume's "Of Money" (1752: 37–8), which he quotes on the preceding page. Thus, the view that Thornton introduced the forced-saving doctrine into economic analysis in contrast with Hume's "strictly neutral" money analysis (Robert Ekelund and Robert Hébert 2014: 148) is incorrect.

8 It thus appears unwarranted for Jacob Viner (1937: 197) to conclude that Ricardo did not accept the forced-saving doctrine as being operational; see also Ahiakpor (1985). Mark Blaug (1996: 159) makes a similar claim about Ricardo, which is evidently unjustifiable: "[Ricardo] admitted that an increase in paper money may redistribute income to entrepreneurs by means of wages lagging behind prices; this is not quite the same thing as 'forced saving' because here the increase in saving is perfectly voluntary." Yet Blaug accepts Pigou's description of the inflationary transfer of real income from wage- and interest-income earners as "forced levies" or the "doctoring of contracts" as the equivalent of forced saving.

9 This conflicts with Viner's (1937: 197) claim that "Although Ricardo conceded that a sharp fall in prices was a serious evil, the only undesirable consequence of such a fall which he emphasized was the arbitrary redistribution of wealth which resulted therefrom."

10 The modern attitude in seeking to exploit the possible short-term trade-off between inflation and unemployment appears to reflect Malthus's sentiments.

11 Mill's statements contradict Humphrey's (1991: 6) claim that "Mill … dismissed Hume's [forced-saving] mechanism with the assertion that money cannot exert even the briefest stimulus to output since prices instantly rise to absorb all the stimulus." However, Humphrey (1991: 11–2) also quotes Mill as arguing that unanticipated money growth produces "an increase in production" in the short run.

12 Laidler's claim echoes that of M.A. Hudson (1965) who argues, "So far as the mainstream of classical economic thought was concerned, the [forced-saving] doctrine was never utilized to any important extent in monetary theorizing. This is as true of the work of Thornton and Malthus as it is of Ricardos" (245). Also, Hudson argues, "The neoclassicals [including Hayek and Schumpeter] … were as disposed to play up the importance of the doctrine as Ricardo was to play it down" (246). However, Laidler (1999) does not refer to Hudson's work.

13 Chapter 4 in Ahiakpor (2019) discusses the problem with some Hume interpreters, including Morris Perlman, Eugene Rotwein, Margaret Schabas, and Carl Wennerlind.

14 Hayek (1935, Lecture 1) credits Richard Cantillon for the inspiration of this account. Hume's essay, "Of Interest" (esp. 57–8) also explains that a sudden increase in the quantity of money may lower interest rates in the short run but raise them again in the long run as the price level rises; see also Ricardo (*Works*, 1: 363–4).

15 Garrison (2004) argues a concurrent "overconsumption" and "overinvestment," which he attributes to Mises's version of forced saving. That is, there is no reduction in real consumption during the process of forced saving even by fixed-income earners. Ahiakpor (2008) argues that Garrison's claim is implausible, besides its not being consistent with Mises's own discussion of forced saving, e.g. Mises (1963: 548–9, 556–7).

10 The future of Keynesian economics

Struggling to sustain a dimming light

Introduction[1]

In my 2004 article, I argue that Keynesians will face a future of struggling to sustain a dimming light. However, the 2008 Great Financial crisis in the US that spread to several other industrialized economies appears to have sparked a resurgence of faith in the relevance of Keynesian economics among many Keynes adherents. Thus, David Laidler (2011: 33), for example, observes: "Fortunately, there is no need to wonder what distinguishing sartorial symbols the modern Keynesian should display, because the current crisis seems to have made Keynesians of everybody." This, after having acknowledged the unreliability of some of Keynes's claims, also noting Keynes to be "a notoriously agile and unscrupulous debater" (31).[2] Even before the financial crisis, Roger Backhouse and Bradley Bateman's 2006 edited volume, *The Cambridge Companion to Keynes*, which includes contributions from such notable Keynes scholars as David Laidler, Axel Leijonhufvud, and Don Moggridge, mostly lauds Keynes's macro-monetary analysis. In their *Capitalist Revolutionary: John Maynard Keynes* (2011), Roger Backhouse and Bradley Bateman also mostly recount the relevance of Keynes's arguments regarding the instability of financial markets and the need for government regulation or intervention.

In his defense of the massive infusion of Federal Reserve money into the US economy, intended to deal with the 2008 financial crisis under the so-called Quantitative Easing, Ben Bernanke (2015) contrasts Adam Smith's alleged belief that "markets are *always* in supply and demand balance, *except* in the *very short run*" (28; italics added) and "the capacity of free markets to allocate resources efficiently" (417) with Keynes's belief in the need for governments to correct economic dislocations. A journal, *Review of Keynesian Economics*, whose principal aim is "to provide a forum for developing and disseminating Keynesian ideas," was established in 2012, and the *Journal of the History of Economic Thought* published in September 2016, Roy Grieve's article, claiming that Keynes could have made a compelling critique of John Stuart Mill's restatement of Say's law of markets.[3] In 2019 Robert Dimand and Harald Hagemann also edited *The Elgar Companion to John Maynard Keynes* that celebrates the life, work, and influence of Keynes on modern macroeconomic analysis, while Alain Béraud and Guy Numa (2019) argue that Keynes and Jean-Baptiste Say had common grounds upon which to agree on macroeconomic analysis.[4] These are but a few examples of the resurgence of belief in the relevance of Keynesian macroeconomics since the 2008 financial crisis.

However, none of the above revivals of the Keynesian faith confronts the fundamental errors in Keynes's macroeconomic analysis that my 2004 article explains. The errors include (a) the inaccuracy of Keynes's definition of saving; (b) the invalidity of Keynes's multiplier argument; (c) the inaccuracy of Keynes's liquidity (cash) preference theory of interest rates; (d) the invalidity of Keynes's claiming that classical economics assumes an automatic and quick adjustment out of economic recessions; and (e) the inaccuracy of Keynes's interpretation of Say's law of markets as being founded upon the assumption of permanent full employment of labor. Some earlier chapters in this book have elaborated Keynes's errors regarding the above assertions about classical macro-monetary analysis. This chapter restates the difficulties Keynes adherents will have in sustaining acceptance of his arguments when they confront them. We first recount a brief history of Keynesian economics.

A brief history of Keynesian economics

Keynesian economics took over macroeconomic analysis with lightning speed following the publication of Keynes's *General Theory* in 1936. Keynes himself intended his work to cause a revolution in economic thought and took steps to make sure that the book got the most exposure possible. He publicized the fact that he was writing a revolutionary book and subsidized its price to sell for only five shillings (the equivalent of $2 US), instead of the fifteen shillings several reviewers of the book expected it at least to cost (Backhouse 1999). Reviewed in at least 40 magazines, from newspapers to literary and professional journals in its year of publication (1936), the book's message, that Keynes had discovered the causes and cures for persistent unemployment, quickly reached a wide audience.

From Backhouse's (1999) collection of the book's reviews we find that most reviewers praised this book, including Jacob Viner (1936), who credited it with "outstanding intellectual achievement," even as he acknowledged Keynes's changed meaning of economic terms, such that "if old terms are used new meanings are generally assigned to them." Charles Hardy (1936) considers the book's "purely theoretical sections [to be] fresh, coherent and consistent," while Roy Harrod (1936) credits Keynes with unsurpassed "analytic and constructive powers" and that Keynes's "knowledge of the development of economic doctrine is far-reaching." Joseph Schumpeter (1936) even considers his "unfavorable review" of the *General Theory* to be yet "a tribute to one of the most brilliant men who ever bent their energies to economic problems," but he welcomes Keynes's "purely monetary [liquidity preference] theory of interest ..., the first to follow upon [his] own."[5] Henry Simons (1936), who believed that Keynes's criticisms of classical economics "will impress only the incompetent," also acknowledges that "Keynes is popularly accepted as one of the most authentic geniuses of his generation" and that the book "is full of brilliant insights." Dennis Robertson (1936) treacherously attributes to Alfred Marshall an "automatic process of trade recovery," ignoring Marshall's explanation of economic disorganization and unemployment caused by shaken confidence that requires its restoration as the cure in the *Principles* (1920: esp. 591–2). J.R. Hicks (1936) considers as the "most revolutionary thing about the book" Keynes's use of "the method of expectations" and that Keynes had applied the Marshallian technique to "problems never tackled by Marshall and his contemporaries."[6] Wassily Leontief (1936; italics added) also incorrectly attributes to classical economics the assumption that "our economic system is absolutely free from any kind of frictions and time-lag effects" and that the economy adjusts to "any primary variation … *instantaneously*." All these commentators on Keynes's *General Theory* have had their influence on the development of modern macroeconomics.

A.C. Pigou's (1936) review, among the specialist academic journals, was about the most consistently critical, which he directed at "six dominant themes" in Keynes's book, besides noting Keynes's "loose and inconsistent use of terms." The themes include "the 'multiplier,' the rate of interest, the problem of saving, the relation of money wages to real wages and employment … Mr. Keynes's vision of the day of judgment, and his view that it is practicable for State and Bank action to abolish all unemployment." Nevertheless, Pigou credits Keynes, "on many secondary matters," with having "made illuminating and suggestive observations," adding that "even those parts of [Keynes's] discussion which least command agreement are a strong stimulus to thought." Pigou's November 1949 conciliatory memorial remarks about Keynes's contributions to macroeconomic analysis also have undermined subsequent efforts to clarify Keynes's misrepresentations of classical macro-monetary analysis. Pigou writes:

> Whatever imperfections there may be in [Keynes's] working out of the fundamental conception embodied [in the *General Theory*], the conception itself is an extremely germinal idea. In my original review article on the *General Theory*[,] I failed to grasp its significance and did not assign to Keynes the credit for it. Nobody before him, so far as I know, had brought all the relevant factors, real and monetary at once, together in a single formal scheme, through which their interplay could be coherently investigated".
>
> (Pigou 1950, cited in Richard Kahn 1978: 550–1)

It was as if Pigou had forgotten all about Say's law of markets, which explains the coordination of markets for produced goods and services, credit, and money through variations in relative commodity prices, interest rates, and the value of money (Ahiakpor 2003a, 2018b); recall Chapter 2.

By the 1960s communicating Keynes's macroeconomics through formalized models—equations and diagrams—had become the standard fare in universities across the world, following especially the work of J.R. Hicks (1937), Franco Modigliani (1944), Paul Samuelson (1948), Alvin Hansen (1949, 1953), and Don Patinkin (1965). The 1970s saw a significant erosion of the Keynesian dominance in macroeconomics, following the experience of significant inflation and economic recession, particularly among the industrialized countries hitherto believed to be more suitable for the application of Keynesian aggregate demand management policies to stabilize economies. The failure of such policies greatly aided the emergence of monetarism in the 1970s as well as the new classical and supply-side economics, further challenging the remnants of Keynesianism in the 1980s. Keynesian macroeconomics at the turn of the twenty-first century had lost most of its influence on public policymaking until the onset of the financial crisis, although it is now represented by three different strands in academia: (1) the neoclassical Keynesianism in the lineage of Hicks, Hansen, and Samuelson; (2) post-Keynesianism of the Kahn-Robinson-Harcourt tradition; and (3) the new Keynesianism espoused by the younger generation, mainly of American Keynesians.

The persistence of neoclassical Keynesianism seems to be due mainly to the ease with which its formalization of Keynes's arguments in mathematical models can be taught in the classroom (the IS-LM model and the income-expenditure diagrams), although the monetarists and new classical economists also employ the same models to criticize the Keynesian conclusions. This is the sense in which Milton Friedman declares: "We are all Keynesians now... We all use the Keynesian language and apparatus," although he also adds the incorrect observation that "none of us any longer accepts the initial Keynesian conclusions" (1968b: 15). Indeed, monetarism is best viewed as an extension of Keynesian macroeconomics over a broader range of assets than only financial (Friedman 1970a: 28–9; 1987).

The equilibrating processes inherent in the neoclassical Keynesian models and their apparent lack of emphasis on income inequality and the need to pursue redistributive policies as a means of promoting economic growth and increased employment seem to have been the principal reasons for the development of post-Keynesianism (Davidson 1991).[7] On the other hand, the new Keynesians seek to provide micro-foundations for Keynes's conclusions in response to criticisms of the neoclassical Keynesian models (Mankiw 1993, 1997).[8] Their model adjustments include recognizing (1) the non-instantaneous adjustment of product prices, (2) imperfect knowledge, and (3) non-clearing labor markets. But these adjustments in assumptions are all conditions recognized in classical macroeconomics. Some Keynesians also now appear to accept the importance of savings for economic growth as well as the role of excessive money creation in causing inflation in conditions of unemployment, e.g., Gregory Mankiw (2013), Frank and Bernanke (2011) and Brad DeLong and Martha Olney (2006). These acknowledgments are a significant deviation from Keynes's own views, which regard saving as a negative force in the growth process and inflation as arising from excessive aggregate demand only in a situation of full employment.

Meanwhile, there appears to be a near insulation of macroeconomists within their identifiable seven schools, including three varieties of Keynesianism— neoclassical Keynesians, new Keynesians, and post-Keynesians—monetarism, new classical macroeconomics, real business cycle theorists, and Austrians. But they all employ Keynes's new definitions of such important macroeconomic concepts as saving, investment, capital, and money. Their adoption of Keynes's "language and apparatus" (Friedman 1968b: 15) appears to have hindered their confronting Keynes's fundamental misrepresentations of classical macro-monetary analysis in the *General Theory* that Friedman (1970a: 133) considers "a great book, at once more naïve and more profound than the 'Keynesian economics' that Leijonhufvud contrasts with the 'economics of Keynes.'" The rest of the chapter elaborates.

The faulty founding pillars of Keynesian macroeconomics

Keynes founded his new macroeconomics on five principal pillars, all of which are faulty:

(1) Savings are not spent; they do not provide the funds for investment spending as classical economics argues;
(2) Consumption spending sustains and drives an economy's expansion through a multiplier process;
(3) The rate of interest is determined by the supply and demand for money (cash) or liquidity, and not by the supply and demand for "capital" or savings;
(4) There are no equilibrating tendencies in a monetary economy to restore it to full employment once involuntary unemployment has occurred; and
(5) The classical theories of interest, the price level, inflation, and the law of markets (Say's Law) are all founded on the premise that full employment of labor always exists.

Keynes successfully persuaded most of his audience, including many economists, of the above claims about classical economics mainly by changing the meaning of some key economic terms (Ahiakpor 1998b), although none of his claims is correct. Neither does a monetary economy work the way Keynes claims nor are the classical principles founded on the assumption of full employment.

Keynes's saving

Keynes (1930, 1936) defines saving as the non-spending of one's income on consumption, rather than spending on or acquiring interest- and/or dividend-earning assets, as in classical economics. Thus, Keynes's new definition turns saving essentially into the hoarding of cash (1936: 167). Now hoarded cash withdraws the purchasing power of income from circulation. If saving meant cash hoarding, there would be some currently produced goods and services for which there would be inadequate purchasing power to sustain their prices above costs. Producers must lose profits, be discouraged, and reduce their rate of production and therefore lay off some workers. As Keynes argues, saving does not only reduce the demand for currently produced goods and services, it also denies investors the funds they need to purchase materials for production as well as hiring workers (1936: 210). This is why increased saving has only a negative effect on an economy at less than full employment, according to him.

Keynes's new definition of saving as equivalent to the hoarding of cash has been incorporated into macroeconomic models. His paradox of thrift argument (Keynes 1936: 30–1) appears convincing when illustrated as an upward shift of a saving function against an investment function, thus producing a fall in equilibrium national income. The IS-LM model achieves the same result by a left-ward shift of the IS curve against a fixed LM curve. But when saving is defined according to the classics and Alfred Marshall (which is also consistent with what people actually do when they save), namely, purchasing interest- and/or dividend-earning assets, Keynes's negative conclusions about savings are shown to be false (Ahiakpor 1995). That is, $S = Y(1 - t) - C - \Delta H_h = \Delta FA^d$, where S = saving, $Y(1 - t)$ = disposable income, C = consumption, ΔH_h = household's accumulation of cash balances from current income,[9] and ΔFA^d = the purchase of newly supplied financial assets (demand deposits, savings and time deposits, money market mutual fund shares, money market deposit accounts, bonds, and stocks).

Thus correctly understood, savings provide the funds for lending by financial institutions, which hold a portion as reserves against future withdrawals as well as for satisfying legal reserve requirements ($D - R = BC$, where D = deposits, R = reserves, and BC = bank credit or loans and investments). Savings also are the source of funds for purchasing other financial assets, including stocks and bonds. But in Keynes's mistaken view, "The investment market can become congested through the shortage of cash. It can never become congested through the shortage of saving. This is the most fundamental of my conclusions within this field" (1937c: 669). It is partly on the basis of this mistaken Keynesian view that Minsky (1985: 45), for example, builds his financial instability hypothesis in which a country's central bank and commercial banks are the sources of the "supply of finance," independent of savings, and that the supply could be infinitely elastic.

Consumption spending

The Keynesian focus on consumption spending as the sustaining and driving force of an economy gives the appearance of validity for several reasons. One is that expected demand is the reason firms engage in production. Moreover, purchases for consumption constitute by far the largest single component of total spending (Gross Domestic Product, GDP) of an economy; as Adam Smith observes: "Consumption is the sole end and purpose of all production … The maxim is so perfectly self-evident, that it would be absurd to attempt to prove it" (*WN*, 2: 179). Thus, the greater the level of consumption demand, the greater will be the total demand for goods and services in the marketplace, validating producers' plans. Were the market demand for some commodities to exceed their producers' expectations, increased profits would be made as their prices rise. This will encourage increased production and the subsequent hiring of more workers in the affected industries. The opposite occurs when producers' expectations are disappointed by the actual market or "effectual demand" (Smith *WN*, 1: 63–8).

Richard Kahn (1931) turned the apparently positive relation between purchases for consumption and income generation for producers into a multiplier analysis, which Keynes (1936) subsequently adopts. The analysis has become a staple of modern macroeconomics. The argument, simply put, is that an individual's consumption spending (C_0) becomes another's (seller's) income ($C_0 = Y_1$). The seller also consumes a fraction (β) of that income ($C_1 = \beta Y_1$), which then becomes another's income ($C_1 = \beta Y_1 = Y_2$). Subsequent consumption spending out of Y_2 generates further income ($C_2 = \beta Y_2 = \beta^2 Y_1 = Y_3$), and so on, until the initial consumption spending has generated a geometric series whose summation equals kC_0, where $k = 1/(1-\beta)$ is the multiplier. Clearly, the larger is the fraction consumed out of income, the larger will be the size of the multiplier: if $\beta = .8$, $k = 5$, and if $\beta = .9$, $k = 10$.

The multiplier analysis is fundamental to modern Keynesian macroeconomics, including the income-expenditure model in which the slope of the expenditure curve reflects the size of β (the marginal propensity to consume). Given some value for β, Keynesian analysis suggests that changes in business investment (I) and government expenditures (G) are multiplied by the factor k to determine changes in equilibrium national income: $\Delta Y = k\Delta I$ or $\Delta Y = k\Delta G$. The same results are obtained in the IS-LM model.

But as has been shown (Ahiakpor 2001), the Keynesian multiplier argument is incorrect. Without having produced or sold anything, the initial consumer in the multiplier model would have no means by which to make the purchase. (If spending is from a gift, the donor must first have earned income from production.) Furthermore, to have sold anything to acquire the purchasing power, the buyer of the product also must have earned income with which to make the purchase. Clearly then, it is production which makes consumer spending possible, as J.-B. Say clarifies in the law of markets: *productions can only be purchased by productions* (1821b: 15; italics original), elaborated in Chapter 2.[10] Also, the part of income not directly consumed is not lost from the expenditure stream as the Keynesian multiplier argument presumes. Savings are borrowed for purchasing goods and services for consumption or for production by issuers of loan-notes or the sellers of financial securities (IOUs). Thus, if there is an expansionary force or multiplier process going on, it starts with production, not from consumption spending.

The Keynesian derivation of an expansionary effect from government spending through the multiplier process also depends on the false assumption that government spending does not depend on current income or savings and thus can be autonomous, even for a closed economy. But government spending must be financed either by tax revenues or the sale of debt instruments (bonds). Unless the bonds are sold to a central bank or to foreigners, the public must pay for them out of their current savings, which depends on their income ($\Delta FA^d_G = \gamma Y = \Delta FA^s_G = (G - T)$), just as the public supplies loanable funds to private investors by purchasing their debt instruments ($\Delta FA^d_p = \lambda Y = \Delta FA^s_p = I$). Therefore, the usual process of generating the government or investment expenditure multiplier is invalid. $Y = AD = C + I + G$ becomes $Y = \beta Y + \lambda Y + \gamma Y$, taking into account the fact that there cannot be any autonomous consumption spending in a closed economy. Whatever anyone spends first must have been earned from production. Thus, the simple Keynesian multiplier analysis yields a zero outcome: $Y = [1/(1 - \beta - \lambda - \gamma)] \cdot 0 = 0$; see Ahiakpor (2001 or 2003b, Chapter 12).

The Theory of Interest

Keynes's supply and demand for money (liquidity) theory of interest seems plausible partly because it uses language readily understood by most people: interest is paid for borrowing "money," e.g. Say (1821a: 352) and John Stuart Mill (*Works*, 3: 508). Thus, the more money made available to borrowers, the cheaper must be the cost to borrow it. It also sounds reasonable to argue that a lender parts with money and may hold a loan-note, which renders the lender illiquid for the duration of the loan. This is why claiming that "the rate of interest is the reward for parting with liquidity for a specified period" (Keynes 1936: 167) appears to be a reasonable alternative theory of interest.

But the Keynesian explanation of interest rate determination from the supply and demand for money or liquidity derives from a misunderstanding, arising from an "ambiguity of language" (Smith *WN*, 1: 306–7). The lender who parts with money must first have acquired it with income. Thus, it is the lender's non-consumed income or savings that is loaned out. The money (cash) is merely the instrument of conveyance (Smith *WN*, 1: 374; Pigou 1927: 121). Furthermore, the lender regards the loan-note as part of his or her wealth. Also, in the business person's language, it is "capital" which is obtained in a loan. It is to recognize this fundamental process of borrowing and lending "capital" through the medium of money that the classical economists explained the theory of interest in terms of the supply and demand for "capital" or savings, e.g. Smith (*WN*, 1: 372–6), Ricardo (*Works*, 1: 363–4; 2: 331; 3: 89–92), and Mill (*Works*, 3: 647–55)

It was mainly Keynes's failure to interpret "capital" as funds in the classical theory of interest explained in Marshall's *Principles* that led to his rejecting the theory as nonsensical and his offering the liquidity-preference alternative (Keynes 1936: 186–7; 1937a; Ahiakpor 1990 or 2003b, Chapter 5). The subsequent acceptance of Keynes's criticism of the classical theory also was influenced by Irving Fisher's warning that "the student should ... forget all former notions concerning the so-called supply and demand of capital as the causes of interest" (1930: 32), while arguing the Austrian alternative theory of interest in terms of time-preference or the degree of impatience. Fisher himself had been influenced or misled by Böhm-Bawerk's (1890) criticism of the classical theory of interest, which also was founded on the latter's misinterpretation of "capital" as capital goods in the classical theory (Ahiakpor 1997b or 2003b, Chapter 6).

Adjustment to full employment

Keynes relied heavily on the experience of persistent unemployment initially following Britain's return to the gold standard at the pre-war parity in 1925, which got worse with the Great Depression until Britain left the gold standard in September 1931, to focus on the problem of unemployment. The slow recovery in many economies around the world, particularly those that stayed longer on the gold standard, further strengthened Keynes's doubts about the ability of a market economy to recover from a depression and promote increased employment without the intervention of government to increase aggregate demand by its increased spending. Otherwise, it is possible for an economy to be stuck in less than full employment equilibrium, Keynes reasoned.

A part of Keynes's theoretical argument for the claim is that an unemployed worker does not have the ability to determine their nominal or real wage rate. Certainly, it is difficult for an individual to find employment merely by offering to work for less than the going rate in a firm. Keynes compounded the problem of wage rate determination and unemployment by also suggesting that it must take an authoritarian government to lower money wage rates across the board to solve the unemployment problem since workers typically resist nominal wage reductions. In this, Keynes believed, "the workers ... are instinctively more reasonable economists than the classical school, inasmuch as they resist reductions in money-wages ... even though the existing real equivalent of these wages exceeds the marginal disutility of the existing employment" (1936: 14); see also Chapter 19 in Keynes (1936). Keynes claimed that a reduction in wage rates would not reduce the rate of unemployment but would rather increase it since a lower wage rate would reduce aggregate demand for output, lower the level of prices, and decrease the demand for labor in turn. Keynes's claims have been formalized into a model of aggregate supply and demand for labor in which the supply curve is horizontal at the existing wage rate until full-employment when the supply curve either slopes upwards or becomes vertical. However, carefully considered, Keynes's argument is incorrect.

Indeed, we may apply the classical theory of value to labor and derive the conclusion that in a flexible (nominal) wage regime with an upward sloping labor supply curve, a fall in the demand for labor would yield a new equilibrium with less employment and lower average wage rate. The decreased demand for labor may arise, say, from the introduction of labor-replacing machinery or a fall in the general level of prices, resulting from an excess demand for currency. But the decreased demand for labor must first produce some involuntary unemployment before the nominal wage rate falls. In time, the demand for labor may increase as the rate of production increases, including the increased production of labor-replacing machinery. On the other hand, an increase in the supply of labor, following the fall in the level of commodity prices, would lower the nominal wage rate, thereby increasing the quantity of labor employed.

No "classical" economist, including Pigou in the *Theory of Unemployment* (1933) that Keynes (1936) held up representative of the classical view of the labor market, claims that the labor market is always at full employment or that a fall in the demand for labor would not cause involuntary unemployment.[11] Pigou (1913: 14; italics added) also concerns himself with "only that part of [the idleness of prospective wage-earners] which is, from their point of view and in their existing condition at the time, *involuntary*." Marshall (1920: 572–3, 590–2) recognizes the "enforced idleness" or "compulsory idleness" of some potential workers resulting from the disorganization of credit or high wage demands of labor unions when prices fall. But in Keynes's understanding, "The classical postulates do not admit of the possibility of ... 'involuntary' unemployment" (1936: 6).[12] Furthermore, the notion of a perfectly elastic labor supply curve at an existing wage rate may be a meaningful depiction of a firm's or a sub-set of an industry's circumstances—"different employment centres"—as Pigou (1933: 63) characterizes them. Thus, an apple orchard or a machine tool company may be able to increase its hiring of workers without an increase in the nominal wage rate because it draws from other industries paying lower wages. But a horizontal labor supply curve for a whole industry or the economy defies sound logic.

Were the modern economy to be characterized by daily wage contracting, it may be possible for wage rates to adjust quickly for the rate of involuntary unemployment to approach zero. Indeed, in the face of uncertainty about demand in the goods market, there is no guarantee that all prospective employees would always be hired, a point Pigou (1933: 10, 222, 252) makes in his explanations of unemployment. Contrast this with Keynes's (1936: 24, n. 3; 1937a: 222) view of classical analysis as presuming entrepreneurs form expectations about the future with certainty.

Keynes (1936) also makes an incorrect argument, claiming that a fall in the nominal wage rate may not decrease the real wage rate but would rather increase the rate of unemployment. This because, according to his reasoning, total consumption spending would be reduced when the wage rate falls, and this would cause the price level to fall and the real wage rate to rise (1936: 262–9). First, the level of prices is determined by the supply and demand for money (currency), not by the consumption spending of wage earners. Second, consumption spending out of wages is not the only determinant of the total demand for goods and services. Some consumers borrow funds from savers for consumption purposes. Moreover, profit earners also are consumers and so are rental- and interest-income earners. Besides, the demand for non-consumption goods also generates demand for hiring labor to produce them. Furthermore, a fall in the nominal wage rate, by reducing the cost of production, increases the rate of profit at the current rate of production, encouraging producers to hire more workers.

Thus, Keynes's (1936: 261) requirement that the "community's marginal propensity to consume [be] equal to unity" for a cut in the nominal wage rate not to decrease total employment is just red herring. So are his claims that the type of wage cuts that may be helpful to an economy "could only be accomplished by administrative decree [which] is scarcely practical politics under a system of free wage-bargaining" (1936: 265) or could only be achieved in "a highly authoritarian society" (1936: 269). Labor unions in non-authoritarian societies sometimes negotiate wage cuts in order to minimize lay-offs among their members in times of economic recession. Thus, Keynes's (1936: 268–9) requirement that wage rate reductions cause a lowering of interest rates for that to help increased employment of labor has no correct theoretical basis. Interest rates are determined by the supply and demand for credit (savings) rather than by the level of wage rates.

Keynes is further incorrect in claiming that a cut in the nominal wage rate may keep prospective employers waiting for more cuts before hiring additional employees (1936: 263). The foregone production entails a cost to producers, namely, the revenue to meet the cost of borrowed "capital." The threat of bankruptcy keeps producers operating for as long as they can cover their direct or variable costs in the short run, that is, while there are contractual obligations to hire some other factors of productions. Keynes's argument may have provided an excuse for the behavior of British labor unions that were resisting wage cuts in the face of increasing unemployment in the early 1930s. Keynes even praised such resistance to wage rate reductions as labor union leaders being wiser than were the economists of the classical school. He argues:

> Thus it is fortunate that the workers, though unconsciously, are instinctively more reasonable economists than the classical school, inasmuch as they resist reductions of money-wages, which are seldom or never of an all-round character, even though the existing real wage equivalent of these wages exceeds the marginal disutility of the existing employment.
>
> (1936: 14)

The conflicting interests of workers and employers regarding wage rates have long been understood. As Adam Smith (*WN*, 1:74) explains,

> What are the common wages of labour, depends every where upon the contract usually made between these two parties, whose interests are by no means the same. The workmen desire to get as much, the masters to give as little as possible. The former are disposed to combine in order to raise, the latter in order to lower the wages of labour.

R. G. Hawtrey employs the same understanding to explain the difficulty of adjusting quickly out of business fluctuations:

> If the working classes would accept an early reduction of wages when a period of bad trade begins and if the employers would give an early

increase of wages when a period of good trade begins, not only would the harmful consequences of a trade fluctuation be avoided, but the fluctuation itself might even be prevented.

(1913: 266)

It appears that political or social considerations drove much of Keynes's reasoning regarding the need for wage rate reductions to aid in reducing unemployment in a recession than sound economic analysis. He argues that the series of "irregular changes" in wage rates needed to reduce unemployment would not be justifiable on any "criterion of social justice or economic expediency" as these would leave "those in the weakest bargaining position [to] suffer relatively to the rest" (1936: 267).

Attributing the full employment always assumption to classical analysis

Finally, Keynes attracted adherence to his theories of interest, the price level and inflation, and aggregate demand management by claiming that the classical alternatives he sought to replace were valid only under the condition of full employment. Thus, he dubbed David Ricardo's (*Works*, 1: 363–4) explanation that increases in the quantity of money by a central bank would not permanently lower interest rates but would only lower the value of the currency issued (increased level of prices) as being founded on the assumption of full employment: "Once again the assumption required ['as always with Ricardo'] is the usual classical assumption, that there is always full employment" (Keynes 1936: 191). Such a claim enabled Keynes to canvass the view that a central bank could drive the rate of interest to zero or hold it down permanently to relieve society of the need for paying positive rates of interest to attract savings.[13] Similarly, Keynes (1936, Chapter 21) argues against the inflationary consequences of a central bank's excessive money (currency) creation by suggesting that, in conditions of "widespread unemployment," the increased money supply would primarily increase the rate of production and the hiring of labor rather than be a source of inflation.[14] Also, claiming that Say's law of markets assumes full employment and does not recognize the demand for money to hold other than for transactions purposes (Keynes 1936: 18–20, 26), Keynes argues that, in conditions of less than full employment, there is the need for increased government spending to increase aggregate demand. But all of these claims are founded on Keynes's misunderstandings or outright misrepresentations of classical arguments (Ahiakpor 1997a or 2003b, Chapter 10).

Ricardo's explanation that increases in the quantity of money (currency) do not permanently lower the rate of interest is based simply on the fact that money is not "capital" but only a means whereby "capital" may be transferred from savers to borrowers. It is by increasing the supply of credit (S_{CR} = S_c + ΔH, where CR = credit, S_c = supply of "capital" or savings, and ΔH = increased quantity of currency or high-powered money) that the rate of interest is lowered in the short run, as Ricardo pointed out. But as prices rise the demand for loans increases, driving interest rates back up. Real-world economies confirm the classical argument, especially in those countries where interest rates are free to adjust to the conditions of market demand and supply of credit. See Friedman (1972) for some examples relating to the 1960s and 1970s where high currency (central bank credit) growth is associated with high rates of inflation and high interest rates. The experience of high currency growth and high rates of inflation and interest rates in Argentina, Brazil, and Peru in the late 1980s and early 1990s also confirms the argument.

In Argentina, the currency growth rate rose from 418% in 1988 to 7,446% in 1989 and declined to 589% in 1990. The bank deposit interest rate rose from 372% to 17,236% and declined to 1,515% in those years, respectively. In Brazil, in those same years, currency growth rates were 306%, 2,415%, and 1,835%, while bank deposit interest rates rose from 859% in 1988 to 5,845% in 1989 and to 9,394% in 1990. In Peru, the currency growth rate was 568% in 1988 and soared to 1,437% in 1989 and to 7,783% in 1990, while the deposit interest rate rose from 162% in 1988 to 1,136% in 1989 and to 2,440% in 1990. By 1994, the currency growth rate in Argentina had declined to 8.5% while the deposit interest rate also decreased to 8.1 %. Currency growth rate that year was 31% in Peru while that country's bank deposit interest rate also declined 22.4%. Only in Brazil did the deposit rate stay high at 5,175% along with a high currency growth rate of 2,242%. (See the International Monetary Fund's *International Financial Statistics Yearbook*, 2001.)

Keynes's denial that the supply and demand for money (currency) determine the level of prices rather than the rate of interest stems from his difficulties with the classical Quantity Theory of money as well as his misunderstanding the classical forced-saving doctrine. From the Cambridge version of the quantity theory ($H = kPy$), we derive the price level as $P = H/ky$, where $k =$ the proportion of income the public wants to hold as currency, $y =$ real income or output, and $H =$ currency. Clearly, changes in H, k, and y must affect P, the price level, as explained in previous chapters. Also, from Fisher's version ($HV = PT$), which Fisher (1913: 26n) attributes first to Ricardo's formulation of the quantity theory, we derive the price level as $P = HV/T$, where $V =$ velocity of money's circulation and $T =$ the volume of transactions requiring the use of currency. Again, there is little doubt that changes in the quantity of money, money's velocity, or the volume of transactions requiring the use of cash must affect the level of prices. And, none of such effects on prices requires the assumption of full employment. If that assumption were required, we would observe changes in the level of prices or inflation only in economies with no unemployment. Reality or experience refutes the Keynesian view.

As elaborately explained in Chapter 2 earlier, Say's Law is an explanation of how production of a commodity creates a market or a vent for other productions and thus relative prices and interest rates adjust to changes in excess demands or supplies in different markets in an economy. Prices rise in markets experiencing excess demands while they fall in those with excess supplies.

The self-interested behavior of producers leads them to adjust their supplies to meet market demand by reallocating productive resources, including "capital." Interest rates also may rise from the excess demand for credit or "capital" while the adjustments are taking place in the product markets.

Were an excess demand to develop for money (currency), especially in a condition of shaken confidence in the economy, the level of prices would fall, raising the value of money in response to its excess demand (Marshall 1923: 42–6). It would require a sufficient increase in the quantity of money to meet its excess demand for the level of prices to be restored. As Mill well explains:

> At such times there is really an excess of all commodities above the money demand: in other words, there is an under-supply of money. From the sudden annihilation of a great mass of credit, every one dislikes to part with ready money, and many are anxious to procure it at any sacrifice. Almost everybody therefore is a seller, and there are scarcely any buyers: so that there may really be, though only while the crisis lasts, an extreme depression of general prices, from what may be indiscriminately called a glut of commodities or a dearth of money. But it is a great error to suppose, with Sismondi, that a commercial crisis is the effect of a general excess of production. … its immediate cause is a contraction of credit, and the remedy is, not a diminution of supply, but the restoration of confidence.
>
> (*Works*, 3: 574)

Keynes's version of Say's Law as "supply creates its own demand" or that the supply price of commodities is always equal to their demand price arises from his misunderstanding or misinterpretation of what the classics actually wrote (see Ahiakpor 1997a, 2001, 2003a, 2018b, 2020; Jonsson 1995, 1997; Kates 1997, 1998). It is the failure of many modern interpreters carefully to address Keynes's misrepresentations of classical writings that his distorted version of Say's Law has been so much popularized, e.g., Samuelson and Nordhaus (1998), Jansen, Delorme, and Ekelund (1994), Baumol (1999, 2003), Ekelund and Tollison (2000), Schiller (2000), and Davidson (1991).

Keynesianism in the future

In the face of the declining influence of neoclassical Keynesianism, post-Keynesians and new Keynesians have been attempting to sustain the relevance of Keynes's macroeconomics. Post-Keynesians focus on issues of income distribution (and unemployment) and see economic problems, including inflation and recessions, as arising from the maldistribution of income between profits and wages or the misguided exercise of economic power by the capitalist class over labor, a kind of Marxism without Karl Marx. They appear to find relevance for their work in Keynes's concerns over the distribution of income in the *General Theory,* including his argument that increased taxation of the rich to finance public spending to favor the poor would ensure enough aggregate demand to sustain full employment or prevent recessions (1936: 321, 372–5). The poor have a higher marginal propensity to consume, thus such redistribution would increase aggregate demand. But, again, the argument follows from Keynes's mistaken presumption that savings are not spent or consumed, but they are (Smith *WN*, 1: 359).

A variant of the post-Keynesian argument is Hyman Minsky's (1985: 51–2) claim that "the emphasis upon growth through investment, the bias towards bigness in business, business styles that emphasize advertising and overheads, and the explosion of transfer payments are the main causes of our current inflation." Like Keynes, this view has no room for the classical Quantity Theory of money as the basis for explaining inflation. Thomas Piketty (2014) is a recent focus on income and wealth inequality as a danger to economic prosperity, unless governments intervened with redistributive policies. Like Keynes (1930, 1936), Piketty does not fully reckon that wealth is accumulated out of significant productivity increases and that the savings of the wealthy provide the capital (funds) for hiring labor (the Wages Fund) and financing other business investments.

However, the post-Keynesian theories of inflation, interest rates, and market prices provide little consistency with experience to command the serious attention of most economists. When they come to recognize the fundamental flaws in the conceptions upon which Keynes based his income redistribution arguments, particularly the fact that (1) saving is not hoarding but spending on financial assets, (2) interest rates are determined mainly by the flow of saving relative to its demand, and not by the rate of a central bank's money (currency) creation, (3) taxation does not change total spending or "aggregate demand" but only redistributes total spending, and (4) the level of prices and its changes are determined by the supply of money (currency) relative to its demand rather than the relation between wages and profits, they may be willing to give up their allegiance to their doctrine.

Some among the post-Keynesians also emphasize the effect of changing expectations about future profitability of investment in determining current rates of investment, employment, and growth, following Keynes's arguments in the *General Theory* and his mistaken claim that "orthodox theory assumes that we have a knowledge of the future of a kind quite different from that which we actually possess" (1937a: 222). Hyman Minsky combines the problem of uncertainty with the nature of the financial system in advanced capitalist economies to build his so-called financial instability hypothesis. But the "classical" economists recognized the problem of uncertainty in economic calculations, contrary to Keynes's claims. Pigou's *Industrial Fluctuations* (1927, esp. Chapters 6 and 7) and *Theory of Unemployment* (1933), and Marshall's *Principles* (1920) explain economic fluctuations and unemployment partly by the uncertainties of economic agents. Marshall also includes "the rapidity of invention, the *fickleness of fashion*, and above all the *instability of credit*" among the factors that "certainly introduce disturbing elements into modern industry," creating the "inconstancy of employment" (1920: 572–3; italics added).

Mill (1874: 55, 58) bases the idleness of productive capacity and lack of full employment on the failure of producers to estimate accurately future demand for their products. Mill explains that "the calculations of producers and traders being of *necessity imperfect*, there are always some commodities which are more or less in excess, as there are always some which are in deficiency" (1874: 67; italics added). Furthermore, Mill writes:

> In the present state of the commercial world, mercantile transactions being carried on upon an immense scale, but the *remote causes of fluctuations* in prices being *very little understood*, so that unreasonable hopes and unreasonable fears alternately rule with tyrannical sway over the minds of a majority of the mercantile public; general eagerness to buy and general reluctance to buy, succeed one another in a manner more or less marked, at brief intervals. Except during short periods of transition, there is almost always either great briskness of business or great stagnation; either the principal producers of almost all the leading articles of industry have as many orders as they can possibly execute, or dealers in almost all commodities have their warehouses *full of unsold goods*.
>
> (Mill 1874: 68; italics added)[15]

If economic agents were presumed to have perfect foresight in classical economics, the classics would have argued that market prices are always equal to their natural or normal values instead of gravitating towards the latter, e.g., Adam Smith (*WN*, Bk 1: Ch. 7); see also Marshall (1920: 287–9), who notes that "we cannot foresee the future perfectly" (289). It is truly astounding the degree to which Keynes misrepresented classical macroeconomic analysis and badly has misled many modern macroeconomists!

However, pointing out that classical economists did not assume a world of certainty is not to give credence to Hyman Minsky's "financial instability hypothesis." The hypothesis pays no attention to the classical forced-saving mechanism, which better explains the business cycle phenomenon it seeks to address. Minsky's argument is also founded on the false (but rather common) notion that banks' credit expansion is not based on savings deposited with them;[16] there is a false separation of "capital assets" from "current output," as if current output does not include capital goods; and a strange equation of profits with "financed investment" (1985: 42).

Minsky's treatment of banking has a foundation in Keynes's (1930: 25–6) claim that it is bank lending which creates customers' deposits, rather than the other way around. Of course, Keynes's argument follows those of Knut Wicksell (1898: 110–1) and A.C. Pigou (1927: 123–4); see Ahiakpor (2003b, Chapter 4, esp. 47–52). But banks only lend a fraction of their customers' deposits, keeping the unlent portion in readiness to pay cash on demand or to fulfill legal reserve requirements. Indeed, the so-called bank deposit multiplier process works only if all recipients of the spent borrowed funds make new deposits with them; see Chapter 7. But the most significant defect of Minsky's hypothesis is that it blames the failure of an economy to attain equilibrium on "the prices of current output – and the employment offered in producing output – [depending] upon shorter-run expectations" whereas "capital asset prices reflect long-run expectations" (29) and that these expectations can be misaligned.

Minsky's alleged problem of disequilibrium arises partly from his using Keynes's (1930, 2: 207; 1936: 62) definition of investment to mean only the purchase of capital goods, following the Böhm-Bawerkian tradition (Ahiakpor 1997b or 2003b, Chapter 6). As the classics explained, investment on the part of producers means spending savings or borrowed funds to purchase capital goods (fixed capital), raw materials, hiring the services of land and labor (the Wages Fund), and keeping some cash on hand to run an enterprise (circulating capital). Conceived this way, we can appreciate that the same investor of borrowed funds must hold expectations over both the short run and the long run, with the long run predominantly ruling. Few entrepreneurs enter into a business venture with the intent to fold within a year or two. Even when hiring workers, most employers would like to keep them over the long haul or for as long as the business survives and the employees meet their contractual expectations.

Should a business enterprise experience persistent losses, the capital goods may be sold to liquidate the venture. The markets for capital goods, land, labor, and credit are the venues through which unrealized expectations are resolved, resulting in changing prices and interest rates. Only by failing to recognize the equilibrating functions of these markets (as illustrated in Say's Law) does Minsky claim the existence of "financial instability [as] a normal functioning, internally-generated result of the behavior of a capitalist economy" (1985: 26). He then argues that it requires changes in government spending or a shift to "the achievement of full employment through consumption production" (ibid: 53) in order to stabilize that economy.[17] As explained in Chapter 4, a government's spending of its tax and/or bond revenues merely substitutes for private sector spending, particularly for a closed economy.

The new Keynesians do not address the fundamental flaws of Keynes's arguments noted above. Rather, they have responded quite correctly to some arguments advanced by the new classicals and real business cycle theorists denying the usefulness of interventionist policies of government popularized by the Keynesian revolution. The new classicals argue that only unanticipated changes in monetary policy could affect employment and output in an economy since rationally acting individuals would not stand to lose their real purchasing power, which such policies require to produce their effects. But the existence of overlapping contracts enables changes in the quantity of money to have real effects over longer periods than would appear consistent with the new classicals' argument. Similarly, real business cycle theorists tend to argue that short-run fluctuations in employment and output are only the result of supply-side shocks, denying demand-side arguments. Building upon the rationality of individual-choice arguments, they also suggest that practically all unemployment is voluntary.

The new Keynesian responses to these arguments include (1) noting that product prices tend to be sticky over fairly long periods, as observed for restaurant menus, (2) claiming that some firms pay higher than market-clearing wages in order to avoid the costliness of training new employees and also encouraging the higher productivity of existing workers, the so-called efficiency-wage hypothesis, and (3) that unionized employees resist wage reductions in times of falling output demand, thus causing involuntary unemployment of some of their members, an "insider-outsider" modeling of the labor market.[18] The basic thrust of all these arguments is to deny the existence of perfect competition in product as well as labor markets, and thus the failure of markets to adjust quickly enough to prevent involuntary unemployment. But the arguments would constitute a valid negation of the classical theories against which Keynes reacted if the "classics," including Marshall (1920) and Pigou (1933), had assumed the existence of perfect competition in these markets. They did not. Such characterization of classical economics was one of Keynes's successful misrepresentations of their work.

The classics explained what would be the nature of an economy's adjustment process if competition were *perfectly free*, especially from government intervention. But such perfectly free competition depicts the freedom of entry and exit of firms in an industry rather than the modern perfect competition model in which firms themselves do not change prices but take them from some mythical market, and prices adjust instantaneously. Thus Adam Smith posits the condition of "perfect liberty, or where [a man] may change his trade as often as he pleases" (*WN*, 1: 63; see also 1: 70, 111) as one under which firms would earn normal profits and the market price frequently would equal the long-run or natural price. And in contrasting free competition with monopoly, Smith explains that "Monopoly ... is a great enemy to good management, which can never be universally established but in consequence of that *free and universal competition* which forces everybody to have recourse to it for the sake of self-defense" (*WN*, 1: 165; italics added). David Ricardo also describes a "system of perfectly free commerce" under which "each country naturally devotes its capital and labor to such employments as are most beneficial to each" (*Works*, 1: 133).

Thus, the model of mark-up pricing, which some post-Keynesians seem to construe as constituting a major refutation of classical macroeconomics, because it does not fit the perfectly competitive model, is not alien to classical analysis. In principle, the mark-up price has to have some relation to a product's price elasticity of demand as well as its marginal cost, if a firm seeks to maximize profits. But since the relevant variables are hard to estimate in practice, mark-up pricing is a trial-and-error process on the part of firms, a process quite consistent with the classical view of firms' adjustment of prices in the marketplace, e.g., Smith (*WN*, Bk 1, Ch. 7) and John Stuart Mill (*Works*, 3: 467–70). Of course, the attempt to use mark-up theory to explain the level of prices (inverse of the value of money), as if an economy were one giant factory whose owner marks up direct input costs to determine "the economy's price" (Galbraith and Darity 1994: 396–7), is not meaningful or sound analysis.

Also, contrary to the perfect knowledge assumption of the neoclassical perfect competition model and which Keynes wrongly attributes to the "classics," the latter made no such assumption.[19] Adjusting quantities or prices in the marketplace is a learning process in classical economics. Indeed, writing in the classical tradition, Marshall (1920: 448–9) rejects the applicability of the perfect competition model, along with its perfect knowledge assumption, to the classics and to any real economy. With respect to the labor market, Marshall notes: "if a man had sufficient ability to know everything about the market for his labor, he would have too much to remain long in a low grade. The older economists, in constant contact as they were with the actual facts of business life, must have known this well enough" (1920: 449). Marshall goes on to explain how the perfect knowledge assumption may have mistakenly been applied to the classics: "partly for brevity and simplicity, partly because of the term 'free competition' had become almost a catchword, partly because they had not sufficiently classified and conditioned their doctrines, they often seemed to imply that they did assume this perfect knowledge" (1920: 449). Marshall here does little justice to Mill's explicit statements rejecting the perfect foresight or knowledge assumption noted above, including Mill (1874: 67, 68).

A.C. Pigou also rejects the perfect competition assumption, noting that:

> With *perfectly free competition* among workpeople and labor perfectly mobile, the nature of the relation [between the demand function for labor and the real wage rate][20] will be very simple. There will always be at work a *strong tendency* for wage-rates to be so related to demand that everybody is employed. Hence, in stable conditions every one will actually be employed. The implication is that such unemployment as exists at any time is due wholly to the fact that changes in demand conditions are continually taking place and that frictional resistances prevent the appropriate wage adjustments from being made instantaneously.
>
> (1933: 252; italics added)

Crucially, we should note, Pigou continues to argue: "In the absence of perfectly free competition among workpeople the functional relation, if such exists, between the wage-rate stipulated for and the state of demand need not be of the above simply sort" (1933: 252).

Furthermore, Pigou (1933: 254) explains that trade unions in "industries ... sheltered from foreign competition" create unemployment among their members by insisting on higher wage rates because "the leaders in charge of the bargaining... prefer smaller aggregate earnings that give good incomes to a comparatively small number of men to larger aggregate earnings made up of a great number of poor incomes." He notes that the system of "State-aided unemployment insurance with substantial rates of benefit" (1933: 254) tends to encourage such behavior among trade unions.

Pigou (1933: 293–4) also describes conditions in the marketplace that make it hard for wages to adjust to changes in the demand for goods and services, again showing the irrelevance of the perfect competition assumption. They include the fact that "Employers are unwilling to grant real wage increases in good times for fear that, if they do so, they will be unable to recall them when the good times pass: workpeople are unwilling to accept reductions in bad times for fear that employers will refuse to rescind them when the bad times pass" (1933: 294). These arguments by Pigou are in clear contradiction of Keynes's (1936: 257) attribution to the "classics" a belief in the "fluidity of money-wages." Only by ignoring the classical literature and Pigou's (1941: 78, 91) invitation that we examine such literature carefully could one continue to accept Keynes's version of what they wrote.

Following Keynes's claim that the classics argued the neutrality of money or dichotomized the pricing process (1936: 292–3), David Romer (1993) harps incessantly on the non-neutrality of money on real variables in the short run as one of the distinguishing features of the new Keynesian response to the new classical and real business cycle theorists. The latter are believed to be elaborating the alleged classical tradition of money's neutrality both in the short run and in the long run. Paul Davidson (1991) also harps on the non-neutrality of money on real variables as one of the fundamental disagreements Keynes had with classical economics and which the neoclassical Keynesians are willing to accept for the long run, but which the post-Keynesians reject. Fontana (2001) also claims that the non-neutrality of money in Keynes's work is a distinguishing feature of his method of analysis from that of the classics. But the alleged neutrality of money in classical analysis in the short run is only a figment of Keynes's imagination

The classics explained that changes in the quantity of money (currency) have real effects in the short run; they change real output and employment until all prices, including wage rates, have adjusted to the changed quantity. This is what the classical forced-saving doctrine is all about (Ahiakpor 1985, 1997a, 2009); see also Chapter 9. David Ricardo also explains that in an economy in which there are proportional as well as absolute taxes, changes in the amount of money do change relative prices and the composition of output in the long run, even if the level of output and employment is unchanged (Ahiakpor 1985). Keynes (1936: 80), on the other hand, misrepresents Jeremy Bentham's explanation of the forced-saving mechanism, claiming that it implies the existence always of full employment, and attributes the same argument to "All the nineteenth-century writers who dealt with this matter" (1936: 80–81). But Keynes's claims are a misrepresentation of the classics.

Finally, the classics, Marshall, and Pigou did focus on involuntary unemployment as a policy problem, contrary to Keynes's misrepresentation of their work (Ahiakpor 1997a). David Ricardo and J.-B. Say also explicitly noted the problem of involuntary unemployment when new machinery is introduced into the workplace. Ricardo observes: "the substitution of machinery for human labor, is often very injurious to the interests of the class of laborers.

... the same cause which may increase the net revenue of the country, may at the same time render the population redundant, and deteriorate the condition of the laborer" (*Works*, 1: 388; see also 1: 25–6, 36, 44, 80, 388–97; 5: 303). Say recognizes the same phenomenon and explains:

> Whenever a new machine, or a new more expeditious process is substituted in the place of human labor previously in activity, part of the industrious human agents, whose service is thus ingeniously dispensed with, must needs be thrown out of employ. Whence many objections have been raised against the use of machinery, which has been often obstructed by popular violence, and sometimes by the act of authority itself.
>
> ... A new machine supplants a portion of human labor, but does not diminish the amount of the product; if it did, it would be absurd to adopt it.
>
> (Say 1821a: 86)

That Keynes grossly misrepresented the classicals' recognition of involuntary unemployment in a monetary economy can hardly be in doubt when we consult the classical literature.

Evidently, the neoclassical Keynesians, such as Tobin (1993) and Gordon (2000); the post-Keynesians; and the new Keynesians must be unaware of the extent of Keynes's misrepresentations of classical economics. Otherwise, they may simply have chosen not to deal with the textual evidence contradicting Keynes's claims as well as the fundamental flaws in the pillars upon which Keynes founded his macroeconomics.[21] It is truly remarkable how little reference the post-Keynesians make to the classical literature itself rather than simply repeating Keynes's allegations. As I argue in Ahiakpor (2019), none of the recent texts lauding the relevance of Keynes's ideas to current problems, especially since the 2008 financial crisis in the US, mentions Keynes's changed meaning of economic terms and misattributions of assumptions to classical macro-monetary analysis. But it is going to be hard for the upcoming generation of economists exposed to the evidence contradicting Keynes's claims to continue to take Keynesian macroeconomics in any of its forms seriously. Like Marxism, Keynesianism may yet continue to exist as a viewpoint in search of theoretical or empirical validation. Keynesians may continue to urge the activist role of government in economies in hopes of curing unemployment without acknowledging the pricing of labor as a major factor in explaining how much of it is demanded by prospective employers in a market economy.

Notes

1 This chapter draws heavily on my 2004 article, "On the Future of Keynesian Economics: Struggling to Sustain a Dimming Light," in the *American Journal of Economics and Sociology* 63, No. 3 (July): 583–608.

2　In Samuel Hollander's (2011) presentation, on which Laidler was commenting, Hollander notes that Keynes "misrepresented his predecessors disgracefully" (27).

3　Ahiakpor (2018b) explains that Grieve's defense of Keynes's critique of Say's Law is founded upon his own misrepresentations of John Stuart Mill's arguments, besides his failing to recognize Keynes's misrepresentations of such classical concepts as saving, capital, investment, and money, as well as Keynes's misapplication of the law of markets to labor, which is not a produced commodity. Chapter 3 elaborates Grieve's misinterpretations of Say's Law, as discussed by Mill; see also Ahiakpor (forthcoming).

4　Their incredible claim does not take into account the gulf between Keynes's definitions of saving, capital, investment, and Say's usage of those terms in concert with Adam Smith's; see Chapter 2.

5　Schumpeter's (1954) very influential book, *History of Economic Analysis*, mostly praises Keynes's contributions to modern macroeconomic analysis (see [1954] 1994: 1170–84), while being rather critical of classical macro-monetary analysis, as explained in Chapter 1 of this book.

6　Hicks here appears to have accepted Keynes's (1936: 26) charge that the "classics" assumed entrepreneurs form expectations of future profits with certainty, but which they, including Marshall (1920: 281–2) and John Stuart Mill (*Works*, 2: 165), did not.

7　See Landreth and Colander (2002: 490–3) for a brief history of post-Keynesianism. Hyman Minsky has championed an argument he calls the "financial instability hypothesis" as a "variant of Keynesian theory" (1985: 38) in reaction to neoclassical Keynesianism. The argument is often associated with post-Keynesianism, although he also employs the equilibrating mechanism of supply and demand to determine capital asset prices.

8　For an extensive summary of their work, see Froyen (2013: 226–41). King (1993) argues that the new Keynesians' efforts to sustain the life of Keynesian economics are a waste of research time and talent as they divert attention from relevant research. This without noting the fundamental flaws of Keynesian economics discussed in some earlier chapters in this book and summarized again below.

9　From the Cambridge equation, we derive the demand for money (currency) as $H = kY$ and $\Delta H = k\Delta Y + \Delta kY$. The total amount of currency is held by households (h) and non-households (nh), including financial institutions, $H - H_h + H_{nh}$. The classics as well as their early neoclassical followers recognized that households hold or hoard cash, contrary to Keynes's claims, also repeated by Fontana (2001: 723) without contradiction. See Ricardo (*Works*, 3: 172; 6: 289, 300–1), Mill (*Works*, 3: 574) and Marshall (1923: 42, 44, 46).

10　Ricardo (*Works*, 1: 290) and John Stuart Mill (*Works*, 3: 571–2) also affirm the point. Keynes (1936: 18, 369) mentions the arguments by Ricardo and Mill but he evidently failed to appreciate their logic.

11　Pigou (1941: 78) categorically rejects Keynes's attribution of the full-employment assumption to classical analysis: "The classical view is not one which either asserts or implies that full employment always exists." Pigou also urges understanding of the "classical view as it really is—to be carefully distinguished from current caricatures of it" (1941: 91); Ahiakpor (1997a) elaborates. See also Aslanbeigui (1992, 1998) on Keynes's misrepresentation of Pigou's analysis of unemployment.

12　Such mischaracterization of classical analysis was too much even for Joseph Schumpeter who was praising Keynes's contributions to modern macroeconomic analysis. Schumpeter argues that Keynes's "indictment that the classical theory knows no unemployment except a frictional one is true only if the term frictional is defined so widely as to rob the indictment of all significance" ([1954] 1994: 1177, n12).

13　In the *Treatise* (1930, 2: 207), Keynes also claims, "the greatest evil of the moment and the greatest danger to economic progress in the near future are to be found in the unwillingness of the Central Banks of the world to allow the market-rate of interest to fall fast enough."

14 Keynes here may be repeating John Stuart Mill's explanation of the need to increase the quantity of money during an economic distress and falling prices: "An increase of the circulating medium, conformable in extent and duration to the temporary stress of business, does not raise prices, but merely prevents this fall" (*Works*, 3: 516).

15 Mill's argument here does not negate the proposition in Say's Law of there not being an overproduction of all commodities at the same time. Mill mentions "almost all commodities." Besides, money is also a commodity in Say's explanation, which Mill restates: "In order to render the argument for the impossibility of an excess of all commodities applicable to the case in which a circulating medium is employed, *money must itself be considered as a commodity*. It must, undoubtedly, be admitted that there cannot be an excess of all other commodities, and an excess of money at the same time" (1874: 71; italics added).

16 Keynes (1930) and Irving Fisher (1935) have been very influential in promoting this false claim, as discussed in Chapter 7 earlier. Meir Kohn (1993: 207) is among the few textbook authors to insist, "But banks cannot lend without taking in deposits."

17 There are some other aspects of Minsky's hypothesis that need not be discussed here, including his mischaracterization of some financial activities in advanced capitalist economies as "Ponzi schemes."

18 See Froyen (2013, Chapters 11 and 12) and Blanchard and Johnson (2013: 547–50) for some informative summaries.

19 Fontana (2001: 720–5) repeats Keynes's mistaken charge without contradiction. Of course, Fontana does not refer to the classical literature itself.

20 Pigou's (1933) switching between the nominal wage rate and "the real wage rate for which people stipulate" gave much ammunition for Keynes's criticism. Keynes correctly notes, "Now ordinary experience tells us, beyond doubt, that a situation where labour stipulates (within limits) for a money wage-wage rather than a real wage, so far from being a mere possibility, is the normal case" (1936: 9). Indeed, Marshall's (1920) discussions of the labor market are in terms of nominal wage rates, just as in classical macro-monetary analysis; see also Chapter 9 .

21 I confronted participants on the Post-Keynesian Thought network with some evidence of Keynes's misrepresentations of classical economics in the summer of 1995, after I had been invited to join. Rather than dealing with the textual evidence, some of the leading lights simply took themselves off the discussion list. Perhaps, part of their displeasure came from my urging them not to read Keynes as "cult literature." Some others talked past the evidence. Some of those that remained described me as a "lunatic" or a "skunk" that had strayed onto a garden party and caused the desertion of some participants!

11 Conclusion

Some policy implications of ridding
macroeconomics of Keynes's influence

Keynes's principal focus in his *General Theory* was to find the solution to the problem of persistent unemployment. He did not think extant classical macro-monetary analysis had the solution since that analysis, he believed, applies only to an economy operating at full capacity with no involuntary unemployment. He identified that analysis with Say's Law: "Thus Say's law, that the aggregate demand price of output as a whole is equal to its aggregate supply price for all volumes of output, is equivalent to the proposition that there is no obstacle to full employment" (1936: 26). But the experience of high unemployment in Britain, the US, and many other countries around the world during the Great Depression proved Say's Law wrong, in Keynes's judgment. Thus, he argued, "If [Say's Law] is not the true law relating the aggregate demand and supply functions, there is a vitally important chapter of economic theory which *remains to be written* and without which all discussions concerning the volume of aggregate employment are futile" (ibid; italics added).

However, as we have seen in Chapters 2 and 3 earlier, Keynes's reading of Say's Law was incorrect. The meanings of saving, capital, investment, and money with which Keynes read versions of the law from John Stuart Mill and Alfred Marshall impaired his correct interpretation of Say's Law. J.-B. Say himself also specified among the "greatest obstructions" to an economy's well-functioning "wars, embargoes, oppressive duties, the dangers and difficulties of transportation ... times of alarm and uncertainty ... and times of jobbing and speculation" (1821a: 142). Keynes apparently was not aware of Say's argument. These obstructions are capable of rendering an economy into a miserable state, according to Say, where "The labouring classes experience a want of work [unemployment]; families before in tolerable circumstances are more cramped and confined and those before in difficulties are left altogether destitute. Depopulation, misery, and returning barbarism, occupy the place of abundance and happiness" (1821a: 140). The First World War (1914–18), Britain's returning to the gold standard at pre-war parity for the pound in 1925, the 1930s (Smoot-Hawley) tariff wars between the US and other nations, the differential adherence of nations to the rules of the gold standard (Edie 1932, Viner 1932, and Friedman and Schwartz 1963), and the US stock bubble's bursting in October 1929 all appear to fit the kinds of contributory factors to economic disruption in Say's list.

Say also prescribes the needed remedies to economic malaise, almost exactly following Adam Smith's laissez-faire or free-enterprise policy conclusions. They include, in broad outlines, "frugality, intelligence, activity, and freedom" (1821a: 140). Thus, correcting Keynes's changed meanings of key economic concepts and his incorrect attributions of full employment and expectations of the future with certainty to classical macro-monetary analysis, we can recognize the relevant policies to promote economic prosperity and increased employment from the classical literature.

First among the appropriate policies is for governments to give up aggregate demand management through changes in taxation and spending. This derives from recognizing that savings are consumed (spent) reproductively by borrowers, as Adam Smith (*WN*, 1: 359) explains and subsequent classical economists have affirmed. Say also notes, "It is the aim of good government to stimulate production, of bad government to encourage consumption" (1821a: 139). This is because "the creation of a new product is the opening of a new market for other products, the consumption or destruction of a product is the stoppage of a vent for them" (ibid.). When an economy gets into a recession, it is a wise government that seeks to discover the impediments to the economy's normal functioning and to relieve them. So-called expansionary (pure) fiscal policies are ineffective, not because people base their consumption expenditures on their perceived permanent incomes. Rather, it is because whatever the government spends must be financed by the public, except when the government borrows from the central bank or from abroad.

The second policy implication from interpreting classical macro-monetary analysis correctly is that governments should not pursue economic growth by substituting their increased spending for private investment. They would thus keep their tax collection or budget deficits low. As Smith explains, "Little else is requisite to carry a state to the highest level of opulence from the lowest barbarism but peace, easy taxes, and a tolerable administration of justice: all the rest being brought about by the natural course of things."[1] David Ricardo also explains in his contemporaneous equivalence between taxation and government debt that it is the size of the government budget (spending) that is the true burden for an economy. A high government budget substitutes less efficient spending by bureaucrats for private investment spending that is more efficient. Also, the smaller the size of government spending, requiring a smaller level of taxation or debt, the greater will be the disposable incomes of the public, enabling their greater rate of saving and investment.

The third policy follows from our understanding that saving takes various forms, including holding checkable bank deposits. Holders of checkable deposits are seeking (a) to take advantage of being able cheaply to settle their indebtedness by writing checks rather than remitting money (cash), (b) to utilize a banking firm's facility of processing checks they receive, (c) to be relieved of the information gathering cost on borrowers, and (d) to earn interest along with the liquidity of the right to withdraw their short-term savings without notice. A government's providing the public with security for their deposits through deposit insurance while maintaining supervision of banks over their investments contributes to increased saving. The pursuit of 100% reserve requirement for banks as a means of controlling the volume of their loans, on the premise that banks create deposits "out of thin air," rather retards the growth of saving and investment. Commercial banks truly are intermediaries between savers and borrowers. They do not manufacture loanable funds out of nothing, any more than they can destroy the public's savings in checkable deposits at will and cause recessions.

A fourth policy implication is for central banks to employ variations in the quantity of high-powered money, especially through open market operations, to meet the variations in money's demand so as to maintain the level of prices or to target a zero inflation rate. The classical Quantity Theory of money is the application of the classical theory of value to money, not to money's substitute means of payment such as checkable deposits or traveler's checks. Thus, there is no need to control the growth of savings held in checkable deposits as part of monetary policy. Central bank money has replaced classical specie money whose variation depended upon a country's net exports. In the absence of the gold standard, central banks can vary the rate of their own currency creation to stabilize the level of their domestic prices and attenuate business fluctuations and unemployment.

Keynes was impressed with mercantilist arguments linking the increase of money in an economy with economic prosperity. He thus claimed to have turned the classical Quantity Theory from explaining the level of prices to a theory of "output as a whole" (1936, Chapter 21; [1936] 1974: xxxv). Encountering David Hume's warning about the short-term positive impact of increased quantity of money in an economy, Keynes claimed Hume had "a foot and a half in the classical world" because "he was still enough of a mercantilist not to overlook the fact that it is in the transition [short run] that we actually have our being" (1936: 343, n. 2). Keynes was impressed with Hume's arguing that "It is only in [the] interval or intermediate situation, between the acquisition of money and the rise of prizes, that the increasing quantity of gold and silver [money] is favourable to industry" (1752: 38; quoted in Keynes 1936: 343, n. 2). Hume's arguing the ultimate neutrality of money on output and employment did not much matter to Keynes:

> The influence which a greater abundance of coin [money] has in the kingdom ... [is to heighten] the price of commodities, and [oblige] every one to pay a greater number of these little yellow or white pieces for every thing he purchases. And as for foreign trade, it appears, that great plenty of money is rather disadvantageous, by raising the price of every kind of labour.
>
> (Hume 1752: 37)[2]

Thus, to attribute economic growth to the abundance of money, Hume added, is to mistake "a collateral effect ... for a cause, and [to ascribe] a consequence to the plenty of money; though it be really owing to a change in the manners and customs of the people" (ibid: 46). The world has seen examples of high increases in central bank money, high rates of inflation, and economic contraction and high unemployment instead, as noted in Chapter 10 earlier.

A fifth policy deriving from the fourth is for central banks to leave the level of interest rates in various credit or "capital" markets to their determination by supply and demand rather than attempting to manipulate them through variations in the quantity of money. There may be temporary liquidity effects of variations in the quantity of money on the level of interest rates. Interest rates may fall in the short run from increases in the quantity of central bank money, but they will rise from an increased demand for credit when prices rise subsequently—the price-level effect. On the other hand, interest rates may rise from a contraction of the quantity of money, but they would fall from a decreased demand for credit when prices fall subsequently. Adding the public's inflation (deflation) expectations effect to those reversals in the level of interest rates would intensify further the opposite movement of interest rates from that initiated by the central bank action.[3]

From the classical analysis of wage rate determination by the supply and demand for labor (Smith *WN*, 1: 74–5), we derive the appropriate policy on wage rates. These should be left to their determination at the various "employment centers," as A.C. Pigou (1933) describes them. Labor is in constant competition with machinery for employment. Thus mandating wage rates that place labor at a competitive disadvantage with the use of machinery can only keep the rate of unemployment higher than it otherwise would be. Labor union leaders may find it more favorable to maintaining their positions with higher average wage rates and higher rates of unemployment for the union membership than lower average wage rates and lower unemployment for their membership. But government policy regarding wage rates should not add to such tendency of union leaders by legislating minimum wage rates— higher than the equilibrium rate, by definition—and thus sustain higher rates of unemployment. Keynes's linking the level of prices to the level of nominal wage rates derives partly from his having misapplied the classical Quantity Theory of money to explaining interest rates along the lines of mercantilist thought (Keynes 1936: 341; 1974: xxxiv), having disregarded David Hume's (1752) essay, "Of Interest," contradicting the same.

It is instructive that in his 1946 article, Keynes also regretted "how much modernist stuff, gone wrong and turned sour and silly, is circulating in our system" (185), referring to arguments being made by some of his ardent followers, and reminded economists of the wisdom of Adam Smith. Keynes argues, "I find myself, not for the first time, to remind contemporary economists that the *classical teaching* embodied some *permanent truths* of great significance, which we are liable to-day to overlook because we associate them with other doctrines which we cannot now accept without much qualification" (ibid; italics added). The Classical literature has adequate guidance for policy formulation to deal with a modern monetary economy. The classical policies are relevant for an economy's efficient functioning both in the short run and in the long run in which there are more people alive, not dead as Keynes ([1923] 1924: 88) mistakenly quips. We just need to read their explanations with their meanings of saving, capital, investment, and money rather than those of John Maynard Keynes's to understand them.

Notes

1 The Adam Smith Institute credits Dugald Stewart as having cited the quote from a 1755 lecture by Smith.
2 This is a statement of the Quantity Theory of money, yielding $P = H/ky$, using the Cambridge equation.
3 Ahiakpor (2019, Chapter 7) elaborates from works by David Hume, Adam Smith, David Ricardo, John Stuart Mill, and Alfred Marshall.

Bibliography

Abel, Andrew B., Bernanke, Ben S., and Croushore, Dean (2014) *Macroeconomics*. 8th ed. New York: Pearson, Addison-Wesley.

Ahiakpor, James C. W. (1985) "Ricardo on Money: The Operational Significance of the Non-neutrality of Money in the Short Run." *History of Political Economy* 17 (Spring): 17–30.

_____ (1990) "On Keynes's Misinterpretation of 'Capital' in the Classical Theory of Interest." *History of Political Economy* 22 (Fall): 507–28.

_____ (1995) "A Paradox of Thrift or Keynes's Misrepresentation of Saving in the Classical Theory of Growth?" *Southern Economic Journal* 62 (July): 16–33.

_____ (1997a) "Full Employment: A Classical Assumption or Keynes's Rhetorical Device?" *Southern Economic Journal* 64 (July): 56–74.

_____ (1997b) "Austrian Capital Theory: Help or Hindrance?" *Journal of the History of Economic Thought* 19 (Fall): 261–85.

_____ ed. (1998a) "Keynes on the Classics: A Revolution mainly in Definitions?" In *Keynes and the Classics Reconsidered*. Boston, Dordrecht, and London: Kluwer Academic Publishers.

_____ (1998b) "Keynes and the Classics Reconsidered: A Revolution Mainly in Definitions?" In *Keynes and the Classics Reconsidered*, edited by James C. W. Ahiakpor. Boston, Dordrecht, and London: Kluwer Academic Publishers: 13–32.

_____ (1999) "Wicksell on the Classical Theories of Money, Credit, Interest and the Price Level: Progress or Retrogression?" *American Journal of Economics and Sociology* 58, No. 3 (July): 435–57.

_____ (2001) "On the Mythology of the Keynesian Multiplier." *American Journal of Economics and Sociology* 60 (October): 745–73.

_____ (2003a) "Say's Law: Keynes's Success with it Misrepresentation." In *Two Hundred Years of Say's Law: Essays on Economic Theory's Most Controversial Principle*, edited by Kates, Steven. Edward Elgar: 107–32.

_____ (2003b) *Classical Macroeconomics: Some Modern Variations and Distortions*. New York and London: Routledge.

_____ (2008) "Garrison on Mises and Forced Saving: Arguing the Implausible?" *History of Political Economy* 40, No. 2 (Summer): 383–95.

_____ (2009) "The Phillips Curve Analysis: An Illustration of the Classical Forced-Saving Doctrine." *Journal of the History of Economic Thought* 31, No. 2 (June): 143–60.

_____ (2010) "On the Similarities between the 1932 Harvard Memorandum and the Chicago Antidepression Recommendations." *History of Political Economy* 42, No. 3 (Fall): 547–71.

_____ (2013) "The Modern Ricardian Equivalence Theorem: Drawing the Wrong Conclusions from David Ricardo's Analysis." *Journal of the History of Economic Thought* 35, No. 1 (March): 77–92.

_____ (2018a) "On the Impossibility of Keynes's Liquidity Trap: Classical Monetary Analysis Helps to Explain." *History of Economic Ideas* 26, No. 1: 31–58.

_____ (2018b) "Keynes, Mill, and Say's Law: A Comment on Roy Grieve's Mistaken Criticisms of Mill." *Journal of the History of Economic Thought* 40, No. 2 (June): 267–73.

_____ (2019) *Macroeconomics without the Errors of Keynes*. London and New York: Routledge.

_____ (2020) "Disputing the Correct Interpretation of Say's Law: A Comment on Roy Grieve's and Steven Kates's Arguments." *History of Economics Review* (forthcoming). https://doi.org/10.1080/10370196.2020.1784649.

Allen, William B. (1993) "Irving Fisher and the 100 Percent Reserve Proposal." *Journal of Law and Economics* 36, No. 2 (October): 703–17.

Arias, Maria A. and Wen, Yi (2014) "The Liquidity Trap: An Alternative Explanation for Today's Low Inflation." *The Regional Economist* 22, No. 2 (April): 10–11.

Aslanbeigui, Nahid (1992) "Pigou's Inconsistencies or Keynes's Misconceptions?" *History of Political Economy* 24, No. 2 (Summer): 413–33.

_____ (1998) "Unemployment through the Eyes of a Classic." In *Keynes and the Classics Reconsidered*, edited by James C.W. Ahiakpor. Boston, Dordrecht, and London: Kluwer: 85–99.

Backhouse, Roger E. (1999) "Introduction." In *Keynes: Contemporary Responses to the General Theory*, edited by Roger Backhouse. South Bend, IN: St Augustine's Press.

_____ (2006) "The Keynesian Revolution." In *The Cambridge Companion to Keynes*, edited by Roger E. Backhouse and Bradley W. Bateman. Cambridge: Cambridge University Press.

Backhouse, Roger E. and Bateman, Bradley W. eds. (2006) *The Cambridge Companion to Keynes*. Cambridge: Cambridge University Press.

_____ (2011) *Capitalist Revolutionary: John Maynard Keynes*. Cambridge, MA: Harvard University Press.

Bagehot, Walter (1873) *Lombard Street: A Description of the Money Market*. Reprinted Homewood, IL: Richard D. Irwin, 1962.

Bailey, Martin J. (1962) *National Income and the Price Level*. New York: McGraw-Hill.

_____ (1971) *National Income and the Price Level*. 2nd ed. New York: McGraw-Hill.

Barro, Robert J. (1974) "Are Government Bonds Net Wealth?" *Journal of Political Economy* 82, No. 6 (Nov.–Dec.): 1095–117.

_____ (1976) "Perceived Wealth in Bonds and Social Security and the Ricardian Equivalence Theorem: Reply to Feldstein and Buchanan." *Journal of Political Economy* 84, No. 2 (April): 343–50.

_____ (1989) "The Ricardian Approach to Budget Deficits." *Journal of Economic Perspectives* 3 No. 2 (Spring): 37–54.

_____ (2010) *Intermediate Macroeconomics*. Mason, OH: South-Western Cengage Learning.

Barton, John (1817) *Observations on the Circumstances which Influence the Condition of the Labouring Classes of Society*. London: Arch.

Batini, Nicoletta, Jackson, Brian, and Nickell, Stephen (2005) "An Open-Economy New Keynesian Phillips Curve for the U.K." *Journal of Monetary Economics* 52: 1061–71.

Baumol, William J. (1977) "Say's (At Least) Eight Laws, or What Say and James Mill May Really Have Meant." *Economica* 44 (May): 145–61.

_____ (1999) "Say's Law." *Journal of Economic Perspectives* 13, No. 1 (Winter): 195–204.

_____ (2003) "Say's Law and More Recent Macro Literature: Some Afterthoughts." In *Two Hundred Years of Say's Law*, edited by Steven Kates. Cheltenham, UK and Northampton, MA: 34–49.

Becker, Gary S. and Baumol, William J. (1952) "The Classical Monetary Theory: The Outcome of the Discussion." *Economica*, NS, 19, No. 76 (November): 355–76.

Bernanke, Ben S. (1984) "Permanent Income, Liquidity, and Expenditure on Automobiles: Evidence from Panel Data." *Quarterly Journal of Economics* 99, No. 3 (August): 587–614.

—— (2000) *Essays on the Great Depression*. Princeton, NJ: Princeton University Press.

—— (2009) "The Stamp Lecture, London School of Economics, London, England, January 13, 2009." http://www.federalreserve.gov/newsevents/speech/bernanke2009 113a.htm

—— (2015) *The Courage to Act: A Memoir of a Crisis and its Aftermath*. New York: W.W. Norton.

Bentham, Jeremy (1951, 1954) *Jeremy Bentham's Economic Writings*. Edited by W. Stark, 3 vols. London: Allen & Unwin.

Béraud, Alain and Numa, Guy (2018a) "Beyond Say's Law: The Significance of J.-B. Say's Monetary Views." *Journal of the History of Economic Thought* 40, No. 2 (June): 217–41.

—— (2018b) "Keynes, J.-B. Say, J.S. Mill, and Say's Law: A Note on Kates, Grieve, and Ahiakpor." *Journal of the History of Economic Thought* 40, No. 2 (June): 285–9.

—— (2019) "Lord Keynes and Mr. Say: A Proximity of Ideas." *Journal of Economic Perspectives* 33, No. 3 (Summer): 228–42.

Blanchard, Olivier and Johnson, David R. (2013) *Macroeconomics*. 6th ed. New York: Pearson.

Blaug, Mark (1996) *Economic Theory in Retrospect*. 5th ed. Cambridge: Cambridge University Press.

Blinder, Alan S. and Solow, Robert (1973) "Does Fiscal Policy Matter?" *Journal of Public Economics* 2, No. 4: 319–37.

Boianovsky, Mauro (2004) "The IS-LM Model and the Liquidity Trap Concept: From Hicks to Krugman." *History of Political Economy* 36, Annual Supplement: 92–126.

Bordo, Michael D. and Haubrich, Joseph G. (2017) "Deep Recessions, Fast Recoveries, and Financial Crises: Evidence from the American Record." *Economic Inquiry* 55, No. 1 (January): 527–41.

Brady, Dorothy S. and Friedman, Rose D. (1947) "Savings and the Income Distribution." In *Studies in Income and Wealth*, Vol. 10. New York: National Bureau of Economic Research: 247–65.

Brady, Michael Emmett (1986) "A Note on Milton Friedman's Application of His 'Methodology of Positive Economics'." *Journal of Economic Issues* 20, No. 3 (September): 845–51.

Branson, William H. (1972) *Macroeconomic Theory and Policy*. New York: Harper & Row.

Bridel, Pascal (1987) *Cambridge Monetary Thought: Development of Saving-Investment Analysis from Marshall to Keynes*. New York: St. Martin's Press.

Brown, Douglas V. (1934) "Helping Labor." In *The Economics of the Recovery Program*. New York and London: Whittlesey House and McGraw-Hill: 64–89.

Brown, Douglas V., et al. (1934) *The Economics of the Recovery Program*. New York and London: Whittlesey House and McGraw-Hill.

Brown, Harry G. (1940) "Objections to the 100 Percent Plan." *American Economic Review* 30, No. 3, Part 1 (June): 309–14.

Buchanan, James M. (1958) Public Principles of Public Debt. Homewood, IL: Richard D. Irwin.

—— (1976) "Barro on the Ricardian Equivalence Theorem." *Journal of Political Economy* 84, No. 2 (April): 337–42.

Cantillon, Richard (1755) *Essay on the Nature of Trade in General*. Edited with an English translation and other material by Henry Higgs. London: Frank Cass, 1959.

Chamberlin, Edward (1934) "Purchasing Power." In *The Economics of the Recovery Program.* New York and London: Whittlesey House and McGraw-Hill: 23–37.

Churchman, Nancy (2001) *David Ricardo on Public Debt.* New York: Palgrave.

Clower, Robert W. and Leijonhufvud, Axel (1973) "Effective Demand Failures." In *Sweedish Economic Journal* (March). Reprinted in *Information and Coordination*, edited by Axel Leijonhufvud. New York: Oxford University Press: 103–29.

Colander, David (1995) "The Stories We Tell. A Reconsideration of AS/AD Analysis." *Journal of Economic Perspectives* 9, No. 3: 169–88.

Cory, B. A. (1962) *Money, Saving and Investment in English Economics 1800–1850.* London: Macmillan.

Cristiano, Carlo and Fiorito, Luca (2016) "Two Minds that Never Met: Frank H. Knight on John M. Keynes Once Again—A Documentary Note." *Journal of Keynesian Economics* 4, No. 1 (Spring): 67–98.

Currie, Lauchlin (1933) "Treatment of Credit in Contemporary Monetary Theory." *Journal of Political Economy* 41, No. 1 (February): 58–79.

_____ (1934a) "The Failure of Monetary Policy to Prevent the Depression of 1929–1932." *Journal of Political Economy* 42, No. 2 (April): 145–77.

_____ (1934b) *The Supply and Control of Money in the United States.* Cambridge: Harvard University Press.

_____ (1935) *The Supply and Control of Money in the United States.* 2nd revised ed. Cambridge: Harvard University Press.

_____ (1972) "The Keynesian Revolution and its Pioneers." *American Economic Review* 62, No. 2 (May): 139–41.

_____ (1978) "Comments and Observations." *History of Political Economy* 10, No. 4 (Winter): 341–48.

Davidson, Paul (1991) *Controversies in Post Keynesian Economics.* Aldershot: Edward Elgar.

Davis, J. Ronnie (1968) "Chicago Economists, Deficit Budgets, and the Early 1930s." *American Economic Review* 58, No. 3 (June): 476–81.

_____ (1971) *The New Economics and the Old Economics.* Ames, IA: Iowa State University Press.

DeLong, J. Bradford and Olney, Martha L. (2006) *Macroeconomics.* 2nd ed. New York: McGraw-Hill Irwin.

Diamond, Douglas W. and Dybvig, Philip H. (1986) "Banking Theory, Deposit Insurance, and Bank Regulation." *Journal of Business* 59, No. 1: 55–68.

Dimand, Robert W. (1990) "The New Economics and American Economists in the 1930s Reconsidered." *Atlantic Economic Journal* 18, No. 4 (December): 42–7.

_____ (1993a) "Irving Fisher's Debt-Deflation Theory of Depressions." *Review of Social Economy* 52, No. 1 (Spring): 92–107.

_____ (1993b) "100 Percent Money: Irving Fisher and Banking Reform in the 1930s." *History of Economic Ideas* 1, No. 2: 59–76.

Dimand, Robert W. and Hagemann, Harald eds. (2019) *The Elgar Companion to John Maynard Keynes.* Cheltenham: Edward Elgar.

Dominguez, Kathryn M. (1998) "Comments on 'It's Baaack.'" *Brookings Papers on Economic Activity* No. 2: 188–94.

Duesenberry, James S. (1949) *Income, Saving, and the Theory of Consumer Behavior.* Cambridge, MA: Harvard University Press.

Edie, Lionel D. (1932) "The Future of the Gold Standard." In *Gold and Monetary Stabilization,* edited by Quincy Wright. Chicago: University of Chicago Press.

Eggertsson, Gauti B. (2006) "The Deflation Bias and Committing to Being Irresponsible." *Journal of Money, Credit, and Banking.* 38, No. 2 (March): 282–321.

_____ (2008) "Liquidity Trap." In *The New Palgrave Dictionary of Economics*, edited by Steven N. Durlauf and Lawrence E. Blume, 2ⁿᵈ ed. New York: Palgrave Macmillan.

Ekelund, Jr., Robert B. and Hébert, Robert F. (2014) *A History of Economic Method and Method*. 6ᵗʰ ed. Long Grove, IL: Waveland Press.

Ekelund, Robert B. and Tollison, Robert D. (2000) *Macroeconomics: Private Markets and Public Choice*. 6ᵗʰ ed. New York: Addison-Wesley.

Feldstein, Martin (1982) "Government Deficit and Aggregate Demand." *Journal of Monetary Economics* 9 (January): 1–20.

Fisher, Irving (1912) *Elementary Principles of Economics*. New York: Macmillan.

_____ (1913) *The Purchasing Power of Money*. New and revised ed., reprinted. New York: August M. Kelley, 1971.

_____ (1926) "A Statistical Relation between Unemployment and Price Changes." *International Labour Review* 13 (June): 785–92, reprinted in *Journal of Political Economy* 81, No. 2, Part 1. (March-April) 1973: 496–502.

_____ (1930) *The Theory of Interest*. New York: Macmillan.

_____ (1932) *Booms and Depressions*. New York: Adelphi

_____ (1933) "The Debt-Deflation Theory of the Great Depressions." *Econometrica* 1, No. 4 (October): 337–57.

_____ (1935) *100% Money*. New York: Adelphi.

Flavin, Marjorie (1981) "The Adjustment of Consumption to Changes in Expectations about Future Income." *Journal of Political Economy* 89, No. 5 (October): 974–1009.

Fontana, Giuseppe (2001) "Keynes on the 'Nature of Economic Thinking'." *American Journal of Economics and Sociology* 60 (October): 711–43.

Forget, Evelyn (2003) "Jean-Baptiste Say and the Law of Markets: Entrepreneurial Decision-Making in the Real World." In *Two Hundred Years of Say's Law: Essays on Economic Theory's Most Controversial Principle*, edited by Steven Kates. Cheltenham, UK and Northampton, MA: 50–66.

Frank, Robert H. and Bernanke, Ben S. (2011) *Principles of Macroeconomics*. 2ⁿᵈ ed. New York: McGraw-Hill.

Frenkel, Jacob A. (1981) "Adjustment Lags Versus Information Lags: A Test of Alternative Explanations of the Phillips Curve Phenomenon: A Comment." *Journal of Money, Credit and Banking* 13, No. 4 (November): 490–93.

Friedman, Milton (1956) "The Quantity Theory of Money: A Restatement." In *Studies in the Quantity Theory of Money*. Chicago: University of Chicago Press.

_____ (1957) *A Theory of the Consumption Function*. Princeton, NJ: Princeton University Press.

_____ (1960) *A Program for Monetary Stability*. New York: Fordham University Press.

_____ (1967) "The Monetary Theory and Policy of Henry Simons." *Journal of Law and Economics* 10 (October): 1–13.

_____ (1968a) "The Role of Monetary Policy." *American Economic Review* 58 (March): 1–17.

_____ (1968b) *Dollars and Deficits*. Englewood Cliffs, NJ: Prentice-Hall.

_____ (1969) *The Optimum Quantity of Money and Other Essays*. Chicago: Aldine Publishing.

_____ (1970a) "A Theoretical Framework for Monetary Analysis." In *Milton Friedman's Monetary Framework*, edited by Robert J. Gordon. Chicago: University of Chicago Press: 1–62.

_____ (1970b) *The Counter-Revolution in Monetary Theory*. London: Institute of Economic Affairs.

_____ (1972) "Factors Affecting the Level of Interest Rates." In *Money Supply, Money Demand, and Macroeconomic Models*, edited by John T. Boorman and Thomas M. Havrilesky. Boston: Allyn and Bacon: 200–18.

_____ (1974) "Comments on the Critics." In *Milton Friedman's Monetary Framework*, edited by Robert J. Gordon. Chicago: University of Chicago Press.

_____ (1977) "Nobel Lecture: Inflation and Unemployment." *Journal of Political Economy* 85, No. 3 (June): 451–72.

_____ (1983) *Bright Promises, Dismal Performance: An Economist's Protest*. San Diego, New York, and London: Harcourt Brace Jovanovich.

_____ (1984) "Monetary Policy for the 1980s." In *To Promote Prosperity—U.S. Domestic Policy in the Mid–1980*, edited by Moore, John H. Stanford, CA: Hoover Institution Press: 23–60.

_____ (1985) "The Case for Overhauling the Federal Reserve." *Challenge* (July–August): 4–12.

_____ (1987) "Quantity Theory of Money." In *The New Palgrave*, edited by John Eastwell, Murray Milgate, and Peter Newman, Vol. 4. London and Basingstoke: Macmillan: 3–20.

_____ (1997) "John Maynard Keynes." *Federal Reserve Bank of Richmond Economic Quarterly* 83, No. 2: 1–23.

_____ (2008) "The Quantity Theory of Money." In *The New Palgrave Dictionary of Economics*, edited by Steven N. Durlauf and Lawrence E. Blume, 2nd ed, Vol. 6. New York: Palgrave Macmillan: 792–815.

Friedman, Milton and Schwartz, Anna J. (1963) *A Monetary History of the United States, 1867–1960*. Princeton, NJ: Princeton University Press.

_____ (1970) *Monetary Statistics of the United States*. New York: National Bureau of Economic Research.

Froyen, Richard T. (2013) *Macroeconomics: Theories and Policies*. 10th ed. Upper Saddle River, NJ: Pearson Education.

Galbraith, James K. and Darity, William, Jr. (1994) *Macroeconomics*. Boston: Houghton Mifflin.

Garrison, Roger W. (1990) (2004) "Overconsumption and Forced Saving in the Mises-Hayek Theory of Business Cycle." *History of Political Economy* 36, No. 2 (Summer): 323–49.

Gibson, William E. (1970) "Interest Rates and Monetary Policy." *Journal of Political Economy* 78, No. 3 (May/June): 431–55.

Gilboy, Elizabeth W. (1938) "The Propensity to Consume." *Quarterly Journal of Economics* 53, No. 1 (November): 120–40.

Goodhart, Charles A. E. (1988) *The Evolution of Central Banks*. Cambridge, MA: MIT Press.

Gordon, Robert J. (2000) *Macroeconomics*. 8th ed. New York: Addison-Wesley.

_____ (2006)

_____ (2012) *Macroeconomics*. 12th ed. New York: Pearson, Addison-Wesley.

Graham, Frank D. (1941) "100 Per Cent Reserves: Comment." *American Economic Review* 31, No. 2 (June): 338–40.

Grieve, Roy (2016) "Keynes, Mill, and Say's Law: The Legitimate Case Keynes Didn't make Against J.S. Mill." *Journal of the History of Economic Thought* 38, No. 3 (September): 329–49.

_____ (2017) "Kates on Mill's Fourth Proposition on Capital: Why All the Fuss?" *Journal of the History of Economic Thought* 39, No. 2 ((June): 271–2.

_____ (2018) "Off Target: Professor Ahiakpor on Keynes, Mill, and Say's Law." *Journal of the History of Economic Thought* 40, No. 2 (June):275–8.

Gwartney, James D., Stroup, Richard L., Sobel, Russell S., and Macpherson, David A. (2018) *Macroeconomics: Private and Public Choice*. 16th ed. Boston: Cengage.

Haberler, Gottfried (1932) "Gold and the Business Cycle." In *Gold and Monetary Stabilization*, edited by Quincy Wright. Chicago: University of Chicago Press.

_____ (1941) *Prosperity and Depression*. 3rd ed. Geneva: League of Nations.

_____ (1960) *Prosperity and Depression*. 4th ed. Cambridge, MA: Harvard University Press.

Hackett, William T. G. (1945) *A Background of Banking Theory*. Toronto: Canadian Bankers Association.

Hall, Robert E. (1978) Stochastic Implications of the Life-Cycle Permanent Income Hypothesis." *Journal of Political Economy* 86, No. 2 (April): 249–87.

Hansen, Alvin H. (1949) *Monetary Theory and Fiscal Policy*. New York: McGraw-Hill.

_____ (1953) *A Guide to Keynes*. New York: McGraw-Hill.

Hansson, Björn (1987) "Forced Saving." In *The New Palgrave*, edited by John Eastwell, Murray Milgate, and Peter Newman, Vol. 2. London and Basingstoke: Macmillan: 398–9.

Hardy, Charles O. (1936) "Review of the General Theory of Employment, Interest and Money." *American Economic Review* 26, No. 3 (September): 490–3.

Harris, Seymour (1934) "Higher Prices." In *The Economics of the Recovery Program*. New York and London: Whittlesey House and McGraw-Hill: 90–138.

Harrod, Roy F. (1936) "Review of the General Theory of Employment, Interest and Money." *Political Science Quarterly* 7 (April/June): 293–8.

_____ (1937) "Mr. Keynes and Traditional Theory." *Econometrica* 5 (January): 74–86.

_____ (1951) *The Life of John Maynard Keynes*. London: Macmillan.

Hart, Albert G. (1935) "A Proposal for Making Monetary Management Effective in the United States." *Review of Economics Studies* 2, No. 2 (February): 104–16.

Hartfield, Henry R. (1934) "The Early Use of 'Capital'." *Quarterly Journal of Economics* 49 (November): 162–3.

Hayek, Friedrich A. (1932) "A Note on the Development of the Doctrine of 'Forced Saving'." *Quarterly Journal of Economics* 47 (November): 123–33.

_____ (1933) *Monetary Theory and the Trade Cycle*. Reprinted. New York: Augustus M. Kelley, 1966.

_____ (1935) *Prices and Production*. 2nd revised and enlarged ed. London: Routledge.

_____ (1939) *Profits, Interest and Investment*. Reprinted. New York: Augustus M. Kelley, 1969.

_____ (1941) *The Pure Theory of Capital*. London: Routledge & Kegan Paul.

_____ (1976) *Choice of Currency: A Way to Stop Inflation*. London: Institute for Economic Affairs.

_____ (1984) *Money, Capital, and Fluctuations: Early Essays*. Chicago: University of Chicago Press.

Hawtrey, R. G. (1913) *Good and Bad Trade: An Inquiry into the Causes of Trade Fluctuations*. Reprinted. New York: Augustus M. Kelley, 1970.

_____ (1919) *Currency and Credit*. 4th ed. London: Longmans, Green, 1950.

_____ (1933) *Trade Depression and the Way Out*. 2nd ed. London: Longmans, Green.

_____ (1937) "Alternative Theories of the Rate of Interest." *Economic Journal* 47: 436–43.

_____ (1939) "Interest and Bank Rate." *The Manchester School of Economics and Social Studies* 10, No. 2 (December): 144–52.

_____ (1950) *Currency and Credit*. 4th ed. London: Longmans, Green.

Henry, John F. (2003) "Say's Economy." In *Two Hundred Years of Say's Law: Essays on Economic Theory's Most Controversial Principle*, edited by Steven Kates. Cheltenham, UK and Northampton, MA: 187–98.

Hicks, John R. (1936) "Mr. Keynes' Theory of Employment." *Economic Journal* 46 (June): 238–53.

_____ (1937) "Mr. Keynes and the 'Classics': A Suggested Interpretation." *Econometrica* 5 (April): 147–59.

_____ (1967) *Critical Essays in Monetary Theory*. Oxford: Clarendon Press.

_____ (1980/1) "ISLM: an explanation." *Journal of Post Keynesian Economics* 3: 139–54.

Higgins, Benjamin (1941) "Comment on 100 Per Cent Money." *American Economic Review* 31, No. 1 (March): 91–6.

Hollander, Samuel (1979) *The Economics of David Ricardo*. London: Heinemann.

_____ (1985) *The Economics of John Stuart Mill*. Oxford: Basil Blackwell.

_____ (1987) *Classical Economics*. New York: Basil Blackwell.

_____ (2005a) *Jean-Baptiste Say and the Classical Canon in Economics: The British Connection in French Classicism*. London and New York: Routledge.

_____ (2005b) "Review of Two Hundred Years of Say's Law: Essays on Economic Theory's Most Controversial Principle ed. by S. Kates." *History of Political Economy* 37, No. 2 (Summer): 382–5.

_____ (2011) "Making the Most of Anomalies in the History of Economic Thought: Smith, Marx-Engels, and Keynes." In *Perspectives on Keynesian Economics*, edited by Arie Arnon, et al. Berlin and Heidelberg: Springer-Verlag: 15–30.

Horwitz, Steven (2003) "Say's Law of Markets: An Austrian Appreciation." In *Two Hundred Years of Say's Law: Essays on Economic Theory's Most Controversial Principle*, edited by Steven Kates. Cheltenham, UK and Northampton, MA: 82–98.

Hubbard, R. Glenn and O'Brien, Anthony P. (2018) *Money, Banking and the Financial System*. 3rd ed. New York: Pearson.

Hudson, M. A. (1965) "Ricardo on Forced Saving." *Economic Record* 41 (June): 240–7.

Hume, David (1752) *Hume's Writings on Economics*. Edited by Eugene Rotwein, 1955. Reprinted. Madison: University of Wisconsin Press, 1970.

Hume, David [1711–1776] *Essays Moral, Political, and Literary*. Edited by Eugen F. Miller. Revised. Indianapolis, IN: Liberty Fund, 1985, 1987.

Humphrey, Thomas M. (1971) "Role of Non-Chicago Economists in the Evolution of the Quantity Theory in America, 1930–1950." *Southern Economic Journal* 38, No. 1 (July): 12–18.

_____ (1982a) "Of Hume, Thornton, the Quantity Theory, and the Phillips Curve. Federal Reserve Bank of Richmond Economic Review (November/December): 13–18. Reprinted in *Money, Banking and Inflation: Essays in the History of Monetary Thought*. Aldershot, UK: Edward Elgar, 1993: 242–7.

_____ (1982b) "The Real Bills Doctrine." *Economic Review* (Federal Reserve Bank of Richmond) 68, No. 5: 3–33.

_____ (1985) "From Trade-Offs to Policy Ineffectiveness: A History of the Phillips Curve. Federal Reserve Bank of Richmond Economic Review, 5–12. Reprinted in *Money, Banking and Inflation: Essays in the History of Monetary Thought*, 234–41.

_____ (1991) "Nonneutrality of Money in Classical Monetary Thought. Federal Reserve Bank of Richmond Economic Review (April/March): 3–15. Reprinted in *Money, Banking and Inflation: Essays in the History of Monetary Thought*, 251–63.

Hutchison, Terrence W. (1977) *Keynes v. the 'Keynesians' …?* Hobart Paperback. London: Institute of Economic Affairs.

_____ (1981) *The Politics and Philosophy of Economic: Marxians, Keynesians and Austrians*. Oxford: Basil Blackwell.

Hutt, William H. (1974) *A Rehabilitation of Say's Law*. Athens, OH: Ohio University Press.

International Monetary Fund (1995) *International Financial Statistics Yearbook 1995.* Washington, DC.

_____ (2001) *International Financial Statistics Yearbook 2001.* Washington, DC.

_____ (2005) *International Financial Statistics Yearbook 2005.* Washington, DC.

_____ (2009) *International Financial Statistics Yearbook 2009.* Washington, DC.

_____ (2014) *International Financial Statistics Yearbook 2014.* Washington, DC.

Jansen, Dennis W., Delorme, Charles D., and Ekelund, Jr., Robert B. (1994) *Intermediate Macroeconomics.* New York: West.

Jones, Byrd L. (1978) "Lauchlin Currie, Pump Priming, and New Deal Fiscal Policy, 1934–1936." *History of Political Economy* 10, No. 4 (Winter): 509–23.

Jonsson, Petur O. (1995) "On the Economics of Say and Keynes's Interpretation of Say's Law." *Eastern Economic Journal* 21 (June): 147–55.

_____ (1997) "On Gluts, Effective Demand and the True Meaning of Say's Law." *Eastern Economic Journal* 23 (Spring): 203–18.

_____ (1999) Review of Steven Kates's "Say's Law and the Keynesian Revolution: How Macroeconomics Lost Its Way." *Southern Economic Journal* 65, No. 4: 967–70.

Kahn, Richard (1931) "The Relation of Home Investment to Unemployment." *Economic Journal* 41 (June): 173–98.

_____ (1978) "Some Aspects of the Development of Keynes' Thought." *Journal of Economic Literature* 16 (June): 545–59.

Kates, Steven (1997) "On the True Meaning of Say's Law." *Eastern Economic Journal* 23, No. 2 (Spring): 191–202.

_____ (1998) *Say's Law and the Keynesian Revolution.* Cheltenham, UK: Edward Elgar.

_____ ed. (2003) *Two Hundred Years of Say's Law: Essays on Economic Theory's Most Controversial Principle.* Cheltenham, UK and Northampton, MA.

_____ (2015) "Mill's Fourth Fundamental Proposition on Capital: A Paradox Explained." *Journal of the History of Economic Thought* 37, No. 1 (March): 39–56.

_____ (2018) "Making Sense of Classical Theory." *Journal of the History of Economic Thought* 40, No. 2 (June): 279–83.

_____ (2019) "Letter to the Editor: Say's Law, Its Origins and Meaning." *Journal of the History of Economic Thought* 41, No. 1 (March): 123–8.

Keynes, John Maynard (1911) Review of "The Purchasing Power of Money by Irving Fisher." *Economic Journal* 21 (September): 393–8.

_____ (1919) *The Economic Consequences of the Peace.* Reprinted in the *Collected Writings of John Maynard Keynes,* Vol. 2. London and Basingstoke: Macmillan, for the Royal Economic Society, 1971.

_____ (1923) *Monetary Reform.* New York: Harcourt Brace, 1924.

_____ (1930) *A Treatise on Money.* Vols. 1–2. London: Macmillan.

_____ (1933) *Essays in Biography.* London: Macmillan.

_____ (1936) *The General Theory of Employment, Interest and Money.* Paperbound ed. London and Basingstoke: Macmillan, 1974.

_____ (1937a) "The General Theory of Employment." *Quarterly Journal of Economics* 51 (February): 209–23.

_____ (1937b) "Alternative Theories of the Rate of Interest." *Economic Journal* 47 (June): 241–52.

_____ (1937c) "The 'ex-ante' Theory of the Rate of Interest." *Economic Journal* 47 (December): 663–9.

_____ (1938) "Mr. Keynes and 'Finance': Comment." *Economic Journal* 48 (June): 318–22.

_____ (1939) "Preface to the French Edition." *The General Theory of Employment, Interest and Money*. Paperbound ed. London and Basingstoke: Macmillan, 1974.

_____ (1946) "The Balance of Payments of the United States." *Economic Journal* 56, No. 222 (June): 172–87.

_____ (1972) *The Collected Writings of John Maynard Keynes*. Vol. IX. Edited by Don E. Moggridge. London: Macmillan.

_____ (1973) *The Collected Writings of John Maynard Keynes*. Vol. XIII. Edited by Don E. Moggridge. London: Macmillan.

_____ (1983) *The Collected Writings of John Maynard Keynes*. Vol. XII: *Economic Articles and Correspondence*. Edited by Donald Moggridge. London and Basingstoke: Macmillan.

King, Robert G. (1993) "Will the New Keynesian Macroeconomics Resurrect the IS-LM Model?" *Journal of Economic Perspectives* 7 (Winter): 67–82.

Knight, Frank (1937) "Unemployment: An Mr. Keynes's Revolution in Economic Theory." *Canadian Journal of Economics and Political Science* 3 (February): 100–23.

Kochin, Levis A. (1974) "Are Future Taxes Anticipated by Consumers?: Comment." *Journal of Money, Credit and Banking* 6, No. 2 (August): 385–94.

Kohn, Meir (1993) *Money, Banking, and Financial Markets*. 2nd ed. Fort Worth: Dryden Press.

Kotlikoff, Laurence J. (2010) *Jimmy Stewart is Dead: Ending the World's Ongoing Financial Plague with Limited Purpose Banking*. Hoboken, NJ: John Wiley & Sons.

Krugman, Paul (1998) "It's Baaack: Japan's Slump and the Return of the Liquidity Trap." *Brookings Papers on Economic Activity* No. 2: 137–87, 204–5.

_____ (2013) "Monetary Policy in a Liquidity Trap." *The New York Times* at http://krugman.blogs.nytimes.com/2013/04/11

Kuznets, Simon (1952) "Proportion of Capital Formation to National Product." *American Economic Review, Papers and Proceedings* 42 (May): 507–26.

Laidler, David (1969) "The Definition of Money: Theoretical and Empirical Problems." *Journal of Money, Credit and Banking* 1 (August): 508–25.

_____ (1991) *The Golden Age of the Quantity Theory*. Princeton, NJ: Princeton University Press.

_____ (1993a) "Hawtrey, Harvard, and the Origins of the Chicago Tradition." *Journal of Political Economy* 101, No. 6 (December): 1068–104.

_____ (1993b) *The Demand for Money: Theories, Evidence, and Problems*. 4th ed. New York: Harper Collins.

_____ (1999) *Fabricating the Keynesian Revolution: Studies of the Inter-war Literature on Money, the Cycle, and Unemployment*. New York: Cambridge University Press.

_____ (2004) "Monetary Policy after Bubbles Burst: The Zero Lower Bound, the Liquidity Trap and the Credit Deadlock." *Canadian Public Policy/Analyse de Politiques* 30, No. 3 (September): 333–40.

_____ (2006) "Keynes and the Birth of Modern Macroeconomics." In *The Cambridge Companion to Keynes*, edited by Roger E. Backhouse and Bradley W. Bateman. Cambridge: Cambridge University Press.

_____ (2011) "Hollander on Anomalies in the History of Economic Thought: Some Comments." In *Perspectives on Keynesian Economics*, edited by Arie Arnon, et al. Berlin and Heidelberg: Springer-Verlag: 31–4.

Laidler, David and Sandilands, Roger (2002a) "An Early Harvard Memorandum on Anti-depression Policies: An Introductory Note." *History of Political Economy* 34, No. 3 (Fall): 515–32.

_____ eds. (2002b) "Memorandum Prepared by L.B. Currie, P.T Ellsworth, and H.D. White (Cambridge, Mass., January 1932)." *History of Political Economy* 34, No. 3 (Fall): 533–52.

_____ (2010) "Harvard, the Chicago Tradition, and the Quantity Theory: A Reply to James Ahiakpor." *History of Political Economy* 42, No. 3 (Fall): 573–92.

Landreth, Harry and Colander, David C. (2002) *History of Economic Thought.* 4th ed. Boston: Houghton Mifflin.

Lavington, Frederick (1921) *English Capital Market.* Reprinted. New York: Augustus M. Kelley, 1968.

Lawlor, Michael S. (2006) *The Economics of Keynes in Historical Context: An Intellectual History of the General Theory.* New York: Palgrave Macmillan.

Leijonhufvud, Axel (1968) *On Keynesian Economics and the Economics of Keynes.* New York: Oxford University Press.

Leontief, Wassily (1934) "Helping the Farmer." In *The Economics of the Recovery Program.* New York and London: Whittlesey House and McGraw-Hill: 139–59.

_____ (1936) "The Fundamental Assumption of Mr. Keynes' Monetary Theory of Employment." *Quarterly Journal of Economics* 51 (November): 192–7.

Lesson, Robert (1997) "The Trade-Off Interpretation of Phillips's Dynamic Stabilization Exercise." Economica, NS, 64, No. 253 (February): 155–71.

_____ (1998) "The Consequences of the 'Klassical' Caricature for Economics." In *Keynes and the Classics Reconsidered,* edited by James C.W. Ahiakpor. Boston, Dordrecht, and London: Kluwer Academic Publishers.

Levy, David (1986) "The Paradox of the Sinking Fund." In *Deficits,* edited by Buchanan, James M., Rowley, Charles K. and Rollison, Robert D. New York, NY: Blackwell: 93–113.

Lipsey, Richard G. (1960) "The Relation between Unemployment and the Rate of Change of Money Wage Rates in the United Kingdom, 1862–1957: A Further Analysis." Economica, NS, 27 (February): 1–31.

Lucas, Jr., Robert E. (1996) "Nobel Lecture: Monetary Neutrality." *Journal of Political Economy* 104, No. 4 (August): 661–82.

Malthus, Thomas R. (1811) "The Question Concerning the Depreciation of Our Currency Stated and Examined." In *Occasional Papers of T.R. Malthus,* edited by Bernard Semmel. New York: Burt Franklin, 1963.

_____ (1836) *Principles of Political Economy.* 2nd ed. New York: Augustus M. Kelley, 1964.

Mankiw, N. Gregory (1992) "The Reincarnation of Keynesian Economics." In *European Economic Review* 36 (April): 559–65, excerpted in *A Macroeconomics Reader,* edited by Brian Snowdon and Howard R. Vane. London and New York: Routledge.

_____ (1993) "Symposium on Keynesian Economics Today." *Journal of Economic Perspectives* 7 (Winter): 3–4.

_____ (1997) *Macroeconomics.* 3rd ed. New York: Worth Publishers.

_____ (2010) *Macroeconomics.* 7th ed. New York: Worth.

_____ (2013) *Macroeconomics.* 8th ed. New York: Worth.

Mankiw, N. Gregory and Shapiro, Matthew D. (1985) "Trends, Random Walks, and Tests of the Permanent Income Hypothesis." *Journal of Monetary Economics* 16, No. 2 (September): 165–74.

Marshall, Alfred (1887) "Memoranda and Evidence before the Gold and Silver Commission." In *Official Papers by Alfred Marshall,* edited by J. M Keynes. London: Macmillan: 1926.

_____ (1907) *Principles of Economics.* 5th ed. London: Macmillan.

_____ (1920) *Principles of Economics*. 8th ed. Reprinted. Philadelphia, PA: Porcupine Press, 1990.

_____ (1923) *Money, Credit and Commerce*. Reprinted. New York: Augustus M. Kelley, 1960.

_____ (1926) *Official Papers*. London: Palgrave Macmillan.

Marshall, Alfred and Marshall, Mary Paley (1879) *The Economics of Industry*. London: Macmillan.

Mason, Edward S. (1934) "Controlling Industry." In *The Economics of the Recovery Program*. New York and London: Whittlesey House and McGraw-Hill.

Mathews, Don (2019) "Did Irving Fisher Really Discover the Phillips Curve?" *Journal of the History of Economic Thought* 41, No. 2 (June): 255–71.

Mayer, Thomas (1980) "David Hume and Monetarism." *Quarterly Journal of Economics* 95, No. 1 (August): 89–101.

Meghir, Costas (2004) "A Retrospective on Friedman's Theory of Permanent Income." *Economic Journal* 114, No. 496 (June): F293–F306.

Mill, James (1808) *Commerce Defended*. Reprinted. New York: Augustus M. Kelley, 1965.

Mill, John S. (1874) *Essays on Some Unsettled Questions of Political Economy*. 2nd ed. Reprinted. Augustus M. Kelley, 1968.

_____ (1961, 1965) *Collected Works*. Edited by J. M. Robson. London: University of Toronto Press.

Minsky, Hyman P. (1985) "The Financial Instability Hypothesis: A Restatement." In *Post Keynesian Economic Theory*, edited by Philip Arestis and Thanos Skouras. Sussex: Wheatsheaf Books: 24–55.

Mints, Lloyd W. (1945) *A History of Banking Theory in Great Britain and the United States*. Chicago, IL: University of Chicago Press.

Mises, Ludwig von (1934) *The Theory of Money and Credit*. Translated by H.E. Batson. London: Jonathan Cape.

_____ (1963) *Human Action*. New Revised Edition. New Haven, CT: Yale University Press.

Mishkin, Frederic S. (2015) *Macroeconomics*. 2nd ed. New York: Pearson.

Modigliani, Franco (1944) "Liquidity Preference and the Theory of Interest and Money." *Econometrica* 12 (January): 45–88.

_____ (1949) "Fluctuations in the Saving-Income Ratio: A Problem in Economic Forecasting." In *Studies in Income and Wealth*, Vol. 11. New York: National Bureau of Economic Research: 371–441.

_____ (1961) "Long-run Implications of Alternative Fiscal Policies and the Burden of the National Debt." *Economic Journal* 71 (December): 730–55.

Modigliani, Franco and Brumberg, Richard (1954) "Utility Analysis and the Consumption Function: An Interpretation of Cross-Section Data." In *Post-Keynesian Economics*, edited by Kenneth K. Kurihara. New Brunswick: Rutgers University Press: 383–436.

Moggridge, Donald E. (1992) *Maynard Keynes: An Economist's Biography*. London and New York: Routledge.

Mundell, Robert A. (1968) *Man and Economics*. New York: McGraw-Hill.

Nelson, Charles R. (1981a) "Adjustment Lags Versus Information Lags: A Test of Alternative Explanations of the Phillips Curve Phenomenon." *Journal of Money, Credit and Banking* 13, No.1 (Feb): 1–11.

_____ (1981b) "Adjustment Lags Versus Information Lags: A Test of Alternative Explanations of the Phillips Curve Phenomenon: Reply." *Journal of Money, Credit, and Banking* 13, No. 4 (November): 494–6.

Nelson, Edward (2007) "Milton Friedman and U.S. Monetary History, 1961–2006." *Federal Reserve Bank of St. Louis Review* 89, No. 3 (May/June): 153–82.

O'Brien, Denis P. (1975) *The Classical Economists.* Oxford: Clarendon Press.

_____ (2004) *The Classical Economists Revisited.* Princeton and Oxford: Princeton University Press.

O'Driscoll, Gerald P. (1977) "The Ricardian Nonequivalence Theorem." *Journal of Political Economy* 84, No. 1 (February): 207–10.

Patinkin, Don (1965) *Money, Interest and Prices: An Integration of Monetary and Value Theory.* 2nd ed. New York: Harper & Row.

_____ (1969) "The Chicago Tradition, the Quantity Theory, and Friedman." *Journal of Money, Credit, and Banking* 1 (February): 46–70.

_____ (1973) "On the Monetary Economics of Chicagoans and Non-Chicagoans: Comment." *Southern Economic Journal* 39, No. 3 (January): 454–59.

_____ (1976) *Keynes' Monetary Thought.* Durham, NC: Duke University Press.

Perlman, Morris (1987) "Of a Controversial Passage in Hume." *Journal of Political Economy* 95, No. 2 (April): 274–89.

Persons, Warren M. (1931) *Forecasting Business Cycles.* New York: John Wiley.

Phelps, Edmund S. (1967) "Phillips Curves, Expectations of Inflation and Optimal Unemployment over Time." Economica, NS, 34, No. 135 (August): 254–81.

Phillips, A. W. (1950) "Mechanical Models in Economic Dynamics." Economica, NS, 17, No. 67 (August): 283–305.

_____ (1958) "The Relation between Unemployment and the Rate of Change of Money Wage Rates in the United Kingdom, 1861–1957." Economica, NS, 25, No.100 (November): 283–99.

_____ (1961) "A Simple Model of Employment, Money and Prices in a Growing Economy." Economica, NS, 28, No. 112 (November): 360–70.

Pigou, Arthur C. (1912) *Wealth and Welfare.* London: Macmillan.

_____ (1913) *Unemployment.* London: Williams & Norgate.

_____ (1917) "The Value of Money." *Quarterly Journal of Economics* 37 (November): 38–65.

_____ (1920) *The Economics of Welfare.* London: Macmillan.

_____ (1927) *Industrial Fluctuations.* London: Macmillan.

_____ (1933) *The Theory of Unemployment.* Reprinted. New York: Augustus Kelley, 1968.

_____ (1936) "Mr. J.M. Keynes's General Theory of Employment, Interest and Money." *Economica* 3 (May): 115–32.

_____ (1941) *Employment and Equilibrium.* Reprinted. Westport, CT: Greenwood Publishing Group, 1979.

_____ (1943) "The Classical Stationary State." *Economic Journal* 53 (December): 343–51.

_____ (1945) *Lapses from Full Employment.* London: Macmillan.

Piketty, Thomas (2014) *Capital in the Twenty-First Century.* Cambridge, MA: Harvard University Press.

Posner, Richard (2009) "How I Became a Keynesian: Second Thoughts in the Middle of a Crisis." *New Republic* 23 (September): 28–32.

Ricardo, David (1951, 1957) *Works and Correspondence.* Edited by Piero Sraffa. Cambridge: Cambridge University Press.

Roberts, R. O. (1942) *Ricardo's Theory of Public Debts. Economica* 9, No. 35 (August): 257–66.

Robertson, D. H. (1922) *Money.* Chicago: University of Chicago, 1957.

_____ (1926) *Banking Policy and the Price Level.* Reprinted. New York: Augustus M. Kelley, 1949.

_____ (1936) "Some Notes on Mr. Keynes' General Theory of Employment." *Quarterly Journal of Economics* 51, No. 1 (November): 168–91.

_____ (1937) "Alternative Theories of Interest." *Economic Journal* 47 (September): 428–36.

_____ (1940) *Essays in Monetary Theory*. London: Staples.

_____ (1922) *Money*. 4th ed. Chicago: University of Chicago, 1957.

_____ (1966) *Essays in Money and Interest*. Manchester: Collins.

Robinson, George B. (1937) "One Hundred Per Cent Bank Reserves." *Harvard Business Review* 15: 438–47.

Rogoff, Kenneth (1998) "Comments on 'It's Baaack.'" *Brookings Papers on Economic Activity*, No. 2: 194–9.

Roll, Eric (1938) *A History of Economic Thought*. 5th revised ed. London and Boston: Faber and Faber, 1992.

Romer, David (1993) "The New Keynesian Synthesis." *Journal of Economic Perspectives* 7 (Winter): 5–22

Rotwein, Eugene (1955) "Editor's Introduction." In *David Hume: Writings on Economics*. Reprinted. Madison: University of Wisconsin Press, 1970: ix–cxi.

Samuelson, Paul A. (1948) *Economics*. New York: McGraw-Hill.

_____ (1985) "Succumbing to Keynesianism." *Challenge* 27, No. 6 (January/February): 4–11.

Samuelson, Paul A. and Nordhaus, William D. (1998) *Economics*. 16th ed. New York: Irwin McGraw-Hill

Samuelson, Paul A. and Solow, Robert M. (1960) "Analytical Aspects of Anti-Inflation Policy." *American Economic Review* 50, No. 2 (May): 177–94.

Sandilands, Roger (2010) "Hawtreyan 'Credit Deadlock' or Keynesian 'Liquidity Trap? Lessons for Japan from the Great Depression." In *David Laidler's Contributions to Economics*, edited by Robert Leeson. Basingstoke, England and New York: Palgrave Macmillan: 329–63.

Say, Jean-Baptiste (1821a) *A Treatise on Political Economy*. Reprinted. New York: Augustus M. Kelley, 1964.

_____ (1821b) *Letters to Mr. Malthus*. Reprinted. New York: Augustus M. Kelley, 1967.

Schiller, Robert (2000) *The Macroeconomy Today*, 8th ed., New York: Irwin-McGraw-Hill.

Schumpeter, Joseph A. (1934) "Depressions." In *The Economics of the Recovery Program*. New York and London: Whittlesey House and McGraw-Hill: 3–21.

_____ (1936) "The General Theory of Employment, Interest and Money by John Maynard Keynes." *Journal of the American Statistical Association* 31, No. 196 (December): 791–5.

_____ (1946) "John Maynard Keynes 1883–1946." *American Economic Review* 36, No. 4 (September): 495–518.

_____ (1954) *History of Economic Analysis*. New York: Oxford University Press, 1994.

Seater, John J. (1993) "Ricardian Equivalence." *Journal of Economic Literature* 31, No. 1 (March): 142–190.

Simons, Henry C. (1936) "Keynes Comments on Money." *Christian Century* 53 (July): 1016–7.

_____ (1948) "Rules versus Authorities in Monetary Policy." In *Economic Policy for a Free Society*. Chicago: University of Chicago Press: 160–83.

Simpson, J. A. and Weiner, E. S. C. (1989) *Oxford English Dictionary*. Oxford: Clarendon Press.

Smith, Adam (1776) *The Wealth of Nations*. Edited by E. Cannan. Vols. 1 and 2. Chicago: University of Chicago Press, 1976.

_____ (1978) *Lectures in Jurisprudence*. Edited by R. L. Meek, D. D. Raphael, and P. G. Stein. Oxford: Clarendon Press.

Snowdon, Brian and Vane, Howard R. (1997) "Modern Macroeconomics and Its Evolution from a Monetarist Perspective: An Interview with Professor Milton Friedman." *Journal of Economic Studies* 24, No. 4: 191–221.

Solow, Robert M. (2002) "'Analytical Aspects of Anti-Inflation Policy' After 40 Years." In *Paul Samuelson & The Foundations of Modern Economics*, edited by K. Puttaswamaiah. New Brunswick, NJ: Transaction Publishing: 71–7.

Souleles, Melvin (1999) "The Response of Household Consumption to Income Tax Refunds." *American Economic Review* 89, No. 4 (September): 947–58.

Sowell, Thomas (1972) *Say's Law: An Historical Analysis.* Princeton, NJ: Princeton University Press.

Steindl, Frank G. (1995) *Monetary Interpretations of the Great Depression.* Ann Arbor, MI: University of Michigan Press.

Stephens, Jr, Melvin (2003) "'3rd of the Month': Do Social Security Recipients Smooth Consumption between Checks?" *American Economic Review* 93, No. 1 (March): 406–22.

Sumner, Scott (2002) "Some Observations on the Return of the Liquidity Trap." *Cato Journal* 21, No. 3 (Winter): 481–90.

Svensson, Lars E.O. (2003) "Escaping from a Liquidity Trap and Deflation: The Foolproof Way and Others." *Journal of Economic Perspectives.* 17, No. 4 (Autumn): 145–66.

Taussig, Frank W. (1921) *Principles of Economics.* 3rd ed. New York: Macmillan.

_____ (1936) "Employment and the National Dividend." *Quarterly Journal of Economics* 51 (November): 198–203.

Tavlas, George S. (1998) "Was the Monetarist Tradition Invented?" *Journal of Economic Perspectives* 12, No. 4 (Fall): 211–22.

_____ (2019) "'The Group': The Making of the Chicago Monetary Tradition, 1927–36." *History of Political Economy* 51, No. 2 (Summer): 259–96.

Taylor, Fred M. (1921) *Principles of Economics,* 9th ed. New York: Ronal Press, 1925.

Taylor, Overton H. (1934) "Economics versus Politics." In *The Economics of the Recovery Program.* New York and London: Whittlesey House and McGraw-Hill: 160–88.

Thomas, Rollin G. (1940) "100 Per Cent Money: The Present Status of the 100 Per Cent Plan." *American Economic Review* 30, No. 2 Part 1 (January): 315–23.

Thornton, Henry (1802) *Paper Credit in Great Britain.* Edited by F. A. Hayek. Reprinted. New York: Augustus M. Kelley, 1965.

Timberlake, Jr., Richard (1999) "The Reserve Requirement Debacle of 1935–1938." The *Freeman/Ideas on Liberty* 49 (June): 23–9.

Tobin, James (1951) "Relative Income, Absolute Income, and Savings." In *Money, Trade, and Economic Growth,* in honor of John Henry Williams. New York: Macmillan: 135–51.

_____ (1963) "Commercial Banks as Creators of 'Money'." In *Banking and Monetary Studies,* edited by Dean Carson. Homewood, IL: Richard D. Irwin: 408–19.

_____ (1971) *Essays in Economics.* Vol. 1. *Macroeconomics.* Amsterdam: North-Holland.

_____ (1985) "Financial Innovation and Deregulation in Perspective." *Bank of Japan Monetary and Economic Studies* 3: 19–29. Reprinted in James Tobin (1987) *Policies for Prosperity.* Cambridge, MA: MIT Press: 255–64.

_____ (1993) "Price Flexibility and Output Stability: An Old Keynesian View." *Journal of Economic Perspectives* 7 (Winter): 45–65.

Tullio, Giuseppe (1989) "Smith and Ricardo on the Long-Run Effects of the Growth of Government Expenditure, Taxation, and Debt: Is Their Theory Relevant Today?" *History of Political Economy* 21, No. 4 (Winter): 723–36.

Viner, Jacob (1932) "International Aspects of the Gold Standard." In *Gold and Monetary Stabilization,* edited by Quincy Wright. Chicago: University of Chicago Press: 3–42.

_____ (1936) "Mr. Keynes on the Causes of Unemployment." *Quarterly Journal of Economics* 51 (November): 147–67.

_____ (1937) *Studies in the Theory of International Trade.* New York: Harper.

Walker, Francis A. (1895) "The Quantity-Theory of Money." *Quarterly Journal of Economics* 9, No. 4 (July): 372–9.

_____ (1878) *Money.* Reprinted. New York: Augustus M. Kelley, 1968.

Walter, John R. (2005) "Depression-Era Bank Failures: The Great Contagion or the Great Shakeout?" *Federal Reserve Bank of Richmond Economic Quarterly* 91, No. 1 (Winter): 39–54.

Webster's New Collegiate Dictionary (1980) Springfield, MA: G. & C. Merriam.

Wennerlind, Carl (2005) "David Hume's Monetary Theory Revisited: Was He Really a Quantity Theorist and an Inflationist?" *Journal of Political Economy* 113, No. 1 (February): 223–37.

Wicker, Elmus (1996) *The Banking Panics of the Great Depression.* New York: Cambridge University Press.

Wicksell, Knut Wicksell, Knut (1898) *Interest and Prices.* Translated by R.F. Kahn. Reprinted. New York: Augustus M. Kelley, 1965.

_____ (1935) *Selected Papers on Economic Theory.* Edited with an Introduction by Erik Lindhal. Cambridge, MA: Harvard University Press, 1958.

Willis, H. Parker (1932) "Federal Reserve Policy in the Depression." In *Gold and Monetary Stabilization,* edited by Quincy Wright. Chicago: University of Chicago Press: 77–108.

Williams, John H. (1932) "Monetary Stability and the Gold Standard." In *Gold and Monetary Stabilization,* edited by Quincy Wright. Chicago: University of Chicago Press: 133–58.

Wright, Quincy (1932) *Gold and Monetary Stabilization: Lectures on the Harris Foundation,* Editor. Chicago: University of Chicago Press.

Young, Allyn (1927) *Economic Problems: New and Old.* Boston: Houghton Mifflin.

Index

Printed in the United States
By Bookmasters